SCHAUM'S OUTLINE OF

THEORY AND PROBLEMS

of

DATA STRUCTURES
WITH JAVA

•

JOHN R. HUBBARD, Ph.D.

Professor of Mathematics and Computer Science
University of Richmond

•

SCHAUM'S OUTLINE SERIES

McGRAW-HILL

New York   San Francisco   Washington, D.C.   Auckland   Bogotá   Caracas
Lisbon   London   Madrid   Mexico City   Milan   Montreal
New Delhi   San Juan   Singapore   Sydney   Tokyo   Toronto

JOHN R. HUBBARD is Professor of Mathematics and Computer Science at the University of Richmond. He received his Ph.D. from the University of Michigan in 1973 and has been a member of the Richmond faculty since 1983. His primary interests are in numerical algorithms and database systems. Dr. Hubbard's other *Schaum's Outline* books include *Programming with C++, Programming with Java, Fundamentals of Computing with C++*, and *Data Structures with C++*.

Schaum's Outline of Theory and Problems of

DATA STRUCTURES WITH JAVA

3 4 5 6 7 8 9 10 11 12 13 14 15 16 17 18 19 20   PRS   PRS   0 9 8 7 6 5 4 3 2

ISBN 0-07-136128-6

Sponsoring Editor: Barbara Gilson
Production Supervisor: Tina Cameron
Editing Supervisor: Maureen Walker

Library of Congress Cataloging-in-Publication Data applied for.

McGraw-Hill

A Division of The McGraw·Hill Companies

Preface

Like all Schaum's Outline Series books, this volume is intended to be used primarily for self study, preferably in conjunction with a regular course in data structures. However, it is also well-suited for use in independent study or as a reference.

The book includes over 200 examples and solved problems. I firmly believe that the principles of data structures can be learned from a well-constructed collection of examples with complete explanations. This book is designed to provide that support.

Source code for all the examples and solved problems in this book may be downloaded from the author's Web page `http://www.mathcs.richmond.edu/~hubbard/schaums`, or at his sites `http://jhubbard.net/schaums` or `http://www.projectEuclid.net/schaums`. These sites also contain any corrections and addenda for the book.

I wish to thank all my friends, colleagues, students, and the McGraw-Hill staff who have helped me with the critical review of this manuscript. Special thanks to my wife and colleague, Anita H. Hubbard, for her advice, encouragement, and creative ideas for this book. Many of the original problems used here are hers.

JOHN R. HUBBARD
Richmond, Virginia

Dedicated to

Anita H. Hubbard

Contents

v

CONTENTS vii

Chapter 1

Review of Java

This chapter outlines those features of the Java programming language that are essential to the design and implementation of data structures. For more details, see the book **[Hubbard]** listed in Appendix D on page 362.

1.1 OBJECT-ORIENTED PROGRAMMING

Java is an *object-oriented* programming language:
- Every data item is encapsulated in some object.
- Every executable statement is inside some method.
- Every object is an instantiation of some class or is an array.
- Every class is defined within a single inheritance hierarchy.

Java's single inheritance hierarchy is a tree structure whose root is the `Object` class. (See Section 3.2 on page 55.) This single structure might seem to render Java a simple language. However, that structure includes the Java 1.3 Class Libraries, which contain 2,130 classes with 23,901 members.

Object orientation makes Java particularly well-suited for the design and implementation of data structures. Its Collections Framework (see Chapter 4) provides an excellent platform for the programmer to construct data structures.

1.2 THE JAVA PROGRAMMING LANGUAGE

A *Java program* is a collection of one or more text files, at least one of which contains a unique `public` class with a unique method whose signature is

```
public static void main(String[] args)
```

Each file in the program must contain a unique `public` class or `public` interface. Each file is named *X*`.java`, where *X* is the name of its unique `public` class or `public` interface. Each file *X*`.java` is compiled into a corresponding class file named *X*`.class`. Then the program is run by executing the *X*`.class` file that contains the `main(String[])` method that in turn contains the statements to be executed. This programming can be done from the command line or from within an IDE. (See Appendix C.)

1.3 VARIABLES AND OBJECTS

In any programming language, data are accessed through variables. In Java, a variable is either a reference to an object or one of the eight primitive types, as shown in the diagram at the top of the next page. If it is a reference, then its value is either `null` or it contains the address of an instantiated object.

1

Each object belongs to a unique class. The class defines its objects' properties and operations, just as a primitive type defines its variables' properties and operations.

A variable is created by a declaration that specifies its type and optional initial value. An object is created by the new operator invoking its class constructor.

EXAMPLE 1.1 Creating Variables and Objects

```java
public class Ex0101
{ public static void main(String[] args)
  { boolean flag=true;
    char ch='B';
    short m;
    int n=22;
    float x=3.14159F;
    double y;
    String str;
    String nada=null;
    String country = new String("United States");
    System.out.println("flag = " + flag);
    System.out.println("ch = " + ch);
    System.out.println("n = " + n);
    System.out.println("x = " + x);
    System.out.println("nada = " + nada);
    System.out.println("country = " + country);
  }
}
```

```
flag = true
ch = B
n = 22
x = 3.14159
nada = null
country = United States
```

Java Types
└─ Primitive Types
   ├─ boolean
   └─ Numeric Types
      ├─ Integer Types
      │ ├─ byte
      │ ├─ short
      │ ├─ int
      │ ├─ long
      │ └─ char
      └─ Floating-Point Types
         ├─ float
         └─ double
└─ Reference Types
   ├─ Array Type
   ├─ Class Type
   └─ Interface Type

This program declares nine variables and then prints the six that were initialized. The first six variables are primitive types. The last three variables are references to String objects.

The program contains only one object: the String object named country. (Technically, country is the name of the variable that refers to the String object.)

The picture here shows the nine variables and the one object. Each variable has a name and a type. If the type is a class, then the variable is a reference to an instance (i.e., an object) of that class. The uninitialized variables appear empty; the others contain their values. The only possible value of a

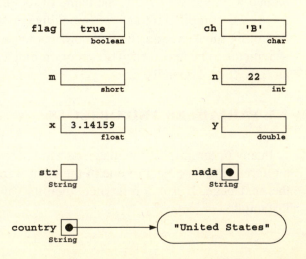

reference variable is a reference, drawn as a black dot. If the reference is not `null`, then the dot has an arrow pointing to the object to which it refers. In Java, an object cannot exist unless some reference variable refers to it.

1.4 PRIMITIVE TYPES

Java defines eight primitive types:

> `boolean`either `false` or `true`
>
> `char`16-bit Unicode character; e.g., `'B'` or `'π'`
>
> `byte`8-bit integer: `-128` to `127`
>
> `short`16-bit integer: `-32768` to `32767`
>
> `int`32-bit integer: `-2147483648` to `2147483647`
>
> `long`64-bit integer: `-9223372036854775808` to `9223372036854775807`
>
> `float`32-bit floating-point decimal: (plus or minus) `1.4E-45F` to `3.4E38F`
>
> `double`64-bit floating-point decimal: (plus or minus) `4.9E-324` to `1.8E308`

Note that `float` literals require an `F` suffix to distinguish them from values of type `double`.

Every Unicode character literal can be expressed in the form `'\uxxxx'`, where x is any hexadecimal digit. For example, `'B'` is `'\u0042'`, and `'π'` is `'\u03C0'`.

In addition to their numeric values, floating-point variables can also have any of the three special values `NEGATIVE_INFINITY`, `POSITIVE_INFINITY`, and `NaN` (for "not a number"). These special values result from improper arithmetic operations.

EXAMPLE 1.2 Special Values for Floating-Point Types

```
public class Ex0102
{ public static void main(String[] args)
  { double x=1E200;  // x=10000...0 (1 followed by 200 zeros)
    System.out.println("x = " + x);
    System.out.println("x*x = " + x*x);
    System.out.println("(x*x)/x = " + (x*x)/x);
    System.out.println("(x*x)/(x*x) = " + (x*x)/(x*x));
  }
}
```

```
x = 1.0E200
x*x = Infinity
(x*x)/x = Infinity
(x*x)/(x*x) = NaN
```

The value of `x*x` is `Infinity` because $(10^{200})(10^{200}) == 10^{400}$, which is greater than the maximum value $1.3(10^{308})$ for `double` type.

Algebraically, $(xx)/x = x$, but not so when x is infinite: `Infinity` divided by any nonnegative finite value will still be `Infinity`.

Finally, `Infinity` divided `Infinity` is not even infinite; it is algebraically indeterminate, so its Java value is `NaN`.

For each of the eight primitive types, Java defines a *wrapper class* that provides object-oriented services for manipulating primitive types. For example, the wrapper class for type `double` is `Double`, and the wrapper class for type `int` is `Integer`.

EXAMPLE 1.3 Using Wrapper Classes

```
public class Ex0103
{ public static void main(String[] args)
  { String s = "2.7182818284590";
    System.out.println("s = " + s);
    Double x = new Double(s);
    System.out.println("x = " + x);
    double y = x.doubleValue();
    System.out.println("y = " + y);
    s += 45;
    System.out.println("s = " + s);
    y += 45;
    System.out.println("y = " + y);
    int n = x.intValue();
    System.out.println("n = " + n);
    n = Integer.parseInt("3A9",16);
    System.out.println("n = " + n);
  }
}
```

```
s = 2.7182818284590
x = 2.718281828459
y = 2.718281828459
s = 2.718281828459045
y = 47.718281828459
n = 2
n = 937
```

The constructor `Double(s)` creates the `Double` object x from the `String` object s, storing the numeric value 2.7182818284590 inside the object x. The second `println()` statement implicitly invokes the `Double.toString()` method, which converts that numeric value back into a string to be printed. The `x.doubleValue()` invocation returns the stored numeric value that is assigned to y. Then the `+=` operator is applied to `String` object s and to the double variable y, with very different results. For strings, "+=" means "append to," but for numbers, it means "add to."

Next, the `Double.intValue()` method truncates that stored numeric value to the integer 2 and initializes n with it. Finally, `Integer.parseInt("3A9",16)` returns the `int` value (in decimal form) for the integer whose hexadecimal representation is `3A9`. That is $3(16^2) + 10(16) + 9 = 937$.

Note that the + operator automatically converts the number y into its string equivalent when combined with a string, as in the call `System.out.println("y = " + y)`.

1.5 FLOW CONTROL

Java supports the `if` statement, the `if..else` statement, the `switch` statement, and the *conditional expression operator* `? . . :`.

EXAMPLE 1.4 Using Conditional Statements

This program generates random integers in the range 0 to 99 and then uses conditional statements to classify them.

```
public class Ex0104
{ public static void main(String[] args)
  { int n = (int)Math.round(100*Math.random());
    System.out.println("n = " + n);
```

```
      if (n>25 && n<75) System.out.println(n + " is between 25 and 75");
      else System.out.println(n + " is not between 25 and 75");
      switch ((int)n/20)
      { case  0: System.out.println(n + " < 20");
        case  1: System.out.println(n + " < 40");
        case  2: System.out.println(n + " < 60");   break;
        case  3: System.out.println(n + " < 80");   break;
        default: System.out.println(n + " >= 80");
      }
      System.out.println(n + (n%2>0 ? " is odd" : " is even"));
    }
  }
n = 19
19 is not between 25 and 75
19 < 20
19 < 40
19 < 60
19 is odd
```

Note how the absence of the `break` statement in `case  0` and `case  1` allows control to "fall through" each of those cases on to `case  2`, executing all three of those `println()` statements.

The expression `(n%2>0 ? " is odd" : " is even")` evaluates to the string `" is odd"` if the condition `n%2>0` is true (i.e., `n` is not divisible by 2); otherwise it evaluates to the string `" is even"` (when `n` is divisible by 2).

Java supports the `while` statement, the `do..while` statement, and the `for` statement.

EXAMPLE 1.5 Using Loops

This program empirically tests Gauss's Prime Number Theorem: if $p(n)$ is the number of prime numbers that are less than n, then the ratio $p(n)(\ln n)/n$ approaches 1.0 as n grows without bound. It counts the number `p(n)` of prime numbers for each odd `n` in the range 3 to 1,000,000. As $p(n)$ increases, each time it passes a multiple of 5,000, the program prints the values of n, $p(n)$, $\ln n$ (the natural logarithm) and the ratio $p(n)(\ln n)/n$, which gets close to 1.0.

```
public class Ex0105
{ public static void main(String[] args)
  { System.out.println("n\tp(n)\tln(n)\t\t\tp(n)*ln(n)/n");
    final String DASHES18="\t------------------";
    System.out.println("------\t-----" + DASHES18 + DASHES18);
    int p=1;   // p = number of primes that are <= n
    for (int n=3; n<1000000; n += 2)
    { int d=3;
      while (d<=Math.sqrt(n) && n%d>0)
        d += 2;
      if (n%d==0) continue;
      ++p;
      if (p%5000>0) continue;
      double ln=Math.log(n);
      System.out.println(n + "\t" + p + "\t" + ln + "\t" + p*ln/n);
    }
    System.out.println("------\t-----" + DASHES18 + DASHES18);
  }
}
```

n	c(n)	ln(n)	c(n)*ln(n)/n
------	-----	------------------	------------------
48619	5000	10.79176967999097	1.109830486023054
104743	10000	11.559265009775785	1.1035835339617717
163847	15000	12.006688344529985	1.0991981859170432
224743	20000	12.322712806131365	1.0966048158235286
287137	25000	12.567714732761953	1.0942263390613152
350381	30000	12.766776412829921	1.093105198012728
414991	35000	12.936012112230687	1.091012633835611
479939	40000	13.08141429147497	1.0902564110418174
545749	45000	13.209911442069696	1.0892299388420983
611957	50000	13.324417297588104	1.0886726761511107
679279	55000	13.428787220525182	1.087304770394617
746777	60000	13.52352189210366	1.0865510232990836
814309	65000	13.610095179831822	1.0863888114819662
882389	70000	13.690388280841916	1.0860597533048737
951193	75000	13.765472265206315	1.085384795609801
------	-----	------------------	------------------

The `for` loop iterates 499,999 times, for each value of n = 3, 5, 7, 9, ..., 999999. The loop's block tests n for primality by dividing it by d = 3, 5, 7, 9, ..., $\sqrt{n}$. If it finds a d that divides n evenly (i.e., the remainder n%d is zero), then the first `continue` statement executes, starting the next iteration of the `for` loop. If no divisor of n is found, then n must be a prime number, so the counter p is incremented.

Java supports the use of subprograms, called *methods*.

EXAMPLE 1.6 Using Methods

This program has the same output as the one in Example 1.5, But it uses a separate method to determine whether each integer n is prime.

```
public class Ex0106
{ public static void main(String[] args)
  { System.out.println("n\tp(n)\tln(n)\t\t\tp(n)*ln(n)/n");
    final String DASHES18="\t------------------";
    System.out.println("------\t-----" + DASHES18 + DASHES18);
    int p=1;  // p = number of primes that are <= n
    for (int n=3; n<1000000; n += 2)
      if (isPrime(n))
      { ++p;
        if (p%5000>0) continue;
        double ln=Math.log(n);
        System.out.println(n + "\t" + p + "\t" + ln + "\t" + p*ln/n);
      }
    System.out.println("------\t-----" + DASHES18 + DASHES18);
  }

  private static boolean isPrime(int n)
  { int d=3;
    while (d<=Math.sqrt(n) && n%d>0)
      d += 2;
    if (n%d==0) return false;
    return true;
  }
}
```

The `isPrime(s)` method encapsulates the code that tests n for primality. It returns `false` if a divisor d of n is found; otherwise, it returns `true`.

Note that the method is declared to be `private static`. It is `private` because it is not meant to be used outside of its class. It is `static` because it has to be invoked from within the `static` method `main()`. (See Section 1.7 on page 9.)

1.6 CLASSES

A *class* in an implementation of an abstract data type. Objects are created by instantiating classes. The class definition specifies the kind of data that its objects maintain and the operations that its objects can perform. These specifications are the *members* of the class.

As the diagram on the right shows, there are four kinds of members that a class can have. A *field* is a variable that holds data. A *method* is a function that performs operations. A class may also define local "inner" classes and interfaces within itself.

```
member
  ├─ field
  ├─ method
  │    ├─ constructor
  │    ├─ accessor
  │    ├─ mutator
  │    └─ utility
  ├─ class
  └─ interface
```

The diagram lists four common kinds of specialized methods: constructors, accessor methods, mutator methods, and utility methods. A *constructor* is a function that creates the objects of the class. This process is called *instantiation*, and the resulting objects are called *instances* of the class. It is the duty of the constructor also to initialize the fields of the objects it creates.

An *accessor* method is a read-only function. It may return the value of a class field without allowing it to be changed externally. In Java, an accessor method that accesses a field X is usually named `getX()`. For this reason, accessor methods are often called "getty" methods in Java.

A *mutator* method is a read-write function that allows external invokers to change the value of a field. In Java, a mutator method that changes a field X is usually named `setX()`. For this reason, mutator methods are often called "setty" methods in Java.

A *utility* method is a private function that is used internally by other methods in its class.

EXAMPLE 1.7 A `Point` Class

This defines a class whose instances represent points in the Euclidean plane:

```java
public class Point
{ protected double x, y;

  public Point(double x, double y)
  { this.x = x;
    this.y = y;
  }

  public double getX()
  { return x;
  }

  public double getY()
  { return y;
  }

  public Point getLocation()
  { return new Point(x,y);
  }
```

```
    public void setLocation(double x, double y)
    { this.x = x;
      this.y = y;
    }

    public void translate(double dx, double dy)
    { x += dx;
      y += dy;
    }

    public boolean equals(Object object)
    { if (object == this) return true;
      if (object.getClass() != this.getClass()) return false;
      Point point = (Point)object;
      return (x == point.x && y == point.y);
    }

    public int hashCode()
    { return (new Double(x)).hashCode() + (new Double(y)).hashCode();
    }

    public String toString()
    { return new String("(" + (float)x + ","  + (float)y + ")");
    }

  }
```

This class has three fields (x, y, and origin), one constructor, five accessor methods (getX(), getY(), getLocation(), hashCode(), and toString()), and one mutator method (translate(double,double)).

Here is a test driver for the class:

```
    public class Ex0107
    { public static void main(String[] args)
      { Point p = new Point(2,3);
        System.out.println("p = " + p);
        System.out.println("p.hashCode() = " + p.hashCode());
        Point q = p.getLocation();
        compare(p,q);
        q.translate(5,-1);
        compare(p,q);
        q = p;
        compare(p,q);
      }
      private static void compare(Point p, Point q)
      { System.out.println("q = " + q);
        System.out.println("q.hashCode() = " + q.hashCode());
        if (q.equals(p)) System.out.println("q equals p");
        else System.out.println("q does not equal p");
        if (q == p) System.out.println("q == p");
        else System.out.println("q != p");
      }
    }
```

```
p = (2.0,3.0)
p.hashCode() = -2146959360
q = (2.0,3.0)
q.hashCode() = -2146959360
q equals p
q != p
q = (7.0,2.0)
q.hashCode() = -2145648640
q does not equal p
q != p
q = (2.0,3.0)
q.hashCode() = -2146959360
q equals p
q == p
```

The test driver includes the utility method compare(Point,Point) to facilitate testing.

The point p has hashCode() value –2,146,959,360. This number has no intrinsic meaning; it is merely used as an identification number. It is computed from the corresponding hashCode() values of the point's two coordinate objects (x and y).

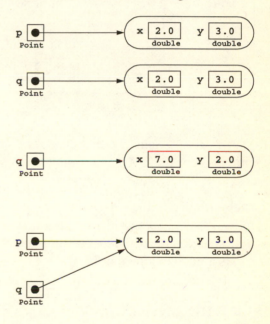

The point q is defined to be a copy of p. So it has the same hashCode() value, and the equals(Object) method returns true. However, the test q == p evaluates to false because p and q are different objects. The equality operator == really tests for identity rather than equality: It is true only when you have two different references to the same single object.

After q is translated to the location (7,2), the equals(Object) method returns false.

Finally, when the reference p is assigned to the reference q, the equality q == p evaluates to true, because at that moment only one Point object remains: the original point (2,3). The other point (7,2) was "garbage collected"; i.e., when it lost its reference variable q, it was destroyed.

1.7 MODIFIERS

Classes, interfaces, and their members can be declared using the modifiers public, protected, private, package, abstract, static, and final. The table at the top of the next page summarizes the meanings of these six modifiers.

The public, protected, and private modifiers are called *access modifiers* because they determine from where the class or member can accessed. Generally, public means accessible from anywhere, protected means accessible only from within the class and its subclasses, and private means accessible only from within the class itself.

A member is declared abstract if it is incomplete. So an abstract method is one whose implementation is not included. An abstract class is one that has at least one abstract method. Interfaces are abstract by default, and so the modifier is not used on them. Fields cannot be abstract.

Modifiers for Classes, Interfaces, and their Members

Modifier	Interface	Class	Nested Class	Field	Method
`public`	Accessible from any class.				
`protected`	Accessible only from this class and its subclasses.				
`private`	Accessible only from this class.				
`abstract`	N/A	Contains at least one `abstract` method		N/A	Its implementation is not defined; only its signature and return type are declared.
`final`	N/A	Cannot be subclassed.		Its value cannot be changed.	It cannot be overridden by a subclass.
`static`	N/A	N/A	Not an inner class.	Exactly one instance exists for all objects of the class.	Exactly one instance exists for all objects of the class.

A `final` class is one that cannot be subclassed (see Section 3.1 on page 53). A `final` field is simply a constant. A `final` method is one that cannot be overridden in a subclass.

A `static` field is one that belongs to the class itself instead of generating a separate copy for each instance of the class. Similarly, a `static` method is one that is bound to the class instead of to its objects. If X is a class with `static` field x and `static` method $y()$, then they are accessed by $X.x$ and $X.y()$, independent of any objects. The `java.lang.Math` class (Section 1.9 on page 13) is a good example of how `static` methods are used.

1.8 THE `String` CLASS

A *string* is an object that contains a sequence of characters usually used for processing text. Java provides a `String` class for creating and processing strings. The class contains over 50 methods, including more than 10 constructors. The most commonly used methods are shown in the class definition at the top of the next page.

Although strings are objects instead of primitive types, they are in some ways similar to primitive types. The system recognizes string literals such as `"blue"` and `"'Tis so."` just as it recognizes numeric literals such as `8388608` and `3.14159`. Moreover, string references can be assigned to these literals, like this:

```
String color="blue";
```

Since literals are unique, any other reference to `"blue"` will test equal to the `color` reference.

Also like numeric types, strings are the only class of objects that can be manipulated by operators. (See Example 1.8.)

```
    public final class String
    { public char      charAt()
      public boolean endsWith(String suffix)
      public boolean equals(Object object)
      public int      indexOf(char ch)
      public int      indexOf(char ch, int start)
      public int      indexOf(String str)
      public int      indexOf(String str, int start)
      public int      lastIndexOf(char ch)
      public int      lastIndexOf(char ch, int start)
      public int      lastIndexOf(String str)
      public int      lastIndexOf(String str, int start)
      public int      length()
      public String   replace(char ch, char ch2)
      public boolean startsWith(String prefix)
      public boolean startsWith(String prefix, int start)
      public          String()
      public          String(char[] chars)
      public          String(char[] chars, int start, int len)
      public String   substring(int start)
      public String   substring(int start, int stop)
      public char[]   toCharArray()
      public String   toLowerCase()
      public String   toUpperCase()
      public String   trim()
    }
```

In addition, the `String` class defines the two concatenation operators + and +=. These are illustrated in the following example.

EXAMPLE 1.8 Testing the `String` Class

```
    public class Ex0108
    { public static void main(String[] args)
      { String s="ABCDEFG";
        System.out.println("s = \"" + s + "\"");
        s = s + "HIJK";
        System.out.println("s = \"" + s + "\"");
        s += "LMNOP";
        System.out.println("s = \"" + s + "\"");
        System.out.println("s.length() = " + s.length());
        System.out.println("s.charAt(6) = " + s.charAt(6));
        System.out.println("s.indexOf('G') = " + s.indexOf('G'));
        System.out.println("s.indexOf('Z') = " + s.indexOf('Z'));
        System.out.println("s.indexOf('G',8) = " + s.indexOf('G',8));
        System.out.println("s.indexOf(\"GHIJ\") = " + s.indexOf("GHIJ"));
        if (s.startsWith("DE"))
          System.out.println("s.startsWith(\"DE\")");
        else System.out.println("s does not start with \"DE\"");
        if (s.startsWith("DE",3))
          System.out.println("s.startsWith(\"DE\",3)");
        else
          System.out.println("s does not start with \"DE\" after 3 chars");
```

```
        if (s.endsWith("IJK")) System.out.println("s.endsWith(\"IJK\")");
        else System.out.println("s does not end with \"IJK\"");
        if (s.endsWith("NOP")) System.out.println("s.endsWith(\"NOP\")");
        else System.out.println("s does not end with \"NOP\"");
        s += "DABBADABBADO";
        System.out.println("s = \"" + s + "\"");
        s = s.replace('B','T');
        System.out.println("s = \"" + s + "\"");
        s = s.substring(7,10);
        System.out.println("s = \"" + s + "\"");
        s = s.toLowerCase();
        System.out.println("s = \"" + s + "\"");
        s = "  W XY  Z   ";
        System.out.println("s = \"" + s + "\"");
        System.out.println("s.length() = " + s.length());
        s = s.trim();
        System.out.println("s = \"" + s + "\"");
        System.out.println("s.length() = " + s.length());
    }
}
```

```
s = "ABCDEFG"
s = "ABCDEFGHIJK"
s = "ABCDEFGHIJKLMNOP"
s.length() = 16
s.charAt(6) = G
s.indexOf('G') = 6
s.indexOf('Z') = -1
s.indexOf('G',8) = -1
s.indexOf("GHIJ") = 6
s does not start with "DE"
s.startsWith("DE",3)
s does not end with "IJK"
s.endsWith("NOP")
s = "ABCDEFGHIJKLMNOPDABBADABBADO"
s = "ATCDEFGHIJKLMNOPDATTADATTADO"
s = "HIJ"
s = "hij"
s = "  W XY  Z   "
s.length() = 12
s = "W XY  Z"
s.length() = 7
```

Note that `String` objects are *immutable*; so the only way to change a string is to assign to it the return value of a method like `replace(char,char)` that returns a new string.

Java requires the computer's operating system to maintain a pool of string literals, thereby guaranteeing that in any runtime environment there is only one occurrence of any string literal in use. This is similar to numeric literals: there is only one 27. The consequence of this unusual requirement is that the equality operator `==` always works "correctly" for strings.

EXAMPLE 1.9 Testing the Uniqueness of `String` Literals

```
public class Ex0109
{ public static void main(String[] args)
```

```
    { String s1="ABCDEFG";
      System.out.println("s1 = \"" + s1 + "\"");
      System.out.println("(s1 == \"ABCDEFG\") = " + (s1 == "ABCDEFG"));
      System.out.println("(s1 == \"ABCD\"+\"EFG\") = "
                          + (s1 == "ABCD"+"EFG"));
      String s2="ABCDEFG";   // makes s2 a synonym for s1
      System.out.println("s2 = \"" + s2 + "\"");
      System.out.println("(s1 == s2) = " + (s1 == s2));
      s2 = new String("ABCDEFG");   // now s2 refers to a separate object
      System.out.println("s2 = \"" + s2 + "\"");
      System.out.println("(s1 == s2) = " + (s1 == s2));
      System.out.println("s1.equals(s2) = " + s1.equals(s2));
    }
}
```

```
s1 = "ABCDEFG"
(s1 == "ABCDEFG") = true
(s1 == "ABCD"+"EFG") = true
s2 = "ABCDEFG"
(s1 == s2) = true
s2 = "ABCDEFG"
(s1 == s2) = false
s1.equals(s2) = true
```

This shows that there is only one string literal `"ABCDEFG"` no matter how it is formed. So if two different references (i.e., references with different names) are both assigned that literal, they must be equal: The equality operator "==" evaluates to `true`. But note that two different strings can have the same literal value. In that case, the equality operator evaluates to false, but the `equals()` method still returns `true`.

Compare this with the results of Example 1.7 on page 7.

These special properties distinguish the `String` class from all other classes:
- `String` objects are immutable (read-only); their values cannot be changed.
- `String` literals are maintained in a "string pool" by the operating system.
- The `String` class defines the special operators + and +=.
- The length is accessed by a `length()` method instead of by a `length` field as used by arrays or by a `size()` method as used by `Collection` objects.

1.9 THE `Math` CLASS

The Java `Math` class defines mathematical constants and methods that implement the common mathematical functions. Its definition in the `java.util` package looks like this:

```
public final class Math
{ public static final double       E=2.7182818284590452354;
  public static final double       PI=3.14159265358979323846;
  public static double             abs(double x)   // absolute value
  public static native double      atan(double x)  // arctangent
  public static native double      ceil(double x)  // ceiling
  public static native double      cos(double x)
  public static native double      exp(double x)   // base e
  public static native double      floor(double x)
  public static native double      log(double x)   // base e
```

```
        public static native double        max(double x, double y)
        public static native double        min(double x, double y)
        public static native double        pow(double x, double y)  // power
        public static synchronized double random()
        public static long                 round(double x)
        public static native double        sin(double x)
        public static native double        sqrt(double x)  // square root
        public static native double        tan(double x)
}
```

Note that all these members are `static`. That means that they are invoked with the "`Math.`" prefix instead of using a `Math` object.

EXAMPLE 1.10 Testing the `Math` Class

```
public class Ex0110
{ public static void main(String[] args)
  { final double PI=Math.PI;
    final double E=Math.E;
    System.out.println("E                   = " + E);
    System.out.println("Math.exp(1.0)       = " + Math.exp(1.0));
    System.out.println("PI                  = " + PI);
    System.out.println("4*Math.atan(1.0)    = " + 4*Math.atan(1.0));
    System.out.println("Math.cos(2*PI)      = " + Math.cos(2*PI));
    System.out.println("Math.sin(PI/2)      = " + Math.sin(PI/2));
    System.out.println("Math.tan(PI/4)      = " + Math.tan(PI/4));
    System.out.println("Math.log(E)         = " + Math.log(E));
    System.out.println("Math.abs(-13.579)   = " + Math.abs(-13.579));
    System.out.println("Math.floor(13.579)  = " + Math.floor(13.579));
    System.out.println("Math.ceil(13.579)   = " + Math.ceil(13.579));
    System.out.println("Math.round(13.579)  = " + Math.round(13.579));
    System.out.println("Math.pow(25.0,0.5)  = " + Math.pow(25.0,0.5));
    System.out.println("Math.sqrt(25.0)     = " + Math.sqrt(25.0));
    System.out.println("Math.random()       = " + Math.random());
    System.out.println("Math.random()       = " + Math.random());
  }
}
```

```
E                   = 2.718281828459045
Math.exp(1.0)       = 2.718281828459045
PI                  = 3.141592653589793
4*Math.atan(1.0)    = 3.141592653589793
Math.cos(2*PI)      = 1.0
Math.sin(PI/2)      = 1.0
Math.tan(PI/4)      = 0.9999999999999999
Math.log(E)         = 1.0
Math.abs(-13.579)   = 13.579
Math.floor(13.579)  = 13.0
Math.ceil(13.579)   = 14.0
Math.round(13.579)  = 14
Math.pow(25.0,0.5)  = 5.0
Math.sqrt(25.0)     = 5.0
Math.random()       = 0.9279776738566742
Math.random()       = 0.4493770111566855
```

Note the round-off error in the computation of `Math.tan(PI/4)`; the correct value is exactly 1.0. Also note that the `Math.round(double)` method returns a `long` integer instead of a `double` precision floating-point decimal number like all the other `Math` methods.

The `Math.random()` method returns randomly generated `double` precision floating-point decimal numbers that are uniformly distributed in the interval from 0.0 to 1.0. The following example tests that distribution.

EXAMPLE 1.11 Testing the `Math.random()` Method

This program generates 50,000 random numbers in the range 0.0 to 1.0 and then counts how many fall within each of the 100 equally spaced subintervals of length 0.01 in that range. It uses a `frequency[]` array to accumulate these counts. For example, the random number $x = 0.7294416115902632$ falls in the interval $0.72 \leq x < 0.73$, so it is counted by incrementing `frequency[72]`.

```
public class Ex0111
{ public static void main(String[] args)
    { final int SUBINTERVALS=100;
      final int TOTAL=50000;
      int[] frequency = new int[SUBINTERVALS];
      for (int k=0; k<SUBINTERVALS; k++)
        frequency[k] = 0;
      for (int j=0; j<TOTAL; j++)
      { double x = Math.random();   // 0.0 < x < 1.0
        x *= SUBINTERVALS;          // 0.0 < x < 100.0
        x = Math.floor(x);          // 0.0 <= x <= 99.0
        long m = Math.round(x);     // 0 <= m <= 99
        int k = (int)m;             // 0 <= k <= 99
        ++frequency[k];             // count k
      }
      for (int i=0; i<SUBINTERVALS; i++)
        System.out.print(frequency[i]+(i%10==9?"\n":"    "));
    }
}
```

515	506	515	454	495	512	502	542	506	514
475	529	483	504	476	496	471	524	508	489
501	499	477	498	500	498	517	482	438	492
491	480	566	487	512	485	489	461	524	504
500	527	482	506	498	475	519	517	466	509
473	503	497	483	522	468	505	510	488	532
499	533	499	488	511	468	506	476	510	498
552	504	507	478	512	521	484	479	480	487
514	489	511	512	464	487	499	506	497	526
511	501	522	468	524	505	508	533	530	504

If the 50,000 numbers were uniformly distributed exactly then there would be exactly 500 in each subinterval. Since all of these 100 frequency counts are close to 500, we have empirical evidence that the `Math.random()` method does indeed produce a uniform distribution.

EXAMPLE 1.12 Testing the `Math.sqrt()` Method

This program tests the `Math.sqrt()` method by comparing its results with a locally defined square root method and also by squaring its output.

```
public class Ex0112
{ public static void main(String[] args)
```

```
{ for (double x=50.0; x<60.0; x++)
  { double y=Math.sqrt(x);
    double z=sqrt(x);
    System.out.println(y + "\t" + y*y);
    System.out.println(z);
  }
}

private static double sqrt(double x)
{ final double EPSILON=1E-14;
  if (x <= 0) return 0.0;
  double y=1.0;
  while (Math.abs(y*y-x) > EPSILON)
    y = (y+x/y)/2;
  return y;
}
}
```

```
7.0710678118654755        50.00000000000001
7.0710678118654755
7.14142842854285          51.00000000000001
7.14142842854285
7.211102550927978         51.99999999999999
7.211102550927979
7.280109889280518         53.0
7.280109889280518
7.3484692283495345        54.0
7.3484692283495345
7.416198487095663         55.0
7.416198487095663
7.483314773547883         56.0
7.483314773547883
7.54983443527075          57.0
7.54983443527075
7.615773105863909         58.00000000000001
7.615773105863909
7.681145747868608         58.99999999999999
7.681145747868609
```

Review Questions

1.1   Why is Java called an "object-oriented" programming language?

1.2   What is required for a Java program?

1.3   What is a primitive type?

1.4   What is a literal?

1.5   What are the three nonnumeric literals for the two floating-point types?

1.6   What is an object reference?

1.7   What is an object?

1.8   What is a class?

1.9   What is an instance?

1.10 What is a field?

1.11 What is a method?

1.12 What is a method signature?

1.13 What is a constructor?

1.14 What is a `static` member?

1.15 What is an access modifier?

1.16 What does `private` mean?

1.17 What does `protected` mean?

1.18 What is a wrapper class?

1.19 What makes the `String` class so different from all the other classes in the Java standard library?

1.20 What does the `Math.random()` method do?

Problems

1.1 Write and test the following method:
```
public static String monthName(int month)
// precondition:  0 < n and n < 13
// example: monthName(2) returns "February"
```

1.2 Write and test the following method:
```
public static int daysInMonth(int month, int year)
// precondition:  0 < n and n < 13
// example: daysInMonth(2,2000) returns 29
```

1.3 Write and test the following method:
```
public static int numberOfDigits(int n)
// example: numDigits(-8036800) returns 7
```

1.4 Write and test the following method:
```
public static int sumOfDigits(int n)
// example: sumOfDigits(-8036800) returns 25
```

1.5 Write and test the following method:
```
public static int reverseDigits(int n)
// example: reverseDigits(-8036800) returns 572038
```

1.6 Write and test the following method:
```
public static double round(double x, int precision)
// example: round(803.505692,4) returns 803.1057
```

1.7 Write and test the following method:
```
public static String signedToBinary(int n)
// examples: signedToBinary( 1289) returns "010100001001"
//           signedToBinary(-1289) returns "101011110111"
```

1.8 Write and test the following method:
```
public static String unsignedToBinary(int n)
// precondition:  n >= 0
// example: unsignedToBinary(1289) returns "10100001001"
```

1.9 Write and test the following method:
```
public static int binaryToSigned(String code)
// preconditions: each character in code is either '0' or '1';
//                code.length <= 32
```

```
// example: binaryToSigned("010100001001") returns  1289
//          binaryToSigned("101011110111") returns -1289
```

1.10   Write and test the following method:
```
public static int binaryToUnsigned(String code)
// preconditions: each character in code is either '0' or '1';
                  code.length <= 32
// example: binaryToUnsigned("010100001001") returns 1289
//          binaryToUnsigned("101011110111") returns 2807
```

1.11   Write and test the following method:
```
public static String format(String s, int len, int d)
// examples:  format("tomato",9,d) for d = -1,0, 1 return
//            respectively:
//            "tomato   " , "  tomato  " , "   tomato"
```

1.12   Write and test the following method:
```
public static int randomInt(int start, int stop)
// preconditions: start < stop;
// returns uniformly distributed integers
// in the range start to stop-1 (inclusive)
```

1.13   Implement this default constructor for the `Point` class (see Example 1.7 on page 7):
```
public Point()
// constructs a point that represents the origin (0,0)
```

1.14   Add a `public static final` object to the `Point` class that represents the origin (0,0).

1.15   Implement the following copy constructor for the `Point` class (see Example 1.7 on page 7):
```
public Point(Point point)
// constructs a point that has the same coordinates as the
// given point
```

1.16   Implement the following method for the `Point` class (see Example 1.7 on page 7):
```
public double distance(Point point)
// returns the Euclidean distance from this point to the
// given point
```

1.17   Implement the following method for the `Point` class (see Example 1.7 on page 7):
```
public double magnitude()
// returns the Euclidean distance from this point to the
// origin
```

1.18   Implement the following method for the `Point` class (see Example 1.7 on page 7):
```
public double amplitude()
// returns the radian measure of the polar angle of this point
```

1.19   Implement the following constructor for the `Point` class (see Example 1.7 on page 7):
```
public void setPolar(double r, double theta)
// moves this point to the given polar coordinates (r,theta)
```

1.20   Implement the following method for the `Point` class (see Example 1.7 on page 7):
```
public static Point polar(double r, double theta)
// returns the point whose polar coordinates are (r,theta)
```

1.21   Implement the following method for the `Point` class (see Example 1.7 on page 7):
```
public void expand(double dr)
// expands this point by the factor dr
```

1.22   Implement the following method for the `Point` class (see Example 1.7 on page 7):
```
public void rotate(double theta)
// rotates this point clockwise by theta radians
```

Answers to Review Questions

1.1 Java is called an "object-oriented" programming language because all data and operations are encapsulated within objects. Furthermore, the objects' classes are all defined within a single inheritance hierarchy.

1.2 A Java program must have a `public` class defined in a file named `X.java`, where `X` is the class name, and that class must include a method declared as

```
public static void main(String[] args)
```

1.3 A *primitive type* is one of `boolean`, `char`, `byte`, `short`, `int`, `long`, `float`, or `double`.

1.4 A *literal* is an anonymous constant; a symbol that represents a constant value for the type. For example, `44`, `3.14`, and `"East Anglia"` are literals.

1.5 The three nonnumeric literals for the two floating-point types are `NEGATIVE_INFINITY`, `POSITIVE_INFINITY`, and `NaN`.

1.6 An *object reference* is a variable whose value is either `null` or the address of some object.

1.7 An *object* is a contiguous block of storage in memory that is typed by a class and accessed by a reference variable for that class. It may have fields that contain data and it may have methods that perform operations.

1.8 A *class* is blueprint for creating its objects. The class definition specifies the fields and the methods for each instance of the class.

1.9 An *instance* of a class is an object of that class type. The creation of an instance is called *instantiating* the class.

1.10 A *field* is a member variable of a class. When the class is instantiated, the resulting object's fields hold data for the object.

1.11 A *method* is a member function of a class. When the class is instantiated, the resulting object's methods perform operations for the object.

1.12 A *method signature* is the part of the method's definition that the compiler needs in order to compile statements that invoke the method. For example, the signature of the main method is

```
main(String[])
```

1.13 A *constructor* is a method that instantiates its class. It has the same name as the class itself and it has no return type. It is invoked by the `new` operator.

1.14 A `static` member of a class is one that applies to the entire class itself instead of to individual instances of the class. It is invoked with the class name instead of with the name of an instance. For example, the `sqrt(double)` method of the `Math` class is static. It is invoked as `Math.sqrt()`. A `static` field has exactly one data value, regardless of how many objects of the class exist, including none.

1.15 An *access modifier* is one of the three Java keywords `public`, `protected`, or `private`. They are used to modify a class, a field, a method, or an interface when it is defined.

1.16 The access modifier `private` means that the entity being defined will be accessible only from within the class in which it is defined.

1.17 The access modifier `protected` means that the entity being defined will be accessible only from within the class in which it is defined or any descendant subclasses.

1.18 A *wrapper class* is a class who purpose is to provide constants and methods for processing one of the eight primitive types. For example, the `Double` class is a wrapper class for the `double` primitive type.

1.19 The `String` class is distinct because its instances are immutable (read-only), its literals are unique, and it has the two operators `+` and `+=` used for concatenation.

1.20 The `Math.random()` method returns `double` precision floating-point random numbers that are uniformly distributed in the range 0.0 to 1.0.

Solutions to Problems

1.1
```java
public static String monthName(int month)
{ switch (month)
    { case  1: return "January";
      case  2: return "February";
      case  3: return "March";
      case  4: return "April";
      case  5: return "May";
      case  6: return "June";
      case  7: return "July";
      case  8: return "August";
      case  9: return "September";
      case 10: return "October";
      case 11: return "November";
      case 12: return "December";
    }
  return "";
}
```

1.2
```java
public static int daysInMonth(int month, int year)
{ if (month==4 || month==6 || month==9 || month==11) return 30;
  if (month==2)
    if (year%400==0 || year%100!=0 && year%4==0) return 29;
    else return 28;
  return 31;
}
```

1.3
```java
public static int numberOfDigits(int n)
{ if (n<0) n = -n;
  int count=0;
  while (n>0)
  { n /= 10;
    ++count;
  }
  return count;
}
```

1.4
```java
public static int sumOfDigits(int n)
{ if (n<0) n = -n;
  int sum=0;
  while (n>0)
  { sum += n%10;
    n /= 10;
  }
  return sum;
}
```

1.5
```java
public static int reverseDigits(int n)
{ if (n==0) return 0;
  int sign = (n<0?-1:1);
  if (n<0) n = -n;
  int reverse=0;
  while (n>0)
  { reverse = 10*reverse + n%10;
    n /= 10;
  }
  return sign*reverse;
}
```

1.6   ```
public static double round(double x, int precision)
{ double pow10 = Math.pow(10,precision);
  return Math.round(x*pow10)/pow10;
}
```

**1.7**    ```
public static String signedToBinary(int n)
{ if (n==0) return "0";
  if (n>0) return "0" + unsignedToBinary(n); // Problem 1.8
  int mod=1;
  while(mod+2*n<0)
    mod *= 2;
  return unsignedToBinary(mod+n);
}
```

1.8   ```
public static String unsignedToBinary(int n)
{ // PRECONDITION: n > 0
  String code="";
  while (n > 0)
  { code = "" + (n%2) + code; // append next bit to left of code
    n /= 2;   // remove current least significan bit
  }
  return code ;
}
```

**1.9**    ```
public static int binaryToSigned(String code)
{ int len = code.length();
  int unsigned = binaryToUnsigned(code);  // Problem 1.10
  if (code.charAt(0) == '0') return unsigned;
  return  unsigned - (int)Math.pow(2,len);
}
```

1.10   ```
public static int binaryToUnsigned(String code)
{ int n = code.length();
  int answer = 0;
  for (int i=0; i<n; i++)
    answer = answer*2 + (code.charAt(i)=='1' ? 1 : 0);
  return answer;
}
```

**1.11**    ```
public static String format(String s, int len, int d)
{ int spaces = (len - s.length());
  if (spaces <= 0) return s;
  String formatS = "";
  int leftSpaces = (d<0)? 0 : ((d>0)? spaces : spaces/2);
  int rightSpaces = spaces - leftSpaces;
  for (int i=0; i<leftSpaces; i++)
    formatS += " ";
  formatS += s ;  // s comes after spaces on left
  for (int i=0; i<rightSpaces; i++)
    formatS += " ";
  return formatS;
}
```

1.12   ```
static java.util.Random random = new java.util.Random();
public static int randomInt(int start, int stop)
{ return start + random.nextInt(stop-start);
}
```

**1.13**    A default constructor for the Point class:
```
public Point()
{ this.x = 0;
  this.y = 0;
}
```
```

1.14   A `public static final` field for the `Point` class:

```
     public static final Point ORIGIN = new Point();
```

1.15   A copy constructor for the `Point` class:

```
    public Point(Point q)
    { this.x = q.x;
      this.y = q.y;
    }
```

1.16   A distance method for the `Point` class:

```
    public double distance(Point point)
    { double dx = this.x - point.x;
      double dy = this.y - point.y;
      return Math.sqrt(dx*dx+dy*dy);
    }
```

1.17   A magnitude method for the `Point` class:

```
    public double magnitude()
    { return distance(ORIGIN);
    }
```

1.18   An amplitude method for the `Point` class:

```
    public double amplitude()
    { return Math.atan(y/x);
    }
```

1.19   A `Point` class method for polar coordinates:

```
    public void setPolar(double r, double theta)
    { this.x = r*Math.cos(theta);
      this.y = r*Math.sin(theta);
    }
```

1.20   Another `Point` class method for polar coordinates:

```
    public static Point polar(double r, double theta)
    { double x = r*Math.cos(theta);
      double y = r*Math.sin(theta);
      return new Point(x,y);
    }
```

1.21   An expand method for the `Point` class:

```
    public void expand(double dr)
    { x *= dr;
      y *= dr;
    }
```

1.22   A rotate method for the `Point` class:

```
    public void rotate(double theta)
    { double xx = x;
      double yy = y;
      double sin = Math.sin(theta);
      double cos = Math.cos(theta);
      x = xx*cos - yy*sin;
      y = xx*sin + yy*cos;
    }
```

Chapter 2

Review of Arrays

An *array* is an object that consists of a sequence of numbered elements, all of the same type. The elements are numbered beginning with 0 and can be referenced by their number using the *subscript operator* `[]`. Arrays are widely used because they are so efficient.

2.1 PROPERTIES OF ARRAYS

Here are the main properties of arrays in Java:
1. Arrays are objects.
2. Arrays are created dynamically (at run time).
3. Arrays may be assigned to variables of type `Object`.
4. Any method of `Object` class may be invoked on an array.
5. An array object contains a sequence of variables, all of the same type.
6. The variables are called the *components* of the array.
7. If the component type is T, then the array itself has type $T[]$.
8. An array type variable holds a reference to the array object.
9. The component type may itself be an array type.
10. An array *element* is a component whose type is not an array type.
11. An element's type may be either primitive or reference.
12. The *length* of an array is its number of components.
13. An array's length is set when the array is created, and it cannot be changed.
14. An array's length can be accessed as a `public final` instance variable.
15. Arrays must be indexed by integral values in the range $0..length-1$.
16. An `ArrayIndexOutOfBoundsException` is thrown if Property 15 is violated.
17. Variables of type `short`, `byte`, or `char` can be used as indexes.
18. Arrays can be duplicated with the `Object.clone()` method.
19. Arrays can be tested for equality with the `Arrays.equals()` method.
20. Array objects implement `Cloneable` and `java.io.Serializable`.

Property 3 follows from Property 1. Although array types are not classes, they behave this way as extensions of the `Object` class. Property 7 shows that array types are not the same as class types. (See the diagram on page 2.) They are, in fact, derived types: for every class type T there is a corresponding array type $T[]$. Also, for each of the eight primitive types, the corresponding array type exists.

Property 9 allows the existence of arrays of arrays. Technically, Java allows multidimensional arrays only with primitive types. But for objects, an array of arrays is essentially the same thing. Since arrays themselves are objects, an array of arrays is an array of objects, and some of those component objects could also be nonarrays. (See Example 2.1.)

Note that a consequence of Property 13 is that changing a reference component value to `null` has no effect upon the length of the array; `null` is still a valid value of a reference component.

EXAMPLE 2.1 Some Array Definitions

Here are some valid array definitions:

```
public class Ex0201
{ public static void main(String[] args)
  { float x[];
    x = new float[100];
    args = new String[10];
    boolean[] isPrime = new boolean[1000];
    int fib[] = { 0, 1, 1, 2, 3, 5, 8, 13 };
    short[][][] b = new short[3][8][5];
    double a[][] = { {1.1,2.2}, {3.3,4.4}, null, {5.5,6.6}, null };
    a[4] = new double[66];
    a[4][65] = 3.14;
    Object[] objects = { x, args, isPrime, fib, b, a };
  }
}
```

The first line declares x[] to be an array of floats but does not allocate any. The second line defines x[] to have 100 float components.

The third line declares args[] to be an array of String objects. Note the two different (equivalent) ways to declare an array: the brackets may be a suffix on the type identifier or on the array identifier. The fourth line defines args[] to have 10 String components.

The fifth line defines isPrime[] to be an array of 1000 boolean variables.

The sixth line defines fib[] to be an array of 8 ints, initializing them to the 8 values listed. So, for example, fib[4] has the value 3, and fib[7] has the value 13.

The eighth line defines a[][] to be an array of five components, each of which is an array of elements of type double. Only three of the five component arrays are allocated. Then the next line allocates a 66-element array of doubles to a[4], and the last line assigns 3.14 to its last element.

The last line defines the array objects to consist of six components, each of which is itself an array. The components of the first four component arrays are elements (non-arrays). But the components of the components b and a are not elements because they are also arrays. The actual elements of the objects array include 2, 5, and 13 (components of the component fib), null (components of the component a), and 2.2 and 3.14 (components of the components of the component a).

The array a[][] defined in Example 2.1 is called a *ragged array* because it is a two-dimensional array with rows of different lengths.

The element type of an array in Java can be a primitive type, a reference type, or an array type. The simplest, of course, are arrays of primitive type elements, such as x[], isPrime[], and fib[] in Example 2.1. These are arrays that can be sorted.

2.2 DUPLICATING AN ARRAY

Since it is an object, an array can be duplicated by invoking the Object.clone() method, as shown in Example 2.2.

EXAMPLE 2.2 Duplicating an Array

```
public class Ex0202
{ public static void main(String[] args)
  { int[] a = { 22, 44, 66, 88 };
    print(a);
```

```
        int[] b = (int[])a.clone();   // duplicate a[] in b[]
        print(b);
        String[] c = { "AB", "CD", "EF" };
        print(c);
        String[] d = (String[])c.clone();   // duplicate c[] in d[]
        print(d);
        c[1] = "XYZ";   // change c[], but not d[]
        print(c);
        print(d);
    }

    public static void print(int[] a)
    { for (int i=0; i<a.length; i++)
        System.out.print(a[i] + " ");
      System.out.println();
    }

    public static void print(Object[] a)
    { for (int i=0; i<a.length; i++)
        System.out.print(a[i] + " ");
      System.out.println();
    }
}
```

```
22 44 66 88
22 44 66 88
AB CD EF
AB CD EF
AB XYZ EF
AB CD EF
```

The array a[] contains four int elements. The array b[] is a duplicate of a[]. Similarly, the array d[] is a duplicate of the array c[], each containing three String elements. In both cases, the duplication is obtained by invoking the clone() method. Since it returns a reference to an Object, it must be cast to the array type being duplicated, int[] or String[].

The last part of the example shows that the cloned array d[] is indeed a separate copy of c[]: changing c[1] to "XYZ" has no effect upon the value "CD" of d[1].

2.3 THE Arrays CLASS

The java.util.Arrays class defines the following methods:
```
    public static List asList(Object[])
    public static int binarySearch(...)
    public static boolean equals(...)
    public static void fill(...)
    public static void sort(...)
```
Here, the ellipses "..." indicate that the method is overloaded for various parameter types, both primitive and reference. For example, there are nine versions of the binarySearch(...) method: one for array of every primitive type except boolean, and two for arrays of type Object[].

Note that all the methods in the `Arrays` class are `static`. Thus, they are invoked using the prefix `Arrays.` instead of with the name of an instance of the class. In fact, it is not possible to instantiate the `Arrays` class because its constructor is declared to be `private`.

EXAMPLE 2.3 Testing the Methods in the `Arrays` Class

```java
import java.util.Arrays;

public class Testing
{ public static void main(String[] args)
    { char[] a = new char[64];
      Arrays.fill(a,'H');
      String s = new String(a);
      System.out.println("s = \"" + s + "\"");
      Object[] objects = new Object[8];
      Arrays.fill(objects,2,5,"Java");
      System.out.println("objects = " + Arrays.asList(objects));
      int[] x = { 77, 44, 99, 88, 22, 33, 66, 55 };
      int[] y = (int[])x.clone();
      System.out.print("x = ");   print(x);
      System.out.print("y = ");   print(y);
      System.out.println("Arrays.equals(x,y) = " + Arrays.equals(x,y));
      System.out.println("y.equals(x) = " + y.equals(x));
      y[4] = 0;
      System.out.print("y = ");   print(y);
      System.out.println("Arrays.equals(x,y) = " + Arrays.equals(x,y));
      System.out.print("x = ");   print(x);
      Arrays.sort(x);
      System.out.print("x = ");   print(x);
      int i = Arrays.binarySearch(x,44);
      System.out.println("Arrays.binarySearch(x,44) = " + i);
      i = Arrays.binarySearch(x,47);
      System.out.println("Arrays.binarySearch(x,47) = " + i);
    }

  private static void print(int[] a)
  { System.out.print("{ " + a[0]);
    for (int i=1; i<a.length; i++)
      System.out.print(", " + a[i]);
    System.out.println(" }");
  }
}
```

```
s = "HHHHHHHHHHHHHHHHHHHHHHHHHHHHHHHHHHHHHHHHHHHHHHHHHHHHHHHHHHHHHHHH"
objects = [null, null, Java, Java, Java, null, null, null]
x = { 77, 44, 99, 88, 22, 33, 66, 55 }
y = { 77, 44, 99, 88, 22, 33, 66, 55 }
Arrays.equals(x,y) = true
y.equals(x) = false
y = { 77, 44, 99, 88, 0, 33, 66, 55 }
Arrays.equals(x,y) = false
x = { 77, 44, 99, 88, 22, 33, 66, 55 }
x = { 22, 33, 44, 55, 66, 77, 88, 99 }
Arrays.binarySearch(x,44) = 2
Arrays.binarySearch(x,47) = -4
```

The first three lines show how to construct a `String` object with repeated instances of a single character. First we define a to be an array of 64 `chars`. Then we use the `Arrays.fill()` method to fill it with the desired character; in this case, an `'H'`. Then we use the appropriate `String` constructor to produce a `String` object with the same contents.

Next, we construct an array named objects of eight references. Then we fill the elements indexed from 2 to 4 with the `String` object `"Java"`. Note that the integer parameters 2 and 5 are used to indicate the subrange of values to be filled: The first integer, 2, is the starting index, and the second integer is the index of the first element thereafter that is not to be changed. This protocol for indicating subranges is commonly used in standard libraries. A consequence is that the number of elements in the subrange is always equal to the difference between the two parameters; in this case $5 - 2 = 3$ elements were changed.

There is no `toString()` method for arrays, so unlike other objects, they cannot be printed directly. However, the `Arrays.toList()` method produces a `List` object that can be passed to the `System.out.println()` method because it does have a `toString()` method. This is a simple way to print an array of objects.

The next part of the example creates two `int` arrays, x and y, using the `Object.clone()` method to duplicate x in y. (See Section 2.2 on page 24.) Then it invokes the `Arrays.equals()` method and the `Object.equals()` method to check their equality. Notice that only the first of these two methods returns the correct answer. Then we change `y[4]` to check that the `Arrays.equals()` method also works correctly when the two arrays are not equal.

The `Arrays.sort()` method is used to sort x. Then we can use the `Arrays.binarySearch()` method to search for a specific `int` in x. If the element is in the array, then the method returns its index, 2 in this case. Otherwise, the method returns a negative integer to signal that the element is not in the array. The general Binary Search Algorithm is outlined in Section 2.5 on page 31.

Note that the `Arrays.binarySearch()` method will not work properly unless the array is sorted first.

The `Arrays.equals()` method is meant to be used in place of the `Object.equals()` method for arrays. The latter method returns true only when the two references refer to the same object; i.e., it tests identity instead of equality.

To illustrate the array algorithms presented in this book, we define another `Arrays` class. To avoid a name conflict, we define this class in a separate package named `schaums.dswj` (for "Schaum's Outline of Data Structures with Java").

EXAMPLE 2.4 An `Arrays` Utility Class

```
package schaums.dswj;
import java.util.Random;

public class Arrays
{ private static Random random = new Random();

  public static int load(int start, int range)
  { return random.nextInt(range) + start;
  }

  public static void load(int[] a, int start, int range)
  { int n=a.length;
    for (int i=0; i<n; i++)
      a[i] = random.nextInt(range) + start;
  }
```

```
   public static void print(int[] a)
   { for (int i=0; i<a.length; i++)
       System.out.print("  " + (i>9?"":" ") + i);
     System.out.print("\n{ " + a[0]);
     for (int i=1; i<a.length; i++)
       System.out.print(", " + a[i]);
     System.out.println(" }");
   }
 }
```

Initially, this testing class has only three methods: two `load()` methods for initializing variables and arrays with random integers and a `print()` method for printing arrays of integers. The `load()` methods restrict the integer values to the `range` start to `load−1`. This facilitates the production of duplicate values. The `print()` method annotates the array list with a row of index numbers to facilitate locating individually indexed elements.

Here is a test driver to illustrate how the class works:

```
   import schaums.dswj.Arrays;

   public class Testing
   { private static final int SIZE = 16;
     private static final int START = 40;
     private static final int RANGE = 20;
     private static int[] a = new int[SIZE];

     public static void main(String[] args)
     { Arrays.load(a,START,RANGE);
       Arrays.print(a);
       Arrays.load(a,START,RANGE);
       Arrays.print(a);
     }
   }
```

```
    0   1   2   3   4   5   6   7   8   9  10  11  12  13  14  15
{ 49, 56, 46, 43, 40, 57, 47, 43, 43, 43, 46, 57, 47, 53, 44, 46 }
    0   1   2   3   4   5   6   7   8   9  10  11  12  13  14  15
{ 58, 55, 40, 45, 56, 46, 59, 59, 57, 45, 46, 42, 52, 47, 42, 54 }
```

This generates two random arrays of 16 elements each. The elements are bound to the range 40 to 59, so they are likely to have duplicates. For example, in the first array, a[2] = a[10] = 46.

2.4 THE SEQUENTIAL SEARCH ALGORITHM

The *Sequential Search* (also called the *Linear Search*) is the simplest search algorithm. It is 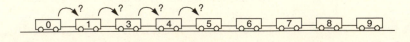 also the least efficient. It simply examines each element sequentially, starting with the first element, until it finds the key element or it reaches the end of the array.

If you were looking for someone on a moving passenger train, you would use a Sequential Search.

Algorithm 2.1 The Sequential Search

(Precondition: $s = \{s_0, s_1, s_2, \ldots, s_{n-1}\}$ is a sequence of n ordinal values of the same type as x.)

(Postcondition: either the index i is returned where $s_i = x$, or -1 is returned.)

1. Repeat steps 2–3 n times, for $i = 0$ to $n - 1$.
2. (Invariant: none of the elements in the subsequence $\{s_0..s_{i-1}\}$ is equal to x.)
3. If $s_i = x$, return i.
4. Return -1.

In Algorithm 2.1 (and in all the algorithms in this book), we use preconditions and postconditions to specify exactly what the algorithm does, and we use loop invariants to prove that the algorithm is correct. We also provide for each algorithm an example of its Java code:

EXAMPLE 2.5 The Sequential Search

```
public static int sequentialSearch(int[] a, int x)
{ // POSTCONDITIONS: returns i; if i >= 0, then a[i] == x;
  //                 otherwise i == -1;
  for (int i=0; i<a.length; i++)                    // step 1
    // INVARIANT: if a[k]==x then i <= k < a.length;  // step 2
    // INVARIANT: a[k] != x, for 0 <= k < i;          // step 2
    if (a[i]==x) return i;                           // step 3
  return -1;                                         // step 4
}
```

Theorem 2.1 The Sequential Search is correct.

Proof: If $n = 0$, then the sequence is empty and the loop does not execute at all. Only step 4 executes, immediately returning -1. This satisfies the postconditions: x cannot equal any of the elements because there aren't any.

If $n = 1$, then the loop iterates only once, with $i = 0$. On that iteration, either $s_0 = x$ or $s_0 \neq x$. If $s_0 = x$, then 0 is returned and the postcondition is satisfied. If $s_0 \neq x$, then the loop terminates, step 4 executes, and -1 is returned, and that satisfies the postcondition because the single element of the sequence is not equal to x.

Suppose $n > 1$. Then on the first iteration of the loop, $i = 0$, and the loop invariant in step 2 is true "vacuously" because the subsequence $\{s_0..s_{i-1}\}$ is empty. Then in step 3, either $s_0 = x$ or $s_0 \neq x$. If $s_0 = x$, then 0 is returned and the postcondition is satisfied. If $s_0 \neq x$, then the loop continues. If there is a second iteration (i.e., if $s_0 \neq x$), then $i = 1$ and the loop invariant in step 2 is again true because the subsequence $\{s_0..s_{i-1}\} = \{s_0\}$ and $s_0 \neq x$.

Suppose that on the kth iteration of the loop, the loop invariant is true; i.e., none of the elements in the subsequence $\{s_0..s_{k-1}\}$ is equal to x. Then during that iteration, at step 3, either $s_i = x$ or $s_i \neq x$. If $s_i = x$, then k is returned and the postcondition is satisfied. If $s_i \neq x$, then the loop continues.

It follows by the Principle of Mathematical Induction (see Section A.4 on page 336) that after every iteration of the loop, either the algorithm terminates with the postcondition being true, or the loop invariant for the next iteration will be true. So if the algorithm does not terminate during any iteration, then after the last iteration (when $i = n - 1$), the loop invariant for the case $i = n$ will be true; i.e., none of the elements in the subsequence $\{s_0..s_{n-1}\}$ is equal to x. At that point, -1 is returned and the postcondition is satisfied.

The next theorem uses the $O()$ notation. See Section A.3 on page 335 for a review.

Theorem 2.2 The Sequential Search runs in $O(n)$ time.

Proof: If x is in the sequence, say at $x = s_i$ with $i < n$, then the loop will iterate i times. In that case, the running time is proportional to i, which is $O(n)$ since $i < n$. If x is not in the sequence, then the loop will iterate n times, making the running time proportional to n, which is $O(n)$.

EXAMPLE 2.6 Testing the Sequential Search

```
import schaums.dswj.Arrays;

public class Testing
{ private static final int SIZE = 16;
  private static final int START = 40;
  private static final int RANGE = 20;
  private static int[] a = new int[SIZE];

  public static void main(String[] args)
  { Arrays.load(a,START,RANGE);
    Arrays.print(a);
    test();
    test();
    test();
    test();
  }

  public static void test()
  { int x = Arrays.load(START,RANGE);
    System.out.print("Searching for x = " + x + ":\t");
    int i = Arrays.sequentialSearch(a,x);
    if (i >= 0) System.out.println("a[" + i + "] = " + a[i]);
    else System.out.println("i = " + i + " ==> x not found");
  }
}
```

```
    0    1    2    3    4    5    6    7    8    9   10   11   12   13   14   15
{  49,  44,  49,  41,  50,  59,  51,  48,  48,  41,  50,  47,  41,  58,  46,  48 }
Searching for x = 51:    a[6] = 51
Searching for x = 47:    a[11] = 47
Searching for x = 56:    i = -1 ==> x not found
Searching for x = 50:    a[4] = 50
```

This tests the Sequential Search Algorithm four times on the array generated by load(). The first test searches for x = 51 and finds it at a[6]. The second test searches for x = 47 and finds it at a[11]. The third test searches for x = 56 and fails, returning –1. The fourth test searches for x = 50 and finds it at a[4]. Note that this value is also at a[10]. The Sequential Search stops as soon as it finds its target, ignoring the rest of the array.

For easy access, each array algorithm is added to our schaums.dswj.Arrays class. So for example, to test the Sequential Search, we import this class and then invoke the search method as Arrays.sequentialSearch().

2.5 THE BINARY SEARCH ALGORITHM

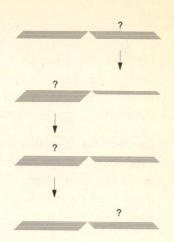

The *Binary Search* is the standard procedure for searching through a sorted sequence. It is much more efficient than the Sequential Search, but it does require that the elements be in order. It repeatedly divides the sequence in two, each time restricting the search to the half that would contain the element.

You might use a binary search to look up a word in a dictionary.

Algorithm 2.2 The Binary Search

(Precondition: $s = \{s_0, s_1, s_2, \ldots, s_{n-1}\}$ is a sorted sequence of n ordinal values of the same type as x.)

(Postcondition: either the index i is returned where $s_i = x$, or -1 is returned.)

1. Let ss be a subsequence of the sequence s, initially set equal to s.
2. If the subsequence ss is empty, return -1.
3. (Invariant: if x is in the original sequence s, then it must be in the subsequence ss.)
4. Let s_i be the middle element of ss.
5. If $s_i = x$, return its index i.
6. If $s_i < x$, repeat steps 2–7 on the subsequence that lies above s_i.
7. Repeat steps 2–7 on the subsequence of ss that lies below s_i.

Note that the precondition in Algorithm 2.2 requires the sequence to be sorted.

The Binary Search is implemented in the `java.util.Arrays` class. (See Section 2.3.) An annotated version is given here:

EXAMPLE 2.7 The Binary Search

```
public static int binarySearch(int[] a, int x)
{ // PRECONDITION:    a[0] <= a[1] <= ... <= a[a.length-1];
  // POSTCONDITIONS: returns i; if i >= 0, then a[i] == x;
  //                 otherwise i == -1;
  int lo=0, hi=a.length-1;
  while (lo <= hi)                                   // step 1
  { // INVARIANT: if a[j]==x then lo <= j <= hi;     // step 3
    int i = (hi + lo)/2;                             // step 4
    if (a[i] == x) return i;                         // step 5
    else if (a[i] < x) lo = i+1;                     // step 6
    else hi = i-1;                                   // step 7
  }
  return -1;                                         // step 2
}
```

Theorem 2.3 The Binary Search is correct.

Proof: The loop invariant is true on the first iteration because the current subsequence is the same as the original sequence. On every other iteration, the current subsequence was defined in the preceding iteration to be the half of the previous subsequence that remained after omitting the half that did not contain x. So if x was in the original sequence, then it must be in the current subsequence. Thus the loop invariant is true on every iteration.

On each iteration, either i is returned where $s_i = x$, or the subsequence is reduced by more than 50%. Since the original sequence has only a finite number of elements, the loop cannot continue indefinitely. Consequently, the algorithm terminates either by returning i from within the loop or at step 6 or step 7 where −1 is returned. If i is returned from within the loop, then $s_i = x$. Otherwise, the loop terminates when hi < lo; i.e., when the subsequence is empty. In that case we know by the loop invariant that s_i is not in the original sequence.

Theorem 2.4 The Binary Search runs in $O(\lg n)$ time.

Proof: In the proof of Theorem 2.3 it is seen that the number of iterations is at most the number (plus 1) of times that n can be divided in two. That number is the integral binary logarithm $\lfloor \lg n \rfloor$ (See page 334.)

EXAMPLE 2.8 Testing the Binary Search

```
import schaums.dswj.Arrays;

public class Ex0208
{ private static final int SIZE = 16;
  private static final int START = 40;
  private static final int RANGE = 20;
  private static int[] a = new int[SIZE];

  public static void main(String[] args)
  { Arrays.load(a,START,RANGE);
    Arrays.print(a);
    test();
    java.util.Arrays.sort(a);
    Arrays.print(a);
    test();
    test();
    test();
  }

  public static void test()
  { int x = Arrays.load(START,RANGE);
    System.out.print("Searching for x = " + x + ":\t");
    int i = Arrays.binarySearch(a,x);
    if (i >= 0) System.out.println("a[" + i + "] = " + a[i]);
    else System.out.println("i = " + i + " ==> x not found");
  }
}
```

```
      0    1    2    3    4    5    6    7    8    9   10   11   12   13   14   15
  { 48,  57,  46,  51,  55,  51,  55,  45,  47,  52,  57,  47,  50,  42,  59,  45 }
  Searching for x = 50:    i = -1 ==> x not found
      0    1    2    3    4    5    6    7    8    9   10   11   12   13   14   15
  { 42,  45,  45,  46,  47,  47,  48,  50,  51,  51,  52,  55,  55,  57,  57,  59 }
  Searching for x = 50:    a[7] = 50
  Searching for x = 47:    a[5] = 47
  Searching for x = 58:    i = -1 ==> x not found
```

This tests the Binary Search Algorithm four times on the array generated by load(). The first test searches for x = 50 and fails, even though a[7] = 50. The Binary Search fails because the array is not sorted yet.

After using `java.util.Arrays.sort(a)` to sort the array, the second test finds x = 50 at a[7]. The third test searches for x = 57 and finds it at a[5]. Note that this is not the leftmost occurrence of this value: it also occurs at a[4]. The Binary Search is not sequential, so when a value occurs more than once in the array, the index returned by algorithm is not easy to predict. (See Review Question 2.9 on page 36)

The fourth test searches for x = 58 and fails, returning –1.

2.6 THE `Vector` CLASS

Mathematically, a *vector* is simply a finite sequence of numbers. Geometrically, we think of a two-dimensional vector (x, y) as representing a point in the plane and a three-dimensional vector (x, y, z) as representing a point in the space. Vectors of an unspecified number n of elements are common in linear algebra: $(x_1, x_2, ..., x_n)$. This requires the use of subscripts.

In Java, a vector is the same thing as an array except:

- A vector is an instance of the `java.util.Vector` class.
- A vector can change its length.

The `Vector` class has been substantially rewritten for Java 1.2. It is defined in the java.util package like this:

```
public class Vector extends AbstractList implements List
{ public boolean   add(Object object)
  public void      add(int index, Object object)
  public boolean   addAll(Collection collection)
  public boolean   addAll(int index, Collection collection)
  public void      addElement(Object object)
  public void      clear()
  public Object    clone()
  public boolean   contains(Object object)
  public boolean   containsAll(Collection collection)
  public void      copyInto(Object[] objects)
  public Object    elementAt(int index)
  public boolean   equals(Object object)
  public Object    firstElement()
  public Object    get(int index)
  public int       hashCode()
  public int       indexOf(Object object)
  public int       indexOf(Object object, int index)
  public void      insertElementAt(Object object, int index)
  public boolean   isEmpty()
  public Object    lastElement()
  public int       lastIndexOf(Object object)
  public int       lastIndexOf(Object object, int index)
  public Object    remove(int index)
  public boolean   remove(Object object)
  public boolean   removeAll(Collection collection)
  public void      removeAllElements()
  public boolean   removeElement(Object object)
  public void      removeElementAt(int index)
  public boolean   retainAll(Collection collection)
  public Object    set(int index, Object object)
  public void      setElementAt(Object object, int index)
```

```
    public int      size()
    public List     subList(int start, int stop)
    public Object[] toArray()
    public Object[] toArray(Object[] objects)
    public String   toString()
    public          Vector()
    public          Vector(Collection collection)
}
```

The `add` methods are used to insert new elements into the vector. The `add(object)` and `addElement(object)` methods have the same effect, except that the former returns `true` (or `false` if unsuccessful). If the location of the new element(s) is not specified, it defaults to the end of the vector.

The `clear()` method reduces the vector to size 0, rendering it empty. Note that an empty vector is not the same as the `null` reference; the vector object still exists.

The `clone()` method duplicates the entire vector, thereby also cloning the objects it contains.

The `contains` methods determine whether the given objects are elements of the vector.

The `copyInto` method copies elements of the vector into the given array.

The `elementAt()` and `get()` methods are analogous to the subscript operator for arrays: They return the vector element at the given index.

The `equals()` tests equality of another object, returning true if and only if the given object is a vector whose elements are equal to the invoked vector.

The `firstElement()` and `lastElement()` methods simply return the first and last elements of the vector.

The `hashCode()` method returns an identification number for the vector object.

The `indexOf` methods use the Sequential Search to find and return the index of the given object in the vector. They return –1 if the object is not found. The two-parameter version begins its search at the given index.

The `insertElementAt()` method inserts the given object into the vector at the given index. This causes it to shift forward all the existing elements from that index forward.

The `lastIndexOf` methods work the same way as the `indexOf()` except that they execute the Sequential Search in reverse.

The `remove` methods remove a segment of one or more elements from the vector. This causes the existing elements that were beyond the removed segment to be shifted back, with the reverse effect as the `insertElementAt()` method. Note that, while there is only one `insert` method, there are six (`public`) `remove` methods. The `remove(index)` and `removeElementAt(index)` methods have the same effect, except that the former returns the object removed (or `null` if unsuccessful) while the latter returns `true` (or `false` if unsuccessful).

The `set(index,object)` and `setElementAt(object,index)` methods both replace the element at the given index with the given object. They have the same effect, except that the former returns the object removed (or `null` if unsuccessful).

The `subList()` method returns a `List` object containing the objects in the vector from the `start` index to the index `stop` – 1. Thus the size of the resulting `List` object is `stop` – `start`.

The `toArray()` methods return an `Object[]` array that contains the same elements as the vector. The no-parameter version creates the returned array, so it has the same size as the vector. The version that has the `Object[]` parameter does the same thing if the size of the given array is less than the size of the vector. Otherwise, it copies the vector's elements into the front of the given array and then changes its remaining components to `null`.

The `toString()` method returns a string that represents the contents of the vector.

EXAMPLE 2.9 Testing the `java.util.Vector` Class

```
import java.util.*;
public class Ex0209
{ private static Vector v = new Vector();
  private static Vector w = new Vector();
  public static void main(String[] args)
  { String[] cities = { "Austin", "Boston", "Fresno", "Toledo" };
    v.addAll(Arrays.asList(cities));
    System.out.println("v = " + v);
    v.add("Tucson");
    System.out.println("v = " + v);
    w = (Vector)v.clone();
    System.out.println("w = " + w);
    System.out.println("w.equals(v) = " + w.equals(v));
    v.set(3,"Ottowa");
    System.out.println("v = " + v);
    System.out.println("w = " + w);
    System.out.println("w.equals(v) = " + w.equals(v));
    v.insertElementAt("London",3);
    System.out.println("v = " + v);
    System.out.println("w = " + w);
    System.out.println("w.equals(v) = " + w.equals(v));
    w.removeElementAt(1);
    w.removeElementAt(3);
    w.remove("Fresno");
    System.out.println("w = " + w);
    v.addAll(5,w);
    System.out.println("v = " + v);
    System.out.println("v.indexOf(\"Austin\") = "
                        + v.indexOf("Austin"));
    System.out.println("v.indexOf(\"Austin\",2) = "
                        + v.indexOf("Austin",2));
    System.out.println("v.indexOf(\"Dublin\") = "
                        + v.indexOf("Dublin"));
  }
}
```

```
v = [Austin, Boston, Fresno, Toledo]
v = [Austin, Boston, Fresno, Toledo, Tucson]
w = [Austin, Boston, Fresno, Toledo, Tucson]
w.equals(v) = true
v = [Austin, Boston, Fresno, Ottowa, Tucson]
w = [Austin, Boston, Fresno, Toledo, Tucson]
w.equals(v) = false
v = [Austin, Boston, Fresno, London, Ottowa, Tucson]
w = [Austin, Boston, Fresno, Toledo, Tucson]
w.equals(v) = false
w = [Austin, Toledo]
v = [Austin, Boston, Fresno, London, Ottowa, Austin, Toledo, Tucson]
v.indexOf("Austin") = 0
v.indexOf("Austin",3) = 5
v.indexOf("Dublin") = -1
```

The array `cities` is used to create the vector `v` by passing the `List` object created by the `Arrays.asList()` method to the `Vector` constructor that takes a `Collection` object as a parameter. (A `List` is a `Collection`.) The `System.out.println()` method invokes the vector's `toString()` method to print it.

The invocation `v.add("Tucson")` appends the new string to the end of the vector, thereby increasing its size. The invocation `v.clone()` returns a duplicate of the vector `v`, but as an `Object` type, so it has to be cast down to type `Vector` with the `(Vector)` cast in order to be assigned to the reference `w`.

The `equals()` method shows that `v` and `w` are equal. The invocation `v.set(3,"Ottowa")` changes `v` but not `w`, verifying that the two vectors were separate but equal.

After removing three elements from `w`, the invocation `v.addAll(5,w)` inserts copies of all of `w` into `v` starting at its fifth position (i.e., immediately after its first five elements). Finally, the `indexOf()` method is used to search for elements in `v`.

Review Questions

2.1   What is the difference between a component and an element of an array?

2.2   What does it mean to say that Java does not allow multidimensional arrays?

2.3   What is an `ArrayIndexOutOfBoundsException` exception, and how does its use distinguish Java from other languages such as C and C++?

2.4   What types are valid for array indexes?

2.5   What's wrong with this definition:
```
Arrays arrays = new Arrays();
```

2.6   What is the simplest way to print an array of objects?

2.7   If the Binary Search is so much faster than the Sequential Search, why would the latter ever be used?

2.8   What happens if the Sequential Search is applied to an element that occurs more than once in the array?

2.9   What happens if the Binary Search is applied to an element that occurs more than once in the array?

2.10 What's the difference between invoking the `clear()` method on a `Vector` object as opposed to setting it to `null`?

Problems

2.1   Run a test program to see how the `Arrays.fill()` method handles an array of objects.

2.2   Run a test program to see how the `Arrays.equals()` method handles an array of objects.

2.3   Run a test program to see how the `Arrays.equals()` method handles an array of arrays.

2.4   If the Sequential Search took 50 ms to run on an array of 10,000 elements, how long would you expect it to take to run on an array of 20,000 elements on the same computer?

2.5   If the Binary Search took 5 ms to run on an array of 1,000 elements, how long would you expect it to take to run on an array of 1,000,000 elements on the same computer?

2.6   Run a test driver for the Binary Search method in Example 2.7 on page 31.

2.7   Run a test driver for the Binary Search method in Example 2.7 on page 31 on an array of 10,000 elements and count the number of iterations.

2.8   Write and test the following method:
```
private static boolean isSorted(int[] a)
// returns true iff a[0] <= a[1] <= ... <= a[a.length-1]
```

2.9   Write and test the following method:
```
private static int minimum(int[] a)
// returns the minimum element of a[]
```

2.10 Write and test the following method:
```
private static double mean(double[] a)
// returns the average value of all the elements in a[]
```

2.11 Write and test the following method:
```
private static int[] withoutDuplicates(int[] a)
// returns an array with same elements as a[] but no duplicates
```

2.12 Write and test the following method:
```
private static Object[] withoutDuplicates(Object[] a)
// returns an array with same components as a[] but no duplicates
```

2.13 Write and test the following method:
```
private static void reverse(int[] a)
// reverses the elements of a[]
```

2.14 Write and test the following method:
```
private static Object[] concatenate(Object[] a, Object[] b)
// returns an array containing all of a[] followed by all of b[]
```

2.15 Write and test the following method:
```
private static void shuffle(Object[] a)
// randomly permutes the elements of a[]
```

2.16 Write and test the following method:
```
private static int[] tally(String string)
// returns an array a[] of 26 integers that count the frequencies
// of the (case insensitive) letters in the given string
```

2.17 Write and test the following method:
```
private static double innerProduct(double[] x, double[] y)
// returns the algebraic inner product (the sum of the component-
// wise products) of the two given arrays as (algebraic) vectors
```

2.18 Write and test the following method:
```
private static double[][] outerProduct(double[] x, double[] y)
// returns the algebraic outer product of the two given arrays
// as (algebraic) vectors: p[i][j] = a[i]*b[j]
```

2.19 Write and test the following method:
```
private static double[][] product(double[][] a, double[][] b)
// returns the matrix product of the two given arrays a matrix:
// p[i][j] = Sum(a[i][k]*b[k][j]:k)
```

2.20 Write and test the following method:
```
private static void transpose(double[][] a)
// transposes the given array as a matrix:
// a[i][j]   <--   a[j][i]
```

2.21 Write and test the following method:
```
private static int[][] pascal(int size)
// returns Pascal's triangle of the given size
```

2.22 The *Sieve of Eratosthenes* is an array of `boolean` elements whose ith element if true if and only if i is a prime number. Use the following algorithm to compute and print a sieve of size 1000:

Algorithm 2.3 The Sieve of Eratosthenes

(Precondition: p is an array of n bits.)

(Postcondition: $p[i]$ is true if and only if i is prime.)

1. Initialize $p[0]$ and $p[1]$ to be false, and all other $p[i]$ to be true.

2. Repeat step 3 for each i from 3 to n, incrementing by 2.

3. If there is a prime $\leq$ the square root of i that divides i, set $p[i]$ false.

2.23 Repeat Problem 2.22 using a `java.util.Vector` object.

2.24 Repeat Problem 2.22 using a `java.util.BitSet` object.

2.25 Define and test a `Primes` class with the following methods:

```
private Primes()
public static void setLast(int last)        // sets last
public static void setLast()                // sets last=1
public static void sizeSize(int size)       // sets size of bitset
public static void sizeSize()               // sets bitset size=1000
public static boolean isPrime(int n)        // true if n is prime
public static int nextPrime()               // next prime after last
public static void printPrimes()            // prints sieve
```

Use the `BitSet` implementation of the Sieve of Eratosthenes from Problem 2.24. Use the following definitions

```
public class Primes
{ private static final int SIZE = 1000;
  private static int size = SIZE;
  private static BitSet sieve = new BitSet(size);
  private static int last = 1;
```

including this static initializer, which implements the Sieve of Eratosthenes:

```
static
{ for (int i=2; i<SIZE; i++)
    sieve.set(i);
  for (int n=2; 2*n<SIZE; n++)
    if (sieve.get(n))
      for (int m=n; m*n<SIZE; m++)
        sieve.clear(m*n);
}
```

2.26 Add the following method to the `Primes` class and then test it:

```
public static String factor(int n)
// precondition: n > 1
// returns the prime factorization of n;
// example:  factor(4840) returns "2*2*2*5*11*11"
```

2.27 Christian Goldbach (1690–1764) conjectured in 1742 that every even number greater than 2 is the sum of two primes. Write a program that tests the *Goldbach Conjecture* for all even numbers less than 100. Use the `Primes` class from Problem 2.25. Your first 10 lines of output should look like this:

```
 4  =  2+2
 6  =  3+3
 8  =  3+5
10  =  3+7  =  5+5
12  =  5+7
14  =  3+11  =  7+7
16  =  3+13  =  5+11
18  =  5+13  =  7+11
20  =  3+17  =  7+13
22  =  3+19  =  5+17  =  11+11
```

2.28 Pierre de Fermat (1601–1665) conjectured that there are infinitely many prime numbers of the form $n = 2^{2^p} + 1$ for some integer p. These numbers are called *Fermat primes*. For example, 5 is a Fermat prime because it is a prime number and it has the form $2^{2^1} + 1$. Write a program that finds all the Fermat primes that are in the range of the `int` type. Use the `Primes` class from Problem 2.25 and the `Math.pow` method. Your first 5 lines of output should look like this:

```
2^2^0 + 1 = 3
2^2^1 + 1 = 5
2^2^2 + 1 = 17
2^2^3 + 1 = 257
2^2^4 + 1 = 65537
```

2.29 Charles Babbage (1792–1871) obtained the first government grant in history when in 1823 he persuaded the British government to provide £1000 pounds to build his Difference Engine. In his grant proposal, Babbage gave the formula $x^2 + x + 41$ as an example of a function that his computer would tabulate. This particular function was of interest to mathematicians because it produces an unusual number of prime numbers. Primes that have this form $n = x^2 + x + 41$ for some integer x could be called *Babbage primes*. Write a program that finds all the Babbage primes that are less than 10,000. Use the `Primes` class from Problem 2.25. Your first 5 lines of output should look like this:

```
0          41 is prime
1          43 is prime
2          47 is prime
3          53 is prime
4          61 is prime
```

2.30 Two consecutive odd integers that are both prime are called *twin primes*. The *Twin Primes Conjecture* is that there are infinitely many twin primes. Write a program that finds all the twin primes that are less than 1000. Use the `Primes` class from Problem 2.25. Your first five lines of output should look like this

```
3          5
5          7
11         13
17         19
29         31
```

2.31 Test the conjecture that there is at least one prime between each pair of consecutive square numbers. (The *square numbers* are 1, 4, 9, 16, 25, ...). Use the `Primes` class from Problem 2.25. Your first 5 lines of output should look like this:

```
1 < 2 < 4
4 < 5 < 9
9 < 11 < 16
16 < 17 < 25
25 < 29 < 36
```

2.32 The Minimite friar Marin Mersenne (1588–1648) undertook in 1644 the study of numbers of the form $n = 2^p - 1$, where p is a prime. He believed that most of these n are also primes, now called *Mersenne primes*. Write a program that finds all the Mersenne primes for $p < 30$. Use the `Primes` class from Problem 2.25. Your first five lines of output should look like this:

```
2          2^2-1 = 3 is prime
3          2^3-1 = 7 is prime
5          2^5-1 = 31 is prime
7          2^7-1 = 127 is prime
11         2^11-1 = 2047 is not prime
```

2.33 A number is said to be *palindromic* if it is invariant under reversion; i.e., the number is the same if its digits are reversed. For example, 3456543 is palindromic. Write a program that checks each of the first 10,000 prime numbers and prints those that are palindromic. Use the `Primes` class from Problem 2.25.

Answers to Review Questions

2.1 An array *component* can be any type: primitive, reference, or array. An array *element* is a component that is not itself an array type. So in, the components of a `[]` are its row arrays, and the elements of `a[][]` are `double` variables.

2.2 A multidimensional array is one that has more than one index. A Java array has only one index variable. However, since a components indexed by that variable can itself be an array (with an index), the original array appears to have more than one index.

2.3 An `ArrayIndexOutOfBoundsException` object is an exception that gets thrown whenever a value less than 0 or greater than or equal to the array's length is attempted to be used as an index on the array. This give the programmer some control over the consequences of such a run-time error. In languages such as C++, such a run-time error normally causes the program to crash.

2.4 An array index can have type `byte`, `char`, `short`, or `int`.

2.5 The `Array` class cannot be instantiated because its constructor is declared `private`.

2.6 The simplest way to print an array of objects is to pass it to the `Arrays.toList()` method which produces a `List` object that can be printed directly with the `System.out.println()` method.

2.7 The Binary Search will not work unless the sequence is sorted first.

2.8 If the Sequential Search is applied to an element that occurs more than once in an array, it will return the index of the one that is closest to the beginning of the array.

2.9 If the Binary Search is applied to an element that occurs more than once in an array, it could return the index of any one of them. It depend upon how close their indexes are to multiples of midpoints of subintervals. For example, if the Binary Search is applied in an array of 10,000 elements, searching for a value that is repeated at locations 0–99, the search would return the index 77 on the 7th iteration.

2.10 The invocation `v.clear()` reduces v to the empty vector, which is still a non-`null` object. The assignment `v = null` destroys the object. In the first case, the expression `v.size()` would evaluate to 0; in the second case, it would through an exception.

Solutions to Problems

2.1 Testing the `java.util.Arrays.fill()` method on arrays of objects:

```
import java.util.Arrays;
public class Pr0201
{ public static void main(String[] args)
  { Object[] a = new Object[4];
    Double x = new Double(Math.PI);
    Arrays.fill(a,x);
    for (int i=0; i<a.length; i++)
      System.out.println("a[" + i + "] = " + a[i]);
    Arrays.fill(a,"Cherry Pie!");
    for (int i=0; i<a.length; i++)
      System.out.println("a[" + i + "] = " + a[i]);
  }
}
```

2.2 Testing the `java.util.Arrays.equals()` method on arrays of objects:

```java
import java.util.Arrays;
public class Pr0202
{ public static void main(String[] args)
  { Double x = new Double(Math.PI);
    Object[] a = new Object[4];
    Arrays.fill(a,x);
    Object[] b = new Object[4];
    Arrays.fill(b,x);
    System.out.println("b.equals(a) = " + b.equals(a));
    System.out.println("Arrays.equals(a,b) = "
                       + Arrays.equals(a,b));
    Arrays.fill(a,"Cherry Pie!");
    Arrays.fill(b,"Cherry Pie!");
    System.out.println("b.equals(a) = " + b.equals(a));
    System.out.println("Arrays.equals(a,b) = "
                       + Arrays.equals(a,b));
  }
}
```

2.3 Testing the `java.util.Arrays.equals()` method on arrays of arrays:

```java
import java.util.Arrays;
public class Pr0203
{ public static void main(String[] args)
  { double[] x = { Math.E, Math.PI };
    String[] s = { "North", "East", "South", "West" };
    Vector[] y = new Vector[0];
    Object[] a = { x, s, null, y };
    Object[] b = { x, s, null, y };
    System.out.println("b.equals(a) = " + b.equals(a));
    System.out.println("Arrays.equals(a,b) = "
                       + Arrays.equals(a,b));
  }
}
```

2.4 The Sequential Search runs in linear time, which means that the time is proportional to the number of elements. So an array with twice as many elements would take twice as long to process: 20 ms.

2.5 The Binary Search runs in logarithmic time, so squaring the size of the problem should only double its running time. So an array with 1000^2 elements would take twice as long to process: 10 ms.

2.6 The Interpolation Search runs in hyperlogarithmic time, so squaring the size of the problem should have no appreciable effect on its running time. So an array with 1,000,000 elements would also take about 2 ms to process.

2.7 Testing the Sequential Search Algorithm:

```java
public class Pr0207
{ private static final int N=16;
  private static int[] a = new int[N];
  private static final int RANGE=2*N;
  private static final int START=10;
  private static Random random = new Random();
  public static void main(String[] args)
  { load(a);
    print(a);
    int x = random.nextInt(RANGE) + START;
    System.out.println("x = " + x);
    int i = sequentialSearch(a,x);
    System.out.println("search(a,x) = " + i);
    if (i >= 0) System.out.println("a[" + i + "] = " + a[i]);
  }
```

```
      private static void load(int[] a)
      { for (int i=0; i<a.length; i++)
          a[i] = random.nextInt(RANGE) + START;
      }
      private static void print(int[] a)
      { for (int i=0; i<a.length; i++)
          System.out.print("   " + (i>9?"":" ") + i);
        System.out.print("\n{ " + a[0]);
        for (int i=1; i<a.length; i++)
          System.out.print(", " + a[i]);
        System.out.println(" }");
      }
      public static int sequentialSearch(int[] a, int x)
      { // Sequential Search:
        for (int i=0; i<a.length; i++)
          if (a[i]==x) return i;
        return -1;
      }
    }
```

2.8   Testing an `isSorted(int[])` method:

```
    public class Pr0208
    { private static final int SIZE = 16;
      private static int[] a = new int[SIZE];
      public static void main(String[] args)
      { schaums.dswj.Arrays.load(a,40,20);
        schaums.dswj.Arrays.print(a);
        System.out.println("isSorted(a) = " + isSorted(a));
        java.util.Arrays.sort(a);
        schaums.dswj.Arrays.print(a);
        System.out.println("isSorted(a) = " + isSorted(a));
      }
      private static boolean isSorted(int[] a)
      { if (a.length<2) return true;
        for (int i=1; i<a.length; i++)
          if (a[i]<a[i-1]) return false;
        return true;
      }
    }
```

2.9   Testing a `minimum(int[])` method:

```
    public class Pr0209
    { private static final int SIZE = 8;
      private static int[] a = new int[SIZE];

      public static void main(String[] args)
      { schaums.dswj.Arrays.load(a,20,80);
        schaums.dswj.Arrays.print(a);
        System.out.println("minimum(a) = " + minimum(a));
      }
      private static int minimum(int[] a)
      { int min = a[0];
        for (int i=1; i<a.length; i++)
          if (a[i]<min) min = a[i];
        return min;
      }
    }
```

2.10 Testing a `mean(double[])` method:

```
public class Pr0210
{ private static final int SIZE = 4;
  private static double[] a = new double[SIZE];
  public static void main(String[] args)
  { schaums.dswj.Arrays.load(a,20,10);
    schaums.dswj.Arrays.print(a);
    System.out.println("mean(a) = " + mean(a));
  }
  private static double mean(double[] a)
  { double sum=0.0;
    for (int i=0; i<a.length; i++)
      sum += a[i];
    return sum/a.length;
  }
}
```

2.11 Testing a `withoutDuplicates(int[])` method:

```
public class Pr0211
{ private static final int SIZE = 16;
  private static int[] a = new int[SIZE];
  public static void main(String[] args)
  { schaums.dswj.Arrays.load(a,10,8);
    schaums.dswj.Arrays.print(a);
    int[] b = withoutDuplicates(a);
    schaums.dswj.Arrays.print(b);
  }
  private static int[] withoutDuplicates(int[] a)
  { if (a.length<2) return a;  // there are no duplicates
    int x = a[0];  // use this value as a dummy marker
    for (int i=1; i<a.length-1; i++)
      for (int j=i+1; j<a.length; j++)
        if (a[j]==a[i]) a[j] = x;
    int count=0;  // count the duplicates
    for (int i=1; i<a.length; i++)
      if (a[i]==x) ++count;
    if (count==0) return a;  // there are no duplicates
    int[] b = new int[a.length-count];
    b[0] = x;
    int shift=0;
    for (int i=1; i<a.length; i++)
      if (shift>0 && a[i] != x) b[i-shift] = a[i];
      else if (a[i]==x) ++shift;
      else b[i] = a[i];
    return b;
  }
}
```

2.12 Testing a `withoutDuplicates(Object[])` method:

```
public class Pr0212
{ private static final int SIZE = 16;
  private static Object[] a = new Object[SIZE];
  public static void main(String[] args)
  { schaums.dswj.Arrays.load(a,10,8);
    schaums.dswj.Arrays.print(a);
    Object[] b = withoutDuplicates(a);
    schaums.dswj.Arrays.print(b);
  }
```

```
        private static Object[] withoutDuplicates(Object[] a)
        { if (a.length<2) return a;   // there are no duplicates
          Object x = a[0];   // use this object as a dummy marker
          for (int i=1; i<a.length-1; i++)
            for (int j=i+1; j<a.length; j++)
              if (a[j].equals(a[i]))
                a[j] = x;
          int count=0;   // count the duplicates
          for (int i=1; i<a.length; i++)
            if (a[i].equals(x)) ++count;
          if (count==0) return a;   // there are no duplicates
          Object[] b = new Object[a.length-count];
          b[0] = x;
          int shift=0;
          for (int i=1; i<a.length; i++)
            if (shift>0 && !a[i].equals(x)) b[i-shift] = a[i];
            else if (a[i].equals(x)) ++shift;
            else b[i] = a[i];
          return b;
        }
      }
```

2.13   Testing a `reverse(int[])` method:

```
      public class Pr0213
      { private static final int SIZE = 16;
        private static int[] a = new int[SIZE];
        public static void main(String[] args)
        { schaums.dswj.Arrays.load(a,60,40);
          schaums.dswj.Arrays.print(a);
          reverse(a);
          schaums.dswj.Arrays.print(a);
        }
        private static void reverse(int[] a)
        { if (a.length<2) return;
          for (int i=0; i<a.length/2; i++)
            schaums.dswj.Arrays.swap(a,i,a.length-1-i);
        }
      }
```

2.14   Testing a `concatenate(Object[],Object[])` method:

```
      public class Pr0214
      { private static final int SIZE = 8;
        private static Object[] a = new Object[SIZE];
        private static Object[] b = new Object[SIZE];
        public static void main(String[] args)
        { schaums.dswj.Arrays.load(a,10,40);
          schaums.dswj.Arrays.load(b,60,40);
          schaums.dswj.Arrays.print("a",a);
          schaums.dswj.Arrays.print("b",b);
          Object[] c = concatenate(a,b);
          schaums.dswj.Arrays.print("a",a);
          schaums.dswj.Arrays.print("b",b);
          schaums.dswj.Arrays.print("c",c);
        }
        private static Object[] concatenate(Object[] a, Object[] b)
        { Object[] c = new Object[a.length+b.length];
          for (int i=0; i<a.length; i++)
            c[i] = a[i];
```

```
      for (int i=0; i<b.length; i++)
        c[i+a.length] = b[i];
      return c;
    }
  }
```

2.15 Testing a `shuffle(Object[])` method:

```
  public class Pr0215
  { private static final int SIZE = 16;
    private static Object[] a = new Object[SIZE];

    public static void main(String[] args)
    { schaums.dswj.Arrays.load(a,10,90);
      schaums.dswj.Arrays.print(a);
      shuffle(a);
      schaums.dswj.Arrays.print(a);
    }
    private static void shuffle(Object[] a)
    { Random random = new Random();
      for (int i=0; i<a.length; i++)
        schaums.dswj.Arrays.swap(a,i,random.nextInt(a.length));
    }
  }
```

2.16 Testing a `tally(String)` method:

```
  public class Pr0216
  { public static void main(String[] args)
    { String string="Welcome to the new millenium";
      System.out.println(string);
      int[] t = tally(string);
      for (int i=0; i<26; i++)
        System.out.println("Frequency of " + (char)('A'+i)
                      + " = " + t[i]);
    }
    private static int[] tally(String s)
    { int[] frequency = new int[26];
      for (int i=0; i<s.length(); i++)
      { char ch = Character.toUpperCase(s.charAt(i));
        if (Character.isLetter(ch))
          ++frequency[(int)ch - (int)'A'];   // count ch
      }
      return frequency;
    }
  }
```

2.17 Testing an `innerProduct(double[],double[])` method:

```
  public class Pr0217
  { public static void main(String[] args)
    { double[] x = { 1.1, 2.2, 3.3, 4.4 };
      double[] y = { 2.0, 0.0, 1.0, -1.0 };
      System.out.println("innerProduct(x,y) = "
                      + innerProduct(x,y));
    }
    private static double innerProduct(double[] x, double[] y)
    { double sum=0.0;
      for (int i=0; i<x.length && i<y.length; i++)
        sum += x[i]*y[i];
      return sum;
    }
  }
```

2.18   Testing an `outerProduct(double[],double[])` method:

```
public class Pr0218
{ public static void main(String[] args)
  { double[] x = { 1.1, 2.2, 3.3, 4.4 };
    double[] y = { 2.0, 0.0, -1.0 };
    double[][] z = outerProduct(x,y);
    for (int i=0; i<x.length; i++)
    { for (int j=0; j<y.length; j++)
        System.out.print("\t" + z[i][j]);
      System.out.println();
    }
  }

  private static double[][] outerProduct(double[] x, double[] y)
  { double[][] z = new double[x.length][y.length];
    for (int i=0; i<x.length; i++)
      for (int j=0; j<y.length; j++)
        z[i][j] = x[i]*y[j];
    return z;
  }
}
```

2.19   Testing a `product(double[][],double[][])` method:

```
public class Pr0219
{ public static void main(String[] args)
  { double[][] x = { {  1.0,   2.0  },
                     {  3.0,   4.0  } };
    double[][] y = { { 20.0, -10.0  },
                     { 10.0,  20.0  } };
    double[][] z = product(x,y);
    for (int i=0; i<x.length; i++)
    { for (int j=0; j<y.length; j++)
        System.out.print("\t" + z[i][j]);
      System.out.println();
    }
  }

  private static double[][] product(double[][] x, double[][] y)
  { double[][] z = new double[x.length][y[0].length];
    for (int i=0; i<x.length; i++)
      for (int j=0; j<y[0].length; j++)
      { double sum=0.0;
        for (int k=0; k<x[0].length; k++)
          sum += x[i][k]*y[k][j];
        z[i][j] = sum;
      }
    return z;
  }
}
```

2.20   Testing a `transpose(double[][])` method:

```
public class Pr0220
{ public static void main(String[] args)
  { double[][] x = { { 1.0, 2.0, 3.0 }, { 4.0, 5.0, 6.0 } };
    double[][] y = transpose(x);
    for (int i=0; i<y.length; i++)
    { for (int j=0; j<y[0].length; j++)
        System.out.print("\t" + y[i][j]);
      System.out.println();
    }
  }
```

```
    private static double[][] transpose(double[][] x)
    { double[][] y = new double[x[0].length][x.length];
      for (int i=0; i<x[0].length; i++)
        for (int j=0; j<x.length; j++)
          y[i][j] = x[j][i];
      return y;
    }
  }
```

2.21 Testing method that returns Pascal's Triangle:

```
    public class Pr0221
    { private static final int N=9;
      public static void main(String[] args)
      { int[][] p = pascal(N);
        for (int i=0; i<N; i++)
        { for (int j=0; j<N; j++)
            System.out.print("\t" + p[i][j]);
          System.out.println();
        }
      }
      private static int[][] pascal(int n)
      { int[][] p = new int[n][n];
        for (int j=0; j<n; j++)
          p[j][0] = p[j][j] = 1;
        for (int i=2; i<n; i++)
          for (int j=1; j<i; j++)
            p[i][j] = p[i-1][j-1] + p[i-1][j];
        return p;
      }
    }
```

2.22 The Sieve of Eratosthenes:

```
    public class Pr0222
    { private static final int SIZE=1000;
      private static boolean[] sieve = new boolean[SIZE];
      public static void main(String[] args)
      { initializeSieve();
        printSieve();
      }
      private static void initializeSieve()
      { for (int i=2; i<SIZE; i++)
          sieve[i] = true;
        for (int n=2; 2*n<SIZE; n++)
          if (sieve[n])
            for (int m=n; m*n<SIZE; m++)
              sieve[m*n] = false;
      }
      private static void printSieve()
      { int n=0;
        for (int i=0; i<SIZE; i++)
          if (sieve[i]) System.out.print((n++%10==0?"\n":"\t")+i);
        System.out.println("\n" + n + " primes less than " + SIZE);
      }
    }
```

2.23 The Sieve of Eratosthenes with a `java.util.Vector` object:

```
    import java.util.Vector;
    public class Pr0223
    { private static final int SIZE=1000;
```

```
    private static Vector sieve = new Vector(SIZE);
    public static void main(String[] args)
    { initializeSieve();
      printSieve();
    }
    private static void initializeSieve()
    { sieve.add(Boolean.FALSE);
      sieve.add(Boolean.FALSE);
      for (int i=2; i<SIZE; i++)
        sieve.add(Boolean.TRUE);
      for (int n=2; 2*n<SIZE; n++)
        if (((Boolean)sieve.get(n)).booleanValue())
          for (int m=n; m*n<SIZE; m++)
            sieve.set(m*n,Boolean.FALSE);
    }

    private static void printSieve()
    { int n=0;
      for (int i=0; i<SIZE; i++)
        if (((Boolean)sieve.get(i)).booleanValue())
          System.out.print((n++%10==0?"\n":"\t")+i);
      System.out.println("\n" + n + " primes less than " + SIZE);
    }
  }
```

2.24 The Sieve of Eratosthenes with a `java.util.BitSet` object:

```
    import java.util.BitSet;
    public class Pr0224
    { private static final int SIZE=1000;
      private static BitSet sieve = new BitSet(SIZE);
      public static void main(String[] args)
      { initializeSieve();
        printSieve();
      }
      private static void initializeSieve()
      { for (int i=2; i<SIZE; i++)
          sieve.set(i);
        for (int n=2; 2*n<SIZE; n++)
          if (sieve.get(n))
            for (int m=n; m*n<SIZE; m++)
              sieve.clear(m*n);
      }
      private static void printSieve()
      { int n=0;
        for (int i=0; i<SIZE; i++)
          if (sieve.get(i))
            System.out.print((n++%10==0?"\n":"\t")+i);
        System.out.println("\n" + n + " primes less than " + SIZE);
      }
    }
```

2.25 A Primes class:

```
    package schaums.dswj;
    import java.util.*;
    public class Primes
    { private static final int SIZE = 1000;
      private static int size = SIZE;
      private static BitSet sieve = new BitSet(size);
      private static int last = 1;
```

```
        static
        { for (int i=2; i<SIZE; i++)
            sieve.set(i);
          for (int n=2; 2*n<SIZE; n++)
            if (sieve.get(n))
              for (int m=n; m*n<SIZE; m++)
                sieve.clear(m*n);
        }
        private Primes()
        {
        }
        public static void setLast(int n)
        { last = n;
        }
        public static void setLast()
        { last = 1;
        }
        public static void setSize(int n)
        { size = n;
        }
        public static void setSize()
        { size = 1000;
        }
        public static boolean isPrime(int n)
        { return sieve.get(n);
        }
        public static int next()
        { while (++last<size)
            if (sieve.get(last)) return last;
          return -1;
        }
        public static void printPrimes()
        { int n=0;
          for (int i=0; i<SIZE; i++)
            if (sieve.get(i))
              System.out.print((n++%10==0?"\n":"\t")+i);
          System.out.println("\n" + n + " primes less than " + SIZE);
        }
    }

    import schaums.dswj.Primes;
    public class Pr0225
    { public static void main(String[] args)
      { Primes.printPrimes();
        for (int n=1; n<=10; n++)
          System.out.println(n + ".\t" + Primes.next());
      }
    }
```

2.26 Testing a prime factorization method:

```
    import schaums.dswj.Primes;
    import java.util.Random;
    public class Pr0226
    { private static final int N=10;
      private static final int RANGE=2000;
      private static Random random = new Random();
      public static void main(String[] args)
```

```
  { for (int i=0; i<N; i++)
    { int n = random.nextInt(RANGE);
      System.out.println(n + " = " + Primes.factor(n));
    }
  }
}
```

Add this method to the `Primes` class:

```
public static String factor(int n)
{ String primes="";
  int p = next();
  while (n>1)
  { if (n%p==0)
    { primes += (primes.length()==0?"":"*") + p;
      n /= p;
    }
    else p = next();
    if (p == -1)
    { primes += " OVERFLOW";
      break;
    }
  }
  setLast();
  return primes;
}
```

2.27 Testing the Goldbach Conjecture:

```
public class Pr0227
{ public static void main(String[] args)
  { final int N=10000;
    Primes.setSize(N);
    System.out.println("4 = 2+2");
    for (int n=6; n<100; n += 2)
    { System.out.print(n);
      for (int p=3; p<=n/2; p += 2)
        if (Primes.isPrime(p) && Primes.isPrime(n-p))
          System.out.print(" = "+p+"+"+(n-p));
      System.out.println();
    }
  }
}
```

2.28 Finding Fermat primes:

```
public class Pr0228
{ public static void main(String[] args)
  { final int N=10000;
    Primes.setSize(N);
    for (int p=0; p<5; p++)
    { int n = (int)Math.pow(2,Math.pow(2,p)) + 1;
      if (Primes.isPrime(n))
        System.out.println("p = "+p+", n = 2^2^p = "+n);
    }
  }
}
```

2.29 Finding Babbage primes:

```
public class Pr0229
{ public static void main(String[] args)
  { final int N=10000;
    Primes.setSize(N);
```

```
        for (int x=0; x<50; x++)
        { System.out.print(x);
          int n = x*x + x + 41;
          if (Primes.isPrime(n))
            System.out.println("\t"+n+" is prime");
          else System.out.println();
        }
      }
    }
```

2.30 Finding twin primes:

```
    public class Pr0230
    { public static void main(String[] args)
      { final int N=1000;
        Primes.setSize(N);
        int n=Primes.next();
        while (n<0.9*N)
        { if (Primes.isPrime(n+2))
            System.out.println(n + "\t" + (n+2));
          n = primes.next();
        }
      }
    }
```

2.31 Finding primes between squares:

```
    public class Pr0231
    { public static void main(String[] args)
      { final int N=10000;
        Primes.setSize(N);
        for (int n=1; n<100; n++)
          for (int i=n*n+1; i<(n+1)*(n+1); i++)
            if (Primes.isPrime(i))
            { System.out.println(n*n + " < " + i + " < " + (n+1)*(n+1));
              break;
            }
      }
    }
```

2.32 Finding Mersenne primes:

```
    public class Pr0232
    { public static void main(String[] args)
      { final int N=10000;
        Primes.setSize(N);
        for (int p = Primes.next(); p<30; p = Primes.next())
        { int n = (int)Math.round(Math.pow(2,p)) - 1;
          System.out.print(p + "\t2^" + p + "-1 = " + n);
          if (Primes.isPrime(n)) System.out.println(" is prime ");
          else System.out.println(" is not prime ");
        }
      }
    }
```

2.33 Finding palindromic primes:

```
    public class Pr0233
    { public static void main(String[] args)
      { final int N=10000;
        Primes.setSize(N);
        for (int i=0; i<N; i++)
        { int p = Primes.next();
          if (isPalindromic(p)) System.out.print(p+"\t");
```

```
    }
    System.out.println();
  }

  private static boolean isPalindromic(int n)
  { if (n<0) return false;
    int p10=1;
    // make p10 is the greatest power of 10 that is < n
    while (p10<n)
      p10 *= 10;
    p10 /= 10;
    while (n>9)
    { if (n/p10 != n%10) return false;
      n /= 10;      // remove rightmost digit from n
      p10 /= 10;
      n %= p10;   // remove leftmost digit from n
    }
    return true;   // single digit integers are palindromic
  }
}
```

Chapter 3

Advanced Java

3.1 INHERITANCE

One of the central principles of object-oriented programming is *inheritance* of classes. We say that class Y *inherits* from class X if it extends class X by using its fields and methods in addition to defining more of its own. In this case, we also call Y a *subclass* of X. We also refer to Y as a *child class* of X and call X the *parent class* of Y. Conceptually, the result is that instances of class Y are more specialized and instances of class X are more general.

EXAMPLE 3.1 Extending the Point Class

This defines ColoredPoint as a subclass of the Point class from Example 1.7 on page 7:

```
public class ColoredPoint extends Point
{ private String color="black";

  public ColoredPoint(double x, double y, String color)
  { super(x,y);  // invokes the parent constructor
    this.color = color;
  }

  public String getColor()
  { return color;
  }

  public void setColor(String color)
  { this.color = color;
  }

  public boolean equals(Object object)
  { if (object == this) return true;
    if (object.getClass() != this.getClass()) return false;
    if (object.hashCode() != this.hashCode()) return false;
    ColoredPoint point = (ColoredPoint)object;
    return (x == point.x && y == point.y && color == point.color);
  }

  public int hashCode()
  { return (new Double(x)).hashCode() + (new Double(y)).hashCode()
           + color.hashCode();
  }

  public String toString()
  { return new String("(" + x + ","  + y + ", " + color + ")");
  }
}
```

53

This subclass defines its own constructor, a new accessor method `getColor()`, and a new mutator method `setColor(String)`. It overrides the `equals(Object)` method, `hashCode()` method, and the `toString()` method that are defined in its parent class.

Note that the fields `x` and `y` in the `Point` class had to be declared as `protected` instead of `private` in order to allow access to them from within the `ColoredPoint` subclass.

Here is a test driver:

```
public class Ex0301
{ public static void main(String[] args)
  { ColoredPoint p = new ColoredPoint(2,3,"green");
    System.out.println("p = " + p);
    ColoredPoint q = new ColoredPoint(2,3,"green");
    System.out.println("q = " + q);
    if (q == p) System.out.println("q == p");
    else System.out.println("q != p");
    if (q.equals(p)) System.out.println("q equals p");
    else System.out.println("q does not equal p");
    q.setColor("red");
    System.out.println("q = " + q);
    if (q.equals(p)) System.out.println("q equals p");
    else System.out.println("q does not equal p");
  }
}
```

```
p = (2.0,3.0, green)
q = (2.0,3.0, green)
q != p
q equals p
q = (2.0,3.0, red)
q does not equal p
```

3.2 POLYMORPHISM

One aspect of inheritance that makes it so useful is the ability of an instance of a subclass to be regarded, when passed as an argument to a method, as an instance of its parent class. This appearance of having several forms is called *polymorphism*.

EXAMPLE 3.2 Using Polymorphism

```
public class Ex302
{ public static void main(String[] args)
  { ColoredPoint p = new ColoredPoint(2,3,"green");
    System.out.println("p = " + p);
    Point q = new Point(-2,0);
    System.out.println("q = " + q);
    System.out.println("distance(p,q) = " + distance(p,q));
  }
  private static double distance(Point p, Point q)
  { double dx = p.getX() - q.getX();
    double dy = p.getY() - q.getY();
    return Math.sqrt(dx*dx + dy*dy);
  }
}
```

```
p = (2.0,3.0, green)
q = (-2.0,0.0)
distance(p,q) = 5.0
```

The object p is an instance of the ColoredPoint class. But the distance(Point,Point) method allows it to be passed to its first parameter as an instance of the parent Point class. Thus, p appears to have several forms (both ColoredPoint and Point); i.e., it is polymorphic.

All Java classes, both those in the standard library and those written independently by the programmer, reside in a very large inheritance hierarchy. This hierarchy is a tree structure with the java.lang.Object class at its root. Every other class lies below a unique parent class. So, directly or indirectly, every Java class is a subclass of the Object class.

The tree diagram here shows the organization of 40 of the 1462 classes in the Java 1.2 standard library (less than 3% of them). It shows, for example, that Integer is a subclass of Number, which is a subclass of Object.

The Java hierarchy tree also shows how polymorphism works. Since instances of any descendant class can be passed to a parameter whose type is an ancestor class, we can simply follow the paths from leaf level toward the Object root to see how polymorphic an object can be. For example, a Frame object could be passed to a parameter that has type Frame, Window, Container, Component, or Object.

Because of this hierarchy, polymorphism in Java means that any object can be passed to a parameter of type Object, and any object can invoke any of the methods that are defined in the Object class (since none is private).

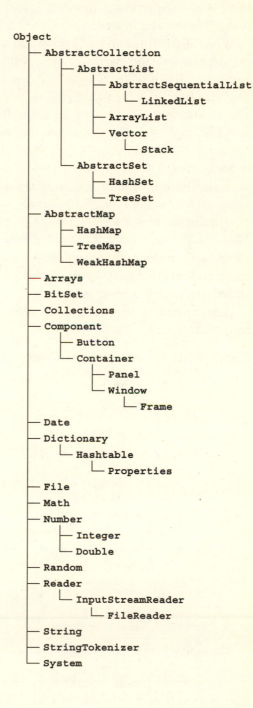

3.3 TYPE CONVERSION

Every expression in Java has a type. A type can be converted by several mechanisms.

The String concatenation operator + automatically converts other types to String type, as in

```
int n = 44;
```

```
String s = "n = " + n;
```
In the expression `"n = " + n`, the + operator converts the `int` n into the `String` object `"44"`.
This is called *string conversion*.

If the non-`String` type is a class type, then that class's
`toString()` method is invoked to perform the conversion. This may be inherited from the `Object` class.

When different numerical types are used in a numerical expression, the narrower type values are converted
automatically to wider type values. For example,
```
double x = 3.14159/4;
```
The expression `3.14159/4` contains the `double` value
3.14159 and the `int` value 4, so the `int` value is
"promoted" to type `double` before the division operation
is performed. This is called *numeric promotion*.

A similar conversion occurs when a narrower type is
assigned to a wider type. For example,
```
double x = 44;
```
This initialization assigns the `int` value 44 to the `double`
variable x. Before the assignment takes place, the `int`
value is converted to its equivalent `double` value. This is
called *assignment conversion*.

Assignment conversion can also occur between
reference types:

Widening Primitive Conversions

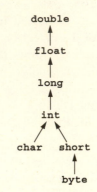

EXAMPLE 3.3 Assignment Conversion

```
class X { int a; }
class Y extends X { int b; }

public class Ex0303
{ public static void main(String[] args)
  { X x = new X();
    System.out.println("x.getClass() = "+ x.getClass());
    Y y = new Y();
    System.out.println("y.getClass() = "+ y.getClass());
    x = y;  // assignment conversion of x to type Y
    System.out.println("x.getClass() = "+ x.getClass());
  }
}
x.getClass() = class X
y.getClass() = class Y
x.getClass() = class Y
```

Narrowing Primitive Conversions

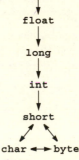

The assignment x = y assigns the narrower type Y to the wider type X, thereby converting x to type Y.

The polymorphism described in Section 3.2 is called *method invocation conversion* because
one type gets converted to another when it is passed to a method being invoked. This kind of
conversion also occurs with primitive types. For example,
```
int n = 44;
double y = Math.sqrt(n);  // method invocation conversion
```

Here the `int` value 44 gets converted to type `double` when the `Math.sqrt(double)` method is invoked because its parameter has type `double`.

Finally, types can be converted explicitly using the type cast operator.

EXAMPLE 3.4 Casting Reference Types

```
class X { public String toString() { return "I am an X."; } }
class Y extends X { public String toString() { return "I am a Y."; } }

public class Ex0304
{ public static void main(String[] args)
  { Y y = new Y();
    System.out.println("y: " + y);
    X x = y;
    System.out.println("x: " + x);
    Y yy = (Y)x;          // casts x as type Y
    System.out.println("yy: " + yy);
    X xx = new X();
    System.out.println("xx: " + xx);
    yy = (Y)xx;        // RUN-TIME ERROR: xx cannot be cast as a Y
    System.out.println("yy: " + yy);
  }
}
```

```
y: I am a Y.
x: I am a Y.
yy: I am a Y.
xx: I am an X.
Exception in thread "main" java.lang.ClassCastException: X
        at Testing.main(Testing.java)
```

The cast `yy = (Y)x` casts x as a type Y. This works because the value of x can be interpreted for type Y since it originally came from y. The cast `yy = (Y)xx` casts xx as a type Y. This compiles, but at run time the `ClassCastException` exception is thrown because the value of xx cannot be interpreted for type Y.

The casting in Example 3.4 illustrates both successful and unsuccessful narrowing conversions of reference types. The next example shows that type casting can also be used, successfully and unsuccessfully, for narrowing conversions of primitive types.

EXAMPLE 3.5 Casting Primitive Types

```
public class Ex0305
{ public static void main(String[] args)
  { double x = 44.0;
    System.out.println("x = " + x);
    float y = (float)x;    // narrowing cast from double to float
    System.out.println("y = " + y);
    int n = (int)y;        // narrowing cast from float to int
    System.out.println("n = " + n);
    short m = (short)n;    // narrowing cast from int to short
    System.out.println("m = " + m);
    n = 65536 + 4444;
    System.out.println("n = " + n);
```

```
    m = (short)n;              // narrowing cast from int to short
    System.out.println("m = " + m);
    y = (float)m;              // widening cast from short to float
    System.out.println("y = " + y);
    y = (float)n;              // widening cast from int to float
    System.out.println("y = " + y);
  }
}
```

```
x = 44.0
y = 44.0
n = 44
m = 44
n = 69980
m = 4444
y = 4444.0
y = 69980.0
```

The first three narrowing casts are successful because the value 44 is appropriate for the narrower types. However, the int value 69980 (65536 + 4444) does not narrow successfully into a short: The erroneous value 4444 is assigned to m. This is because the narrowing from int to short will always result in the remainder from dividing the int value by 65,536, which is 2^{16}.

Similarly, the widening cast y = (float)m from short to float is successful, but the widening cast y = (float)n from int to float fails because the int value 69,980 has too many significant digits for the float type. Note that this is the same numeric value as was obtained by narrowing the int to a short.

3.4 THE Object CLASS

The Object class is the ultimate ancestor class in Java: All other classes are descended from it. Every method in the Object class is inherited by every other class. Here are most of them:

```
public class Object
{ protected Object    clone()
  public boolean      equals(Object)
  public final Class  getClass()
  protective int      hashCode()
  public              Object()
  public String       toString()
}
```

Most of these methods are intended to be overridden by subclasses.

The clone() method returns a duplicate of the object. If the subclass does not override this method, then it simply makes a field-by-field copy.

EXAMPLE 3.6 Incorrect Cloning

```
class Widget implements Cloneable
{ int n;
  Widget w;
  Widget(int n) { this.n = n; }

  public Object clone() throws CloneNotSupportedException
  { return super.clone();
  }
```

```
    public String toString()
    { return "(" + n + "," + w.n + ")";
    }
}
public class Ex0206
{ public static void main(String[] args)
        throws CloneNotSupportedException
    { Widget x = new Widget(44);
      x.w = new Widget(66);
      System.out.println("x = " + x);
      Widget y = (Widget)x.clone();
      System.out.println("y = " + y);
      x.n = 55;
      x.w.n = 77;
      System.out.println("x = " + x);
      System.out.println("y = " + y);
    }
}
```

```
xx = (44,66)
yy = (44,66)
xx = (55,77)
yy = (44,77)
```

The widget x is constructed with its n field initialized to 44. Then its w field is instantiated directly in the second line, initializing x.w.n to 66.

The widget y is constructed as a clone of x. The Object.clone() method simply duplicates x's two fields n and w, without instantiating another widget for y.w. So the widget referenced by x.w does not get duplicated.

When x.n is assigned the value 55, it has no effect upon y.n which keeps its value 44. But when x.w.n is assigned the value 77, that is also the value of y.w.n, So y is not completely independent of x. The cloning was incomplete.

EXAMPLE 3.7 Correct Cloning

Replace the clone() method in Example 3.6 on page 58 with this:

```
    public Object clone() throws CloneNotSupportedException
    { Widget newWidget = new Widget(this.n);
      Widget y = newWidget;
      Widget t = this.w;
      while (t != null)
      { y.w = new Widget(t.n);
        y = y.w;
        t = t.w;
      }
      return newWidget;
    }
}
```

```
xx = (44,66)
yy = (44,66)
xx = (55,77)
yy = (44,66)
```

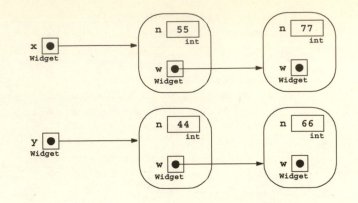

This not only duplicates the widget; it also duplicates every widget that is linked to `this` widget. So no cloned widget is completely independent of this widget, and changing one has no effect upon the other.

The `equals()` method should be overridden in the same manner as the `clone()` method: All corresponding linked elements should be compared. (See Example 1.7 on page 7 and Problem 3.4 on page 70.)

The `getClass()` method returns a `Class` object that represents the class which `this` object instantiates. This is useful in testing for equality of objects. (See Example 1.7 on page 7 and Problem 3.4 on page 70.)

The `hashCode()` method returns an `int` that acts like an identification code for the object. The hash codes for different objects are likely to be different. Hash codes for composite objects should be computed from the hash codes of their components. (See Example 1.7 on page 7 and Problem 3.5 on page 70.)

The `toString()` method returns a `String` that displays the contents of the object. (See Example 1.7 on page 7 and Example 3.6 on page 58.)

3.5 ABSTRACT CLASSES

An *abstract class* is a class that includes at least one abstract method. An *abstract method* is a method without an implementation; it has only its header declaration. The keyword "`abstract`" is required to identify abstract classes and abstract methods.

EXAMPLE 3.8 An `abstract` `Sequence` Class

```java
public abstract class Sequence
{ protected int length=0;

  public int getLength()
  { return length;
  }

  public abstract void append(Object object);
  // adds the given object to end of this sequence

  public int count(Object object)
  { int c=0;
    for (int i=0; i<getLength(); i++)
      if (object.equals(get(i))) ++c;
    return c;
  }
  public abstract Object get(int index);
```

```
        // returns the object at the given index,
        // or null if it is not in this sequence

        public int indexOf(Object object)
        { for (int i=0; i<length; i++)
            if (object.equals(get(i))) return i;
          return -1;
        }


        public abstract Object remove(int index);
        // removes and returns the object at the given index,
        // or returns null if index >= length;

        public abstract boolean remove(Object object);
        // removes the first occurrence of the the object;
        // returns thre iff successful;

        public abstract Object set(int index, Object object);
        // returns the object at the given index after replacing
        // it with the given object, or null is unsuccessful

        public String toString()
        { if (length==0) return "()";
          String s = "(" + get(0);
          for (int i=1; i<length; i++)
            s += "," + get(i);
          return s + ")";
        }
    }
```

This class has five `abstract` methods and four concrete (non-`abstract`) methods. It also has one field.

Note that each abstract method declaration ends with a semicolon ";".

The purpose of defining an `abstract` class is to allow for various different implementations of some of its methods. These are completed in its subclasses.

EXAMPLE 3.9 An `ArraySequence` Subclass of the `Sequence` Class

```
    public class ArraySequence extends Sequence
    { protected Object[] a;
      protected int capacity=16;
      // INVARIANT: a[i] != null for 0 <= i < length;

      public ArraySequence()
      { a = new Object[capacity];
      }

      public void append(Object object)
      { if (length==capacity) // double the capacity
          { Object[] tmp = a;
            capacity *= 2;
            a = new Object[capacity];
```

```
      for (int i=0; i<length; i++)
        a[i] = tmp[i];
    }
    a[length++] = object;
  }

  public Object get(int index)
  { if (index >= length) return null;
    return a[index];
  }

  public Object remove(int index)
  { if (index >= length) return null;
    Object x = a[index];
    for (int i=index; i<length; i++)
      a[i] = a[i+1];
    --length;
    return x;
  }

  public boolean remove(Object object)
  { int i=indexOf(object);
    if (i == -1) return false;
    remove(i);
    return true;
  }

  public Object set(int index, Object object)
  { if (index >= length) return null;
    Object x = a[index];
    a[index] = object;
    return x;
  }
}
```

This subclass implements the sequence structure as an array of `Objects`. It provides a default constructor and implements all five of the `abstract` methods in the `Sequence` class.

Here is a test driver:

```
public class Ex0309
{ public static void main(String[] args)
  { ArraySequence s = new ArraySequence();
    System.out.println("s = " + s);
    s.append("Chile");
    s.append("China");
    s.append("Congo");
    s.append("Egypt");
    s.append("China");
    s.append("India");
    s.append("Italy");
    s.append("China");
    System.out.println("s = " + s);
    System.out.println("s.getLength() = " + s.getLength());
    System.out.println("s.count(\"China\") = " + s.count("China"));
```

```
        System.out.println("s.get(5) = " + s.get(5));
        System.out.println("s.indexOf(\"China\") = "
                          + s.indexOf("China"));
        System.out.println("s.remove(5) = " + s.remove(5));
        System.out.println("s.remove(\"China\") = " + s.remove("China"));
        System.out.println("s.indexOf(\"China\") = "
                          + s.indexOf("China"));
        System.out.println("s.set(2,\"Japan\") = " + s.set(2,"Japan"));
        System.out.println("s = " + s);
        System.out.println("s.getLength() = " + s.getLength());
    }
}
```

```
s = ()
s = (Chile,China,Congo,Egypt,China,India,Italy,China)
s.getLength() = 8
s.count("China") = 3
s.get(5) = India
s.indexOf("China") = 1
s.remove(5) = India
s.remove("China") = true
s.indexOf("China") = 3
s.set(2,"Japan") = Egypt
s = (Chile,Congo,Japan,China,Italy,China)
s.getLength() = 6
```

Example 3.9 uses an array to implement the `Sequence` class defined in Example 3.8. There are other possible implementations. For example, we could use a linked structure similar to the `Widget` class defined in Example 3.6 on page 58. The decision about which implementation to use can be deferred.

3.6 INTERFACES

An *abstract data type*, or ADT, is a description of the behavior of a data type without any details on how the data type is to be implemented. In Java, a data type is a class, and an ADT is an interface.

An *interface* is a like an `abstract` class with no method implementations and no non-`final` fields. It serves as a blueprint or contract; any object of any class that implements the interface is guaranteed to be able to do what the interface specifies through its methods. Consequently, other methods can declare their parameters to have interface types as well as class types and primitive types. The compiler will allow an object to be passed to such a parameter as long as it is an instance of a class that implements the interface, even if that class is abstract.

EXAMPLE 3.10 A `Sequence` Interface

Here is an interface that could be used instead of the abstract class defined in Example 3.8:
```
public interface Sequential
{ public abstract void append(Object object);
  // adds the given object to end of this sequence
  public int count(Object object);
  // returns the number of occurrences of the
  // given object that are in this sequence
```

```
      public abstract Object get(int index);
      // returns the object at the given index,
      // or null if it is not in this sequence

      public int getLength();
      // returns the number of elements in this sequence

      public int indexOf(Object object);
      // returns the number of elements that come before the
      // first occurrence of the given object in this sequence,
      // or -1 if the given object is not in this sequence

      public abstract Object remove(int index);
      // removes and returns the object at the given index,
      // or returns null if index >= length;

      public abstract boolean remove(Object object);
      // removes the first occurrence of the the object;
      // returns thre iff successful;

      public abstract Object set(int index, Object object);
      // returns the object at the given index after replacing
      // it with the given object, or null is unsuccessful

      public String toString();
      // returns a string that displays the contents of this
      // sequence
    }
```

Note that interfaces contain no executable code. By definition, they can contain only method declarations and constant definitions.

Also note that, in concert with the Java standard library, we use nouns for names of classes and adjectives for names of interfaces. This helps us remember that a class is a type, while an interface is a description of behavior. For example, the `Sequential` interface specifies how instances of types that implement it should behave: as "sequential" data structures.

Interfaces can be used the same way classes are used to declare variables and parameters, like this:

```
      public static void print(Sequential sequence)
      { for (int i=0; i<sequence.getLength(); i++)
          System.out.println(i + ": " + sequence.get(i));
      }
```

This will compile, even without any implementation of the `Sequential` interface.

But to be useful, the interface must be implemented. This is done by defining a class that includes definitions for all the method declarations specified in the interface and by appending an "implements" clause to the class declaration.

EXAMPLE 3.11 An `ArraySequence` Class to Implement the `Sequential` Interface

```
      public class ArraySequence implements Sequential
      { protected int length=0;
```

```java
  protected Object[] a;
  protected int capacity=16;
  // INVARIANT: a[i] != null for 0 <= i < length;

  public ArraySequence()
  { a = new Object[capacity];
  }

  public void append(Object object)
  { if (length==capacity) // double the capacity
    { Object[] tmp = a;
      capacity *= 2;
      a = new Object[capacity];
      for (int i=0; i<length; i++)
        a[i] = tmp[i];
    }
    a[length++] = object;
  }

  public int count(Object object)
  { int c=0;
    for (int i=0; i<getLength(); i++)
      if (object.equals(get(i))) ++c;
    return c;
  }

  public Object get(int index)
  { if (index >= length) return null;
    return a[index];
  }

  public int getLength()
  { return length;
  }

  public int indexOf(Object object)
  { for (int i=0; i<length; i++)
      if (object.equals(get(i))) return i;
    return -1;
  }

  public Object remove(int index)
  { if (index >= length) return null;
    Object x = a[index];
    for (int i=index; i<length; i++)
      a[i] = a[i+1];
    --length;
    return x;
  }
  public boolean remove(Object object)
  { int i=indexOf(object);
    if (i == -1) return false;
```

```
    remove(i);
    return true;
}

public Object set(int index, Object object)
{ if (index >= length) return null;
  Object x = a[index];
  a[index] = object;
  return x;
}

public String toString()
{ if (length==0) return "()";
  String s = "(" + get(0);
  for (int i=1; i<length; i++)
    s += "," + get(i);
  return s + ")";
}
```

Note that Example 3.11 uses the same code as in Example 3.8 and Example 3.9. This shows that the main distinction between using an `abstract` class instead of an interface is organizational: where to put the code. With an interface, all the executable code has to be in its implementation. With an `abstract` class, we can have some of the executable code in there and the rest in the subclass.

Interfaces are less flexible than `abstract` class in that they cannot include any executable code. But they are more flexible in that several interfaces can be implemented by a single class. Java does not allow multiple inheritance—one class extending several other classes.

3.7 PACKAGES

A *package* is collection of classes and interfaces. Each class or interface name must be unique within a package. But the same name can be used for different classes or interfaces in different packages. For example, there are two different classes named `Object` in the Java standard library: one in the `java.lang` package and one in the `java.org.omg.CORBA` package. Technically, these two names are different because their complete names are `java.lang.Object` and `java.org.omg.CORBA.Object`. In other words, the name of the package to which the class belongs is actually a prefix on the class name itself.

Packages are organized in tree hierarchies, just as classes, interfaces, and file directories (folders) are. In fact, Java programmers usually map each package into a unique file directory with the package hierarchy matching the directory hierarchy. So for example, all the class files for the `java.awt.event` package would be stored in the

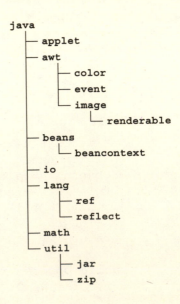

```
java
  ├── applet
  ├── awt
  │     ├── color
  │     ├── event
  │     └── image
  │           └── renderable
  ├── beans
  │     └── beancontext
  ├── io
  ├── lang
  │     ├── ref
  │     └── reflect
  ├── math
  └── util
        ├── jar
        └── zip
```

java/awt/event/ directory (or the java\awt\event\ folder in Windows). The hierarchy for some of the subpackages of the java package is shown here.

Most Java development environments (see Appendix C) encourage the use of packages. They map the fields of a package name to the subdirectory path to the directory where the package is stored. For example, a package named books.schaums.dswj.util would have the Windows path books\schaums\dswj\util.java.

3.8 EXCEPTION HANDLING

> If anything can go wrong, it will.
> —Murphy's Law

An *exception* is a run-time error that causes program execution to be transferred from the source of the condition to an exception handler. The source of the condition is called the *thrower* of the exception, and the handler is called the *catcher*.

Run-time errors in general are encapsulated as instances of the Throwable class and its subclasses. Its two immediate subclasses are the Error class and the Exception class. The inheritance hierarchy here shows the further classification of exceptions according to the conditions that cause them.

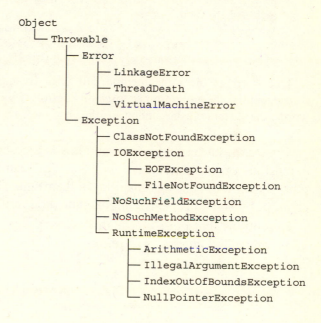

The next two examples illustrate the two ways to handle an exception: either catch it with a try..catch statement, or simple pass it along to the invoker of the current environment by appending a throws clause to the current method.

EXAMPLE 3.12 A Caught Exception

```
public class Ex0312
{ public static void main(String[] args)
  { try
    { int n = Integer.parseInt("Abacadabra!");
      System.out.println("n = " + n);
    }
    catch (Exception e)
    { System.out.println("e = " + e);
    }
  }
}
```

```
e = java.lang.NumberFormatException: Abacadabra!
```

The call Integer.parseInt("Abacadabra!") fails because the string passed does not represent an integer. The method throws a NumberFormatException object which is caught by the main() method. The executable statements in the catch block are executed when the exception is caught.

EXAMPLE 3.13 An Uncaught Exception

```
public class Ex0313
{ public static void main(String[] args)
  { System.out.println("Try this...");
    int n = Integer.parseInt("Abacadabra!");
    System.out.println("n = " + n);
  }
}
Try this...
Exception in thread "main" java.lang.NumberFormatException:
Abacadabra!
        at java.lang.Integer.parseInt(Integer.java:409)
        at java.lang.Integer.parseInt(Integer.java:458)
        at Testing.main(Testing.java:12)
```

This attempts the same method call as in Example 3.12, but it is not done within a `try` block. Consequently, the programmer loses all control of the execution after the exception is thrown. In other words, the system crashes and prints the error message.

The `NumberFormatException` class is a descendant of the `RuntimeException` class. Only extensions of the `RuntimeException` class can be handled benignly, as in Example 3.13. All other exceptions (the vast majority of them) must be caught, either by the method that caused the error, or by some previously invoked method farther back on the calling stack.

Exceptions that must be caught (i.e., any that are not extensions of the `RuntimeException` class) are called *checked exceptions*.

Review Questions

3.1   What is inheritance?

3.2   What is polymorphism?

3.3   What is *type casting*?

3.4   What is *promotion*?

3.5   Why is the `Object` class called "the mother of all classes" in Java?

3.6   What is an `abstract` method?

3.7   What is an `abstract` class?

3.8   What is the difference between an `abstract` class and an interface?

3.9   What is the difference between a subclass and a class extension?

3.10 What is the difference between an interface and an `abstract` class?

3.11 What is the difference between an `abstract` class and a concrete class?

3.12 What is the difference between a class extending another class and a class implementing an interface?

3.13 What is a `try` block?

3.14 What is the difference between a checked exception and an unchecked exception?

Problems

3.1 Extend the `Point` class (see Example 1.7 on page 7) to a `Point3D` class by adding a third coordinate. Override these methods:

```
public boolean equals(Object object);
public int hashCode();
public String toString();
```

and add these methods:

```
private double z;
public Point3D(double x, double y);
public Point3D(double x, double y, double z);
public Point3D(Point3D q);
public double getZ();
public void setLocation(double x, double y, double z);
public void translate(double dx, double dy, double dz);
```

3.2 Modify the `Point3D` class from Problem 3.1 to reflect the additions made to the `Point` class in the previous exercises. Override these methods:

```
public double magnitude();
public void expand(double dr);
```

and add these members:

```
public static final Point3D ORIGIN;
public Point3D();
public double distance(Point3D point);
```

3.3 Try to predict what the following program will print. Then run it to check your prediction.

```
class X
{ protected int a;
  protected int b=22;
  public X()
  { System.out.print("X(): " + this);
    System.out.print(" a = " + a + ", b = " + b);
    a = 33;
    b = 44;
    System.out.println(" a = " + a + ", b = " + b);
  }
  public String toString() { return "I am an X."; }
}
class Y extends X
{ protected int c=55;
  public Y()
  { System.out.print("Y(): " + this);
    System.out.print(" a = " + a + ", b = " + b + ", c = " + c);
    a = 66;
    b = 77;
    c = 88;
    System.out.println(" a = " + a + ", b = " + b + ", c = " + c);
  }
  public String toString() { return "I am a Y."; }
}
public class Testing
{ public static void main(String[] args)
  { Y y = new Y();
  }
}
```

3.4   Implement the `equals(Object)` method for the `Widget` class in Example 3.6 on page 58.

3.5   Implement the `hashCode()` method for the `Widget` class in Example 3.6 on page 58.

Answers to Review Questions

3.1   *Inheritance* describes the relationship between one class and another that extends it. The extension consists of the addition of more fields and/or methods and possibly other methods that override those defined in the first class. The first class is called the *parent class* or *superclass*, and the second is called the *child class* or *subclass*.

3.2   *Polymorphism* is the appearance of one object behaving like another. Its apparent object is really the same object, regarded as a member of its parent or ancestor class.

3.3   *Type casting* is the use of the value of one type as another type. Objects cannot change their types, but their values can be assigned to objects of another type as long as the two types are on the same root-to-leaf path in the inheritance tree. For example:

```
String string1 = "ABCDE";
Object object = (Object)string1;   // casting a String as an Object
String string2 = (String)object;   // casting an Object as a String
```

3.4   *Promotion* is like type casting applied to primitive types. Values of numeric types can be assigned to variables of higher numeric types. For example:

```
int n = 44;       // promoting an int to a float
float x = n;      // promoting a float to a double
double y = x;
```

3.5   The `Object` class is the only class in Java that has no parent class. It is at the root of the Java inheritance tree.

3.6   An `abstract` method is simply the function declaration: the methods modifiers, return type, and signature.

3.7   An `abstract` class is a class that has at least one `abstract` method.

3.8   An `abstract` class may have fields and some implemented methods. An interface has no implementation; only constants and method declarations.

3.9   There is no difference between a subclass and a class extension. They are synonyms.

3.10   An *interface* is a class without any implementation; i.e., only a listing of the method signatures, without any executable statements and without any field definitions. An `abstract` class is like an interface except that some of its methods may be implemented and it may have some field definitions. Those methods of an `abstract` class that are not implemented must be declared with the `abstract` keyword.

3.11   An `abstract` class is a class with one or more abstract (i.e., unimplemented) methods. All the methods of a concrete class are implemented.

3.12   When a class extends another class, it inherits all of its parent class's fields methods, except for those that it overrides. When a class implements an interface, it is obliged to define all the methods whose signatures are specified in the interface.

3.13   A `try` block is the statement block that follows the try keyword in a `try..catch` statement. It is where methods that throw checked exceptions must be called unless the calling method itself throws the exception farther up the calling tree.

3.14   A *checked exception* is an exception that must be caught, either by the method where it occurs or by another method farther up the calling tree. Methods that throw checked exceptions can be called only from with `try` blocks or from other methods that throw the exception. The only unchecked exceptions are those descended from the `RuntimeException` class.

Solutions to Problems

3.1   Extending the `Point` class:

```
public class Point3D extends Point
{ protected double z;
  public Point3D(double x, double y)
  { this.x = x;
    this.y = y;
    this.z = 0;
  }
  public Point3D(double x, double y, double z)
  { this.x = x;
    this.y = y;
    this.z = z;
  }
  public Point3D(Point3D q)
  { this.x = q.x;
    this.y = q.y;
    this.z = q.z;
  }
  public double getZ()
  { return z;
  }
  public void setLocation(double x, double y, double z)
  { this.x = x;
    this.y = y;
    this.z = z;
  }
  public void translate(double dx, double dy, double dz)
  { x += dx;
    y += dy;
    z += dz;
  }
  public boolean equals(Object object)
  { if (object == this) return true;
    if (object.getClass() != this.getClass()) return false;
    if (object.hashCode() != this.hashCode()) return false;
    Point3D point = (Point3D)object;
    return (x == point.x && y == point.y && z == point.z);
  }
  public int hashCode()
  { return (new Double(x)).hashCode() + (new Double(y)).hashCode()
                               + (new Double(z)).hashCode();
  }
  public String toString()
  { return new String("(" + (float)x + ","  + (float)y
                         + ","  + (float)z + ")");
  }
}
```

3.2   Additions to the `Point3D` class:

```
public static final Point3D ORIGIN = new Point3D();
public Point3D()
{ this.x = 0;
  this.y = 0;
  this.z = 0;
```

```
     public double distance(Point3D point)
     { double dx = this.x - point.x;
       double dy = this.y - point.y;
       double dz = this.z - point.z;
       return Math.sqrt(dx*dx+dy*dy+dz*dz);
     }
     public double magnitude()
     { return distance(ORIGIN);
     }
     public void expand(double dr)
     { x *= dr;
       y *= dr;
       z *= dr;
     }
```

3.3 The order of events is:
1. Set fields to default values.
2. Invoke `Y()` constructor.
3. Invoke `X()` constructor.
4. Invoke `Object` constructor.
5. Initialize `X` fields.
6. Execute `X()` constructor.
7. Initialize `Y` fields.
8. Execute `Y()` constructor.

So the output is

```
X(): I am a Y. a = 0, b = 22 a = 33, b = 44
Y(): I am a Y. a = 33, b = 44, c = 55 a = 66, b = 77, c = 88
```

3.4 The `equals(Object)` method for the `Widget` class:

```
     public boolean equals(Object object)
     { if (object == this) return true;
       if (object.getClass() != this.getClass()) return false;
       Widget y = (Widget)object;
       Widget t = this;
       while (y != null || t != null)
       { if (y == null || t == null) return false;
         if (y.n != t.n) return false;
         y = y.w;
         t = t.w;
       }
       return true;
     }
```

3.5 The `hashCode()` method for the `Widget` class:

```
     public int hashCode()
     { int hc = (new Integer(n)).hashCode();
       Widget tw = this.w;
       while (tw != null)
       { hc += (new Integer(tw.n)).hashCode();
         tw = tw.w;
       }
       return hc;
     }
```

Chapter 4

Recursion

A *recursive* function is one that calls itself. This powerful technique produces repetition without using `while` loops, `do..while` loops, or `for` loops. Thus it can produce substantial results from very little code.

Recursion allows elegantly simple solutions to difficult problems. But it can also be misused, producing inefficient code.

Recursive code is usually produced from recursive algorithms.

EXAMPLE 4.1 The Factorial Function

The *factorial* function is defined mathematically by

$$n! = \begin{cases} 1, \text{ if } n = 0 \\ n(n-1)!, \text{ if } n > 0 \end{cases}$$

n	$n!$
0	1
1	1
2	2
3	6
4	24
5	120
6	720
7	5,040
8	40,310
9	362,880

This is a recursive definition because the factorial "recurs" on the right side of the equation. The function is defined in terms of itself.

The first 10 values of the factorial function are shown at right. The first value, 0! is defined by the upper half of the definition: 0! = 1 (for $n = 0$). All the rest of the values are defined by the lower half of the definition:

For $n = 1$, $1! = n! = n(n-1)! = 1(1-1)! = 1(0)! = 1(1) = 1$.
For $n = 2$, $2! = n! = n(n-1)! = 2(2-1)! = 2(1)! = 2(1) = 2$.
For $n = 3$, $3! = n! = n(n-1)! = 3(3-1)! = 3(2)! = 3(2) = 6$.
For $n = 4$, $4! = n! = n(n-1)! = 4(4-1)! = 4(3)! = 4(6) = 24$.
For $n = 5$, $5! = n! = n(n-1)! = 5(5-1)! = 5(4)! = 5(24) = 120$.

Notice how rapidly this function grows.

EXAMPLE 4.2 Recursive Implementation of the Factorial Function

When a function is defined recursively, its implementation is usually a direct translation of its recursive definition. The two parts of the recursive definition of the factorial function translate directly into two Java statement:

```java
public static int f(int n)
{ if (n==0) return 1;  // basis
  return n*f(n-1);     // recursive part
}
```

Here is a simple test driver for the factorial method:

```java
public static void main(String[] args)
{ for (int n=0; n<10; n++)
    System.out.println("f("+n+") = "+f(n));
}
```

It should print the same values as shown in the table above.

EXAMPLE 4.3 Iterative Implementation of the Factorial Function

The factorial function is also easy to implement iteratively:

```
public static int f(int n)
{ int f=1;
  for (int i=2; i<=n; i++)
    f *= i;
  return f;
}
```

Note that the function header is identical to that used in Example 4.2; only the body is different. This allows us to use the same test driver for both implementations. The output should be the same.

4.1 THE BASIS AND RECURSIVE PARTS OF RECURSION

To work correctly, every recursive function must have a *basis* and a *recursive part*. The basis is what stops the recursion. The recursive part is where the function calls itself.

EXAMPLE 4.4 The Basis and Recursive Parts of the Factorial Function

In the Java method that implements the factorial function in Example 4.2, the basis and the recursive parts are labeled with comments. The recursive part invokes the method, passing a smaller value of n. So starting with a positive value like 5, the values on the successive invocations will be 4, 3, 2, 1, and 0. When 0 is passed, the basis executes, thereby stopping the recursion and beginning the chain of returns, returning 1, 1, 2, 6, 24, and finally 120.

EXAMPLE 4.5 The Fibonacci Numbers

The *Fibonacci numbers* are 1, 1, 2, 3, 5, 8, 13, 21, 34, 55, …. Each number after the second is the sum of the two preceding numbers. This is a naturally recursive definition:

n	F_n
0	0
1	1
2	1
3	2
4	3
5	5
6	8
7	13
8	21
9	34
10	55
11	89
12	144
13	233
14	377

$$F_n = \begin{cases} 0, \text{if } n = 0 \\ 1, \text{if } n = 1 \\ F_{n-1} + F_{n-2}, \text{if } n > 1 \end{cases}$$

The first 15 values of the Fibonacci sequence are shown at right. The first two values, F_0 and F_1, are defined by the first two parts of the definition: $F_0 = 0$ (for $n = 0$) and $F_1 = 1$ (for $n = 1$). These two parts form the basis of the recursion. All the other values are defined by the recursive part of the definition:

For $n = 2$, $F_2 = F_n = F_{n-1} + F_{n-2} = F_{(2)-1} + F_{(2)-2} = F_1 + F_0 = 1 + 0 = 1$.
For $n = 3$, $F_3 = F_n = F_{n-1} + F_{n-2} = F_{(3)-1} + F_{(3)-2} = F_2 + F_1 = 1 + 1 = 2$.
For $n = 4$, $F_4 = F_n = F_{n-1} + F_{n-2} = F_{(4)-1} + F_{(4)-2} = F_3 + F_2 = 2 + 1 = 3$.
For $n = 5$, $F_5 = F_n = F_{n-1} + F_{n-2} = F_{(5)-1} + F_{(5)-2} = F_4 + F_3 = 3 + 2 = 5$.
For $n = 6$, $F_6 = F_n = F_{n-1} + F_{n-2} = F_{(6)-1} + F_{(6)-2} = F_5 + F_4 = 5 + 3 = 8$.
For $n = 7$, $F_7 = F_n = F_{n-1} + F_{n-2} = F_{(7)-1} + F_{(7)-2} = F_6 + F_5 = 8 + 5 = 13$.

EXAMPLE 4.6 Recursive Implementation of the Fibonacci Function

```
public static int fib(int n)
{ if (n < 2) return n;          // basis
  return fib(n-1) + fib(n-2);   // recursive part
}
```

Here is a simple test driver for the Fibonacci method:

```
public static void main(String[] args)
{ for (int n=0; n<16; n++)
    System.out.println("fib(" + n + ") = " + fib(n));
}
```

It should print the same values as shown in the table in Example 4.5.

4.2 TRACING A RECURSIVE CALL

Hand tracing the execution of a method usually helps clarify it.

EXAMPLE 4.7 Tracing the Recursive Factorial Function

Here is a trace of the call f(5) to the recursive factorial function defined in Example 4.2:

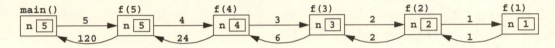

The call originates in the main() function, passing 5 to the f() function. There, the value of the parameter n is 5, so it calls f(4), passing 4 to the f() function. There the value of the parameter n is 4, so it calls f(3), passing 3 to the f() function. This process continues (recursively) until the call f(1) is made from within the call f(2). There, the value of the parameter n is 1, so it returns 1 immediately, without making any more calls. Then the call f(2) returns 2*1 = 2 to the call f(3). Then the call f(3) returns 3*2 = 6 to the call f(4). Then the call f(4) returns 4*6 = 24 to the call f(5). Finally, the call f(5) returns the value 120 to main().

The trace in Example 4.7 shows that the a call f(n) to the recursive implementation of the factorial function will generate $n-1$ recursive calls. This is clearly very inefficient compared to the iterative implementation in Example 4.3.

EXAMPLE 4.8 Tracing the Recursive Fibonacci Function

The Fibonacci function (Example 4.6) is more heavily recursive than the factorial function (Example 4.2) because it includes two recursive calls. The consequences can be seen from the trace of the call fib(5), shown at the top of the next page. The call originates in the main() function, passing 5 to the fib() function. There, the value of the parameter n is 5, so it calls fib(4) and fib(3), passing 4 and 3, respectively. Each of these calls then makes two more recursive calls, continuing down to the basis calls f(1) and f(0). Each of these basis calls returns 1. The recursive calls then return the sum of the two values returned to them, ultimately resulting in the value 8 being returned to main().

4.3 THE RECURSIVE BINARY SEARCH ALGORITHM

The nonrecursive Binary Search Algorithm is given in Section 2.5 on page 31. It uses the Divide-and-Conquer strategy, each time splitting the sequence in half and continuing the search on one half. This is naturally recursive.

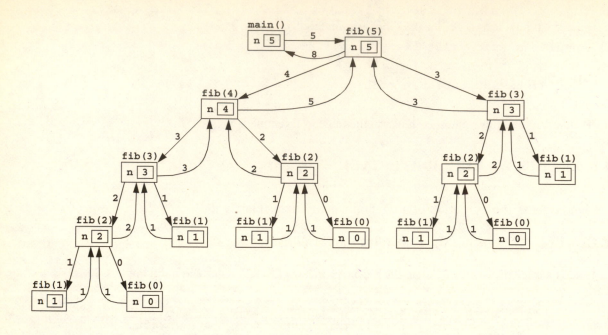

Algorithm 4.1 The Recursive Binary Search

(Precondition: $s = \{s_0, s_1, ..., s_{n-1}\}$ is a sorted sequence of n ordinal values of the same type as x.)

(Postcondition: either the index i is returned where $s_i = x$, or -1 is returned.)

1. If the sequence is empty, return -1.
2. Let s_i be the middle element of the sequence.
3. If $s_i = x$, return its index i.
4. If $s_i < x$, apply the algorithm on the subsequence that lies above s_i.
5. Apply the algorithm on the subsequence of ss that lies below s_i.

Note that the precondition in Algorithm 4.1 requires the sequence to be sorted.

EXAMPLE 4.9 The Recursive Binary Search

```
public static int search(int[] a, int lo, int hi, int x)
{ // PRECONDITION:   a[0] <= a[1] <= ... <= a[a.length-1];
  // POSTCONDITIONS: returns i; if i >= 0, then a[i] == x;
  //                 otherwise i == -1;
  if (lo>hi) return -1;                              // step 1
  int i = (lo+hi)/2;                                 // step 2
  if (a[i] == x) return i;                           // step 3
  else if (a[i] < x) return search(a,i+1,hi,x);      // step 4
  else return search(a,lo,i-1,x);                    // step 5
  }
}
```

Theorem 4.1 The Recursive Binary Search runs in $O(\lg n)$ time.

Proof: The argument here is essentially the same as that in Theorem 2.4 on page 32. The running time is proportional to the number of recursive calls made. Each call processes a subsequence that is half as long as the previous one. So the number of recursive calls is the same as the number of times that n can be divided in two, namely $\lg n$.

EXAMPLE 4.10 Testing the Recursive Binary Search

```
import schaums.dswj.Arrays;
public class Ex0410
{ private static final int SIZE = 16;
  private static final int START = 40;
  private static final int RANGE = 20;
  private static int[] a = new int[SIZE];

  public static void main(String[] args)
  { Arrays.load(a,START,RANGE);
    java.util.Arrays.sort(a);
    Arrays.print(a);
    test();
    test();
    test();
    test();
  }

  public static void test()
  { int x = Arrays.load(START,RANGE);
    System.out.print("Searching for x = " + x + ":\t");
    int i = search(a,x);
    if (i >= 0) System.out.println("a[" + i + "] = " + a[i]);
    else System.out.println("i = " + i + " ==> x not found");
  }

  public static int search(int[] a, int x)
  { return search(a,0,a.length-1,x);
  }

  public static int search(int[] a, int lo, int hi, int x)
  { if (lo>hi) return -1;  // basis
    int i = (lo+hi)/2;
    if (a[i] == x) return i;
    else if (a[i] < x) return search(a,i+1,hi,x);
    else return search(a,lo,i-1,x);
  }
}
```

```
     0   1   2   3   4   5   6   7   8   9  10  11  12  13  14  15
{  45, 45, 45, 45, 48, 48, 49, 50, 51, 52, 53, 54, 54, 58, 58, 59 }
Searching for x = 46:   i = -1 ==> x not found
Searching for x = 48:   a[5] = 48
Searching for x = 54:   a[11] = 54
Searching for x = 57:   i = -1 ==> x not found
```

This test is similar to that in Example 2.8 on page 32.

Note that to have the method signature search(int[],int) with only the two parameters, we have to "wrap" the recursive method in a nonrecursive driver method to get it started.

4.4 BINOMIAL COEFFICIENTS

The *binomial coefficients* are the coefficients that result from the expansion of a binomial expression of the form $(x + 1)^n$. For example,

$$(x + 1)^6 = x^6 + 6x^5 + 15x^4 + 20x^3 + 15x^2 + 6x + 1$$

The seven coefficients generated here are 1, 6, 15, 20, 15, 6, and 1.

The French mathematician Blaise Pascal (1623–1662) discovered a recursive relationship among the binomial coefficients. By arranging them in a triangle, he found that each interior number is the sum of the two directly above it:

For example, $15 = 5 + 10$.

Let $c(n,k)$ denote the coefficient in row number n and column number k (counting from 0). For example, $c(6,2) = 15$. Then Pascal's recurrence relation can be expressed as

$$c(n, k) = c(n-1, k-1) + c(n-1, k), \text{ for } 0 < k < n$$

For example, when $n = 6$ and $k = 2$, $c(6,2) = c(5,1) + c(5,2)$.

EXAMPLE 4.11 Recursive Implementation of the Binomial Coefficient Function

```
public static int c(int n, int k)
{ if (k==0 || k==n) return 1;     // basis
  return c(n-1,k-1) + c(n-1,k);  // recursion
}
```

The basis for the recursion covers the left and right sides of the triangle, where $k = 0$ and where $k = n$.

The binomial coefficients are the same as the *combination* numbers used in combinatorial mathematics and computed explicitly by the formula

$$c(n, k) = \frac{n!}{k!(n-k)!} = \left(\frac{n}{1}\right)\left(\frac{n-1}{2}\right)\left(\frac{n-2}{3}\right)\cdots\left(\frac{n-k+1}{k}\right)$$

In this context, the combination is often written $c(n, k) = \binom{n}{k}$ and is pronounced "n choose k."

For example, "8 choose 3" is $\binom{8}{3} = (8/1)(7/2)(6/3) = 56$.

EXAMPLE 4.12 Iterative Implementation of the Binomial Coefficient Function

This version implements the explicit formula given above. The expression on the right consists of k factors, so it is computed by a loop iterating k times:

```
public static int c(int n, int k)
{ if (n<2 || k==0 || k==n) return 1;
  int c=1;
  for (int j=1; j <= k; j++)
    c = c*(n-j+1)/j;
  return c;
}
```

4.5 THE EUCLIDEAN ALGORITHM

The *Euclidean Algorithm* computes the greatest common divisor of two positive integers. Appearing as Proposition 2 in Book VII of Euclid's *Elements* (c. 300 B.C.), it is probably the oldest recursive algorithm. As originally formulated by Euclid, it says to subtract repeatedly the smaller number n from the larger number m until the resulting difference d is smaller than n. Then repeat the same steps with d in place of n and with n in place of m. Continue until the two numbers are equal. Then that number will be the greatest common divisor of the original two numbers.

```
 494
-130
 364
-130
 234
-130   130
 104  -104    104
       26    -26
              78
             -26
              52
             -26
              26
```

The example on the right applies this algorithm to find the greatest common divisor of 494 and 130 to be 26. This is correct because $494 = 26 \cdot 19$ and $130 = 26 \cdot 5$.

EXAMPLE 4.13 Recursive Implementation of the Euclidean Algorithm

Each step in the algorithm simply subtracts the smaller number from the larger. This is done recursively by calling either `gcd(m,n-m)` or `gcd(m-n,n)`:

```
public static int gcd(int m, int n)
{ if (m==n) return n;                   // basis
  else if (m<n) return gcd(m,n-m);      // recursion
  else return gcd(m-n,n);               // recursion
}
```

For example, the call `gcd(494,130)` makes the recursive call `gcd(364,130)`, which makes the recursive call `gcd(234,130)`, which makes the recursive call `gcd(104,130)`, which makes the recursive call `gcd(104,26)`, which makes the recursive call `gcd(78,26)`, which makes the recursive call `gcd(52,26)`, which makes the recursive call `gcd(26,26)`, which returns 26. The value 26 is then successively returned all the way back up the chain to the original call `gcd(494,130)`, which returns it to its caller.

4.6 INDUCTIVE PROOF OF CORRECTNESS

Recursive functions are usually proved correct by the principle of *mathematical induction*. (See Appendix B.) This principle states that an infinite sequence of propositions can be proved to be true by verifying that (*i*) the first statement is true, and (*ii*) the truth of every other statement in the sequence can be derived from the assumption that its preceding statements are true. Part (*i*) is called the *basis step* and part (*ii*) is called the *inductive step*. The assumption that the preceding statements are true is called the *inductive hypothesis*.

Theorem 4.2 The recursive factorial function is correct.

Proof: To prove that the recursive implementation of the factorial function (Example 4.2 on page 73) is correct, we first verify the basis. The call f(0) returns the correct value 1 because of the first line

```
if (n < 2) return 1;
```
Next, we assume that the function returns the correct value for all integers less than some $n > 0$. Then the second line

```
return n*f(n-1);
```
will return the correct value $n!$ because (by the inductive hypothesis) the call f(n-1) will return $(n-1)!$ and $n! = n \cdot (n-1)$.

Note that we are using the "strong" principle of mathematical induction here (also called the "second" principle). In this version, the inductive hypothesis allows us to assume that *all* of the preceding statements are true. In the "weak" (or "first") principle, we are allowed to assume that only the single preceding statement is true. But since these two principles are equivalent (i.e., they are both valid methods of proof), it is usually better to apply strong induction.

Theorem 4.3 The Euclidean algorithm is correct

Proof: We can use (strong) induction to prove that the Euclidean algorithm (Example 4.13) is correct. If m and n are equal, then that number is their greatest common divisor. So the function returns the correct value in that case because of the line

```
if (m == n) return n;
```
If m and n are not equal then the function returns either gcd(m,n-m) or gcd(m-n,n). To see that this too is the correct value, we need only realize that all three pairs (m,n), (m,n-m), and (m-n,n) will always have the same greatest common divisor. This fact is a theorem from number theory. It is proved in Appendix B.

4.7 COMPLEXITY ANALYSIS OF RECURSIVE ALGORITHMS

The complexity analysis of a recursive algorithm depends upon the solubility of its recurrence relation. The general technique is to let $T(n)$ be the number of steps required to carry out the algorithm on a problem of size n. The recursive part of the algorithm translates into a recurrence relation on $T(n)$. Its solution is then the complexity function for the algorithm.

Theorem 4.4 The recursive factorial function runs in $O(n)$ time.

Proof: Let $T(n)$ be the number of recursive calls made from the initial call f(n) to the function in Example 4.2 on page 73. Then $T(0) = T(1) = 0$, because if $n < 2$ no recursive calls are made. If $n > 1$, then the line

```
return n*f(n-1);
```
executes, making the recursive call f(n-1). Then the total number of recursive calls is 1 plus the number of calls that are made from f(n-1). That translates into the recurrence relation

$$T(n) = 1 + T(n-1)$$

The solution to this recurrence is

$$T(n) = n - 1, \text{ for } n > 0$$

This conclusion is obtained in two stages: first we *find* the solution; then we use induction to *prove* that it is correct.

The simplest technique for finding the solution to a recurrence relation is to make a table of values and look for a pattern. This recurrence relation says that each value if $T(n)$ is 1 more than the previous value. So the solution $f(n) = n - 1$ is pretty obvious.

Now to prove that $T(n) = n - 1$ for all $n > 0$, let $f(n) = n - 1$ and apply the (weak) principle of mathematical induction. The basis case is where $n = 1$. In that case, $T(n) = T(1) = 0$ and $f(n) = f(1) = (1) - 1 = 0$. For the inductive step, we assume that $T(n) = f(n)$ for some $n > 0$ and then deduce from that assumption that $T(n+1) = f(n+1)$:

n	$T(n)$
0	0
1	0
2	1
3	2
4	3
5	4
6	5

$$T(n+1) = 1 + T(n) = 1 + f(n) = 1 + (n-1) = n$$

$$f(n+1) = (n+1) - 1 = n$$

That completes the proof.

Now that we have determined that the complexity function for this recursive implementation of the factorial function $T(n) = n - 1$, we can conclude that this implementation "will run in $O(n)$ time." This means that its execution time will be proportional to the size of its argument n. If it takes 3 milliseconds to compute 8!, then it should take about 6 milliseconds to compute 16!.

4.8 DYNAMIC PROGRAMMING

In most cases, recursion is very inefficient because of its frequent function calls. So an iterative implementation may be better if it is not too complex. Another alternative is to implement the recurrence relation by storing previously computed values in an array instead of recomputing them with recursive function calls. This method is called *dynamic programming*.

EXAMPLE 4.14 Dynamic Programming Implementation of the Fibonacci Function

```
public static int fib(int n)
{ if (n<2) return n;
  int[] f = new int[n];
  f[0] = 0;
  f[1] = 1;
  for (int i=2; i<n; i++)     // store the Fibonacci numbers
    f[i] = f[i-1] + f[i-2];
  return f[n-1] + f[n-2];
}
```

This implementation uses a dynamic array f [] of n integers to store the first n Fibonacci numbers.

4.9 THE TOWERS OF HANOI

We have seen important examples of functions that are more naturally defined and more easily understood using recursion. For some problems, recursion is the only reasonable method of solution.

The Towers of Hanoi game is a classic example of a problem whose solution demands recursion. The game consists of a board with three vertical pegs labeled A, B, and C, and a sequence of n disks with holes in their centers. The radii of the disks are in an arithmetic 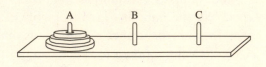 progression (e.g., 5cm, 6cm, 7cm, 8cm, ...) and are mounted on peg A. The rule is that no disk may be above a smaller disk on the same peg. The objective of the game is to move all the disks from peg A to peg C, one disk at a time, without violating the rule.

The general solution to the Towers of Hanoi game is naturally recursive:

- Part I: move the smaller $n-1$ disks from peg A to peg B.
- Part II: move the remaining disk from peg A to peg C.
- Part III: move the smaller $n-1$ disks from peg B to peg C.

The first and third steps are recursive: apply the complete solution to $n-1$ disks. The basis to this recursive solution is the case where $n = 0$: In this case, do nothing.

The solution for the case of $n = 1$ disk is:

1. Move the disk from peg A to peg C.

The solution for the case of $n = 2$ disks is:

1. Move the top disk from peg A to peg B.
2. Move the second disk from peg A to peg C.
3. Move the top disk from peg B to peg C.

The solution for the case of $n = 3$ disks is:

1. Move the top disk from peg A to peg C.
2. Move the second disk from peg A to peg B.
3. Move the top disk from peg C to peg B.
4. Move the remaining disk from peg A to peg C.
5. Move the top disk from peg B to peg A.
6. Move the second disk from peg B to peg C.
7. Move the top disk from peg A to peg C.

Here, steps 1–3 constitute Part I of the general solution, step 4 constitutes Part II, and steps 5–7 constitute Part III.

Since the general recursive solution requires the substitution of different peg labels, it is better to use variables. Then, naming this three-step algorithm $hanoi(n, x, y, z)$, it becomes:

- Part I: move the smaller $n-1$ disks from peg x to peg z.
- Part II: move the remaining disk from peg x to peg y.
- Part III: move the smaller $n-1$ disks from peg z to peg y.

The general solution is implemented in Example 4.15.

EXAMPLE 4.15 The Towers of Hanoi

```
public class Ex0415
{ public static void main(String[] args)
  { runHanoi(4,'A','B','C');
  }

  public static void runHanoi(int n, char x, char y, char z)
  { if (n==1)  // basis
      System.out.println("Move top disk from peg " + x
                          + " to peg " + z);
    else       // recursion
    { runHanoi(n-1,x,z,y);
      runHanoi(1,x,y,z);
      runHanoi(n-1,y,x,z);
    }
  }
}
```

The solution for 4 disks is produced by the call
```
  runHanoi(4,'A','B','C');
```
The output is
```
Move top disk from peg A to peg B
Move top disk from peg A to peg C
Move top disk from peg B to peg C
Move top disk from peg A to peg B
Move top disk from peg C to peg A
Move top disk from peg C to peg B
Move top disk from peg A to peg B
Move top disk from peg A to peg C
Move top disk from peg B to peg C
Move top disk from peg B to peg A
Move top disk from peg C to peg A
Move top disk from peg B to peg C
Move top disk from peg A to peg B
Move top disk from peg A to peg C
Move top disk from peg B to peg C
```

4.10 MUTUAL RECURSION

When a function calls itself, it is call
direct recursion. Another form of recursion
is when a function calls other functions that
call other functions that eventually call the
original function. This is called *indirect
recursion*. Its most common form is when
two functions call each other. This is called
mutual recursion.

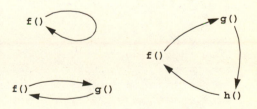

EXAMPLE 4.16 The Sine and Cosine Functions Computed by Mutual Recursion

The sine and cosine functions from trigonometry can be defined in several different ways, and there are several different algorithms for computing their values. The simplest (although not the most efficient) is via mutual recursion. It is based upon the identities

$$\sin 2\theta = 2\sin\theta\cos\theta$$

$$\cos 2\theta = 1 - 2(\sin\theta)^2$$

and the two Taylor polynomials

$$\sin x \approx x - x^3/6$$

$$\cos x \approx 1 - x^2/2$$

which are close approximations for small values of x.

```
    public class Ex0416
    { public static void main(String[] args)
      { for (double x=0. ; x<1.0; x += 0.1)
          System.out.println(s(x) + "\t" + Math.sin(x));
        for (double x=0. ; x<1.0; x += 0.1)
          System.out.println(c(x) + "\t" + Math.cos(x));
      }
      public static double s(double x)
      { if (-0.005 < x && x < 0.005) return x - x*x*x/6;   // basis
        return 2*s(x/2)*c(x/2);                             // recursion
      }
      public static double c(double x)
      { if (-0.005 < x && x < 0.005) return 1.0 - x*x/2;   // basis
        return 1 - 2*s(x/2)*s(x/2);                         // recursion
      }
    }
```

```
0.0         0.0
0.09983341664635367      0.09983341664682815
0.1986693307941265       0.19866933079506122
0.29552020665442036      0.2955202066613396
0.3894183423068936       0.3894183423086505
0.4794255385990945       0.479425538604203
0.5646424733830799       0.5646424733950354
0.6442176872361944       0.644217687237691
0.7173560908968648       0.7173560908995227
0.7833269096232099       0.7833269096274833
0.8414709848016061       0.8414709848078964
1.0         1.0
0.9950041652780733       0.9950041652780258
0.9800665778414311       0.9800665778412416
0.9553364891277464       0.955336489125606
0.9210609940036278       0.9210609940028851
0.8775825618931635       0.8775825618903728
0.8253356149178575       0.8253356149096783
0.7648421872857489       0.7648421872844885
0.6967067093499022       0.6967067093471655
0.6216099682760496       0.6216099682706645
0.5403023058779364       0.5403023058681398
```

This works because on each recursive call x is divided by 2, and eventually it reaches the basis criterion (`-0.005 < x && x < 0.005`), and which stops the recursion. When x is that small, the Taylor polynomials give accurate results to 15 decimal places.

Review Questions

4.1 A recursive function must have two parts: its *basis* and its *recursive part*. Explain what each of these is and why it is essential to recursion.

4.2 How many recursive calls will the call `f(10)` to the recursive factorial function (Example 4.2 on page 73) generate?

4.3 How many recursive calls will the call `fib(6)` to the recursive Fibonacci function (Example 4.6 on page 74) generate?

4.4 What are the advantages and disadvantages of implementing a recursive solution instead of an iterative solution?

4.5 What is the difference between direct recursion and indirect recursion?

Problems

4.1 Write and test a recursive function that returns the sum of the squares of the first n positive integers.

4.2 Write and test a recursive function that returns the sum of the first n powers of a base b.

4.3 Write and test a recursive function that returns the sum of the first n elements of an array.

4.4 Write and test a recursive function that returns the maximum among the first n elements of an array.

4.5 Write and test recursive function that returns the maximum among the first n elements of an array, using at most $\lg n$ recursive calls.

4.6 Write and test a recursive function that returns the power x^n.

4.7 Write and test recursive function that returns the power x^n, using at most $2\lg n$ recursive calls.

4.8 Write and test a recursive function that returns the integer binary logarithm of an integer n (i.e., the number of times n can be divided by 2).

4.9 Write and test a recursive boolean function that determines whether a string is a palindrome. (A *palindrome* is a string of characters that is the same as the string obtained from it by reversing its letters.)

4.10 Write and test a recursive function that returns a string that contains the binary representation of a positive integer.

4.11 Write and test a recursive function that returns a string that contains the hexadecimal representation of a positive integer.

4.12 Write and test a recursive function that prints all the permutations of the first n characters of a string. For example, the call `print("ABC",3)` would print
```
ABC
ACB
BAC
BCA
CBA
CAB
```

4.13 Implement the Fibonacci function iteratively (without using an array).

4.14   Implement the recursive Ackermann function:

$$a(0, n) = 1$$
$$a(1, 0) = 2$$
$$a(m, 0) = m + 2, \text{ if } m > 1$$
$$a(m, n) = a(a(m - 1, n), n - 1), \text{ if } m > 0 \text{ and } n > 0$$

4.15   Prove Pascal's recurrence relation (page 78).

4.16   Trace the recursive implementation of the Euclidean Algorithm (Example 4.6 on page 74) on the call `gcd(385, 231)`.

4.17   Implement the Euclidean Algorithm (page 79) iteratively.

4.18   Implement the recursive Euclidean Algorithm using the integer remainder operator `%` instead of repeated subtraction.

4.19   Implement the Euclidean Algorithm iteratively using the integer remainder operator `%` instead of repeated subtraction.

4.20   Use mathematical induction to prove that the recursive implementation of the Fibonacci function (Example 4.6 on page 74) is correct.

4.21   Use mathematical induction to prove that the recursive function in Problem 4.4 is correct.

4.22   Use mathematical induction to prove that the recursive function in Problem 4.5 is correct.

4.23   Use mathematical induction to prove that the recursive function in Problem 4.8 is correct.

4.24   Use mathematical induction to prove that the recursive function in Problem 4.12 is correct.

4.25   The *computable domain* of a function is the set of inputs for which the function can produce correct results. Determine empirically the computable domain of the factorial function implemented in Example 4.2 on page 73.

4.26   Determine empirically the computable domain of the `sum(b,n)` function implemented in Problem 4.2 on page 85, using b = 2.

4.27   Determine empirically the computable domain of the Fibonacci function implemented in Example 4.3 on page 73.

4.28   Determine empirically the computable domain of the recursive binomial coefficient function (Example 4.11 on page 78).

4.29   The Towers of Hanoi program performs 7 disk moves for 3 disks. How many disk moves are performed for:
a. 5 disks?
b. 6 disks?
c. n disks?

4.30   Prove the formula that you derived in previous problem.

4.31   Determine empirically the computable domain of the Ackermann function (Problem 4.14).

4.32   Show the recursive call tree for the call `hanoi(4,'A','B','C')` in Example 4.15 on page 83.

4.33   Modify the program in Example 4.16 on page 84 so that the results are more accurate by narrowing the bases so that recursion continues until $|x| < 0.00005$.

4.34   Modify the program in Example 4.16 on page 84 so that the results are more accurate by using the more accurate approximations

$$\sin x \approx x - x^3/6 + x^5/120 = x(1 - x^2(1 - x^2/20))$$
$$\cos x \approx 1 - x^2/2 + x^4/24 = 1 - x^2/2 \cdot (1 - x^2/12)$$

4.35 Use mutual recursion to implement the hyperbolic sine and hyperbolic cosine functions. Use these formulas:

$$\sinh 2\theta = 2\sinh\theta\cosh\theta$$

$$\cosh 2\theta = 1 + 2(\sinh\theta)^2$$

$$\sinh x \approx x + x^3/6$$

$$\cosh x \approx 1 + x^2/2$$

Compare your results with the corresponding values of sinh and cosh functions, defined in terms of the exponential function by

$$\sinh x = \frac{(e^x - e^{-x})}{2}$$

$$\cosh x = \frac{(e^x + e^{-x})}{2}$$

4.36 Implement the tangent function recursively using the formulas

$$\tan 2x = \frac{2\tan x}{1 - (\tan x)^2}$$

$$\tan x \approx x + \frac{1}{3}x^3$$

4.37 Implement a recursive function that evaluates a polynomial $a_0 + a_1 x + a_2 x^2 + \cdots + a_3 x^3$, where the $n+1$ coefficients a_i are passed to the function in an array along with the degree n.

Answers to Review Questions

4.1 The basis of a recursive function is its starting point in its definition and its final step when it is being called recursively; it is what stops the recursion. The recursive part of a recursive function is the assignment that includes the function on the right side of the assignment operator, causing the function to call itself; it is what produces the repetition. For example, in the factorial function, the basis is $n! = 1$ if $n = 0$, and the recursive part is $n! = n(n-1)$ if $n > 0$.

4.2 The call `factorial(10)` will generate 10 recursive calls.

4.3 The call `f(6)` to the Fibonacci function will generate $14 + 8 = 22$ recursive calls because it calls `f(5)` and `f(4)`, which generate 14 and 8 recursive calls, respectively.

4.4 A recursive solution is often easier to understand than its equivalent iterative solution. But recursion usually runs more slowly than iteration.

4.5 Direct recursion is where a function calls itself. Indirect recursion is where a group of functions call each other.

Solutions to Problems

4.1 A recursive function that returns the sum of the first n squares:

```
public static int sum(int n)
{ if (n==0) return 0;       // basis
  return sum(n-1) + n*n;   // recursion
}
```

4.2   A recursive function that returns the sum of the first *n* powers of a base *b*:

```
public static double sum(double b, int n)
{ if (n==0) return 1;          // basis
  return 1 + b*sum(b,n-1);  // recursion
}
```

Note that this solution implements Horner's method: $1 + b*(1 + b*(1 + b*(1 + \cdots + b)))$.

4.3   A recursive function that returns the sum of the first *n* elements of an array:

```
public static double sum(double[] a, int n)
{ if (n==0) return 0.0;          // basis
  return sum(a,n-1) + a[n-1];  // recursion
}
```

4.4   A recursive function that returns the maximum among the first *n* elements of an array:

```
public static double max(double[] a, int n)
{ if (n==1) return a[0];        // basis
  double m = max(a,n-1);       // recursion
  if (a[n-1] > m) return a[n-1];
  else return m;
}
```

4.5   A recursive function that returns the maximum among the first *n* elements of an array and makes no more than lg*n* recursive calls:

```
public static double max(double[] a, int lo, int hi)
{ if (lo>=hi) return a[lo];
  int mid=(lo+hi)/2;            // middle index
  double m1=max(a,lo,mid);      // recursion on a[lo..mid]
  double m2=max(a,mid+1,hi);    // recursion on a[mid+1..hi]
  return (m1>m2?m1:m2);         // maximum of {m1,m2}
}
```

4.6   A recursive function that returns the power x^n:

```
public static double pow(double x, int n)
{ if (n==0) return 1.0;        // basis
  return x*pow(x,n-1);         // recursion
}
```

4.7   A recursive function that returns the power x^n and makes no more than lg*n* recursive calls:

```
public static double pow(double x, int n)
{ if (n==0) return 1.0;        // basis
  double p = pow(x,n/2);
  if (n%2==0) return p*p;      // recursion (n even)
  else return x*p*p;           // recursion (n odd)
}
```

4.8   A recursive function that returns the integer binary logarithm of *n*:

```
public static int lg(int n)
{ if (n==1) return 0;        // basis
  return 1 + lg(n/2);        // recursion
}
```

4.9   A recursive function that determines whether a string is a palindrome:

```
public static boolean isPalindrome(String s)
{ int len = s.length();
  if (len<2) return true;
  if (s.charAt(0) != s.charAt(len-1)) return false;
  if (len==2) return true;
  return isPalindrome(s.substring(1,len-1));  // recursion
}
```

4.10   A recursive function that converts decimal to binary:

```
public static String binary(int n)
{ String s;
  if (n%2 == 0) s = "0";
  else s = "1";
  if (n < 2) return s;      // basis
  return binary(n/2) + s;   // recursion
}
```

4.11   A recursive function that converts decimal to hexadecimal:

```
public static String hexadecimal(int n)
{ String s = hex(n%16);
  if (n<16) return s;              // basis
  return hexadecimal(n/16) + s;   // recursion
}
String hex(int n)
{ if (n==0)  return "0";
  if (n==1)  return "1";
  if (n==2)  return "2";
  if (n==3)  return "3";
  if (n==4)  return "4";
  if (n==5)  return "5";
  if (n==6)  return "6";
  if (n==7)  return "7";
  if (n==8)  return "8";
  if (n==9)  return "9";
  if (n==10) return "A";
  if (n==11) return "B";
  if (n==12) return "C";
  if (n==13) return "D";
  if (n==14) return "E";
  else       return "F";
}
```

4.12   A recursive function that prints permutations:

```
public static void print(String str)
{ print("",str);
}

public static void print(String left, String right)
{ int n=right.length();
  if (n==0) return;
  if (n==1)
  { System.out.println(left+right);
    return;
  }
  StringBuffer s = new StringBuffer(right);
  for (int i=0; i<n; i++)
  { char temp = s.charAt(i);
    s.setCharAt(i,s.charAt(0));
    s.setCharAt(0,temp);
    print(left+temp,s.substring(1,n));
  }
}
```

4.13   Iterative implementation of the Fibonacci function:

```
public static int fib(int n)
{ if (n<2) return n;
```

```
      int f0=0, f1=1, f=f0+f1;
      for (int i=2; i<n; i++)
      { f0 = f1;
        f1 = f;
        f = f0 + f1;
      }
      return f;
    }
```

4.14 The Ackermann function:

```
    public static int ackermann(int m, int n)
    { if (m==0) return 1;                          // basis
      if (n==0)
        if (m==1) return 2;                        // basis
        else return m + 2;                         // basis
      return ackermann(ackermann(m-1,n), n-1);     // recursion
    }
```

4.15 Consider the relationship $c(8,3) = 56 = 35 + 21 = c(7,3) + c(7,2)$ from the expansion of $(x + 1)^8$:

$$(x + 1)^8 = (x + 1)(x + 1)^7$$
$$= (x + 1)(x^7 + 7x^6 + 21x^5 + 35x^4 + 35x^3 + 21x^2 + 7x + 1)$$
$$= x^8 + 7x^7 + 21x^6 + 35x^5 + 35x^4 + 21x^3 + 7x^2 + x$$
$$\qquad + x^7 + 7x^6 + 21x^5 + 35x^4 + 35x^3 + 21x^2 + 7x + 1$$
$$= x^8 + 8x^7 + 28x^6 + 56x^5 + 70x^4 + 56x^3 + 28x^2 + 7x + 1$$

The coefficient $c(8,3)$ is for the x^5 term, which is $35x^5 + 21x^5 = 56x^5$. The sum $35x^5 + 21x^5$ came from $(x)(35x^4)$ and $(1)(21x^5)$. So those coefficients are $35 = c(7,3)$ and $21 = c(7,2)$.

The general proof is based upon the same argument: $c(n,k)$ is the coefficient of the term x^k in the expansion of $(x + 1)^n$. Since $(x + 1)^n = (x + 1)(x + 1)^{n-1}$, that term comes from the sum

$$(x)(c(n-1, k-1)\, x^{k-1}) + (1)(c(n-1, k)x^k) = (c(n-1, k-1) + c(n-1, k))x^k$$

Therefore $c(n, k) = c(n-1, k-1) + c(n-1, k)$.

4.16 Trace of the call `gcd(616, 231)`:

4.17 Iterative implementation of the Euclidean algorithm:

```
    public static int gcd(int m, int n)
    { while (m != n)              // INVARIANT: gcd(m,n)
        if (m < n) n -= m;
        else m -= n;
      return n;
    }
```

4.18 Recursive implementation of the Euclidean algorithm using the remainder operator:

```
    public static int gcd(int m, int n)
    { if (m==0) return n;                    // basis
      if (n==0) return m;                    // basis
      else if (m<n) return gcd(m,n%m);       // recursion
      else return gcd(m%n,n);                // recursion
    }
```

4.19 Iterative implementation of the Euclidean algorithm using the remainder operator:

```
    public static int gcd(int m, int n)
    { while (n>0)      // INVARIANT: gcd(m,n)
      { int r = m%n;
        m = n;
        n = r;
```

```
        }
        return m;
    }
```

4.20 To prove that the recursive implementation of the Fibonacci function is correct, first verify the basis. The calls `fib(0)` and `fib(1)` return the correct values `0` and `1` because of the first line

```
    if (n < 2) return n;
```

Next, we assume that the function returns the correct value for all integers less than some $n > 1$. Then the second line

```
    return fib(n-1) + fib(n-2);
```

will return the correct value n! because (by the inductive hypothesis) the calls `fib(n-1)` and `fib(n-2)` return the correct values for F_{n-1} and F_{n-2}, respectively, and $F_n = F_{n-1} + F_{n-2}$ by definition. Note that the basis here required the verification of the first *two* steps in the sequence because the recurrence relation $F_n = F_{n-1} + F_{n-2}$ applies only for $n > 1$.

4.21 If $n = 1$, then the basis executes, returning `a[0]` which is the maximum element because it is the only element. If $n > 1$, then the function correctly computes the maximum m of the first $n-1$ elements (by the inductive hypothesis). If the condition (`a[n-1] > m`) is true, then that element `a[n-1]` is returned, and it is the largest because it is larger than m, which is the largest of all the others. On the other hand, if the condition (`a[n-1] > m`) is false, then m is returned, and that is the largest because it is not smaller than `a[m-1]`, and it is the largest among all the others.

4.22 If $n = 1$, then the basis executes, returning `a[0]` which is the maximum element because it is the only element. If $n > 1$, then the function correctly computes the maxima m1 and m2 of the first and second halves of the array (by the inductive hypothesis). One of these two numbers is the correct maximum for the entire array. The larger is returned.

4.23 If $n = 1$, then the basis executes, returning `0`, which is the number of times n can be divided by 2. If $n > 1$, then the function correctly computes the number of times $n/2$ can be divided by 2 (by the inductive hypothesis). This is 1 less than the number of times n can be divided by 2, so the value returned, `1 + lg(n/2)`, is correct.

4.24 First, we prove the conjectrue that the call `print(left,right)` will print n! distinct strings, all having the same prefix string `left`, where $n = $ `right.length()`. If $n = 1$, the method prints `left+right` and returns; that is 1! (distinct) string. Assume that when `right.length() = n-1`, the call `print(left,right)` prints $(n-1)$! distinct strings all having the same `left` prefix string. Then, when `right.length() = n`, the `for` loop makes n calls of the form `print(left+temp,ss)`, where `temp` is a distinct character and `ss = s.substring(1,n)`. Since the length of `s.substring(1,n)` is $n-1$, each of those calls will print $(n-1)$! distinct strings all having the same `left+temp` prefix string. Therefore, the loop will print $(n)(n-1)$! distinct strings all having the same `left` prefix string. This proves the conjecture by mathematical induction. Now it follows from that conjecture that the call `print(str)` will print n! distict permutations of the characters in the string `str`, where n is its length. Since that is precisely the total number of permutations that the string has, it follows that the method is correct.

4.25 For the factorial function implemented in Example 4.2 on page 73, integer overflow occurs on the return type `long` with $n = 13$ on the author's computer. So the computable domain for this function is $0 \le n \le 12$.

4.26 For the `sum(b,n)` function implemented in Problem 4.2 on page 85 with b = 2, floating point overflow occurs on the return type `double` with $n = 1,023$ on the author's computer. So the computable domain for this function is $0 \le n \le 1,022$.

4.27 For the Fibonacci function implemented in Example 4.6 on page 74, the overhead from the recursive calls degrades the run-time performance noticeably after $n = 36$ on the author's computer. So the computable domain for this function is about $0 \le n \le 40$.

4.28 For the binomial coefficient function implemented in Example 4.7 on page 75, the overhead from the recursive calls degrades the run-time performance noticeably after $n = 25$ on the author's computer. So the computable domain for this function is about $0 \le n \le 30$.

4.29   The Towers of Hanoi program performs:
   a. 31 moves for 5 disks;
   b. 63 moves for 6 disks;
   c. $2^n - 1$ moves for n disks.

4.30   To prove that the Towers of Hanoi program performs $2^n - 1$ disk moves for n disks, use mathematical induction. The basis is established in Example 4.15 on page 83. To move $n + 1$ disks, it takes $2^n - 1$ moves to move all but the last disk to peg B (by the inductive hypothesis). Then it takes 1 move to move the last disk to peg C, and $2^n - 1$ more moves to move the rest of the disks from peg B to peg C on top of that last disk. The total is $(2^n - 1) + 1 + (2^n - 1) = 2^{n+1} - 1$.

4.31   For the Ackermann function implemented in Problem 4.14 on page 86, exceptions are thrown for $m = 17$ when $n = 2$, for $m = 5$ when $n = 3$, for $m = 4$ when $n = 4$, and for $m = 3$ when $n = 5$. So the computable domain for this function is restricted to $0 \le m \le 16$ when $n = 2$, to $0 \le m \le 4$ when $n = 3$, to $0 \le m \le 3$ when $n = 4$, and to $0 \le m \le 2$ when $n = 5$.

4.32   The call tree for Example 4.15 on page 83:

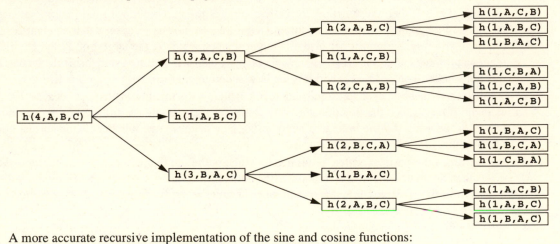

4.33   A more accurate recursive implementation of the sine and cosine functions:
```
public class Pr0433
{ public static void main(String[] args)
  { for (double x=0. ; x<1.0; x += 0.1)
     System.out.println(s(x) + "\t" + Math.sin(x));
   for (double x=0. ; x<1.0; x += 0.1)
     System.out.println(c(x) + "\t" + Math.cos(x));
  }
  public static double s(double x)
  { if (Math.abs(x) < 0.00005) return x - x*x*x/6;
   return 2*s(x/2)*c(x/2);
  }
  public static double c(double x)
  { if (Math.abs(x) < 0.00005) return 1.0 - x*x/2;
   return 1 - 2*s(x/2)*s(x/2);
  }
}
```

4.34   A more accurate recursive implementation of the sine and cosine functions:
```
public class Pr0434
{ public static void main(String[] args)
  { for (double x=0. ; x<1.0; x += 0.1)
     System.out.println(s(x) + "\t" + Math.sin(x));
   for (double x=0. ; x<1.0; x += 0.1)
     System.out.println(c(x) + "\t" + Math.cos(x));
  }
```

```
      public static double s(double x)
    { if (Math.abs(x) < 0.005) return x*(1 - x*x/6*(1-x*x/20));
      return 2*s(x/2)*c(x/2);
    }

      public static double c(double x)
    { if (Math.abs(x) < 0.005) return 1.0 - x*x/2*(1-x*x/12);
      return 1 - 2*s(x/2)*s(x/2);
    }
  }
```

4.35 Mutually recursive implementations of the hyperbolic sine and cosine functions:

```
    public class Pr0435
    { public static void main(String[] args)
      { for (double x=0. ; x<1.0; x += 0.1)
          System.out.println(s(x) + "\t" + sinh(x));
        for (double x=0. ; x<1.0; x += 0.1)
          System.out.println(c(x) + "\t" + cosh(x));
      }

      public static double s(double x)
      { if (Math.abs(x) < 0.005) return x + x*x*x/6;
        return 2*s(x/2)*c(x/2);
      }

      public static double c(double x)
      { if (Math.abs(x) < 0.005) return 1.0 + x*x/2;
        return 1 + 2*s(x/2)*s(x/2);
      }

      public static double sinh(double x)
      { return (Math.exp(x) - Math.exp(-x))/2.0;
      }

      public static double cosh(double x)
      { return (Math.exp(x) + Math.exp(-x))/2.0;
      }
    }
```

4.36 Recursive implementation of the tangent function:

```
    public static double t(double x)
    { if (-0.005 < x && x < 0.005) return x + x*x*x/3;   // basis
      return 2*t(x/2)/(1 - t(x/2)*t(x/2));                // recursion
    }
```

4.37 Recursive evaluation of a polynomial function:

```
    public static double p(double[] a, double x)
    { // returns a[0] + a[1]*x + a[2]*x*x + ...
      return p(a,x,0);
    }

    private static double p(double[] a, double x, int k)
    { // returns a[k] + a[k+1]*x + a[k+2]*x*x + ...
      if (k == a.length) return 0;  // basis
      return a[k] + x*p(a,x,k+1);   // recursion
    }
```

Chapter 5

Collections

A *collection* is a container of objects. Java 1.2 formalized this concept with its *Collections Framework* of interfaces and classes.

5.1 THE JAVA COLLECTIONS FRAMEWORK

The `java.util` package defines the following framework of eight interfaces for collections:

Interface	Description
Collection	A collection of elements.
List	A sequence of elements.
Set	A collection of unique elements.
SortedSet	A sorted collection of unique elements.
Map	A collection of (key,value) pairs. Keys must be unique.
SortedMap	A sorted collection of (key,value) pairs. Keys must be unique.
Iterator	An object that can traverse a collection.
ListIterator	An object that can traverse a sequence.

This chart shows the relationships among these interfaces and the classes that implement them:

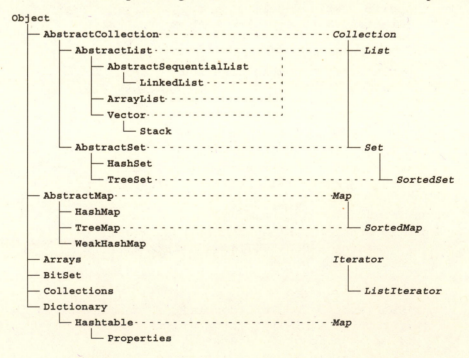

94

The dotted lines connect the interfaces on the right to the classes that directly implement them on the left. For example, the `Hashtable` class implements the `Map` interface. Inheritance, both among classes and among interfaces, is denoted by the solid lines. For example, the `Stack` class extends the `Vector` class, and the `SortedSet` interface extends the `Set` interface.

Note that each of the four primary interfaces (`Collection`, `List`, `Set`, and `Map`) is implemented by a corresponding abstract class (`AbstractCollection`, `AbstractList`, `AbstractSet`, and `AbstractMap`).

Also note that the names of most of the concrete collection classes are concatenations of the data structure used and the interface implemented. For example, the `ArrayList` class uses an array to implement the `List` interface, the `HashSet` class uses a hash table to implement the `Set` interface, and the `TreeMap` class uses a tree to implement the `Map` interface.

This chapter outlines the direct implementations of the `Collection` interface and the `Iterator` interface. The implementations of the other six interfaces are outlined in Chapters 7, 13, and 14.

5.2 THE `Collection` INTERFACE

As the chart indicates, the `Collection` interface defines the framework for all the container classes in Java. Its definition in the `java.util` package looks like this:

```
public interface Collection
{ public boolean   add(Object object);
  public boolean   addAll(Collection collection);
  public void      clear();
  public boolean   contains(Object object);
  public boolean   containsAll(Collection collection);
  public boolean   equals(Object object);
  public int       hashCode();
  public boolean   isEmpty();
  public Iterator  iterator();
  public boolean   remove(Object object);
  public boolean   removeAll(Collection collection);
  public boolean   retainAll(Collection collection);
  public int       size();
  public Object[]  toArray();
  public Object[]  toArray(Object[] objects);
}
```

5.3 THE `AbstractCollection` CLASS

The `AbstractCollection` class is a partial implementation of the `Collection` interface. It implements about as much as possible without specifying the actual storage structure to be used by the collection. Its definition in the `java.util` package looks like this:

```
public class AbstractCollection implements Collection
{ public boolean          add(Object object)
  public boolean          addAll(Collection collection)
  public void             clear()
  public boolean          contains(Object object)
  public boolean          containsAll(Collection collection)
```

```
public boolean              isEmpty()
abstract public Iterator    iterator()
public boolean              remove(Object object)
public boolean              removeAll(Collection collection)
public boolean              retainAll(Collection collection)
abstract public int         size()
public Object[]             toArray()
public Object[]             toArray(Object[] objects)
public String               toString()
}
```

Note that this class implements all 15 of the methods specified by the `Collection` interface except the `equals()` and `hashCode()` methods. These two methods, which are defined in the `Object` class (see Section 3.4 on page 58) are meant to be overridden by extensions of the `AbstractCollection` class. On the other hand, the `AbstractCollection` does override the `Object` class's `toString()` method.

The reason that the `AbstractCollection` does not override the `Object` class's `equals()` and `hashCode()` methods is that those methods cannot be completely defined without knowing what the data structure is that implements the storage of the container's elements. The reason that the `AbstractCollection` does override the `Object` class's `toString()` method is that it can. This is done in the next example.

EXAMPLE 5.1 The `toString()` Method Defined in the `AbstractCollection` Class

```
public String toString()
{ if (isEmpty()) return "[]";
  Iterator it = iterator();
  String str = "[" + it.next();
  while (it.hasNext())
    str += ", " + it.next();
  return str + "]";
}
```

This method uses the iterator returned by the class's `iterator()` method to traverse the collection, accumulating a string image of all its elements. To work on an instance of any concrete subclass of the `AbstractCollection` class, it need only rely upon that subclass's correct implementation of the `iterator()` method. That's why the `AbstractCollection` class defines the `iterator()` method to be `abstract`: to require any concrete subclass to implement it.

The `AbstractCollection` class's `size()` method is defined to be `abstract` for the same reason. Other methods that are implemented here already use it. For example:

EXAMPLE 5.2 The `isEmpty()` Method Defined in the `AbstractCollection` Class

```
public boolean isEmpty()
{ return size() == 0;
}
```

5.4 A `Bag` CLASS

A *bag* (also called a *multiset*) is a collection of elements that may include duplicates. (Ordinary sets do not allow duplicates.) The following example uses an array of `Objects` to implement a `Bag` class.

EXAMPLE 5.3 A Bag Class

```
public class Bag extends AbstractCollection
{ private Object[] objects;
  private int size=0;  // number of objects in the bag
  private static final int CAPACITY=16;  // default capacity

  private void resize(int capacity)
  // increases the length of objects[] to the given capacity
  // See Example 5.4 on page 99.

  public Bag()
  { // constructs an empty bag with the default capacity
    objects = new Object[CAPACITY];
  }

  public Bag(int capacity)
  // constructs an empty bag with the given capacity
  // See Problem 5.1 on page 104.

  public Bag(Collection collection)
  // constructs a bag containing the objects in the
  // given collection and with twice the capacity
  // See Example 5.5 on page 99.

  public Bag(Object[] objects)
  // constructs a bag containing the objects in the
  // given array and with twice the capacity
  // See Problem 5.2 on page 104.

  public boolean add(Object object)
  // adds the given object to this bag
  // See Example 5.6 on page 100.

  public boolean addAll(Collection collection)
  // adds all the objects in the given collection
  // to this bag
  // See Problem 5.3 on page 104.

  public void clear()
  // removes all the objects from this bag
  // See Problem 5.4 on page 105.

  public boolean contains(Object object)
  // returns true iff the given object
  // is equal to some object in this bag
  // See Example 5.7 on page 100.

  public boolean containsAll(Collection collection)
  // returns true iff every object in the given collection
  // is equal to some object in this bag; that is,
  // iff the the given collection is a subset of this bag;
  // See Problem 5.5 on page 105.
```

```
private static int frequency(Collection x, Object object)
// returns the number of objects in the given collection
// that are equal to the given object
// See Problem 5.6 on page 105.

public boolean equals(Object object)
// returns true iff the given object is a Bag
// and has the same content as this bag
// See Example 5.8 on page 101.

public int hashCode()
// returns a hash code for this bag that is the sum
// of the hash codes of its elements
// See Problem 5.7 on page 105.

public boolean isEmpty()
{ // returns true iff this bag is empty
  return size == 0;
}

public Iterator iterator()
// returns an iterator on this bag
// See Example 5.12 on page 104.

public boolean remove(Object object)
// removes one of the given object from this bag;
// returns true iff this bag was modified;
// See Problem 5.8 on page 105.

public boolean removeAll(Object object)
// removes all of the given object from this bag;
// returns true iff this bag was modified;
// See Example 5.9 on page 101.

public boolean removeAll(Collection collection)
// removes from this bag all of the object that are also in
// the given collection, thereby reducing this bag to its
// set-theoretic intersection with that collection;
// returns true iff this bag was modified;
// See Problem 5.9 on page 105.

public boolean retainAll(Collection collection)
// removes from this bag all of the object that are not in
// the given collection, thereby reducing this bag to its
// set-theoretic complement relative to that collection;
// returns true iff this bag was modified;
// See Problem 5.10 on page 105.

public int size()
{ // returns the number of objects in this bag;
  return size;
}
```

```
public Object[] toArray()
// returns an array whose elements are in this bag;
// See Example 5.10 on page 101.

public Object[] toArray(Object[] objects)
// returns an array whose elements are in this bag
// if it is longer than the given object[] array;
// otherwise, the given array is returned after removing
// all of its elements and then loading it with the elements
// of this bag, and padding the rest of it with nulls;
// See Problem 5.11 on page 105.

public String toString()
// returns a String that shows the contents of this bag
// See Problem 5.12 on page 105.
}
```

EXAMPLE 5.4 An Implementation of a `Bag.resize(int)` Method

This is a `private` utility method, included to allow easy expansion of the `objects[]` array as more elements are added to the bag.

```
private void resize(int capacity)
{ // increases the length of objects[] to the given capacity
  if (capacity <= this.capacity) return;
  Object[] temp = objects;
  objects = new Object[capacity];
  for (int i=0; i<size; i++)
    objects[i] = temp[i];
}
```

If the given `capacity` is not larger than the current `capacity`, then the method returns without changing anything. Otherwise, it copies the entire `objects` array into a `temp` array, reassigns the `objects` reference to a new array of length equal to the given `capacity`, and then copies the `temp` array into it.

EXAMPLE 5.5 An Implementation of a `Bag(Collection)` Constructor

```
public Bag(Collection collection)
{ // constructs a bag containing the objects in the
  // given collection and with twice the capacity
  objects = new Object[2*collection.size()];
  for (Iterator it = collection.iterator(); it.hasNext(); )
    objects[size++] = it.next();
}
```

To create a `Bag` containing the elements of the given `collection`, this method first allocates the `objects` array with twice as many components as the given `collection` (to allow growing room). Then it uses an iterator to traverse the given `collection`, copying each of its objects' reference variable to the new bag's `objects` array. Note that the component objects are not duplicated here; we merely have a new data structure of references to them.

Since the given collection implements the `Collection` interface, it is guaranteed to include an `iterator()` method that returns an iterator object that can traverse it. And since that iterator object implements the `java.util.Iterator` interface (see Section 5.5), it is guaranteed to include the `next()` and `hasNext()` methods that we use here. This allows the use of the for loop in that standard fashion to traverse the `collection`, accessing each of its elements through the `next()` method.

EXAMPLE 5.6 An Implementation of a `Bag.add(Object)` Method

```
public boolean add(Object object)
{ // adds the given object to this bag
  if (size == objects.length) resize(2*objects.length);
  objects[size++] = object;
  return true;
}
```

If the bag is full, the `private resize()` method is invoked first to double the capacity of the `objects[]` array. Then the given `object` is appended to the sequence of elements already in the array.

Note that the `Collection` interface requires the `add(Object)` method to return a `boolean` value to indicate whether the add operation was successful. With this implementation, the operation will always be successful (unless the computer runs out of memory), so it automatically returns `true`. But we will see other implementations where `add(Object)` may return `false`.

Here is a test driver of the `add(Object)` method:

```
public class Testing
{ public static void main(String[] args)
  { String[] food = { "egg", "ham", "rum", "tea" };
    Bag foodBag = new Bag(food);
    System.out.println(foodBag);
    foodBag.add("fig");
    System.out.println(foodBag);
  }
}
{ egg, ham, rum, tea }
{ egg, ham, rum, tea, fig }
```

Note that is also tests the `Bag(Object[])` constructor.

EXAMPLE 5.7 An Implementation of a `Bag.contains(Object)` Method

This method implements the Sequential Search Algorithm (see Section 2.4 on page 28) to search the bag for the given `object`. It searches through the `objects[]` array and returns true as soon as one of its elements equals the given `object`. If the loop terminates after checking every element, then the method returns `false`:

```
public boolean contains(Object object)
{ // returns true iff the given object
  // is equal to some object in this bag
  for (int i=0; i<size; i++)
    if (object.equals(objects[i])) return true;
  return false;
}
```

Note that this method uses the `Object.equals()` method to test for equality. That invocation will return `true` only if the two references `object` and `objects[i]` both refer to the same object.

Here is a test driver of the `contains(Object)` method:

```
public class Testing
{ public static void main(String[] args)
  { String[] food = { "egg", "ham", "rum", "tea" };
    Bag foodBag = new Bag(food);
    System.out.println(foodBag);
    if (foodBag.contains("fig")) System.out.println("fig");
    else System.out.println("no fig");
```

```
        if (foodBag.contains("ham")) System.out.println("ham");
        else System.out.println("no ham");
    }
}
{ egg, ham, rum, tea }
no fig
ham
```

Note that the two occurrences of the string literal must be referring to the same object in memory.

EXAMPLE 5.8   An Implementation of a `Bag.equals(Object)` Method

```
public boolean equals(Object object)
{ // returns true iff the given object is a Bag
  // and has the same content as this bag
  if (object == this) return true;
  if (object.getClass() != this.getClass()) return false;
  if (object.hashCode() != this.hashCode()) return false;
  Collection collection = (Collection)object;
  if (collection.size() != this.size()) return false;
  if (!collection.containsAll(this)) return false;
  if (!this.containsAll(collection)) return false;
  for (int i=0; i<size; i++)
  { Object x = objects[i];
    if (frequency(collection,x) != frequency(this,x))
      return false;
  }
  return true;
}
```

EXAMPLE 5.9 An Implementation of a `Bag.removeAll(Object)` Method

```
public boolean removeAll(Object object)
{ // removes all of the given object from this bag;
  // returns true iff this bag was modified;
  boolean modified=false;
  for (int i=0; i<size; i++)
    if (object.equals(objects[i]))
    { objects[i] = objects[--size];
      modified = true;
    }
  return modified;
}
```

EXAMPLE 5.10   An Implementation of a `Bag.toArray()` Method

```
public Object[] toArray()
{ // returns an array whose elements are in this bag;
  Object[] objects = new Object[size];
  for (int i=0; i<size; i++)
    objects[i] = this.objects[i];
  return objects;
}
```

EXAMPLE 5.11 Testing the Bag **Class**

Here is a test driver for the Bag class defined in Example 5.3:

```
public class Ex0511
{ public static void main(String[] args)
  { String[] states = { "Maine", "Idaho", "Iowa", "Ohio", "Utah" };
    Bag myCollection = new Bag(states);
    print(myCollection);
    myCollection.add("Alaska");
    print(myCollection);
    if (myCollection.remove("Ohio")) print(myCollection);
    else System.out.println("Object \"Ohio\" was not found.");
    Iterator it = myCollection.iterator();
    while (it.hasNext())
    { String s = (String)it.next();
      System.out.println("\ts = \""+s+"\"");
      if (s.charAt(0) == 'I')
      { it.remove();
        System.out.println("\tObject \""+s+"\" removed.");
      }
    }
    print(myCollection);
  }
  private static void print(Bag collection)
  { System.out.println("size() = " + collection.size());
    Object[] objects = collection.toArray();
    for (int i=0; i<objects.length; i++)
      System.out.println("\tobjects[" + i + "] = " + objects[i]);
    if (collection.contains("Iowa"))
      System.out.println("\tContains \"Iowa\"");
    else System.out.println("\tDoes not contains \"Iowa\"");
    String[] states = { "Maine", "Idaho", "Iowa", "Ohio", "Utah" };
    Bag newCollection = new Bag(states);
    if (newCollection.containsAll(collection))
      System.out.println("\tnewC contains myC");
    else System.out.println("\tnewC does not contain myC");
    if (collection.containsAll(newCollection))
      System.out.println("\tmyC contains newC");
    else System.out.println("\tmyC does not contain newC");
    if (collection.equals(newCollection))
      System.out.println("\tmyC equals newC");
    else System.out.println("\tmyC does not equal newC");
    if (newCollection.equals(collection))
      System.out.println("\tnewC equals myC");
    else System.out.println("\tnewC does not equal myC");
  }
}
```

```
size() = 5
        objects[0] = Maine
        objects[1] = Idaho
        objects[2] = Iowa
        objects[3] = Ohio
        objects[4] = Utah
```

```
            Contains "Iowa"
            newC contains myC
            myC contains newC
            myC equals newC
            newC equals myC
size() = 6
            objects[0] = Maine
            objects[1] = Idaho
            objects[2] = Iowa
            objects[3] = Ohio
            objects[4] = Utah
            objects[5] = Alaska
            Contains "Iowa"
            newC does not contain myC
            myC contains newC
            myC does not equal newC
            newC does not equal myC
size() = 5
            objects[0] = Maine
            objects[1] = Idaho
            objects[2] = Iowa
            objects[3] = Alaska
            objects[4] = Utah
            Contains "Iowa"
            newC does not contain myC
            myC does not contain newC
            myC does not equal newC
            newC does not equal myC
            s = "Maine"
            s = "Idaho"
            Object "Idaho" removed.
            s = "Utah"
            s = "Iowa"
            Object "Iowa" removed.
            s = "Alaska"
size() = 3
            objects[0] = Maine
            objects[1] = Utah
            objects[2] = Alaska
            Does not contains "Iowa"
            newC does not contain myC
            myC does not contain newC
            myC does not equal newC
            newC does not equal myC
```

5.5 THE Iterator INTERFACE

An *iterator* is an object that traverses a data structure, visiting each element exactly once. Since time is linear, an iterator manifestly linearizes the structure as it traverses it. A structure may have several iterators traversing it simultaneously. At any moment, each iterator identifies a single element of the structure, providing access to it.

Here is the `Iterator` interface defined the `java.util` package:

```
public interface Iterator
{ public boolean  hasNext();
  public Object   next();
  public void     remove();
}
```

Iterators are usually implemented as anonymous inner classes that are defined within the `iterator()` method of its associated collection class, as in the following example.

EXAMPLE 5.12 The `iterator()` Method for the `Bag` Class

Here is the implementation of the `iterator()` method for the `Bag` class defined in Example 5.3:

```
public Iterator iterator()
{ // returns an iterator on this bag
  return new Iterator()  // inline constructor definition:
  { private int cursor=0;
    public boolean hasNext()
    { return cursor<size;
    }
    public Object next()
    { if (cursor>=size) return null;
      return objects[cursor++];
    }
    public void remove()
    { objects[--cursor] = objects[--size];
      objects[size] = null;
    }
  };  // note the required semicolon
}
```

Review Questions

5.1 What is the Java Collections Framework?

5.2 Why are the `iterator()` and `size()` methods declared to be `abstract` in the definition of the `AbstractCollection` class?

5.3 What is an iterator?

Problems

5.1 Implement the following constructor for the `Bag` class (see Example 5.3 on page 97):
```
public Bag(int capacity)
// constructs an empty bag with the given capacity
```

5.2 Implement the following constructor for the `Bag` class (see Example 5.3 on page 97):
```
public Bag(Object[] objects)
// constructs a bag containing the objects in the
// given array and with twice the capacity
```

5.3 Implement the following method for the `Bag` class (see Example 5.3 on page 97):
```
public boolean addAll(Collection collection)
```

```
                              // adds all the objects in the given collection
                              // to this bag
```

5.4   Implement the following method for the Bag class (see Example 5.3 on page 97):

```
              public void clear()
              // removes all the objects from this bag
```

5.5   Implement the following method for the Bag class (see Example 5.3 on page 97):

```
              public boolean containsAll(Collection collection)
              // returns true iff every object in the given collection
              // is equal to some object in this bag; that is,
              // iff the the given collection is a subset of this bag;
```

5.6   Implement the following method for the Bag class (see Example 5.3 on page 97):

```
              private static int frequency(Collection x, Object object)
              // returns the number of objects in the given collection
              // that are equal to the given object
```

5.7   Implement the following method for the Bag class (see Example 5.3 on page 97):

```
              public int hashCode()
              // returns a hash code for this bag that is the sum
              // of the hash codes of its elements
```

5.8   Implement the following method for the Bag class (see Example 5.3 on page 97):

```
              public boolean remove(Object object)
              // removes one of the given object from this bag;
              // returns true iff this bag was modified;
```

5.9   Implement the following method for the Bag class (see Example 5.3 on page 97):

```
              public boolean removeAll(Collection collection)
              // removes from this bag all of the object that are also in
              // the given collection, thereby reducing this bag to its
              // set-theoretic intersection with that collection;
              // returns true iff this bag was modified;
```

5.10 Implement the following method for the Bag class (see Example 5.3 on page 97):

```
              public boolean retainAll(Collection collection)
              // removes from this bag all of the object that are not in
              // the given collection, thereby reducing this bag to its
              // set-theoretic complement relative to that collection;
              // returns true iff this bag was modified;
```

5.11 Implement the following method for the Bag class (see Example 5.3 on page 97):

```
              public Object[] toArray(Object[] objects)
              // returns an array whose elements are in this bag
              // if it is longer than the given object[] array;
              // otherwise, the given array is returned after removing
              // all of its elements and then loading it with the elements
              // of this bag, and padding the rest of it with nulls;
```

5.12 Implement the following method for the Bag class (see Example 5.3 on page 97):

```
              public String toString()
              // returns a String that shows the contents of this bag
```

Answers to Review Questions

5.1   The *Java Collections Framework* is a group of interfaces and classes defined in the java.util package that facilitate the definition of data structure classes through inheritance.

5.2   The `iterator()` and `size()` methods are `abstract` in the `AbstractCollection` class because they are used by other methods (such as `toString()` and `isEmpty()`) that are implemented in that class. This ensures that those other methods will work in concrete subclasses.

5.3   An *iterator* is an object that moves sequentially from one component to the next through a collection structure, providing access to its elements.

Solutions to Problems

5.1   Implementation of the **Bag(int)** constructor for the Bag class:
```
public Bag(int capacity)
{ // constructs an empty bag with the given capacity
  objects = new Object[capacity];
}
```

5.2   Implementation of the **Bag(Object[])** constructor for the Bag class:
```
public Bag(Object[] objects)
{ // constructs a bag containing the objects in the
  // given array and with twice the capacity
  this.objects = new Object[2*objects.length];
  for (int i=0; i<objects.length; i++)
    this.objects[size++] = objects[i];
}
```

5.3   Implementation of the **addAll(Collection)** method for the Bag class:
```
public boolean addAll(Collection collection)
{ // adds all the objects in the given collection
  // to this bag
  resize(2*collection.size());
  for (Iterator it = collection.iterator(); it.hasNext(); )
    objects[size++] = it.next();
  return true;
}
```

5.4   Implementation of the **clear()** method for the Bag class:
```
public void clear()
{ // removes all the objects from this bag
  for (int i=0; i<size; i++)
    objects[i] = null;
  size = 0;
}
```

5.5   Implementation of the **containsAll(Collection)** method for the Bag class:
```
public boolean containsAll(Collection collection)
{ // returns true iff every object in the given collection
  // is equal to some object in this bag; that is,
  // iff the the given collection is a subset of this bag;
  for (Iterator it = collection.iterator(); it.hasNext(); )
    if (!this.contains(it.next())) return false;
  return true;
}
```

5.6   Implementation of the **frequency(Collection,Object)** method for the Bag class:
```
private static int frequency(Collection x, Object object)
{ // returns the number of objects in the given collection
  // that are equal to the given object
  int count=0;
  for (Iterator it = x.iterator(); it.hasNext(); )
    if (object.equals(it.next())) ++count;
```

```
            return count;
          }
```

5.7   Implementation of the **hashCode()** method for the Bag class:

```
          public int hashCode()
          { // returns a hash code for this bag that is the sum
            // of the hash codes of its elements
            int code=0;
            for (int i=0; i<size; i++)
              code += objects[i].hashCode();
            return code;
          }
```

5.8   Implementation of the **remove(Object)** method for the Bag class:

```
          public boolean remove(Object object)
          { // removes one of the given object from this bag;
            // returns true iff this bag was modified;
            for (int i=0; i<size; i++)
              if (object.equals(objects[i]))
              { objects[i] = objects[--size];
                return true;
              }
            return false;
          }
```

5.9   Implementation of the **removeAll(Collection)** method for the Bag class:

```
          public boolean removeAll(Collection collection)
          { // removes from this bag all of the object that are also in
            // the given collection, thereby reducing this bag to its
            // set-theoretic intersection with that collection;
            // returns true iff this bag was modified;
            boolean modified=false;
            for (Iterator it = collection.iterator(); it.hasNext(); )
              if (this.remove(it.next())) modified = true;
            return modified;
          }
```

5.10 Implementation of the **retainAll(Collection)** method for the Bag class:

```
          public boolean retainAll(Collection collection)
          { // removes from this bag all of the object that are not in
            // the given collection, thereby reducing this bag to its
            // set-theoretic complement relative to that collection;
            // returns true iff this bag was modified;
            boolean modified=false;
            for (int i=0; i<size; i++)
              if (!collection.contains(objects[i]))
              { remove(objects[i]);
                modified = true;
              }
            return modified;
          }
```

5.11 Implementation of the **toArray(Object[])** method for the Bag class:

```
          public Object[] toArray(Object[] objects)
          { // returns an array whose elements are in this bag
            // if it is longer than the given object[] array;
            // otherwise, the given array is returned after removing
            // all of its elements and then loading it with the elements
            // of this bag, and padding the rest of it with nulls;
            if (size > objects.length) objects = this.toArray();
            else
```

```
{ for (int i=0; i<size; i++)
    objects[i] = this.objects[i];
  for (int i=size; i<objects.length; i++)
    objects[i] = null;
}
return objects;
}
```

5.12   Implementation of the **toString()** method for the Bag class:

```
public String toString()
{ // returns a String that shows the contents of this bag
  String s="{ ";
  if (size>0) s += this.objects[0];
  for (int i=1; i<size; i++)
    s += ", " + this.objects[i];
  return s + " }";
}
```

Chapter 6

Stacks

A *stack* is a container that implements the last-in-first-out (LIFO) protocol. This means that the only accessible object in the container is the last one among those that were inserted. A stack of books is a good analogy: you can't take a book from the stack without first removing the books that are stacked on top of it.

6.1 THE JAVA Stack CLASS

As shown in the chart on page 94 in Section 5.1, the Java Collections Framework includes a Stack class. It is defined in the java.util package like this:

```
Object
  └─ AbstractCollection
       └─ AbstractList
            └─ Vector
                 └─ Stack
```

```java
public class Stack extends Vector
{
  public boolean empty()
  { return size()==0;
  }

  public Object peek()
  { if (size()==0) throw new EmptyStackException();
    return elementAt(size()-1);
  }

  public Object pop()
  { Object object = peek();
    removeElementAt(size()-1);
    return object;
  }

  public Object push(Object object)
  { addElement(object);
    return object;
  }

  public int search(Object object)
  { int i=lastIndexOf(object);
    if (i<0) return -1;  // object is not on this stack
    return size() - i;
  }

  public Stack()
  {
  }
}
```

The `Stack` class is a subclass of the `Vector` class (see Chapter 2). It implements a stack as a vector, with the last element of the vector being the top of the stack.

The `empty()` method returns `true` iff (if and only if) the number of elements on the stack is zero.

The `peek()` method returns the object on the top of the stack without removing it. It uses the `Vector.elementAt(int)` method to access that object, the last element in the vector. If the stack is empty, it throws an `EmptyStackException` exception.

The `pop()` method returns the object on the top of the stack after removing it. It uses the `Vector.removeElementAt(int)` method. Note that since this method invokes the `peek()` method, it too will throw an `EmptyStackException` exception if the stack is empty.

The `push(Object)` method inserts the given object onto the top of the stack. It uses the `Vector.addElementAt(Object)` method, which adds the element to the end of the vector.

The `search(Object)` method returns the position of the given object on the stack, or it returns −1 if the given object is not on the stack. It invokes the `Vector.lastIndexOf(Object)` method, which uses the `equals()` method to compare the given object with objects in the vector. If it contains several objects that are equal to the given object, the position of the last one is returned. That is the one closest to the top of the stack. Position numbers are computed using "one-based indexing," so the top element on the stack has position 1.

EXAMPLE 6.1 Peeking into an Empty Stack

```
public class Ex0601
{ public static void main(String[] args)
   { java.util.Stack stack = new java.util.Stack();
     System.out.println("stack.size() = " + stack.size());
     System.out.println("stack.peek() = " + stack.peek());
   }
}
stack.size() = 0
java.util.EmptyStackException
        at java.util.Stack.peek(Stack.java:86)
        at Ex0601.main(Ex0601.java:10)
```

This shows that the `EmptyStackException` exception gets thrown if `peek()` is invoked on an empty stack.

EXAMPLE 6.2 Handling an `EmptyStackException` Exception

```
import java.util.Stack;

public class Test
{ public static void main(String[] args)
   { Stack stack = new Stack();
     print(stack);
   }
   private static void print(Stack stack)
   { System.out.println("stack.size() = " + stack.size());
     try
     { System.out.println("stack.peek() = " + stack.peek());
     }
```

```
        catch(java.util.EmptyStackException e)
        { System.out.println(e + ": The stack is empty.");
        }
      }
    }
```
```
stack.size() = 0
java.util.EmptyStackException: The stack is empty.
```

This shows a simple way to handle the `EmptyStackException` exception.

EXAMPLE 6.3 Testing the `push()` and `pop()` Methods

```java
import java.util.Stack;

public class Ex0603
{ public static void main(String[] args)
  { Stack stack = new Stack();
    stack.push("Brazil");
    stack.push("Canada");
    stack.push("France");
    stack.push("Mexico");
    stack.push("Russia");
    stack.push("Sweden");
    stack.push("Brazil");
    stack.push("Turkey");
    print(stack);
    System.out.println("stack.search(\"Brazil\") = "
                       + stack.search("Brazil"));
    System.out.println("stack.pop() = " + stack.pop());
    System.out.println("stack.pop() = " + stack.pop());
    print(stack);
    System.out.println("stack.search(\"Brazil\") = "
                       + stack.search("Brazil"));
  }

  private static void print(Stack stack)
  { System.out.println(stack);
    System.out.println("stack.size() = " + stack.size());
    try
    { System.out.println("stack.peek() = " + stack.peek());
    }
    catch(java.util.EmptyStackException e)
    { System.out.println(e + ": The stack is empty.");
    }
  }
}
```
```
[Brazil, Canada, France, Mexico, Russia, Sweden, Brazil, Turkey]
stack.size() = 8
stack.peek() = Turkey
stack.search("Brazil") = 2
stack.pop() = Turkey
stack.pop() = Brazil
[Brazil, Canada, France, Mexico, Russia, Sweden]
stack.size() = 6
```

```
stack.peek() = Sweden
stack.search("Brazil") = 6
```

After pushing eight objects (all strings) onto the stack, this program invokes its local `print(Stack)` method to display information about the stack. Then it searches for `"Brazil"`, pops `"Turkey"` off the stack, and invokes `print(Stack)` again. Note that `search(Object)` returns 2, meaning that one copy of `"Brazil"` is second from the top of the stack. (Another copy is on the bottom of the stack.)

Next it invokes the `pop()` method twice, thereby removing first `"Turkey"` and then `"Brazil"` from the stack. Then the final call to `print(Stack)` shows that the stack has six elements, with `"Sweden"` at the top and `"Brazil"` sixth from the top.

Note that the call `System.out.println(stack)` invokes the `Vector.toString()` method, which returns a string displaying a list of the elements delimited with brackets `[ ]`.

6.2 APPLICATIONS OF STACKS

Although the `stack` data structure is one of the simplest, it is essential in certain important applications. Some of these are illustrated in the following examples.

An arithmetic expression is said to be in *postfix* notation (also called *reverse Polish notation*, or *RPN*) if each operator is placed after its operands. For example, the postfix expression for `3*(4 + 5)` is `3 4 5 + *`. (The expression `3*(4 + 5)` is called an *infix expression*.) Postfix expressions are easier to process by machine than infix. Calculators that process postfix expressions are called *RPN calculators*.

EXAMPLE 6.4 An RPN Calculator

This program parses postfix expressions, performing the indicated arithmetic. It uses a stack to accumulate the operands.

```java
import java.util.Stack;
import java.io.*;

public class Ex0604
{ public static void main(String[] args)
  { boolean quit=false;
    String input;
    double x, y, z;
    Stack operands = new Stack();
    while (!quit)
    { input = getString("RPN> ");
      switch (input.charAt(0))
      { case 'Q':
          quit = true;
          break;
        case '+':
          y = Double.parseDouble((String)operands.peek());
          operands.pop();
          x = Double.parseDouble((String)operands.peek());
          operands.pop();
          z = x + y;
          System.out.println("\t" + x + "+" + y + " = " + z);
          operands.push(new Double(z).toString());
          break;
```

```
                case '-':
                  y = Double.parseDouble((String)operands.peek());
                  operands.pop();
                  x = Double.parseDouble((String)operands.peek());
                  operands.pop();
                  z = x - y;
                  System.out.println("\t" + x + "-" + y + " = " + z);
                  operands.push(new Double(z).toString());
                  break;
                case '*':
                  y = Double.parseDouble((String)operands.peek());
                  operands.pop();
                  x = Double.parseDouble((String)operands.peek());
                  operands.pop();
                  z = x * y;
                  System.out.println("\t" + x + "*" + y + " = " + z);
                  operands.push(new Double(z).toString());
                  break;
                case '/':
                  y = Double.parseDouble((String)operands.peek());
                  operands.pop();
                  x = Double.parseDouble((String)operands.peek());
                  operands.pop();
                  z = x / y;
                  System.out.println("\t" + x + "/" + y + " = " + z);
                  operands.push(new Double(z).toString());
                  break;
                default:
                  operands.push(input);
              }
            }
          }
      private static String getString(String prompt)
      { System.out.print(prompt);
        InputStreamReader iSReader = new InputStreamReader(System.in);
        BufferedReader bReader = new BufferedReader(iSReader);
        String input="";
        try { input = bReader.readLine(); }
        catch(IOException e) { System.out.println(e); }
        return input;
      }
    }
```

This run processes the postfix expression 3 4 5 + * 10 / 1 -, which represents the infix expression 3*(4 + 5)/10 - 1. Each intermediate calculation is printed.

On each iteration of the while loop, the program prints the RPN> prompt and then reads an input string. If the first character of that string is a 'Q', then the program terminates. If it is a '+', '-', '*', or '/', then the corresponding arithmetic operation is performed. Otherwise, the input string is assumed to hold a numeric operand, which then gets pushed onto the operand stack.

When one of the four operators is input, the last two numbers are popped off the operand stack, the arithmetic operation is performed and printed, and the result pushed onto the operand stack.

```
RPN> 3
RPN> 4
RPN> 5
RPN> +
        4.0+5.0 = 9.0
RPN> *
        3.0*9.0 = 27.0
RPN> 10
RPN> /
        27.0/10.0 = 2.7
RPN> 1
RPN> -
        2.7-1.0 = 1.7000000000000002
RPN> Q
```

Human readers tend to prefer infix to postfix notation for arithmetic expressions. The following example converts a given infix expression to postfix.

EXAMPLE 6.5 Converting Infix to Postfix

```java
import java.util.Stack;
import java.io.*;

public class Ex0605
{ public static void main(String[] args)
  { try
    { Stack stack = new Stack();
      InputStreamReader reader = new InputStreamReader(System.in);
      StreamTokenizer tokens = new StreamTokenizer(reader);
      tokens.ordinaryChar('/');  // otherwise, this would be a comment
      tokens.eolIsSignificant(true);  // default is false
      int tokenType;
      System.out.print("Enter an infix expression: ");
      while ((tokenType=tokens.nextToken()) != StreamTokenizer.TT_EOL)
      { char ch = (char)tokenType;
        if (tokenType==StreamTokenizer.TT_NUMBER)
          System.out.print(tokens.nval + " ");
        else if (ch=='+' || ch=='-' || ch=='*' || ch=='/')
          stack.push(new Character(ch));
        else if (ch==')')
          System.out.print((Character)stack.pop()+" ");
      }
      while (!stack.empty())
        System.out.print((Character)stack.pop()+" ");
    }
    catch (Exception e)
    { System.out.println(e);
    }
  }
}
Enter an infix expression: (80 - 30)*(40 + 50/10)
80.0 30.0 - 40.0 50.0 10.0 / + *
```

The input is parsed by a `StreamTokenizer` object `tokens` bound to the `InputStreamReader` object. It invokes `ordinaryChar('/')` so that it can recognize the division operator "/" as a character, and it invokes `eolIsSignificant(true)` so that it can use its class's `TT_EOL` constant to control the parsing loop, terminating it when the end-of-line character is detected.

On each iteration of the `while` loop, the `tokens` object obtains the next token from the input stream, extracts its `char` representation into the variable `ch`, and then acts according to whether it is a numeric operand, one of the four arithmetic operators, or the right parenthesis character `')'`. If it is a numeric operand, it is printed immediately, because in postfix notation, the operands appear before their operators. If it is an arithmetic operator, it is pushed onto the stack. If it is the right parenthesis character, the top operator on the stack is popped and printed.

Note that this version requires the input expression to be completely parenthesized. It also requires a space before the subtraction operator so that it can be recognized as the binary subtraction operator instead of the unary negation operator.

6.3 REMOVING RECURSION

A computer's operating system executes a recursive function by using a stack to store the current run-time state each time it makes a recursive call. Then each time it returns from a recursive call, it pops the top state off the run-time stack so it can continue where it left off. Since stacks are used by the operating system to execute a recursive function, it stands to reason that the programmer should be able to rewrite a recursive function so that it uses an explicit stack instead of making recursive calls.

EXAMPLE 6.6 Iterative Towers of Hanoi

This program is equivalent to the recursion program in Example 4.15 on page 83:

```
public class Ex0606
{ public static void main(String[] args)
  { hanoi(3,'A','B','C');  // play the game with 3 disks
  }

  private static void hanoi(int n, char x, char y, char z)
  { java.util.Stack stack = new java.util.Stack();
    stack.push(new Quad(n,x,y,z));
    while (!stack.empty())
    { Quad quad = (Quad)stack.pop();
      n = quad.n;
      x = quad.a;
      y = quad.b;
      z = quad.c;
      if (n == 1) System.out.println
        ("Move top disk from peg " + quad.a + " to peg " + quad.c);
      else
      { stack.push(new Quad(n-1,y,x,z));
        stack.push(new Quad(1,x,y,z));
        stack.push(new Quad(n-1,x,z,y));
      }
    }
  }
}
```

```
class Quad
{ public int n;
  public char a, b, c;
  public Quad(int n, char a, char b, char c)
  { this.n = n; this.a = a; this.b = b; this.c = c;
  }
}
Move top disk from peg A to peg C
Move top disk from peg A to peg B
Move top disk from peg C to peg B
Move top disk from peg A to peg C
Move top disk from peg B to peg A
Move top disk from peg B to peg C
Move top disk from peg A to peg C
```

Each recursive invocation in the recursive version of the `hanoi(int,char,char,char)` method is replaced by a `stack.push(Quad)` invocation, and each return from a recursive invocation is replaced by a `stack.pop(Quad)` invocation.

The `Quad` class us used to hold a quadruple containing an integer and three characters.

Review Questions

6.1 Why are stacks called LIFO structures?

6.2 Would it make sense to call a stack
    a. a LILO structure?
    b. a FILO structure?

6.3 What is
    a. prefix notation?
    b. infix notation?
    c. postfix notation?

6.4 Determine whether each of the following is true about postfix expressions:
    a. $x\,y + z + = x\,y\,z + +$
    b. $x\,y + z - = x\,y\,z - +$
    c. $x\,y - z + = x\,y\,z + -$
    d. $x\,y - z - = x\,y\,z - -$

Problems

6.1 Trace the following code, showing the contents of the `stack` after each invocation:

```
Stack stack = new Stack();
stack.push(new Character('A'));
stack.push(new Character('B'));
stack.push(new Character('C'));
stack.pop();
stack.pop();
stack.push(new Character('D'));
stack.push(new Character('E'));
stack.push(new Character('F'));
```

```
stack.pop();
stack.push(new Character('G'));
stack.pop();
stack.pop();
stack.pop();
```

6.2   Translate each of the following prefix expressions into infix:

  a. $- / + * a\ b\ c\ d\ e$

  b. $/ - a\ b\ * c + d\ e$

  c. $/ a + b\ * c - d\ e$

6.3   Translate the prefix expressions in Problem 6.2 into postfix.

6.4   Translate each of the following infix expressions into prefix:

  a. $(a + b) - (c / (d + e))$

  b. $a / ((b / c) * (d - e))$

  c. $(a / (b / c)) * (d - e)$

6.5   Translate the infix expressions in Problem 6.4 into postfix.

6.6   Translate each of the following postfix expressions into prefix:

  a. $a\ b + c\ d - / e +$

  b. $a\ b\ c + d\ e - * -$

  c. $a\ b\ c\ d\ e / / / /$

6.7   Translate the postfix expressions in Problem 6.6 into infix.

6.8   Write the following method using only the constructor and the `push()`, `peek()`, `pop()`, and `empty()` methods of the `Stack` class:

```
private static void reverse(Stack stack);
// reverses the contents of the given stack
```

6.9   Write the following method using only the constructor and the `push()`, `peek()`, `pop()`, and `empty()` methods of the `Stack` class:

```
private static Stack reversed(Stack stack);
// returns a new stack that contains the same elements
// as the given stack, but in reversed order
```

6.10   Write the following method using only the constructor and the `push()`, `peek()`, `pop()`, and `empty()` methods of the `Stack` class:

```
public Object penultimate(Stack stack);
// returns the second from the top element of the given stack
```

6.11   Write the following method using only the constructor and the `push()`, `peek()`, `pop()`, and `empty()` methods of the `Stack` class:

```
public Object bottom();
// returns the bottom element of this stack
```

6.12   Write the following method using only the constructor and the `push()`, `peek()`, `pop()`, and `empty()` methods of the `Stack` class:

```
public Object popBottom();
// removes and returns the bottom element of this stack
```

6.13   Write the `reverse()` method of Problem 6.8, using inherited `Vector` methods.

6.14   Write the `reverse()` method of Problem 6.9, using inherited `Vector` methods.

6.15   Write the `penultimate()` method of Problem 6.10, using inherited `Vector` methods.

6.16   Write the `bottom()` method of Problem 6.11, using inherited `Vector` methods.

6.17   Write the `popBottom()` method of Problem 6.12, using inherited `Vector` methods.

6.18 Modify Example 6.5 on page 114 so that it uses a stack of primitive `char` values instead of `Object` references. Implement your own `Stack` class for this purpose. Use an array to store the `char` values.

Answers to Review Questions

6.1 Stacks are called LIFO structures because the last element that is inserted into a stack is always the first element to be removed. LIFO is an acronym for Last-In-First-Out.

6.2 *a.* No, because a LILO structure would mean Last-In-Last-Out, which is just the opposite of the "Last-In-First-Out" protocol.

b. Yes, because a FILO structure would mean First-In-Last-Out, which is the same as a Last-In-First-Out protocol.

6.3 *a.* The prefix notation for arithmetic expressions places binary operators ahead of both of their operands. For example, the expression "$x + 2$" is written "$+ \, x \, 2$" in prefix notation. The standard functional notation used in mathematics uses prefix notation: $f(x)$, $\sin x$, etc.

b. The infix notation for arithmetic expressions places binary operators between their operands. Infix notation is the usual format for arithmetic expressions; e.g., $x + 2$.

c. The postfix notation for arithmetic expressions places binary operators after both of their operands. For example, the expression "$x + 2$" is written "$x \, 2 \, +$" in postfix notation. The factorial function in mathematics uses postfix notation: $n!$.

6.4 *a.* True, because $(x + y) + z = x + (y + z)$.

b. True, because $(x + y) - z = x + (y - z)$.

c. False, because $(x - y) + z \neq x - (y + z)$.

d. False, because $(x - y) - z \neq x - (y - z)$.

Solutions to Problems

6.1   Trace:

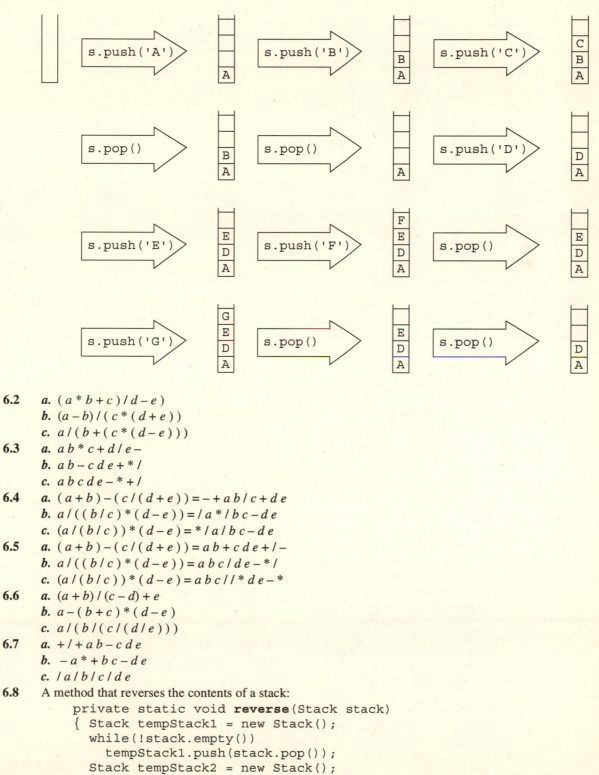

6.2   **a.** $(a*b+c)/d-e)$
        b. $(a-b)/(c*(d+e))$
        c. $a/(b+(c*(d-e)))$

6.3   **a.** $ab*c+d/e-$
        b. $ab-cde+*/$
        c. $abcde-*+/$

6.4   **a.** $(a+b)-(c/(d+e))=-+ab/c+de$
        b. $a/((b/c)*(d-e))=/a*/bc-de$
        c. $(a/(b/c))*(d-e)=*/a/bc-de$

6.5   **a.** $(a+b)-(c/(d+e))=ab+cde+/-$
        b. $a/((b/c)*(d-e))=abc/de-*/$
        c. $(a/(b/c))*(d-e)=abc//*de-*$

6.6   **a.** $(a+b)/(c-d)+e$
        b. $a-(b+c)*(d-e)$
        c. $a/(b/(c/(d/e)))$

6.7   **a.** $+/+ab-cde$
        b. $-a*+bc-de$
        c. $/a/b/c/de$

6.8   A method that reverses the contents of a stack:

```
        private static void reverse(Stack stack)
      { Stack tempStack1 = new Stack();
        while(!stack.empty())
          tempStack1.push(stack.pop());
        Stack tempStack2 = new Stack();
```

```
    while(!tempStack1.empty())
      tempStack2.push(tempStack1.pop());
    while(!tempStack2.empty())
      stack.push(tempStack2.pop());
}
```

6.9   A method that returns the reversed contents of a stack:
```
private static Stack reversed(Stack stack)
{ Stack tempStack = new Stack();
  Stack newStack = new Stack();
  while(!stack.empty())
  { Object x = stack.pop();
    tempStack.push(x);
    newStack.push(x);
  }
  while(!tempStack.empty())
    stack.push(tempStack.pop());
  return newStack;
}
```

6.10   A method that returns the second element from the top of a stack:
```
private static Object penultimate(Stack stack)
{ Object x1 = stack.pop();
  Object x2 = stack.pop();
  stack.push(x2);
  stack.push(x1);
  return x2;
}
```

6.11   A method that returns the bottom element of a stack:
```
private static Object bottom(Stack stack)
{ Object x = null;
  Stack tempStack = new Stack();
  while(!stack.empty())
  { x = stack.pop();
    tempStack.push(x);
  }
  while(!tempStack.empty())
    stack.push(tempStack.pop());
  return x;
}
```

6.12   A method that removes and returns the bottom element of a stack:
```
private static Object popBottom(Stack stack)
{ Stack tempStack = new Stack();
  Object x = null;
  if (!stack.empty()) x = stack.pop();
  while(!stack.empty())
  { tempStack.push(x);
    x = stack.pop();
  }
  while(!tempStack.empty())
    stack.push(tempStack.pop());
  return x;
}
```

6.13   A method that uses Vector methods to reverse the contents of a stack:
```
private static void reverse(Stack stack)
{ Stack copiedStack = (Stack)stack.clone();
  stack.clear();
  while(!copiedStack.empty())
```

```
          stack.push(copiedStack.pop());
    }
```

6.14 A method that uses `Vector` methods to return the reversed contents of a stack:

```
    private static Stack reversed(Stack stack)
    { Stack copiedStack = (Stack)stack.clone();
      Stack newStack = new Stack();
      while(!copiedStack.empty())
        newStack.push(copiedStack.pop());
      return newStack;
    }
```

6.15 A method that uses `Vector` methods to return the second element from the top of a stack:

```
    private static Object penultimate(Stack stack)
    { if (stack.size()<2) return null;
      return stack.elementAt(stack.size()-2);
    }
```

6.16 A method that uses `Vector` methods to return the bottom element of a stack:

```
    private static Object bottom(Stack stack)
    { return stack.firstElement();
    }
```

6.17 A method that uses `Vector` methods to remove and return the bottom element of a stack:

```
    private static Object popBottom(Stack stack)
    { return stack.remove(0);
    }
```

6.18 Example 6.5 modified using a stack of primitive `char` values:

```
    import java.io.*;

    class CharStack
    { private char[] s = new char[1000];
      private int top=-1;
      public boolean empty() { return top<0; }
      public char peek() { return s[top]; }
      public char pop() { return s[top--]; }
      public void push(char ch) { s[++top] = ch; }
    }

    public class Tmp
    { public static void main(String[] args)
      { try
        { CharStack stack = new CharStack();
          InputStreamReader reader = new InputStreamReader(System.in);
          StreamTokenizer tokens = new StreamTokenizer(reader);
          tokens.ordinaryChar('/');
          tokens.eolIsSignificant(true);
          int tokenType;
          System.out.print("Enter an infix expression: ");
          while ((tokenType=tokens.nextToken())
                     != StreamTokenizer.TT_EOL)
          { char ch = (char)tokenType;
            if (tokenType==treamTokenizer.TT_NUMBER)
              System.out.print(tokens.nval + " ");
            else if (ch=='+' || ch=='-' || ch=='*' || ch=='/')
              stack.push(ch);
            else if (ch==')')
              System.out.print(stack.pop()+" ");
```

```
      }
    while (!stack.empty())
       System.out.print(stack.pop()+" ");
  }
catch (Exception e)
{ System.out.println(e);
  }
 }
}
```

Chapter 7

Queues

A *queue* is a container that implements the first-in-first-out (FIFO) protocol. That means that the only accessible object in the container is the one among them that was inserted first. A good analogy is a group of people waiting in line for a movie: the next one admitted is the person in the line who got there ahead of every one else.

7.1 A FRAMEWORK FOR QUEUES

A *framework* is a set of interfaces and `abstract` classes that are related by extension and implementation and which provide for various implementations of abstract data types. The Java Collections Framework (see Section 5.1 on page 94) is a framework for lists, sets, and maps.

There is no framework for queues in the Java standard library. However, its Collections Framework suggests how the programmer can build one.

Like the `List` and `Set` interfaces, a `Queue` interface should be a subinterface of the `Collection` interface (see page 95 in Section 5.2), allowing it to inherit these 15 method specifications:

```
Object
  └─ AbstractCollection - - - - - - - - - - - - - - - - - - Collection
        └─ AbstractQueue - - - - - - - - - - - - - - - - - └─ Queue
              ├─ ArrayQueue
              └─ LinkedQueue
```

```
public interface Collection
{ public boolean   add(Object);
  public boolean   addAll(Collection);
  public void      clear();
  public boolean   contains(Object);
  public boolean   containsAll(Collection);
  public boolean   equals(Object);
  public int       hashCode();
  public boolean   isEmpty();
  public Iterator  iterator();
  public boolean   remove(Object);
  public boolean   removeAll(Collection);
  public boolean   retainAll(Collection);
  public int       size();
  public Object[]  toArray();
  public Object[]  toArray(Object[]);
}
```

EXAMPLE 7.1 A `Queue` Interface

Here is an interface for queues that adds the four methods that traditionally define the specialized behavior of queues.

```
public interface Queue extends Collection
{ public Object dequeue();
  public Object enqueue(Object object);
  public Object getBack();
  public Object getFront();
}
```

Here "dequeue" means remove the object that is in the front of the queue, and "enqueue" means insert the new object at the back of the queue.

EXAMPLE 7.2 Using a Queue

The diagram on the right shows how a queue grows and shrinks as its `enqueue(Object)` and `dequeue()` methods are invoked in this order:

```
q.enqueue("Amin");
q.enqueue("Bush");
q.enqueue("Chen");
q.enqueue("Diaz");
q.dequeue();
q.dequeue();
q.enqueue("Ford");
q.enqueue("Gore");
q.dequeue();
```

Here, the front of the queue is shown on the left and the back on the right. So after that third `dequeue()`, a call to `getFront()` would return `"Diaz"` and a call to `getBack()` would return `"Gore"`.

Following the pattern of the Java Collection Framework (see page 94 in Section 5.1), we implement the `Queue` interface as an `abstract` subclass of the `AbstractCollec-tion` class. Then specific array and linked implementations will be subclasses of this base class:

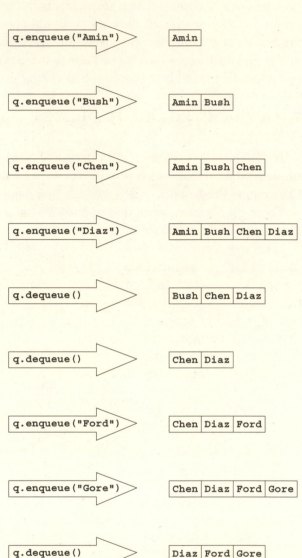

EXAMPLE 7.3 An `AbstractQueue` Class

```
import java.util.*;

public abstract
class AbstractQueue extends AbstractCollection implements Queue
{
  protected AbstractQueue() { }
```

```
      public abstract Object dequeue();

      public abstract Object enqueue(Object object);

      public boolean equals(Object object)
      { if (object == this) return true;
        if (!(object instanceof AbstractQueue)) return false;
        AbstractQueue abstractQueue = (AbstractQueue) object;
        if (abstractQueue.size() != size()) return false;
        return containsAll(abstractQueue);
      }

      public abstract Object getBack();

      public abstract Object getFront();

      public int hashCode()
      { int n = 0;
        for (Iterator it = iterator(); it.hasNext(); )
        { Object object = it.next();
          if (object != null) n += object.hashCode();
        }
        return n;
      }

      public abstract Iterator iterator();

      public abstract int size();

  }
```

This abstract class implements the default constructor and it overrides the equals(Object) and hashCode() methods from the Object class. The other six methods are declared abstract, thereby deferring their implementations to concrete subclasses. The dequeue(), enqueue(Object), getBack(), and getFront() methods are required by the Queue interface. The iterator() and size() methods are required by the AbstractCollections base class.

As a subclass of the AbstractCollections base class, the AbstractQueue class inherits the following concrete methods (see Section 5.3 on page 95):

```
      public boolean    addAll(Collection);
      public void       clear();
      public boolean    contains(Object);
      public boolean    containsAll(Collection);
      public boolean    isEmpty();
      public boolean    remove(Object);
      public boolean    removeAll(Collection);
      public boolean    retainAll(Collection);
      public Object[]   toArray();
      public Object[]   toArray(Object[]);
      public String     toString();
```

The isEmpty() method uses the size() method. The other ten concrete methods all use the iterator() method. So any subclass should implement the size() and iterator() methods.

7.2 A CONTIGUOUS IMPLEMENTATION

The simplest way to implement a queue is with an array.

EXAMPLE 7.4 An `ArrayQueue` Class

```java
import java.util.*;

public class ArrayQueue extends AbstractQueue
{ protected Object[] objects;
  protected int front=0;
  protected int back=0;
  protected int capacity=16;
  // INVARIANTS: objects[i] == null for 0 <= i < front;
  //             objects[i] != null for front <= i < back;
  //             objects[i] == null for back <= i < capacity;

  public ArrayQueue()
  { objects = new Object[capacity];
  }

  public ArrayQueue(int capacity)
  { this.capacity = capacity;
    objects = new Object[capacity];
  }

  public Object dequeue()
  { if (isEmpty()) throw new NoSuchElementException("Queue is empty");
    Object object = objects[front++];
    if (2*front>=capacity)  // shift left
    { for (int i=0; i<size(); i++)
        objects[i] = objects[i+front];
      back -= front;
      front = 0;
    }
    return object;
  }

  public Object enqueue(Object object)
  { if (back>=capacity)
    { Object[] temp = objects;
      capacity *= 2;  // double the capacity
      objects = new Object[capacity];
      for (int i=0; i<back-front; i++)
        objects[i] = temp[i+front];
      back -= front;
      front = 0;
    }
    objects[back++] = object;
    return object;
  }
```

```java
    public Object getBack()
    { if (isEmpty()) throw new NoSuchElementException("Queue is empty");
      return objects[back-1];
    }

    public Object getFront()
    { if (isEmpty()) throw new NoSuchElementException("Queue is empty");
      return objects[front];
    }

    public Iterator iterator()
    { return new Iterator()   // anonymous inner class
        { private int cursor=front;
          public boolean hasNext()
          { return cursor<back;
          }
          public Object next()
          { if (cursor>=back) throw new NoSuchElementException();
            return objects[cursor++];
          }
          public void remove()
          { throw new UnsupportedOperationException();
          }
        };
    }

    public int size()
    { return back-front;
    }
  }
```

The `objects` array holds the elements of the queue. As the class invariant comment says, only the subarray `objects[front..(back-1)]` is used; all the other elements are `null`.

The class has two constructors: a default constructor that sets the initial capacity of the array to 16, and another constructor that lets the user set the initial capacity.

The `getFront()` and `getBack()` methods returns `objects[front]` and `objects[back-1]`, respectively. The `size()` method returns `back-front`, which is the number of elements in the subarray `objects[front..(back-1)]`.

The `enqueue(Object)` method inserts the given object into `objects[back]` and then increments the `back` index. If `objects[back]` does not exist (i.e., `back` has reached the end of the array), then before the insertion, a new array is created with twice the capacity, and the `back-front` elements are copied into it, starting at index 0.

The `dequeue()` method removes the object at `objects[front]` and then increments the `front` index. If, after the removal, the `front` index is at least halfway to the end of the array (i.e., at least half the array elements are unused), then the `back-front` elements are all shifted down toward the beginning of the array, so that they start at index 0.

Finally, the `iterator()` method returns an iterator for traversing the queue. Since the queue is implemented as a subarray, the iterator need only keep track of an index, named `cursor`, that advances through the subarray. The returned iterator is created by the constructor of an anonymous inner class that defines the three methods that the `Iterator` interface requires. The cursor is initialized to the `front` index. Then each call to `next()` returns `objects[cursor]` and increments the cursor. If `next()` is invoked when `hasNext()` is false (i.e., when the cursor has reached the end of the queue), then a

NoSuchElementException exception is thrown. The remove() method automatically throws a UnsupportedOperationException exception because a queue should not allow its elements to be removed by any method other than dequeue().

EXAMPLE 7.5 Testing the `ArrayQueue` Class

Here is a test driver for this queue implementation:

```
public class TestQueue
{ public static void main(String[] args)
  { ArrayQueue q = new ArrayQueue();    System.out.println(q);
    q.enqueue("Amin");                   System.out.println(q);
    q.enqueue("Bush");                   System.out.println(q);
    q.enqueue("Chen");                   System.out.println(q);
    q.enqueue("Diaz");                   System.out.println(q);
    q.dequeue();                         System.out.println(q);
    q.dequeue();                         System.out.println(q);
    q.enqueue("Ford");                   System.out.println(q);
    q.enqueue("Gore");                   System.out.println(q);
    q.dequeue();                         System.out.println(q);
    System.out.println("q.getFront() = " + q.getFront());
    System.out.println("q.getBack() = " + q.getBack());
    System.out.println("q.size() = " + q.size());
    for (java.util.Iterator it=q.iterator(); it.hasNext(); )
      System.out.println("\tit.next() = " + it.next());
    for (;;)   // force an exception
    {  q.dequeue();
       System.out.println(q);
    }
  }
}
```

```
[]
[Amin]
[Amin, Bush]
[Amin, Bush, Chen]
[Amin, Bush, Chen, Diaz]
[Bush, Chen, Diaz]
[Chen, Diaz]
[Chen, Diaz, Ford]
[Chen, Diaz, Ford, Gore]
[Diaz, Ford, Gore]
q.getFront() = Diaz
q.getBack() = Gore
q.size() = 3
        it.next() = Diaz
        it.next() = Ford
        it.next() = Gore
[Ford, Gore]
[Gore]
[]
java.util.NoSuchElementException: queue is empty
        at LinkedQueue.dequeue(LinkedQueue.java:26)
        at TestQueue.main(TestQueue.java, Compiled Code)
Exception in thread "main"
```

7.3 A LINKED IMPLEMENTATION

Although the array implementation is simplest, the linked implementation is probably more efficient.

EXAMPLE 7.6 A `LinkedQueue` Class

```java
import java.util.*;
import AbstractQueue;

public class LinkedQueue extends AbstractQueue
{ private static class Node
  { Object object;
    Node next, previous;
    Node()
    { this.next = this.previous = this;
    }
    Node(Object object, Node next, Node previous)
    { this.object = object;
      this.next = next;
      this.previous = previous;
    }
  }
  private Node header = new Node();
  private int size = 0;

  public Object dequeue()
  { if (isEmpty()) throw new NoSuchElementException("queue is empty");
    Object object = header.next.object;
    header.next = header.next.next;
    header.next.previous = header;
    --size;
    return object;
  }

  public Object enqueue(Object object)
  { Node p = header.previous;  // last element in queue
    header.previous = p.next = new Node(object,header,p);
    ++size;
    return object;
  }

  public Object getBack()
  { if (isEmpty()) throw new NoSuchElementException("queue is empty");
    return header.previous.object;
  }

  public Object getFront()
  { if (isEmpty()) throw new NoSuchElementException("queue is empty");
    return header.next.object;
  }
```

```
      public Iterator iterator()
      { return new Iterator()   // anonymous inner class
        { private Node cursor=header;
          public boolean hasNext()
          { return cursor.next != header;
          }
          public Object next()
          { if (cursor.next==header) throw new NoSuchElementException();
            cursor = cursor.next;
            return cursor.object;
          }
          public void remove()
          { throw new UnsupportedOperationException();
          }
        };
      }

      public LinkedQueue()
      {
      }

      public int size()
      { return size;
      }
}
```

7.4 SIMULATION WITH QUEUES

Queues occur naturally in situations where the rate at which clients' demands for services can exceed the rate at which those services can be supplied. For example, cars arriving at a toll booth may have to wait in a queue before proceeding to the booth. The diagram here shows a queue of four cars waiting at a toll plaza with three booths. The same kind of situation can occur on a local area network where many computers share only a few printers: the print jobs may accumulate in a print queue. Supermarket checkout counters and barber shops are similar.

EXAMPLE 7.7 A Client/Server Simulation

This program simulates a general client/server system. The clients could be cars, print jobs, or people, and the servers could be toll booths, printers, or barbers, respectively.

The first part of the output from a sample run of the simulation is shown on the next page:

```
Job #1 arrives at time 2 with 7 pages.
The queue now contains 1 job: [#1(7)]
Printer A(89%,84%) begins Job #1 at time 2.
The queue is now empty.
Job #2 arrives at time 10 with 39 pages.
The queue now contains 1 job: [#2(39)]
Printer B(97%,91%) begins Job #2 at time 10.
The queue is now empty.
Printer A(89%,84%) ends Job #1 at time 11.
Job #3 arrives at time 18 with 36 pages.
The queue now contains 1 job: [#3(36)]
Printer A(89%,87%) begins Job #3 at time 18.
The queue is now empty.
Job #4 arrives at time 44 with 126 pages.
The queue now contains 1 job: [#4(126)]
Printer C(106%,102%) begins Job #4 at time 44.
The queue is now empty.
Printer B(97%,91%) ends Job #2 at time 53.
Printer A(89%,87%) ends Job #3 at time 60.
Job #5 arrives at time 78 with 170 pages.
The queue now contains 1 job: [#5(170)]
Printer A(89%,92%) begins Job #5 at time 78.
The queue is now empty.
Job #6 arrives at time 113 with 172 pages.
The queue now contains 1 job: [#6(172)]
Printer B(97%,95%) begins Job #6 at time 113.
The queue is now empty.
Job #7 arrives at time 121 with 40 pages.
The queue now contains 1 job: [#7(40)]
Printer D(128%,124%) begins Job #7 at time 121.
The queue is now empty.
Job #8 arrives at time 127 with 30 pages.
The queue now contains 1 job: [#8(30)]
Job #9 arrives at time 136 with 41 pages.
The queue now contains 2 jobs: [#8(30), #9(41)]
Job #10 arrives at time 140 with 20 pages.
The queue now contains 3 jobs: [#8(30), #9(41), #10(20)]
Job #11 arrives at time 147 with 31 pages.
The queue now contains 4 jobs: [#8(30), #9(41), #10(20), #11(31)]
Printer D(128%,124%) ends Job #7 at time 154.
Printer D(128%,126%) begins Job #8 at time 155.
The queue now contains 3 jobs: [#9(41), #10(20), #11(31)]
Job #12 arrives at time 160 with 63 pages.
The queue now contains 4 jobs: [#9(41), #10(20), #11(31), #12(63)]
Printer C(106%,102%) ends Job #4 at time 168.
Printer C(106%,104%) begins Job #9 at time 169.
The queue now contains 3 jobs: [#10(20), #11(31), #12(63)]
Printer D(128%,126%) ends Job #8 at time 179.
Printer D(128%,118%) begins Job #10 at time 180.
The queue now contains 2 jobs: [#11(31), #12(63)]
Printer D(128%,118%) ends Job #10 at time 197.
Printer D(128%,138%) begins Job #11 at time 198.
The queue now contains 1 job: [#12(63)]
Printer C(106%,104%) ends Job #9 at time 209.
Printer C(106%,96%) begins Job #12 at time 210.
The queue is now empty.
```

This output is phrased in the context of the clients being print jobs and the servers being printers.

In this run, the simulation has four servers: Printer A, Printer B, Printer C, and Printer D. Each printer has a different print rate, expressed as a percentage. For example, Printer A has a print rate of 89%, meaning that it averages 0.89 page per second. Each printer's print job also has a print rate. For example, on Job #1, Printer A has a print rate of 84%, meaning that it is printing 0.84 page per second on that job. A single printer's print rates vary among jobs because of other factors such as network traffic. For example, Printer B, which has an average print rate of 0.97 page per second, prints Job #2 at 0.91 pps and Job #6 at 0.95 pps.

The print jobs arrive at the print queue random times. In this run of the simulation, Job #1 arrived at time 2 (i.e., 2 seconds after the start time), Job #2 arrived at time 10, and Job #3 arrived at time 18.

When jobs arrive faster than the printers can begin printing them, they accumulate in the print queue. In this simulation, that happens when Job #8 arrives at time 127, when all four printers are busy. Prior to that time, there was always at least one idle printer that could begin printing a job as soon as it arrived:

>Printer A begins printing Job #1 as soon as it arrives at time 2.
>Printer B begins printing Job #2 as soon as it arrives at time 10.
>Printer A begins printing Job #3 as soon as it arrives at time 18.
>Printer C begins printing Job #4 as soon as it arrives at time 44.
>Printer A begins printing Job #5 as soon as it arrives at time 78.
>Printer B begins printing Job #6 as soon as it arrives at time 113.
>Printer D begins printing Job #7 as soon as it arrives at time 121.

But Job #8 has to wait 28 seconds before Printer D can begin printing it at time 155. It waits in the print queue. And of course, all the other jobs that arrive during that 28-second period must also wait in the print queue. By the time 155, the queue contains four jobs: #8, #9, #10, and #11.

In the output, each print job is identified by its ID number and also its size. For example, #1(7) means that Job #1 has 7 pages to be printed, and #8(30) means that Job #8 has 30 pages.

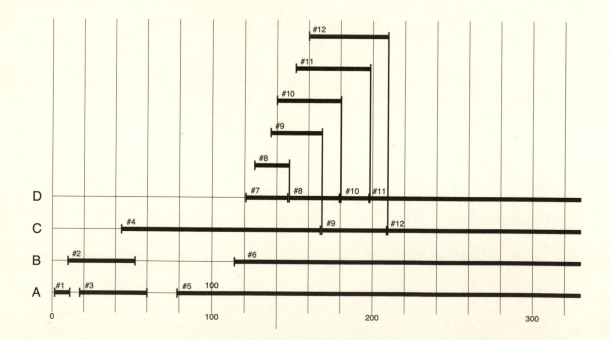

Effective simulation requires the use of randomly generated numeric input. This simulation uses three random number generators: one to generate the average print rates for each printer, one to generate the actual print rates for each printer's print jobs, and one to generate the time elapsed between job arrivals. They are instances of the following extension of the `java.util.Random` class.

```java
public class Random extends java.util.Random
{ private double mean;
  private double standardDeviation;
  public Random(double mean)
  { this.mean = mean;
    this.standardDeviation = mean;
  }
  public Random(double mean, double standardDeviation)
  { this.mean = mean;
    this.standardDeviation = standardDeviation;
  }
  public double nextGaussian()
  { double x = super.nextGaussian();  // x = normal(0.0, 1.0)
    return x*standardDeviation + mean;
  }
  public double nextExponential()
  { return -mean*Math.log(1.0 - nextDouble());
  }
  public int intNextExponential()
  { return (int)Math.ceil(nextExponential());
  }
}
```

The `nextGaussian()` method returns random numbers that are normally distributed with the given mean and standard deviation. It invokes and overrides the synonymous method in the `java.util.Random` class, which returns random numbers that are normally distributed with mean 0.0 and standard deviation 1.0. The `nextExponential()` method returns random numbers that are exponentially distributed with the given mean. This is the correct distribution for unbiased interarrival times. It is also used to generate the job sizes, which determine the service times.

Each print job is an instance of the following class.

```java
public class Client
{ private static final int MEAN_JOB_SIZE = 100;
  private static Random randomJobSize = new Random(MEAN_JOB_SIZE);
  private static int nextId = 0;
  private int id, jobSize;
  private Server server;

  public Client(int time)
  { id = ++nextId;
    jobSize = randomJobSize.intNextExponential();
    print(id,time,jobSize);
  }

  public double getJobSize()
  { return jobSize;
  }

  public void beginService(Server server, int time)
  { this.server = server;
    printBegins(server,id,time);
  }
```

```
      public void endService(int time)
      { printEnds(server,id,time);
        server = null;
      }


      public String toString()
      { return "#" + id + "(" + (int)Math.round(jobSize) + ")";
      }


      private static void print(int job, int time, double size)
      { System.out.println("Job #" + job + " arrives at time " + time
          + " with " + (int)Math.round(size) + " pages.");
      }


      private static void printBegins(Server server, int job, int time)
      { System.out.println("Printer " + server + " begins Job #" + job
          + " at time " + time + ".");
      }


      private static void printEnds(Server server, int job, int time)
      { System.out.println("Printer " + server + " ends Job #" + job
          + " at time " + time + ".");
      }
    }
```

The random number generator `randomJobSize` generates the exponentially distributed job sizes with a mean of 100 pages. It is declared `static` because only one instance is needed to produce all the job sizes. Similarly, the `static int nextId` is used to generate identification numbers for all the jobs.

The constructor uses the `nextId` counter to set the job id, and it uses the `randomJobSize` generator to set the `jobSize`. Then it prints one line of output, announcing that that job has arrived.

The `beginService()` method assigns the `server` reference to the printer that invoked it and then prints one line of output, announcing that the printing has begun. Similarly, the `endService()` method nullifies the `server` reference after printing one line of output that announces that the printing has ended.

Each printer is represented by an instance of this class:

```
    public class Server
    { private static Random randomMeanServiceRate = new Random(1.00,0.20);
      private static char nextId = 'A';
      private Random randomServiceRate;
      private char id;
      private double meanServiceRate, serviceRate;
      private Client client;
      private int timeServiceEnds;

      public Server()
      { id = (char)nextId++;
        meanServiceRate = randomMeanServiceRate.nextGaussian();
        randomServiceRate = new Random(meanServiceRate,0.10);
      }

      public void beginServing(Client client, int time)
      { this.client = client;
        serviceRate = randomServiceRate.nextGaussian();
```

```
      client.beginService(this,time);
      int serviceTime = (int)Math.ceil(client.getJobSize()/serviceRate);
      timeServiceEnds = time + serviceTime;
    }

    public void endServing(int time)
    { client.endService(time);
      this.client = null;
    }

    public int getTimeServiceEnds()
    { return timeServiceEnds;
    }

    public boolean isFree()
    { return client == null;
    }

    public String toString()
    { int percentMeanServiceRate = (int)Math.round(100*meanServiceRate);
      int percentServiceRate = (int)Math.round(100*serviceRate);
      return id + "(" + percentMeanServiceRate + "%,"
              + percentServiceRate + "%)";
    }
  }
```

The random number generator `randomMeanServiceRate` generates the normally distributed rates with mean 100.0 and standard deviation 20.0. It produces the `meanServiceRate` for each printer. In the run just shown, it produced the rates 89% for Printer A, 97% for Printer B, 106% for Printer C, and 128% for Printer D. Similarly, the random number generator `randomServiceRate` generates the normally distributed rates for each print job. In the run just shown, it produced the rates 84% for Job #1, 87% for Job #3, and 92% for Job #5. Those came from a normal distribution with mean 89% (for Printer A). The standard deviation is set at 10% for each printer's distribution.

The `beginServing()` method assigns the `client` reference to the client job that it is printing and obtains the normally distributed `serviceRate` from the `randomServiceRate` generator. Then it sends the `beginService` message to its client print job. Next, the assignment

```
      int serviceTime = (int)Math.ceil(client.getJobSize()/serviceRate);
```

computes the time (number of seconds) that it will take to do the print job by dividing the job size (the number of pages) by the printing rate (pages per second). The integer ceiling of this ratio is used as a count of the number of seconds to elapse. This count is then added to the current time to initialize the `timeServiceEnds` field of the `Server` object.

Here is the main class:

```
    public class ClientServerSimulation
    { private static final int NUMBER_OF_SERVERS = 4;
      private static final double MEAN_INTERARRIVAL_TIME = 20.0;
      private static final int DURATION = 100;
      private static Server[] servers = new Server[NUMBER_OF_SERVERS];
      private static Queue clients = new ArrayQueue();
      private static Random random = new Random(MEAN_INTERARRIVAL_TIME);

      public static void main(String[] args)
      { for (int i=0; i<NUMBER_OF_SERVERS; i++)
```

```
    servers[i] = new Server();
  int timeOfNextArrival = random.intNextExponential();
  for (int t=0; t<DURATION; t++)
  { if (t == timeOfNextArrival)
    { clients.enqueue(new Client(t));
      print(clients);
      timeOfNextArrival += random.intNextExponential();
    }
    for (int i=0; i<NUMBER_OF_SERVERS; i++)
      if (servers[i].isFree())
      { if (!clients.isEmpty())
        { servers[i].beginServing((Client)clients.dequeue(),t);
          print(clients);
        }
      }
      else if (t == servers[i].getTimeServiceEnds())
        servers[i].endServing(t);
  }
}

private static void print(Queue queue)
{ int size=queue.size();
  if (size==0) System.out.println("The queue is now empty.");
  else System.out.println("The queue now contains " + size
      + " job" + (size>1?"s: ":": ") + queue);
}
```

The simulation in Example 7.7 is called a *time-driven simulation* because its main loop iterates once for each tick of the clock. In contrast, an *event-driven* simulation is one where the main loop iterates once for each event: a job arrival, a service begin, or a service end. Event-driven simulations are usually simpler, but they require all servers to perform at the same rate.

Review Questions

7.1 Why are queues called LIFO structures?

7.2 Would it make sense to call a queue
    a. a LILO structure?
    b. a FILO structure?

7.3 What are the advantages and disadvantages of the linked implementation of a queue relative to the contiguous implementation?

Problems

7.1 Trace the following code, showing the contents of the queue q after each call:
```
ArrayQueue q;
q.enqueue("A");
q.enqueue("B");
q.enqueue("C");
```

```
q.dequeue();
q.dequeue();
q.enqueue("D");
q.enqueue("E");
q.enqueue("F");
q.dequeue();
q.enqueue("G");
q.dequeue();
q.dequeue();
q.dequeue();
```

For each of the following, implement the following method using only the constructor and the `enqueue()`, `dequeue()`, and `isEmpty()` methods of the `ArrayQueue` class:

7.2   `public static void reverse(ArrayQueue queue)`
            `// reverses the contents of the given queue;`

7.3   `private static ArrayQueue reversed(ArrayQueue queue);`
            `// returns a new queue that contains the same elements`
            `// as the given queue, but in reversed order`

7.4   `public static Object second(ArrayQueue queue)`
            `// returns the second element from the front of the given queue`

7.5   `public static Object last();`
            `// returns the last element of this queue`

7.6   `public static Object removeLast();`
            `// removes and returns the last element of this queue`

7.7   `public static ArrayQueue merge(ArrayQueue q1, ArrayQueue q2);`
            `// merges the two given queues, alternating between them as long`
            `// as they pair, and returns the resulting combined queue`

7.8 Modify the program in Example 7.7 on page 130 so that it computes and prints each of the following statistics.
   a. The average number of jobs in the system
   b. The average number of jobs in the queue
   c. The average time that a job spends in the system
   d. The average time that a job spends waiting in the queue

   Note that theoretically, the answers should be approximately equal to
   a. $L = n/(st - n)$
   b. $(nL)/(st)$
   c. tL
   d. $(nL)/s$

   where n = mean job size, s = number of servers, and t = mean time between arrivals. For example, if $n = 100$, $s = 6$, and $t = 20$, then the answers should be approximately equal to
   a. 5 jobs in the system
   b. 4.17 jobs in the queue
   c. 100 seconds in the system
   d. 83.3 seconds in the queue

7.9 Modify the program in Problem 7.8 so that it also computes and prints each of the following statistics.
   a. The average service time for each server
   b. The average service time among all jobs
   c. The percent of time that each server is idle

Answers to Review Questions

7.1   Queues are called FIFO structures because the first element that is inserted into a queue is always the first element to be removed. FIFO is an acronym for First-In-First-Out.

7.2   *a.* Yes, because a LILO structure would mean Last-In-Last-Out which is just the same as a First-In-First-Out protocol.

   b. No, because a FILO structure would mean First-In-Last-Out which is the opposite of the First-In-First-Out protocol

7.3   The advantage of the linked implementation is that it essentially eliminated the possibility of queue *overflow*; i.e., the number of calls to the enqueue() function is limited only by the amount of computer memory available to the new operator. The only real disadvantage is that the linked implementation uses pointers, so it is more complicated than the contiguous implementation.

Solutions to Problems

7.1   Trace:

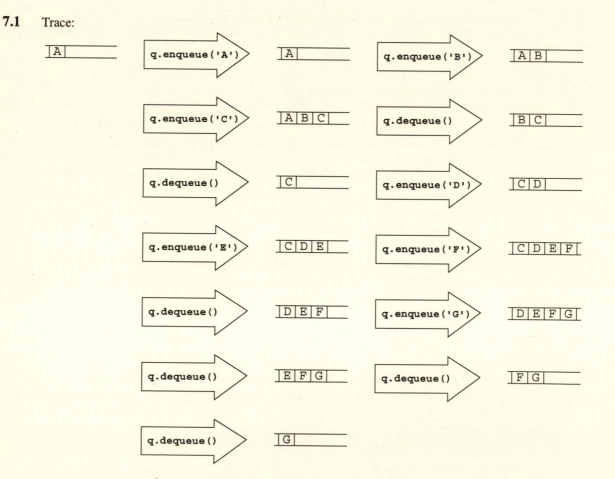

7.2   A method that reverses the contents of a queue:

```
private static void reverse(ArrayQueue queue)
{ Stack tempStack = new Stack();
  while(!queue.isEmpty())
    tempStack.push(queue.dequeue());
```

```
        while(!tempStack.empty())
          queue.enqueue(tempStack.pop());
      }
```

7.3   A method that returns the reversed contents of a queue:

```
      private static ArrayQueue reversed(ArrayQueue queue)
      { ArrayQueue newQueue = new ArrayQueue();
        Stack stack = new Stack();
        while(!queue.isEmpty())
        { Object x = queue.dequeue();
          stack.push(x);
          newQueue.enqueue(x);
        }
        while(!newQueue.isEmpty())
          queue.enqueue(newQueue.dequeue());
        while(!stack.empty())
          newQueue.enqueue(stack.pop());
        return newQueue;
      }
```

7.4   A method that returns the second element from the front of a queue:

```
      private static Object second(ArrayQueue queue)
      { ArrayQueue tempQueue = new ArrayQueue();
        Object x = queue.dequeue();
        tempQueue.enqueue(x);
        x = queue.dequeue();
        tempQueue.enqueue(x);
        while(!queue.isEmpty())
          tempQueue.enqueue(queue.dequeue());
        while(!tempQueue.isEmpty())
          queue.enqueue(tempQueue.dequeue());
        return x;
      }
```

7.5   A method that returns the last element of a queue:

```
      private static Object last(ArrayQueue queue)
      { ArrayQueue tempQueue = new ArrayQueue();
        while(!queue.isEmpty())
          tempQueue.enqueue(queue.dequeue());
        Object x = null;
        while(!tempQueue.isEmpty())
        { x = tempQueue.dequeue();
          queue.enqueue(x);
        }
        return x;
      }
```

7.6   A method that removes and returns the last element of a queue:

```
      private static Object removeLast(ArrayQueue queue)
      { ArrayQueue tempQueue = new ArrayQueue();
        int count=0;
        while(!queue.isEmpty())
        { tempQueue.enqueue(queue.dequeue());
          ++count;
        }
        Object x = null;
        for (int i=0; i<count-1; i++)
          queue.enqueue(tempQueue.dequeue());
        return tempQueue.dequeue();
      }
```

7.7   A method that merges two queues:

```
public static ArrayQueue merged(ArrayQueue q1, ArrayQueue q2)
{ ArrayQueue newQueue = new ArrayQueue();
  while(!q1.isEmpty() && !q2.isEmpty())
  { newQueue.enqueue(q1.dequeue());
    newQueue.enqueue(q2.dequeue());
  }
  while(!q1.isEmpty())
    newQueue.enqueue(q1.dequeue());
  while(!q2.isEmpty())
    newQueue.enqueue(q2.dequeue());
  return newQueue;
}
```

7.8   Modification of the program in Example 7.7 on page 130:

Add the following code to the `Client` class:

```
private int id, jobSize, tArrived, tBegan, tEnded;

public Client(int time)
{ id = ++nextId;
  jobSize = randomJobSize.intNextExponential();
  tArrived = time;
}

public double getJobSize()
{ return jobSize;
}

public int getWaitTime()
{ return tBegan - tArrived;
}

public int getServiceTime()
{ return tEnded - tBegan;
}

public void beginService(Server server, int time)
{ this.server = server;
  tBegan = time;
}

public void endService(int time)
{ tEnded = time;
  server = null;
}
```

Add the following code to the `Server` class:

```
public Client getClient()
{ return client;
}
```

Add the following code to the main class:

```
private static int totalTime, queueTime, totalNumberOfJobs;
private static int[] numberOfJobs = new int[NUMBER_OF_SERVERS];
public static void main(String[] args)
{ for (int i=0; i<NUMBER_OF_SERVERS; i++)
    servers[i] = new Server();
  int timeOfNextArrival = random.intNextExponential();
```

```
        for (int t=0; t<DURATION; t++)
        { if (t == timeOfNextArrival)
          { clients.enqueue(new Client(t));
            timeOfNextArrival += random.intNextExponential();
          }
          for (int i=0; i<NUMBER_OF_SERVERS; i++)
          { Server server = servers[i];
            if (server.isFree())
            { if(!clients.isEmpty())
              { server.beginServing((Client)clients.dequeue(),t);
              }
            }
            else // server is serving a client
            { ++totalTime;   // counting time in system
              if (t == server.getTimeServiceEnds())
              { Client client = server.getClient();
                server.endServing(t);
                int waitTime = client.getWaitTime();
                ++numberOfJobs[i];   // count only those jobs that finish
              }
            }
          }
          totalTime += clients.size();
          queueTime += clients.size();
        }
        for (int i=0; i<NUMBER_OF_SERVERS; i++)
          totalNumberOfJobs += numberOfJobs[i];
        printStatistics();
      }

      private static void printStatistics()
      { System.out.println("Mean interarrival time: " +
                              MEAN_INTERARRIVAL_TIME);
        System.out.println("Mean service time: "
          + Client.MEAN_JOB_SIZE);
        System.out.println("Number of servers: " + NUMBER_OF_SERVERS);
        System.out.println("Average number of jobs in the system: "
          + (float)totalTime/DURATION);
        System.out.println("Average number of jobs in the queue: "
          + (float)queueTime/DURATION);
        System.out.println("Average time a job spent in the system: "
          + (float)totalTime/totalNumberOfJobs);
        System.out.println("Average time a job spent in the queue: "
          + (float)queueTime/totalNumberOfJobs);
      }
```

7.9 For the second modification of the program in Example 7.7 on page 130, add this code:

```
      private static int totalTime, queueTime, totalNumberOfJobs,
                          totalServiceTime;
      private static int[] serviceTime = new int[NUMBER_OF_SERVERS];
      private static int[] numberOfJobs = new int[NUMBER_OF_SERVERS];
      public static void main(String[] args)
      { for (int i=0; i<NUMBER_OF_SERVERS; i++)
        { servers[i] = new Server();
          serviceTime[i] = numberOfJobs[i] = 0;
        }
        int timeOfNextArrival = random.intNextExponential();
```

```
    for (int t=0; t<DURATION; t++)
    { if (t == timeOfNextArrival)
      { clients.enqueue(new Client(t));
        timeOfNextArrival += random.intNextExponential();
      }
      for (int i=0; i<NUMBER_OF_SERVERS; i++)
      { Server server = servers[i];
        if (server.isFree())
        { if(!clients.isEmpty())
          { server.beginServing((Client)clients.dequeue(),t);
          }
        }
        else // server is serving a client
        { ++totalTime;  // counting time in system
          if (t == server.getTimeServiceEnds())
          { Client client = server.getClient();
            server.endServing(t);
            int waitTime = client.getWaitTime();
            serviceTime[i] = client.getServiceTime();
            ++numberOfJobs[i];  // count only those jobs that finish
          }
        }
      }
      totalTime += clients.size();
      queueTime += clients.size();
    }
    for (int i=0; i<NUMBER_OF_SERVERS; i++)
    { totalServiceTime += serviceTime[i];
      totalNumberOfJobs += numberOfJobs[i];
    }
    printStatistics();
}

private static void printStatistics()
{ System.out.println("Mean interarrival time: " +
                      MEAN_INTERARRIVAL_TIME);
  System.out.println("Mean service time: "
    + Client.MEAN_JOB_SIZE);
  System.out.println("Number of servers: " + NUMBER_OF_SERVERS);
  System.out.println("Average number of jobs in the system: "
    + (float)totalTime/DURATION);
  System.out.println("Average number of jobs in the queue: "
    + (float)queueTime/DURATION);
  System.out.println("Average time a job spent in the system: "
    + (float)totalTime/totalNumberOfJobs);
  System.out.println("Average time a job spent in the queue: "
    + (float)queueTime/totalNumberOfJobs);
  System.out.println("Total time spent by all jobs in system: "
    + totalTime);
  System.out.println("Total time spent by all jobs in queue:  "
    + queueTime);
  System.out.println("Duration:                              " + DURATION);
  System.out.println("Total number of jobs completed: "
    + totalNumberOfJobs);
  System.out.println("Average service time for server:");
```

```
    for (int i=0; i<NUMBER_OF_SERVERS; i++)
       System.out.println("\t" + servers[i] + ": "
          + (float)serviceTime[i]/numberOfJobs[i]);
    System.out.println("Average service time among all jobs: "
       + (float)totalServiceTime/totalNumberOfJobs);
    System.out.println("Percent idle time for server:");
    for (int i=0; i<NUMBER_OF_SERVERS; i++)
       System.out.println("\t" + servers[i] + ": "
          + (float)(100.0*(DURATION - serviceTime[i]))/DURATION + "%");
}
```

Chapter 8

Lists

A *list* is a sequential container that can insert and
delete elements locally in *constant time*; i.e., at a rate
that is independent of the size of the container. It is the preferred data structure for applications
that do not need random access. A good analogy is a train of box cars: any car can be removed
simply by disconnecting it from its two neighbors and then reconnecting them.

In Java, the `List` interface is an extension of the `Collection` interface, so it and its
implementations are all part of the Java 1.2 Collections Framework (see Section 5.1 on page 94)
that is defined in the `java.util` package. The `List` interface provides an abstract data type for
the mathematical notion of a sequence. Thus, `List` implementations are characterized in Java as
containers that support an indexed access to their elements.

8.1 THE `java.util.List` INTERFACE

Here is the `List` interface defined in the `java.util` package:

```
public interface List extends Collection
{ public boolean      add(Object object);
  public void         add(int index, Object object);
  public boolean      addAll(Collection collection);
  public boolean      addAll(int index, Collection collection);
  public void         clear();
  public boolean      contains(Object object);
  public boolean      containsAll(Collection collection);
  public boolean      equals(Object object);
  public Object       get(int index);
  public int          hashCode();
  public int          indexOf(Object object);
  public boolean      isEmpty();
  public Iterator     iterator();
  public int          lastIndexOf(Object object);
  public ListIterator listIterator();
  public ListIterator listIterator(int index);
  public Object       remove(int index);
  public boolean      remove(Object object);
  public boolean      removeAll(Collection collection);
  public boolean      retainAll(Collection collection);
  public Object       set(int index, Object object);
  public int          size();
  public List         subList(int start, int stop);
  public Object[]     toArray();
  public Object[]     toArray(Object[] objects);
}
```

Note that this uses a special kind of iterator, called a `ListIterator`, which is bidirectional.

EXAMPLE 8.1 Using the `List` Interface

```
import java.util.*;

public class Ex0801
{ public static void main(String[] args)
    { String[] strings;
        strings = new String[]{"Adams","Tyler","Grant","Hayes","Nixon"};
        List list = Arrays.asList(strings);
        System.out.println("list = " + list);
        System.out.println("list.size() = " + list.size());
        System.out.println("list.getClass().getName() = "
                            + list.getClass().getName());
        System.out.println("list.get(1) = " + list.get(1));
        System.out.println("list.contains(\"Tyler\") = "
                            + list.contains("Tyler"));
        List sublist = list.subList(2,5);
        System.out.println("sublist = " + sublist);
        Object object = list.get(1);
        System.out.println("sublist.get(1) = " + sublist.get(1));
        System.out.println("sublist.contains(\"Tyler\") = "
                            + sublist.contains("Tyler"));
        list.remove(3);
    }
}
```

```
list = [Adams, Tyler, Grant, Hayes, Nixon]
list.size() = 5
list.getClass().getName() = java.util.Arrays$ArrayList
list.get(1) = Tyler
list.contains("Tyler") = true
sublist = [Grant, Hayes, Nixon]
sublist.get(1) = Hayes
sublist.contains("Tyler") = false
Exception in thread "main" java.lang.UnsupportedOperationException
        at java.util.AbstractList.remove(AbstractList.java:174)
        at Testing.main(Testing.java:23)
```

This uses a `String` array to construct the `List` object. The `getClass()` method shows that this object is an instance of the `ArrayList` class.

The `get()` and `sublist()` methods use index numbers for their arguments. The invocation `list.sublist(2,5)` returns a `List` object containing the elements of `list` numbers 2 through 4.

The invocation `list.remove(3)` throws an `UnsupportedOperationException` exception because the `ArrayList` class does not implement the `remove()` method.

The exception thrown in Example 8.1 points to the fact that some of the implementations of the `List` interface do not implement all of the methods specified by the interface. When they don't, they are obliged to throw an `UnsupportedOperationException` exception.

8.2 IMPLEMENTATIONS OF THE `java.util.List` INTERFACE

Example 8.1 illustrates one of the classes in the Java 1.2 Collections Framework that implements the `List` interface: the `ArrayList` class. The `List` interface is also implemented by the `AbstractList`, `LinkedList`, and `Vector` classes.

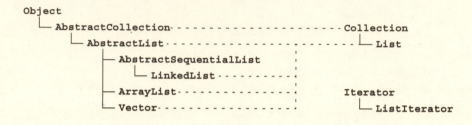

The `AbstractList` class serves the same purpose for lists that the `AbstractCollection` class serves for general collections: as a partial implementation of the corresponding interface, it reduce the amount of code that needs to be written for custom implementations. Since it is defined to be `abstract`, it cannot be instantiated directly. The `AbstractList` class is outlined in Section 8.3.

The `LinkedList` class embodies all the structure and functionality that one would expect from a linked list class. It is outlined in Section 8.6.

The `ArrayList` class implements the `List` interface using a contiguous array. It is outlined in Section 8.5.

The `Vector` class is similar to the `ArrayList` class. It was outlined in Section 2.6 on page 33.

8.3 THE `AbstractList` AND `AbstractSequentialList` CLASSES

The `AbstractList` class is meant to provide a skeletal backbone for complete implementations of the `List` class that use an array to store the list elements. Similarly, the `AbstractSequentialList` class is meant to provide a skeletal backbone for complete implementations of the `List` class that use a noncontiguous linked structure to store the list elements. These two different kinds of storage are opposites in a fundamental sense. The contiguous array structure provides random access for immediate access, but requires substantial movement of data to insertions and deletions. The linked structure can manage immediate insertions and deletions, but at the expense of having no index ("random access') for immediate access. The following table summarizes these differences.

Partial Implementation	Complete Implementation	Data Structure	get(), set()	add(), remove()
AbstractList	ArrayList	array	$O(1)$	$O(n)$
AbstractSequentialList	LinkedList	linked list	$O(n)$	$O(1)$

If your application requires fast access on a rather static sequence, you should either use the `ArrayList` class or extend it or its parent `AbstractList` class. On the other hand, if your application requires a dynamic sequence with frequent insertions and removals, then you should either use the `LinkedList` class or extend it or its parent `AbstractSequentialList` class.

Note that the `LinkedList` class does not implement the `get(int)` method directly.
Here are the `AbstractList` class methods that are defined in the `java.util` package:

```
public abstract class AbstractList extends AbstractCollection
      implements List
{ protected                AbstractList()
  public boolean           add(Object object);
  public void              add(int index, Object object);
  public boolean           addAll(Collection collection);
  public boolean           addAll(int index, Collection collection);
  public void              clear();
  public boolean           equals(Object object);
  abstract public Object   get(int index);
  public int               hashCode();
  public int               indexOf(Object object);
  public Iterator          iterator();
  public int               lastIndexOf(Object object);
  public ListIterator      listIterator();
  public ListIterator      listIterator(int index);
  public Object            remove(int index);
  public void              removeRange(int start, int stop);
  public Object            set(int index, Object object);
  public List              subList(int start, int stop);
}
```

The `get()` method is declared `abstract`, so any concrete extension of this class will have to implement it.

The implementations of the `set()`, `add()`, and `remove()` methods are simply:

```
{ throw new UnsupportedOperationException();
}
```

This makes these methods optional. An extension can override one or more of these three according to the efficiency of its data structure. (See the table on the previous page.) Or, the extension can let one or more of these implementations stand. In that case, the exception will be thrown intentionally if an application uses the method that was not intended to be used.

Here are the `AbstractSequentialList` class methods that are defined in the `java.util` package:

```
public abstract class AbstractSequentialList extends AbstractList
{ protected                      AbstractSequentialList()
  public void                    add(int index, Object object);
  public boolean                 addAll(Collection c);
  public boolean                 addAll(int index, Collection c);
  public Object                  get(int index);
  public Iterator                iterator();
  public int                     lastIndexOf(Object object);
  abstract public ListIterator   listIterator(int index);
  public Object                  remove(int index);
  public Object                  set(int index, Object object);
}
```

The `listIterator()` method and the `size()` method are declared `abstract`, so any concrete extension of this class will have to implement both of them. (The abstract `size()` method is inherited from the `AbstractCollection` class. See Section 5.3.)

8.4 LIST ITERATORS

An *iterator* is an object that is capable of moving through a collection from one element to the next. It is the alternative to a subscript on an array or vector. Just as subscripts are the natural mechanism for processing arrays, iterators are the natural mechanism for processing lists.

Java 1.2 defines the `Iterator` interface and the `ListIterator` subinterface in the `java.util` package. They are part of the Java Collections Framework. The `Iterator` interface specifies how a single-direction iterator should behave on a general linear data structure. (See Section 5.5.) The `ListIterator` extension specifies how a bidirectional iterator should behave on a doubly linked list.

Here is the `ListIterator` interface defined in the `java.util` package:

```
public interface ListIterator extends Iterator
{ public void      add(Object object);
  public boolean hasNext();
  public boolean hasPrevious();
  public Object    next();
  public int       nextIndex();
  public Object    previous();
  public int       previousIndex();
  public void      remove();
  public void      set(Object object);
}
```

EXAMPLE 8.2 Using a List Iterator

```
import java.util.*;
public class Ex0802
{ public static void main(String[] args)
  { String[] planets = new String[]{"Venus","Earth","Mars","Pluto"};
    List list = Arrays.asList(planets);
    System.out.println("list = " + list);
    ListIterator it = list.listIterator();
    System.out.println("it.next() = " + it.next());
    System.out.println("it.next() = " + it.next());
    System.out.println("it.next() = " + it.next());
    System.out.println("it.next() = " + it.next());
    System.out.println("it.previous() = " + it.previous());
    System.out.println("it.previous() = " + it.previous());
    it.add("Saturn");
  }
}
```

```
list = [Venus, Earth, Mars, Pluto]
it.next() = Venus
it.next() = Earth
it.next() = Mars
it.next() = Pluto
it.previous() = Pluto
it.previous() = Mars
Exception in thread "main" java.lang.UnsupportedOperationException
        at java.util.AbstractList.add(AbstractList.java:153)
        at java.util.AbstractList$ListItr.add(AbstractList.java:503)
        at Testing.main(Testing.java:20)
```

This shows how a bidirectional iterator works. It also shows that the `add()` method is not implemented for `ListIterator` objects that iterate on `ArrayList` objects. So the call `it.add("Saturn")` causes the `UnsupportedOperationException` to be thrown.

8.5 THE `ArrayList` CLASS

The `ArrayList` class uses an array to implement the `AbstractList` class. It is defined in the `java.util` package like this:

```
    public class ArrayList extends AbstractList implements List
    { public boolean  add(Object object)
      public void     add(int index, Object object)
      public boolean  addAll(Collection collection)
      public boolean  addAll(int index, Collection collection)
      public          ArrayList()
      public          ArrayList(int initialCapacity)
      public          ArrayList(Collection collection)
      public void     clear()
      public Object   clone()
      public boolean  contains(Object object)
      public void     ensureCapacity(int capacity)
      public Object   get(int index)
      public int      indexOf(Object object)
      public boolean  isEmpty()
      public int      lastIndexOf(Object object)
      public Object   remove(int index)
      public Object   set(int index, Object object)
      public int      size()
      public Object[] toArray()
      public Object[] toArray(Object[] objects)
      public void     trimToSize()
    }
```

The two methods `ensureCapacity(int)` and `trimToSize()` specifically manipulate the private capacity of and `ArrayList` object. That integer is the actual size of the array that stores the elements of the `ArrayList` object. Among the 21 methods that this class implements, only those two and the three constructors are introduced by this class; each of the other 16 methods is an override of the corresponding method in one of the ancestor classes `AbstractList`, `AbstractCollection`, or `Object`.

EXAMPLE 8.3 Using an `ArrayList` to Store Ranked Data

Here is a text file, named `Cities.txt` that lists the nine largest cities in 1990, in decreasing order of their population. (Tokyo is the largest city.)

The following program reads this data into an `ArrayList`, and then uses the `indexOf()` method, the `remove()` method, and the `add()` method to update the data so that it is correct for the populations of 1995:

```
Cities.txt
Tokyo
Mexico City
Sao Paulo
Seoul
New York
Osaka
Bombay
Calcutta
Buenos Aires
```

```
    import java.io.*;
    import java.util.*;

    public class Ex0803
    { private static ArrayList list = new ArrayList();
```

```java
public static void main(String[] args)
{ load("Cities.txt");
  System.out.println(list);
  list.remove(list.indexOf("Seoul"));
  list.remove(list.indexOf("Osaka"));
  list.add(5,"Shanghai");
  list.add(6,"Los Angeles");
  System.out.println(list);
}

private static void load(String filename)
{ try
  { File file = new File(filename);
    FileReader reader = new FileReader(file);
    BufferedReader in = new BufferedReader(reader);
    String city = in.readLine();
    while (city != null)
    { list.add(city);
      city = in.readLine();
    }
  }
  catch(Exception e) { System.out.println(e); }
}
}
```

```
[Tokyo, Mexico City, Sao Paulo, Seoul, New York, Osaka, Bombay,
Calcutta, Buenos
 Aires]
[Tokyo, Mexico City, Sao Paulo, New York, Bombay, Shanghai, Los
Angeles, Calcutt
a, Buenos Aires]
```

8.6 THE `LinkedList` CLASS

The `LinkedList` class uses a linked list to implement the `AbstractSequentialList` class. It is defined in the `java.util` package like this:

```java
public class LinkedList extends AbstractSequentialList implements List
{ public boolean      add(Object object)
  public void         add(int index, Object object)
  public boolean      addAll(Collection collection)
  public boolean      addAll(int index, Collection collection)
  public void         addFirst(Object object)
  public void         addLast(Object object)
  public void         clear()
  public Object       clone()
  public boolean      contains(Object object)
  public Object       getFirst()
  public Object       getLast()
  public int          indexOf(Object object)
  public int          lastIndexOf(Object object)
  public              LinkedList()
  public              LinkedList(Collection collection)
```

```
    public ListIterator  listIterator(int index)
    public Object        remove(int index)
    public boolean       remove(Object object)
    public Object        removeFirst()
    public Object        removeLast()
    public Object        set(int index, Object object)
    public int           size()
    public Object[]      toArray()
    public Object[]      toArray(Object[] objects)
}
```

Of the 24 methods defined in the LinkedList class, only the nine shown here in boldface are not overrides of the corresponding method in one of the ancestor AbstractSequentialList, AbstractList, AbstractCollection, or Object classes.

EXAMPLE 8.4 A Ring Class

This defines a class for circular doubly linked lists. It is similar to the java.util.LinkedList class, except that the next() and previous() methods are able to wrap around from one end of the list to the other.

```
package schaums.dswj;
import java.util.*;

public class Ring extends java.util.AbstractSequentialList
{ private Node header;
  private int size = 0;

  public Ring()
  {
  }

  public Ring(List list)
  { super();
    addAll(list);
  }

  public ListIterator listIterator(int index)
  { return new RingIterator(index);
  }

  public int size()
  { return size;
  }

  private static class Node
  { Object object;
    Node previous, next;

    Node(Object object, Node previous, Node next)
    { this.object = object;
      this.previous = previous;
      this.next = next;
    }
```

```
      Node(Object object)
   { this.object = object;
     this.previous = this.next = this;
   }
}

private class RingIterator implements ListIterator
{ private Node next, lastReturned;
  private int nextIndex;

  RingIterator(int index)
  { if (index<0 || index>size)
      throw new IndexOutOfBoundsException("Index : " + index);
    next=(size==0?null:header);
    for (nextIndex=0; nextIndex<index; nextIndex++)
      next = next.next;
  }

  public boolean hasNext()
  { return size > 0;
  }

  public boolean hasPrevious()
  { return size > 0;
  }

  public Object next()
  { if (size==0) throw new NoSuchElementException();
    lastReturned = next;
    next = next.next;
    nextIndex = (nextIndex==size-1?0:nextIndex+1);
    return lastReturned.object;
  }

  public Object previous()
  { if (size==0) throw new NoSuchElementException();
    next = lastReturned = next.previous;
    nextIndex = (nextIndex==0?size-1:nextIndex-1);
    return lastReturned.object;
  }

  public int nextIndex()
  { return nextIndex;
  }

  public int previousIndex()
  { return (nextIndex==0?size-1:nextIndex-1);
  }
```

```
        public void add(Object object)
        { if (size==0)
          { next = header = new Node(object);
            nextIndex = 0;
          }
          else
          { Node newNode = new Node(object,next.previous,next);
            newNode.previous.next = next.previous = newNode;
          }
          lastReturned = null;
          ++size;
          nextIndex = (nextIndex==size-1?0:nextIndex+1);
        }

        public void remove()
        { if (lastReturned==null) throw new IllegalStateException();
          if (next==lastReturned) next = lastReturned.next;
          else nextIndex = (nextIndex==0?size-1:nextIndex-1);
          lastReturned.previous.next = lastReturned.next;
          lastReturned.next.previous = lastReturned.previous;
          lastReturned = null;
          --size;
        }

        public void set(Object object)
        { if (lastReturned==null) throw new IllegalStateException();
          lastReturned.object = object;
        }
      }
   }
}
```

As a subclass of the `AbstractSequentialList` class, this `Ring` class is required to implement the `listIterator(int)` method and the `size()` method. And since the `listIterator(int)` method must returns a `ListIterator` object, this class must also implement all nine methods of that interface. (See Section 8.4.) It does that with its inner `RingIterator` class.

size 8
header ▣
Ring

The `Ring` class defines two private fields (`header` and `size`), four public methods, and two private classes (`Node` and `RingIterator`).

A linked list is a sequence of linked "nodes," which are distinct objects that hold the list's data, one component per node. So any implementation of a linked list requires an internal `Node` class with a field for the data and at least one link field. In this implementation, the node's data field is an `Object` reference, named `object`. Since these lists are to be doubly linked, the `Node` class has two link fields, named `previous` and `next`. In any linked structure (list, tree, graph, etc.), a link filed must be a reference to the same type as the node class itself. So in this implementation, both `previous` and `next` are `Node` references.

previous ▣
object 'B'
next ▣
Node

The `header` field of the Ring class points to the first node of the list. Note that this implementation uses no "dummy" header node. So the number of nodes is always equal to the actual number of components of the list. That number is stored in the ring's `size` field.

The inner `RingIterator` class implements the `java.util.LinkedList` interface. It has three fields: `next` and `lastReturned`, which are references to the list nodes, and the integer `nextIndex`, which keeps track of the index number of the node that is being located by the iterator. The `next` field points to the next node in the list, that is, the node that would be visited next if the iterator is advanced. The `lastReturned` field points to the node that was returned on the last call to either the `next()` or the `previous()` method. It locates the node that would be affected by a call to either the `remove()` or the `set()` method.

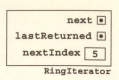

The `ListIterator` interface specifies that the `hasNext()` and `hasPrevious()` methods should return `true` if the list has more components in the corresponding direction. For the `Ring` class, which has no beginning or ending, these two methods will always return `true` except when the list is empty.

The `next()` and `previous()` methods advance the iterator to the next node in the corresponding direction. The statement

```
next = next.next;
```

does that for the forward direction. To understand this assignment, remember that a reference to an object is really the address of that object in main memory. So this assignment statement assigns the address that is stored in `next.next` to the reference variable `next`. The diagram below shows 12 of the objects along with their actual memory addresses during a run of the test driver program in Example 8.5 on page 155:

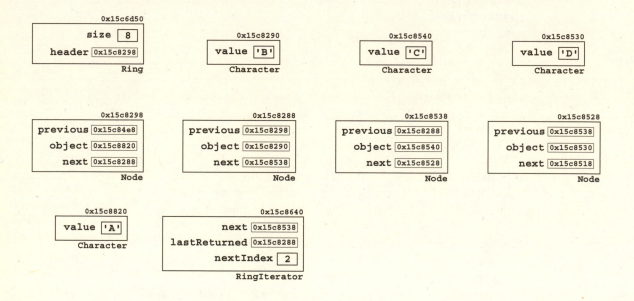

At that moment, the address that was stored in `next.next` was `0x15c8528`, and the address that was stored in `next` was `0x15c8538`. So the assignment

```
next = next.next;
```

changed the value of the reference `next` from `0x15c8538` to `0x15c8528`. In other words, it changed the node that the iterator's `next` field was locating from the third node shown here to the fourth one.

Note that the objects in the diagram are more simply represented as shown in the next diagram where each object reference (memory address) is represented more symbolically by an arrow that points at its referent object:

Notice how the conditional expression operator is used to increment and decrement the `nextIndex` field in the `next()` and `previous()` methods, respectively. For example, the expression

```
nextIndex = (nextIndex==size-1?0:nextIndex+1);
```

either assigns the value 0 to the field or it increments is, according to whether value is size-1. If its value is size-1, then the iterator is at the last element in the list; in that case, advancing the iterator means that it should wrap around to the first element in the list, the one whose index should be 0. Otherwise, the field should simply be incremented.

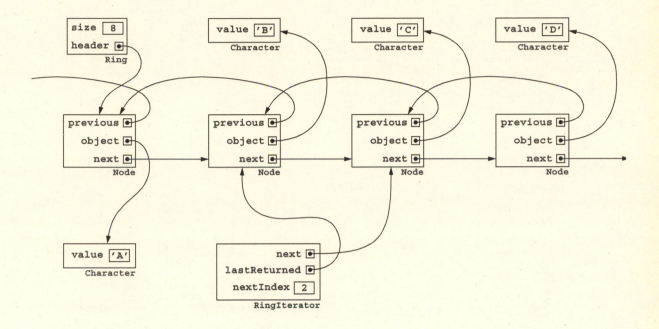

The purpose of the nextIndex() and previousIndex() methods are to return the index values of the next element and the previous element, respectively. The first of these is stored in the iterator's nextIndex field. The other should be 1 less than that, unless the nextIndex value is 0; in that case the previous index should be size-1, again reflecting the wrap-around nature of the circular linked list.

The add() method inserts the given object as a new component of the list. The diagrams on the next page illustrate how the code

```
Node newNode = new Node(object,next.previous,next);
newNode.previous.next = next.previous = newNode;
```

works. The changing pointers are shown as broken lines. Note that after the insertion, the lastReturned pointer is invalidated (set to null), signalling that the last operation performed by the iterator was not a call to next() or previous(). This means that neither the add() nor the remove() method could be invoked next without first invoking the next() or previous() method again. Doing so would cause the UnsupportedOperationException to be thrown, as it was in Example 8.2 on page 148.

EXAMPLE 8.5 Testing the Ring Class

```
import java.util.*;
import schaums.dswj.Ring;

public class Ex0808
{ private static final int SIZE=8;
  private static Ring ring = new Ring();
```

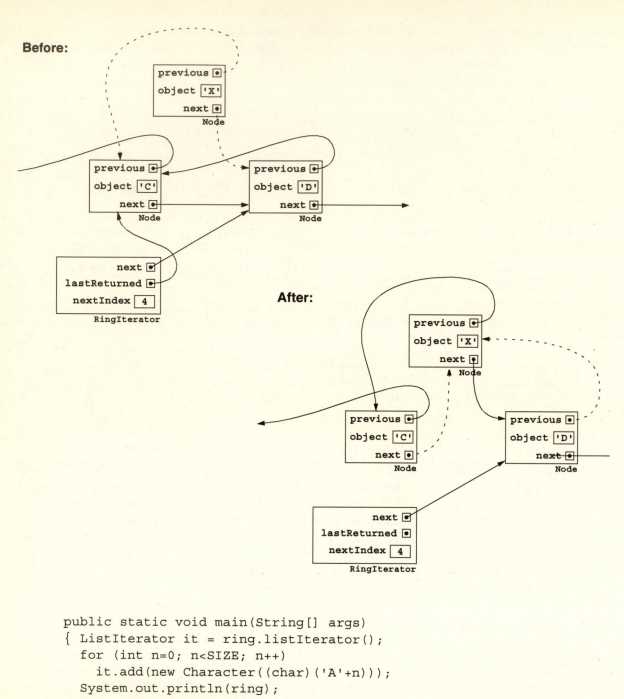

```
public static void main(String[] args)
{ ListIterator it = ring.listIterator();
  for (int n=0; n<SIZE; n++)
    it.add(new Character((char)('A'+n)));
  System.out.println(ring);
  it = ring.listIterator();   // initialize it again
  printNext(it,10);
  printPrevious(it,4);
  System.out.println(ring);
  it = ring.listIterator();   // initialize it again
  printNext(it,2);
  it.remove();      System.out.println(ring);
  printNext(it,3);
  it.remove();      System.out.println(ring);
  printPrevious(it,2);
```

```
        it.remove();     System.out.println(ring);
        printPrevious(it,3);
        it.remove();     System.out.println(ring);
    }


    private static void printNext(ListIterator it, int n)
    { for (int i=0; i<n; i++)
        System.out.println("it.nextIndex() = " + it.nextIndex()
                        + "\tit.next() = " + it.next());
    }
    private static void printPrevious(ListIterator it, int n)
    { for (int i=0; i<n; i++)
        System.out.println("it.previousIndex() = " + it.previousIndex()
                        + "\tit.previous() = " + it.previous());
    }
}
```

```
[A, B, C, D, E, F, G, H]
it.nextIndex() = 0        it.next() = A
it.nextIndex() = 1        it.next() = B
it.nextIndex() = 2        it.next() = C
it.nextIndex() = 3        it.next() = D
it.nextIndex() = 4        it.next() = E
it.nextIndex() = 5        it.next() = F
it.nextIndex() = 6        it.next() = G
it.nextIndex() = 7        it.next() = H
it.nextIndex() = 0        it.next() = A
it.nextIndex() = 1        it.next() = B
it.previousIndex() = 1  it.previous() = B
it.previousIndex() = 0  it.previous() = A
it.previousIndex() = 7  it.previous() = H
it.previousIndex() = 6  it.previous() = G
[A, B, C, D, E, F, G, H]
it.nextIndex() = 0        it.next() = A
it.nextIndex() = 1        it.next() = B
[A, C, D, E, F, G, H]
it.nextIndex() = 1        it.next() = C
it.nextIndex() = 2        it.next() = D
it.nextIndex() = 3        it.next() = E
[A, C, D, F, G, H]
it.previousIndex() = 2  it.previous() = D
it.previousIndex() = 1  it.previous() = C
[A, D, F, G, H]
it.previousIndex() = 0  it.previous() = A
it.previousIndex() = 4  it.previous() = H
it.previousIndex() = 3  it.previous() = G
[A, D, F, H]
```

This program uses two print methods to make it easier to understand. The printNext() method repeatedly invokes the nextIndex() and next() methods the given number of times. The printPrevious() method does the same for the previousIndex() and previous() methods.

First the program loads the ring with eight `Character` objects:

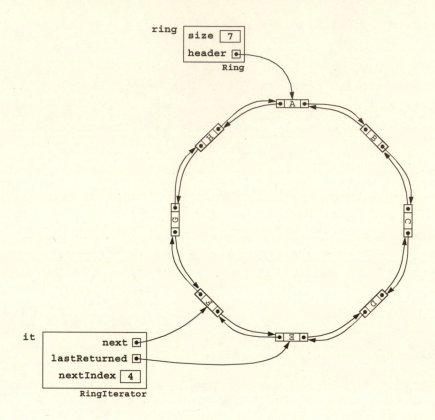

Then it uses its print methods to traverse around the ring both clockwise and counterclockwise. This shows how the index numbers match up with the nodes.

After reinitializing the iterator, it then advances twice, so that its lastReturned field points to the B node. Then the call `it.remove()` removes the B node, as the output from the next `println(ring)` shows. Similarly, advancing three more times and then calling `it.remove()` again removes the E node. Note that just before that call to `it.remove()`, the call to `it.remove()` returned the index 3. Before the first removal, the E node had index 4; but at this point (after removing the B node) there are only 3 nodes ahead of it (A, C, and D), so its index is 3. The index of a sequential element is always equal to the number of elements that precede it.

The next call to `it.remove()` comes after two calls to `it.previous()`, so at that point the node removed (the C node) had index 1. Finally, three more calls to `it.previous()` cause the bidirectional iterator to wrap around the list, making the G node the one that gets removed.

EXAMPLE 8.6 The Josephus Problem

This problem is based upon a report by the historian Joseph ben Matthias ("Josephus") on the outcome of a suicide pact that he had made between himself and 40 soldiers as they were besieged by superior Roman forces in 67 A.D. Josephus proposed that each man slay his neighbor. He cleverly contrived to be the last among his comrades, thus surviving to tell the tale.

We can simulate the problem to solve it using our `Ring` class:

```java
import java.util.*;
import schaums.dswj.*;

public class Ex0806
{ public static void main(String[] args)
  { Ring ring = new Ring();
    ListIterator it = ring.listIterator();
    int N = get("Enter number of soldiers");
    for (int k=0; k<N; k++)
      it.add(new Character((char)('A'+k)));
    System.out.print(N + " soldiers: ");
    System.out.println(ring);
    while (ring.size() > 1)
    { Object killer = it.next();
      System.out.println(killer + " killed " + it.next());
      it.remove();
    }
    System.out.println("The lone survivor is " + it.next());
  }
}
```

```
Enter number of soldiers: 8
8 soldiers: [A, B, C, D, E, F, G, H]
A killed B
C killed D
E killed F
G killed H
A killed C
E killed G
A killed E
The lone survivor is A
```

This program uses the following method for inputting integers:

```java
public static int get(String prompt)
{ int n=0;
  try
  { InputStreamReader reader = new InputStreamReader(System.in);
    BufferedReader in = new BufferedReader(reader);
    System.out.print(prompt + ": ");
    String input = in.readLine();
    n = Integer.parseInt(input);
  }
  catch(Exception e) { System.out.println(e); }
  return n;
}
```

It is defined in the `schaums.dswj.IO` class.

Note that, like all collections data structures in Java, the Ring can store only objects. We have to wrap each `int` in an `Integer` object to store it in the ring.

8.7 INDEPENDENT LIST ITERATORS

More than one iterator can be used on the same linked list, as long as they don't attempt to modify it.

EXAMPLE 8.7 Simulating Random Walks

```java
import java.util.*;

public class Ex0807
{ private static final int SIZE=26;
  private static LinkedList list = new LinkedList();
  private static Random random = new Random();

  public static void main(String[] args)
  { initializeList();
    ListIterator it1 = list.listIterator();
    ListIterator it2 = list.listIterator();
    moveForward(it1);
    moveForward(it2);
    moveBackward(it1);
    moveBackward(it2);
    moveForward(it1);
    moveForward(it2);
  }

  private static void initializeList()
  { ListIterator it = list.listIterator();
    for (int k=0; k<SIZE; k++)
      it.add(new Character((char)('A'+k)));
  }
  private static void moveForward(ListIterator it)
  { int n = random.nextInt(SIZE-it.previousIndex());
    for (int i=0; i<n; i++)
      System.out.print(it.next());
    System.out.println();
  }
  private static void moveBackward(ListIterator it)
  { int n = random.nextInt(it.nextIndex());
    for (int i=0; i<n; i++)
      System.out.print(it.previous());
    System.out.println();
  }
}
```

```
ABCDEFGHIJKLMNOPQR
ABCDE
RQPON
ED
NOP
DEFGHIJKLMNO
```

This program simulates two independent random walks on the same linked list. It uses local methods `moveForward()` and `moveBackward()` to do the walks. Each call moves a random number of steps in the indicated direction. They use the `ListIterator` methods `previousIndex()` and `nextIndex()` to avoid "falling off" the ends of the list.

In this run of the program, iterator `it1` first moves forward 18 elements, to element R. Then iterator `it2` independently moves forward 5 elements, to element E. Then iterator `it1` moves backward 5 elements, from R to element N, and iterator `it2` independently moves backward 2 elements, from E to element D. (Note that when an iterator reverses its direction, it counts the current element again.) Finally, `it1` moves forward 3 elements, from N to element P, and iterator `it2` independently moves forward 12 elements, from D to element O.

Here is how the two iterators look after they make their second sequence of moves:

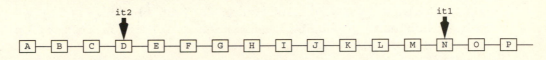

Review Questions

8.1 What is the difference between the `Collection` interface and the `List` interface?

8.2 What is the difference between the `AbstractCollection` class and the `AbstractList` class?

8.3 What is the difference between the `AbstractList` class and the `AbstractSequential-List` class?

8.4 What is the difference between the `Iterator` interface and the `ListIterator` interface?

8.5 What is the difference between the `ArrayList` class and the `LinkedList` class?

8.6 What is the difference between an `ArrayList` object and a `Vector` object?

8.7 In deciding whether to use an `ArrayList` or a `LinkedList` in an application, what factors make one choice better than the other?

Problems

8.1 Implement the following method:
```
public static void loadRandomLetters(LinkedList list, int n)
// fills list with n randomly generated capital letters
```

8.2 Write a method that uses an iterator to print the contents of a linked list, one object per line.

8.3 Write a method that uses an iterator to print the contents of a linked list in reverse order, one object per line.

8.4 Write the following method:
```
public static void exchange(LinkedList list, int i, int j)
// swaps the elements indexed at i and j
```

8.5 Modify the solution to the Josephus Problem (Example 8.6 on page 158) so that it also uses a `skip` parameter to generate the output. The value of `skip` is a constant nonnegative integer that specifies whom each soldier should kill. For example, if `skip = 2`, the A would kill D (skipping over B and C), E would kill H, etc. The original solution is then the special case where `skip = 0`.

8.6   Modify the random walk program in Example 8.7 on page 160 so that the iterators walk around a `Ring` object instead of a `LinkedList`. (See Example 8.5 on page 155) Change the move methods so the walking can wrap around the ring.

8.7   Modify the random walk program in Example 8.7 on page 160 so that the iterators walk around a `Ring` object instead of a `LinkedList` (see Problem 8.6), and also change direction at random.

Answers to Review Questions

8.1   The `List` interface includes the following 10 that work with indexes:

```
public void        add(int index, Object object);
public boolean     addAll(int index, Collection collection);
public Object      get(int index);
public int         indexOf(Object object);
public int         lastIndexOf(Object object);
public ListIterator listIterator();
public ListIterator listIterator(int index);
public Object      remove(int index);
public Object      set(int index, Object object);
public List        subList(int start, int stop);
```

8.2   The `AbstractList` class implements the methods of the `List` interface, including the 10 index methods listed above in the answer to Question 8.1 which are not in the `AbstractCollection` class.

8.3   The `AbstractSequentialList` class is designed to serve as a base class for linked list classes. It specifies the two abstract methods `listIterator()` and `size()` which must be implemented by any concrete subclass.

8.4   The `ListIterator` class extends the `Iterator` class in a way that is analogous to the way the `AbstractSequentialList` class extends the `AbstractList` class. (See the answer to Question 8.2 above.) Ordinary `Iterator` objects are unidirectional iterators that iterate on array lists; `ListIterator` objects are bidirectional iterators that iterate on linked lists.

8.5   Instances of the `ArrayList` class use contiguous, indexed, direct access (array) storage. Instances of the `LinkedList` class use linked (sequential) access storage. So array lists provide faster access, while linked lists provide faster modifications (insertions and removals).

8.6   There isn't much difference between an `ArrayList` object and a `Vector` object: they both provide direct indexed access. As part of the Java Collections Framework, the `ArrayList` class was introduced more recently, in Java 1.2, and so it is probably more preferred. The `Vector` class has about twice as many methods, but many are redundant and consequently a bit confusing.

8.7   An `ArrayList` object should be preferred when frequent lookups are expected. A `LinkedList` object should be preferred when frequent additions and/or removals are expected. (See the answer to Question 8.6 above.)

Solutions to Problems

8.1
```
public static void loadRandomLetters( LinkedList list, int n )
{  list.clear();
   while (0 < n--)
     list.add("" + (char)('A' + (int)(Math.random()*26)));
}
```

8.2
```
public static void printForward(LinkedList list )
{ for (ListIterator itr=list.listIterator(); itr.hasNext(); )
    System.out.println(itr.next());
}
```

8.3
```
public static void printBackward(LinkedList list)
{ ListIterator itr=list.listIterator(list.size());
  while (itr.hasPrevious())
    System.out.println(itr.previous());
}
```

8.4
```
public static void exchange(LinkedList list, int i, int j)
{ Object ithObj = list.get(i);
  Object jthObj = list.get(j) ;
  list.set(i,jthObj);
  list.set(j,ithObj);
}
```

8.5   The solution to the generalized Josephus Problem:
```
public class Pr0805
{ public static void main(String[] args)
  { Ring ring = new Ring();
    ListIterator it = ring.listIterator();
    int n = get("Enter number of soldiers");
    int skip = get("Enter skip number");
    for (int k=0; k<n; k++)
      it.add(new Character((char)('A'+k)));
    System.out.print(n + " soldiers: ");
    System.out.println(ring);
    while (ring.size() > 1)
    { Object killer = it.next();
      for (int i=0; i<skip; i++)
        it.next();
      System.out.println(killer + " killed " + it.next());
      it.remove();
    }
    System.out.println("The lone survivor is " + it.next());
  }
}
```

8.6   Modifying the random walk program so that the iterators walk around a `Ring` object:
```
import java.util.*;      // defines the ListIterator class
import schaums.dswj.*;   // defines the Ring class

public class Pr0806
{ private static final int SIZE=10;
  private static final int MAX_WALK=20;
  private static Ring ring = new Ring();
  private static Random random = new Random();

  public static void main(String[] args)
  { initializeRing();
    ListIterator it1 = ring.listIterator();
    ListIterator it2 = ring.listIterator();
    moveForward(it1);
    moveForward(it2);
    moveBackward(it1);
    moveBackward(it2);
    moveForward(it1);
    moveForward(it2);
  }
```

```
      private static void initializeRing()
      { ListIterator it = ring.listIterator();
        for (int k=0; k<SIZE; k++)
          it.add(new Character((char)('A'+k)));
      }

      private static void moveForward(ListIterator it)
      { int n = random.nextInt(MAX_WALK);
        for (int i=0; i<n; i++)
          System.out.print(it.next());
        System.out.println();
      }

      private static void moveBackward(ListIterator it)
      { int n = random.nextInt(MAX_WALK);
        for (int i=0; i<n; i++)
          System.out.print(it.previous());
        System.out.println();
      }
  }
```

8.7   The random walk program where the iterators walk around the `Ring` object in random directions:

```
      import java.util.*;       // defines the ListIterator class
      import schaums.dswj.*;   // defines the Ring class

  public class Pr0809
  { private static final int SIZE=10;
    private static final int MAX_WALK=20;
    private static Ring ring = new Ring();
    private static Random random = new Random();

    public static void main(String[] args)
    { initializeRing();
      ListIterator it1 = ring.listIterator();
      ListIterator it2 = ring.listIterator();
      move(it1);
      move(it2);
      move(it1);
      move(it2);
      move(it1);
      move(it2);
    }

    private static void initializeRing()
    { ListIterator it = ring.listIterator();
      for (int k=0; k<SIZE; k++)
        it.add(new Character((char)('A'+k)));
    }

    private static void move(ListIterator it)
    { int n = random.nextInt(MAX_WALK);
      boolean forward = (random.nextInt(2)==1);
      if (forward)
        for (int i=0; i<n; i++)
          System.out.print(it.next());
      else
```

```
        for (int i=0; i<n; i++)
          System.out.print(it.previous());
        System.out.println();
    }
}
```

Chapter 9

Trees

A tree is a nonlinear data structure that models a hierarchical organization. The characteristic features are that each element may have several successors (called its "children") and every element except one (called the "root") has a unique predecessor (called its "parent"). Trees are common in computer science: Computer file systems are trees, the inheritance structure for Java

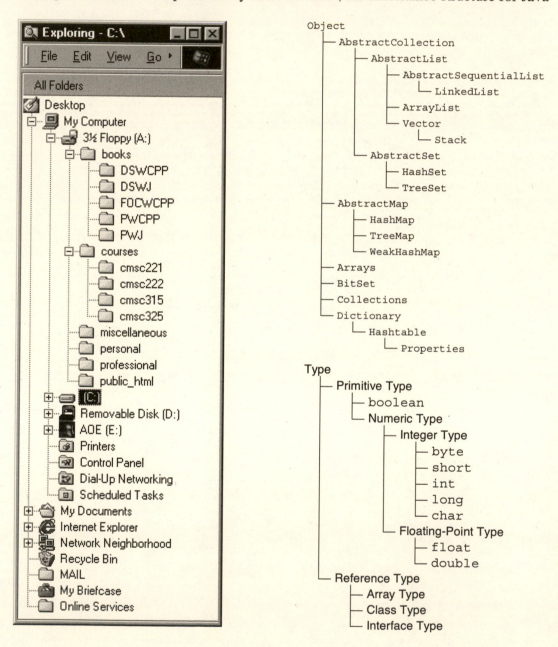

classes is a tree, the run-time system of method invocations during the execution of a Java program is a tree, the classification of Java types is a tree, and the actual syntactical definition of the Java programming language itself forms a tree.

9.1 TREE DEFINITIONS

Here is the recursive definition of an unordered tree:

A *tree* is either the empty set or a pair (r, S), where the first component r is a node and the second component S is a set of disjoint trees, none of which contains r.

The node r is called the *root* of the tree T, and the elements of the set S are called its *subtrees*. The set S, of course, may be empty. The restriction that none of the subtrees contains the root applies recursively: r cannot be in any subtree, or in any subtree of any subtree, etc.

Note that this definition specifies that the second component of a tree be a *set* of subtrees. So the order of the subtrees is irrelevant.

EXAMPLE 9.1 Equal Unordered Trees

The two trees shown here are equal:

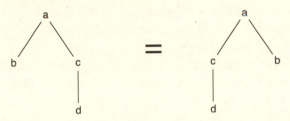

The tree on the left has root a and two subtrees B and C, where B = (b, $\varnothing$), C = (c, {D}), and D is the subtree D = (d, $\varnothing$). The tree on the right has the same root a and the same set of subtrees {B, C} = {C, B}, so (a, {B, C}) = (a, {C, B}).

The elements of a tree are called its *nodes*. Technically, each node is an element of only one subtree, namely the tree of which it is the root. But indirectly, trees consist of nested subtrees, and each node is considered to be an element of every tree in which it is nested. So a, b, c, and d are all considered to be nodes of the tree A shown here. Similarly, c and d are both nodes of the tree C.

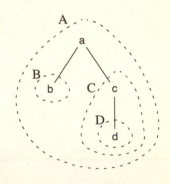

The *size* of a tree is the number of nodes it contains. So the tree A shown here has size 4 and C has size 2. A tree of size 1 is called a *singleton*. The trees B and D shown here are singletons. A tree of size 0 is called the *empty tree* and is denoted by $\varnothing$. Note that this tree is unique; i.e., all empty trees are equal.

If $T = (x, S)$ is a tree, then x is the root of T and S is its set of subtrees $S = \{T_1, T_2, ..., T_n\}$. Each subtree T_j is itself a tree with its own root r_j. In this case, we call the node r the *parent* of each node r_j, and we call the r_j the *children* of r. In general, we say that two nodes are *adjacent* if one is the parent of the other.

A node with no children is called a *leaf*. A node with at least one child is called an *internal node*.

A *path* in a tree is a sequence of nodes $(x_0, x_1, x_2, ..., x_m)$ wherein the nodes of each pair with adjacent subscripts (x_{i-1}, x_i) are adjacent nodes. For example, (a, b, c, d) is a path in the tree shown above, but (a, d, b, c) is not. The *length* of a path is the number m of its adjacent pairs.

It follows from the definition that trees are *acyclic*; i.e., no path can contain the same node more than once.

A *root path* for a node x_0 in a tree is a path $(x_0, x_1, x_2, ..., x_m)$ where x_m is the root of the tree. A root path for a leaf node is called a *leaf-to-root path*.

Theorem 9.1 Every node in a tree has a unique root path.
For a proof, see Problem 9.1 on page 175.

The *depth* of a node in a tree is the length of its root path. Of course, the depth of the root in any tree is 0. We also refer to the *depth* of a subtree in a tree, meaning the depth of its root.

A *level* in a tree is the set of all nodes at a given depth.

The *height* of a tree is the greatest depth among all of its nodes. The Windows directory tree shown on page 166 has height 4. By definition, the height of a singleton is 0, and the height of the empty tree is −1.

A node y is said to be an *ancestor* of another node x if it is on x's root path. Note that the root of a tree is an ancestor of every other node in the tree.

A node x is said to be a *descendant* of another node y if y is an ancestor of x. For each node y in a tree, the set consisting of y and all its descendants form the *subtree* rooted at y. If S is a subtree of T, then we say that T is a *supertree* of S.

The *path length* of a tree is the sum of the lengths of all paths from its root. This is the same as the weighted sum, adding each level times the number of nodes on that level. The path length of the tree shown here is $1\cdot3 + 2\cdot4 + 3\cdot8 = 35$.

EXAMPLE 9.2 Properties of a Tree

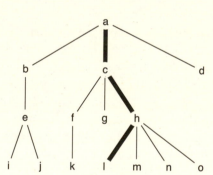

The root of the tree shown here is node a. The six nodes a, b, c, e, f, and h are all internal nodes. The other nine nodes are leaves. The path (m, h, c, a) is a leaf-to-root path. Its length is 3. Node b has depth 1, and node m has depth 3. Level 2 consists of nodes e, f, g, and h.

The height of the tree is 3. Nodes a, c, and h are all ancestors of node m. Node k is a descendant of node c but not of node b.

The subtree rooted at b consists of nodes b, e, i, and j.

The *degree* of a node is the number of its children. In the example above, b has degree 1, d has degree 0, and h has degree 5.

The *order* of a tree is the maximum degree among all of its nodes.

A tree is said to be *full* if all of its internal nodes have the same degree and all of its leaves are at the same level. The tree shown here is a full tree of degree 3. Note that it has a total of 40 nodes.

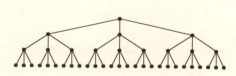

Theorem 9.2 The full tree of order d and height h has $\dfrac{d^{h+1}-1}{d-1}$ nodes.

For a proof, see Problem 9.1 on page 175.

Corollary 9.1 The height of a full tree of order d and size n is $h = \log_d(nd - n + 1) - 1$.

Corollary 9.2 The number of nodes in any tree of height h is at most $\dfrac{d^{h+1}-1}{d-1}$ where d is the maximum degree among its nodes.

9.2 DECISION TREES AND TRANSITION DIAGRAMS

A *decision tree* is a tree diagram that summarizes all the different possible stages of a process that solves a problem by means of a sequence of decisions. Each internal node is labeled with a question, each arc is labeled with an answer to its question, and each leaf node is labeled with the solution to the problem.

EXAMPLE 9.3 Finding the Counterfeit Coin

Five coins that appear identical are to be tested to determine which one of them is counterfeit. The only feature that distinguishes the counterfeit coin is that it weighs less than the legitimate coins. The only available test is to weigh one subset of the coins against another. How should the subsets be chosen to find the counterfeit?

In the decision tree shown below, the symbol $\sim$ means to compare the weights of the two operands. So, for example, $\{a, b\} \sim \{d, e\}$ means to weight coins a and b against coins d and e.

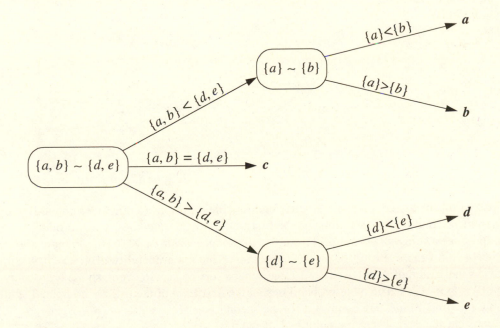

A *transition diagram* is a tree or graph (see Chapter 16) whose internal nodes represent different states or situations that may obtain during a multistage process. As in a decision tree, each leaf represents a different outcome from the process. Each branch is labeled with the conditional probability that the resulting child event will occur, given that the parent event has occurred.

EXAMPLE 9.4 The Game of Craps

The game of *craps* is a dice game played by two players, and X and Y. First X tosses the pair of dice. If the sum of the dice is 7 or 11, X wins the game. If the sum is 2, 3, or 12, Y wins. Otherwise, the sum is designated as the "point," to be matched by another toss. So if neither player has won on the first toss, then the dice are tossed repeatedly until either the point comes up or a 7 comes up. If a 7 comes up first, Y wins. Otherwise, X wins when the point comes up.

The following transition diagram models the game of craps.

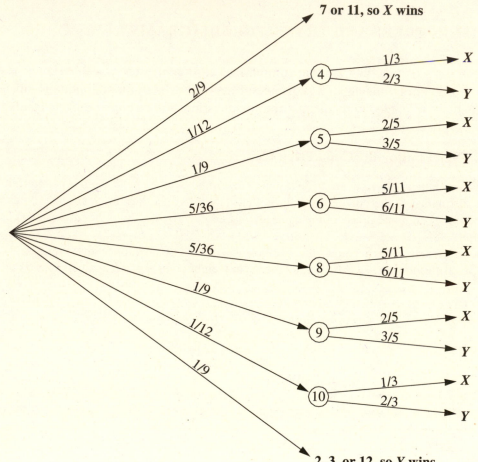

When a pair of dice is tossed, there are 36 different possible outcomes (6 outcomes on the first die, and 6 outcomes on the second for each outcome on the first). Of those 36 outcomes, 1 will produce a sum of 2 (1+1), 2 will produce a sum of 3 (1+2 or 2+1), and 1 will produce a sum of 12 (6+6). So there are a total of 4 chances out of 36 of the event "2, 3, or 12" happening. That's a probability of 4/36 = 1/9. Similarly, there are 6 ways that a sum of 7 will occur and 2 ways that a sum of 11 will occur, so the probability of the event "7 or 11" is 8/36 = 2/9. The other probabilities on the first level of the tree are computed similarly.

To see how the probabilities are computed for the second level of the tree, consider the case where the point is 4. If the next toss comes up 4, X wins. If it comes up 7, Y wins. Otherwise, that step is repeated. The transition diagram shown at right summarizes those three possibilities. The probabilities 1/12, 1/6, and 3/4 are computed as follows:

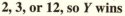

$P(4) = 3/36 = 1/12$

$P(7) = 6/36 = 1/3$

$P(2,3,5,6,8,9,10,11, \text{or } 12) = 27/36 = 3/4$

So once the point 4 has been established on the first toss, X has a probability of 1/12 on winning on the second toss and a probability of 3/4 of getting to the third toss. So once the point 4 has been established on the first toss, X has a probability of (3/4)(1/12) of winning on the third toss and a probability of (3/4)(3/4) of getting to the fourth toss. Similarly, once the point 4 has been established on the first toss, X has a probability of (3/4)(1/12) + (3/4)(3/4)(1/12) of winning on the fourth toss, etc. Summing these partial probabilities, we find that once the point 4 has been established on the first toss, the probability that X wins on *any* toss thereafter is

$$P_4 = \frac{1}{12} + \left(\frac{3}{4}\right)\frac{1}{12} + \left(\frac{3}{4}\right)^2\frac{1}{12} + \left(\frac{3}{4}\right)^3\frac{1}{12} + \left(\frac{3}{4}\right)^4\frac{1}{12} + \left(\frac{3}{4}\right)^5\frac{1}{12} + \cdots$$

$$= \frac{\frac{1}{12}}{1-\frac{3}{4}}$$

$$= \frac{1/12}{1/4}$$

$$= \frac{1}{3}$$

This calculation applies the formula for geometric series. (See Theorem A.10 on page 338.)

If the probability is 1/3 that X wins once the point 4 has been established on the first toss, the probability that Y wins at that point must be 2/3. The other probabilities at the second level are computed similarly.

Now we can calculate the probability that X wins the game from the main transition diagram:

$$P = \frac{2}{9} + \frac{1}{12}(P_4) + \frac{1}{9}(P_5) + \frac{5}{36}(P_6) + \frac{5}{36}(P_8) + \frac{1}{9}(P_9) + \frac{1}{12}(P_{10})$$

$$= \frac{2}{9} + \frac{1}{12}\left(\frac{1}{3}\right) + \frac{1}{9}\left(\frac{2}{5}\right) + \frac{5}{36}\left(\frac{5}{11}\right) + \frac{5}{36}\left(\frac{5}{11}\right) + \frac{1}{9}\left(\frac{2}{5}\right) + \frac{1}{12}\left(\frac{1}{3}\right)$$

$$= \frac{244}{495}$$

$$= 0.4929$$

So the probability that X wins is 49.29%, and the probability that Y wins is 50.71%.

A *stochastic process* is a process that can be analyzed by a transition diagram; i.e., it can be decomposed into sequences of events whose conditional probabilities can be computed. The game of Craps is actually an infinite stochastic process since there is no limit to the number of events that could occur. As with the analysis in Example 9.4, most infinite stochastic processes can be reformulated into an equivalent finite stochastic process that is amenable to (finite) computers.

Note that, unlike other tree models, decision trees and transition trees are usually drawn from left to right to suggest the time-dependent movement from one node to the next.

9.3 ORDERED TREES

Here is the recursive definition of an ordered tree:

> An *ordered tree* is either the empty set or a pair $T = (x, S)$, where the first component x is a node and the second component S is a sequence of disjoint ordered trees, none of which contains x.

The node x is called the *root* of the tree T, and the elements of the set S are called *subtrees*. The set S of course may be empty. The restriction that none of the subtrees contains the root applies recursively: x cannot be in any subtree, or in any subtree of any subtree, etc.

Note that this definition is the same as that for unordered trees except that the subtrees are contained in a sequence instead of a set. So if two trees have the same subsets, then they are equal. But as ordered trees, they won't be equal unless their equal subtrees are in the same order.

EXAMPLE 9.5 Unequal Ordered Trees

The two trees shown here are not equal as ordered trees:

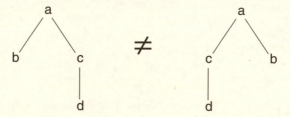

The tree on the left has root a and two subtrees B and C, where B = (b, $\varnothing$) and C = (c, (D)), and D is the subtree D = (d, $\varnothing$). The tree on the right has the same root a and the same subtrees. But the subtrees are not in the same order, so the sequences are not equal: (B, C) $\neq$ (C, B).

Strict adherence to the definition reveals a subtlety often missed, as illustrated by the next example.

EXAMPLE 9.6 Unequal Ordered Trees

The two trees T_1 = (a, (B, C)) and T_2 = (a, (B, $\varnothing$, C)) and are not the same ordered trees, even though they would probably both be drawn as shown here.
Technically, T_1 is a tree of order 2, while T_2 is a tree of order 3.

All the terminology for unordered trees applies the same way to ordered trees. In addition, we can also refer to the *first child* and the *last child* of a node in an ordered tree. It is sometimes useful to think analogously of a human genealogical tree, where the children are ordered by age: oldest first and youngest last.

9.4 TREE TRAVERSAL ALGORITHMS FOR ORDERED TREES

A *traversal algorithm* is a method for processing a data structure that applies a given operation to each element of the structure. For example, if the operation is to print the contents of the element, then the traversal would print every element in the structure. The process of applying the operation to an element is called *visiting* the element. So executing the traversal algorithm causes each element in the structure to be visited. The order in which the elements are visited depends upon which traversal algorithm is used. There are three common algorithms for traversing a general tree.

The *level order traversal* algorithm visits the root, then visits each element on the first level, then visits each element on the second level, and so forth, each time visiting all the elements on one level before going down to the next level. If the tree is drawn in the usual manner with its root at the top and leaves near the bottom, then the level order pattern is the same left-to-right top-to-bottom pattern that you follow to read English text.

EXAMPLE 9.7 The Level Order Traversal

The level order traversal of the tree shown at right would visit the nodes in the following order: a, b, c, d, e, f, g, h, i, j, k, l, m.

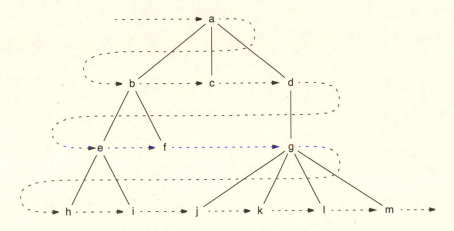

Algorithm 9.1   The Level Order Traversal of an Ordered Tree

To traverse a nonempty ordered tree:
1. Initialize a queue.
2. Enqueue the root.
3. Repeat steps 4–7 until the queue is empty.
4. Dequeue node x from the queue.
5. Visit x.
6. Enqueue all the children of x in order.

The *preorder traversal* algorithm visits the root first and then does a preorder traversal recursively to each subtree in order.

EXAMPLE 9.8 The Preorder Traversal

The preorder traversal of the tree shown in Example 9.8 would visit the nodes in the following order: a, b, e, h, i, f, c, d, g, j, k, l, m.

Note that the preorder traversal of a tree can be obtained by circumnavigating the tree, beginning at the root and visiting each node the first time it is encountered on the left:

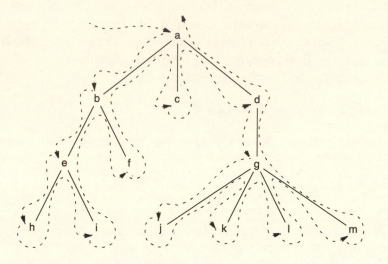

Algorithm 9.2   The Preorder Traversal of an Ordered Tree
To traverse a nonempty ordered tree:
1. Visit the root.
2. Do a recursive preorder traversal of each subtree in order.

The *postorder traversal* algorithm does a postorder traversal recursively to each subtree before visiting the root.

EXAMPLE 9.9   The Postorder Traversal

The postorder traversal of the tree shown in Example 9.8 would visit the nodes in the following order: h, i, e, f, b, c, j, k, l, m, g, d, a.

Algorithm 9.3   The Postorder Traversal of an Ordered Tree
To traverse a nonempty ordered tree:
1. Do a recursive preorder traversal of each subtree in order.
2. Visit the root.

Note that the level order and the preorder traversals always visit the root of each subtree first before visiting its other nodes. The postorder traversal always visits the root of each subtree last after visiting all of its other nodes. Also, the preorder traversal always visits the right-most node last, while the postorder traversal always visits the left-most node first.

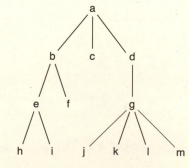

The preorder and postorder traversals are recursive. They also can be implemented iteratively using a stack. The level order traversal is implemented iteratively using a queue.

Review Questions

9.1 All the classes in Java form a single tree, called the *Java inheritance tree*.
    a. What is the size of the Java inheritance tree in Java 1.3?
    b. What is the root of the tree?
    c. What kind of node is a `final` class in the Java inheritance tree?

9.2 True or false:
    a. The depth of a node in a tree is equal to the number of its ancestors.
    b. The size of a subtree is equal to the number of descendants of the root of the subtree.
    c. If *x* is a descendant of *y*, then the depth of *x* is greater than the depth of *y*.
    d. If the depth of *x* is greater than the depth of *y*, then *x* is a descendant of *y*.
    e. A tree is a singleton if and only if its root is a leaf.
    f. Every leaf of a subtree is also a leaf of its supertree.
    g. The root of a subtree is also the root of its supertree.
    h. The number of ancestors of a node equals its depth.
    i. If *R* is a subtree of *S* and *S* is a subtree of *T*, then *R* is a subtree of *T*.
    j. A node is a leaf if and only if it has degree 0.
    k. In any tree, the number of internal nodes must be less than the number of leaf nodes.
    l. A tree is full if and only if all of its leaves are at the same level.
    m. Every subtree of a full binary tree is full.
    n. Every subtree of a complete binary tree is complete.

9.3 For each of the five trees shown at the top of the next page, list the leaf nodes, the children of node C, the depth of node F, all the nodes at level 3, the height, and the order of the tree.

9.4 For the tree shown at right, find:
    a. all ancestors of node F
    b. all descendants of node F
    c. all nodes in the subtree rooted at F
    d. all leaf nodes

9.5 How many nodes are in the full tree of:
    a. order 3 and height 4?
    b. order 4 and height 3?
    c. order 10 and height 4?
    d. order 4 and height 10?

9.6 Give the order of visitation of the tree shown in Example 9.2 on page 168 using the:
    a. level order traversal
    b. preorder traversal
    c. postorder traversal

9.7 Which traversals always visit:
    a. the root first?
    b. the left-most node first?
    c. the root last?
    d. the right-most node last?

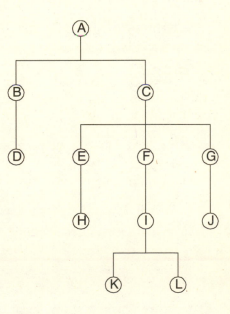

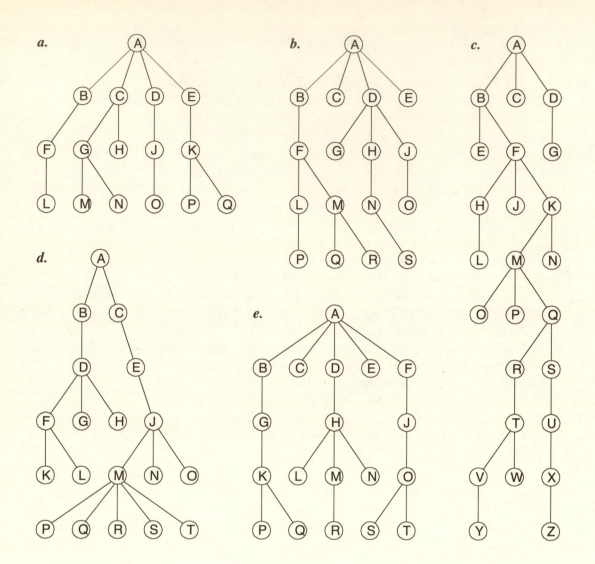

9.8   The level order traversal follows the pattern as reading a page of English text: left-to-right, row-by-row. Which traversal algorithm follows the pattern of reading vertical columns from left to right?

9.9   Which traversal algorithm is used in the call tree for Problem 4.31 on page 86?

Problems

9.1   Prove Theorem 9.1 on page 168.

9.2   Prove Theorem 9.2 on page 169.

9.3   Prove Corollary 9.1 on page 169.

9.4   Prove Corollary 9.2 on page 169.

9.5   Derive the formula for the path length of a full tree of order d and height h.

9.6   Some people play the game of craps allowing 3 to be a possible point. In this version, player *Y* wins on the first toss only if it comes up 2 or 12. Use a transition diagram to analyze this version of the game and compute the probability that *X* wins.

9.7   The *St. Petersburg Paradox* is a betting strategy that seems to guarantee a win. It can be applied to any binomial game in which a win or lose are equally likely on each trial and in which the amount bet on each trial may vary. For example, in a coin-flipping game, the bettor may bet any number of dollars on each flip, and he will win what he bets if a head comes up, and he will lose what he bets if a tail comes up. The St. Petersburg strategy is to continue playing until a head comes up, and to double your bet each time it doesn't. For example, the sequence of tosses is {T, T, T, H}, then the bettor will have bet $1 and lost, then $2 and lost, then $4 and lost, then $8 and won, ending up with a net win of –$1 + –$2 + –$4 + $8 = $1. Since a head has to come up eventually, the bettor is guaranteed to win $1, no matter how many coin flips it takes. Draw the transition diagram for this strategy showing the bettor's winnings at each stage of play. Then explain the flaw in this strategy.

9.8   Seven coins that appear identical are to be tested to determine which one of them is counterfeit. The only feature that distinguishes the counterfeit coin is that it weighs less than the legitimate coins. The only available test is to weigh one subset of the coins against another. How should the subsets be chosen to find the counterfeit? (See Example 9.3 on page 169.)

Answers to Review Questions

9.1   In the *Java inheritance tree:*
   a. The size of the tree in Java 1.3 is 1730.
   b. A `final` class is a leaf node in the Java inheritance tree.

9.2   *a.* True.
   b. False: It's one more because the root of the subtree is in the subtree but is not a descendant of itself.
   c. True
   d. False
   e. True
   f. True
   g. False
   h. True
   i. True
   j. True
   k. False
   l. False
   m. True
   n. True

9.3   *a.* The leaf nodes are L, M, N, H, O, P, Q; the children of node C are G and H; node F has depth 2; the nodes at 3 three are L, M, N, O, P, and Q; the height of the tree is 3; the order of the tree is 4.
   b. The leaf nodes are C, E, G, O, P, Q, R, and S; node C has no children; node F has depth 2; the nodes at level 3 are L, M, N, and O; the height of the tree is 4; the order of the tree is 4.
   c. The leaf nodes are C, E, G, J, L, N, O, P, W, Y, and Z; node C has no children; node F has depth 2; the nodes at level 3 are H, J, and K; the height of the tree is 9; the order of the tree is 3.
   d. The leaf nodes are G, H, K, L, N, O, P, Q, R, S, and T; the only child node C has is node E; node F has depth 3; the nodes at level 3 are F, G, H, and J; the height of the tree is 5; the order is 5.
   e. The leaf nodes are D, E, L, N, P, Q, R, S, and T; node C has no children; node F has depth 1; the nodes at level 3 are K, L, M, N, and O; the height of the tree is 4; the order of the tree is 5.

9.4   *a.* The ancestors of F are C and A
      b. The descendants of F are I, K, and L.
      c. The nodes in the subtree rooted at F are F, I, K, and L.
      d. The leaf nodes are D, H, J, K, and L.

9.5   *a.* $(3^5 - 1)/2 = 121$ nodes
      b. $(4^4 - 1)/3 = 85$ nodes
      c. $(10^5 - 1)/9 = 11{,}111$ nodes
      d. $(4^{11} - 1)/3 = 1{,}398{,}101$ nodes

9.6   *a.* Level order: A, B, C, D, E, F, G, H, I, J, K, L, M, N, O, P.
      b. Preorder: A, B, E, I, J, C, F, G, H, K, L, M, N, O, P, D.
      c. Postorder: I, J, E, B, F, G, K, L, M, N, O, P, H, C, D, A.

9.7   *a.* The level order and the preorder traversals always visit the root first.
      b. The postorder traversal always visits the left-most node first.
      c. The postorder traversal always visits the root last.
      d. The preorder traversal always visits the right-most node last.

9.8   The inorder traversal follows the pattern of reading by column from left to right.

9.9   The inorder traversal is used in Problem 4.31 on page 86.

Solutions to Problems

9.1   Proof of Theorem 9.1 on page 168:

If there were no path from a given node x to the root of the tree, then the definition of tree would be violated, because to be an element of the tree, x must be the root of some subtree. If there were more than one path from x back to the root, then x would be an element of more than one distinct subtree. That also violates the definition of tree, which requires subtrees to be disjoint.

9.2   Proof of Theorem 9.2 on page 169:

If the tree is empty, then its height is $h = -1$ and the number of nodes $n = 0$. In that case, the formula is correct: $n = (d^{(h)+1}-1)/(d-1) = (d^{(-1)+1}-1)/(d-1) = (d^0-1)/(d-1) = (1-1)/(d-1) = 0$.

If the tree is a singleton, then its height is $h = 0$ and the number of nodes $n = 1$. In that case, the formula is again correct: $n = (d^{(h)+1}-1)/(d-1) = (d^{(0)+1}-1)/(d-1) = (d-1)/(d-1) = 1$.

Now assume that the formula is correct for any full tree of height $h-1$, where $h \geq 0$. Let T be the full tree of height h. Then by definition, T consists of a root node and a set of subtrees. And since T is full, it actually consist of a root node and a set of d subtrees each with height $h-1$. Therefore, by the inductive hypothesis, the number of nodes in each subtree is $n_S = (d^{(h-1)+1}-1)/(d-1) = (d^h-1)/(d-1)$. Thus, the total number of nodes in T is

$$n = 1 + (d)(n_S)$$
$$= 1 + d\left(\frac{d^h - 1}{d - 1}\right)$$
$$= \frac{d-1}{d-1} + \frac{d^{h+1}-d}{d-1}$$
$$= \frac{d^{h+1}-1}{d-1}$$

Thus, by the Principle of Mathematical Induction (see Section A.4 on page 336), the formula must be correct for all full trees of any height.

9.3   Proof of Corollary 9.1 on page 169:

This proof is purely algebraic:

$$n = \frac{d^{h+1} - 1}{d - 1}$$

$$n(d-1) = d^{h+1} - 1$$

$$d^{h+1} = n(d-1) + 1$$

$$= nd - n + 1$$

$$h + 1 = \log_d(nd - n + 1)$$

$$h = \log_d(nd - n + 1) - 1$$

9.4   Proof of Corollary 9.2 on page 169:

Let T be a tree of any order d and any height h. Then T can be embedded into the full tree of the same degree and height. That full tree has exactly $\frac{d^{h+1} - 1}{d - 1}$ nodes, so its subtree T has at most that many nodes.

9.5   The path length of a full tree of order d and height h is $\frac{d}{(d-1)^2}[hd^{h+1} - (h+1)d + 1]$. For example, the path length of the full tree on page 168 is 102.

9.6   The version of craps where 3 can be a point:

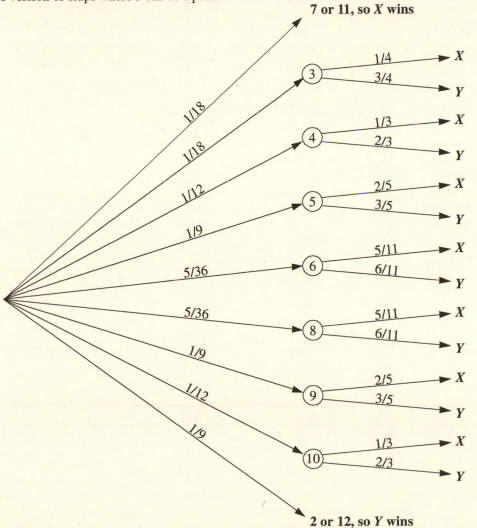

The probability that X wins this version is 0.5068 or 50.68%.

9.7   The tree diagram analysis of the St. Petersburg Paradox is shown below. The flaw in this strategy is

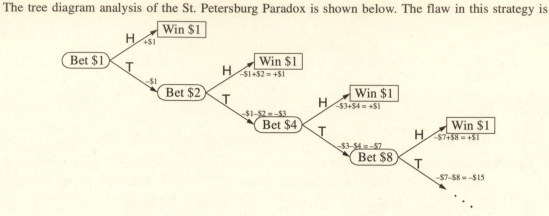

that there is a distinct possibility (i.e., a positive probability) that enough tails could come up in a row to make the required bet exceed the bettor's stake. After n successive tails, the bettor must bet 2^n. For example, if 20 tails come up in a row, the next bet will have to be more than a million dollars!

9.8   This decision tree shows all possible outcomes from the algorithm that solves the 7-coin problem:

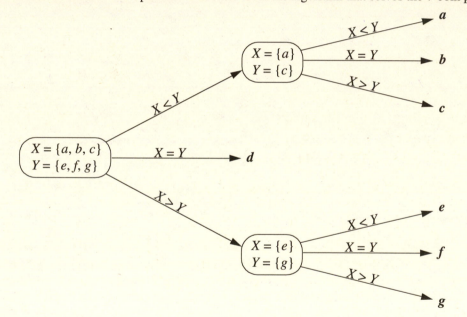

Chapter 10

Binary Trees

10.1 DEFINITIONS

Here is the recursive definition of a binary tree:

> An *binary tree* is either the empty set or a triple $T = (x, L, R)$, where x is a node and
> L and R are disjoint binary trees, neither of which contains x.

The node x is called the *root* of the tree T, and the subtrees L and R are called the *left subtree*
and the *right subtree* of T rooted at x.

Comparing this definition for
ordered trees with the one in
Section 9.3 on page 172, it is easy
to see that a binary tree is just an
ordered tree of order 2. But be
aware that an empty left subtree is
different from an empty right
subtree. (See Example 9.6 on
page 172.) Consequently, the two
binary trees shown here are not the same.

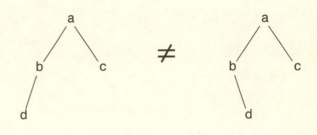

Here is an equivalent, nonrecursive definition for binary trees:

> An *binary tree* is an ordered tree in which every internal node has degree 2.

In this simpler definition, the
leaf nodes are regarded as dummy
nodes whose only purpose is to
define the structure of the tree. In
applications, the internal nodes
would hold data while the leaf
nodes would be either identical
empty nodes, or a single empty
node, or just the `null` reference.
This may seem inefficient and
more complex, but it is usually
easier to implement.

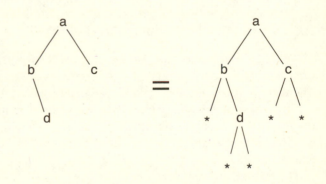

Except where noted, we will in this book adhere to the first definition for binary trees. So
some internal nodes may have only one child, either a left child or a right child.

The definitions of the terms *size*, *path*, *length* of a path, *depth* of a node, *level*, *height*, *interior*
node, *ancestor*, *descendant*, *subtree*, and *supertree* are the same for binary trees as for general
trees. (See page 174.)

EXAMPLE 10.1 Characteristics of a Binary Tree

This is a binary tree of size 10 and height 3. Node a is its root. The path from node h to node b has length 2. Node b is at level 1, and node h is at level 3. b is an ancestor of h, and h is a descendant of b. The part in the shaded region is a subtree of size 6 and height 2. Its root is node b.

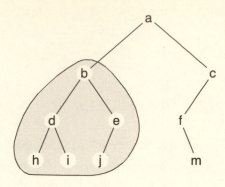

10.2 COUNTING BINARY TREES

EXAMPLE 10.2 All the Binary Trees of Size 3

There are five different binary trees of size $n = 3$:

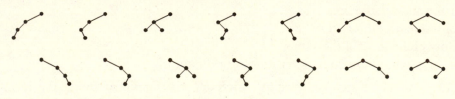

Four have height 2, and the other one has height 1.

EXAMPLE 10.3 All the Binary Trees of Size 4

There are 14 different binary trees of size $n = 4$:

Ten have height 3, and the other four have height 2.

EXAMPLE 10.4 The Binary Trees of Size 5

To find all the binary trees of size 5, apply the recursive definition for binary trees. If t is a binary tree of size 5, then it must consist of a root node together with two subtrees the sum of whose sizes equals 4. There are four possibilities: The left subtree contains either 4, 3, 2, 1, or 0 nodes.

First count all the binary trees of size 5 whose left subtree has size 4. From Example 10.3, we see that there are 14 different possibilities for that left subtree. But for each of those 14 choices, there are no other options because the right subtree must be empty. Therefore, there are 14 different binary trees of size 5 whose left subtree has size 4.

Next, count all the binary trees of size 5 whose left subtree has size 3. From Example 10.2, we see that there are 5 different possibilities for that left subtree. But for each of those 5 choices, there are no other options because the right subtree must be a singleton. Therefore, there are 5 different binary trees of size 5 whose left subtree has size 3.

Next, count all the binary trees of size 5 whose left subtree has size 2. There are only two different possibilities for that left subtree. But for each of those two choices, we have the same two different possibilities for the right subtree because it also must have size 2. Therefore, there are $2 \times 2 = 4$ different binary trees of size 5 whose left subtree has size 2.

By similar reasoning, we find that there are five different binary trees of size 5 whose left subtree has size 1, and there are 14 different binary trees of size 5 whose left subtree has size 0. Therefore, the total number of different binary trees of size 5 is $14 + 5 + 4 + 5 + 14 = 42$.

10.3 FULL BINARY TREES

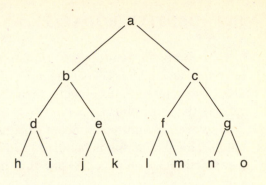

A binary tree is said to be *full* if all its leaves are at the same level and every interior node has two children.

EXAMPLE 10.5 The Full Binary Tree of Height 3

The tree shown at right is the full binary tree of height 3. Note that it has 15 nodes: seven interior nodes and eight leaves.

Theorem 10.1 The full binary tree of height h has $l = 2^h$ leaves and $m = 2^h - 1$ internal nodes.

Proof: The full binary tree of height $h = 0$ is a single leaf node; so it has $n = 1$ node, which is a leaf. Therefore, since $2^h - 1 = 2^0 - 1 = 1 - 1 = 0$, and $2^h = 2^0 = 1$, the formulas are correct for the case where $h = 0$. More generally, let $h > 0$ and assume (the inductive hypothesis) that the formulas are true for all full binary trees of height less than h. Then consider a full binary tree of height h. Each of its subtrees has height $h - 1$, so we apply the formulas to them: $l_L = l_R = 2^{h-1}$ and $m_L = m_R = 2^{h-1} - 1$. (These are the number of leaves in the left subtree, the number of leaves in the right subtree, the number of internal nodes in the left subtree, and the number of internal nodes in the right subtree, respectively.) Then

$$l = l_L + l_R = 2^{h-1} + 2^{h-1} = 2 \cdot 2^{h-1} = 2^h,$$

and

$$m = m_L + m_R + 1 = (2^{h-1} - 1) + (2^{h-1} - 1) + 1 = 2 \cdot 2^{h-1} - 1 = 2^I - 1.$$

Therefore, by the (Second) Principle of Mathematical Induction, the formulas must be true for full binary trees of any height $h \geq 0$.

By simply adding the formulas for m and l, we obtain the first corollary.

Corollary 10.1 The full binary tree of height h has a total of $n = 2^{h+1} - 1$ nodes.

By solving the formula $n = 2^{h+1} - 1$ for h, we obtain the following corollary.

Corollary 10.2 The full binary tree with n nodes has height $h = \lg(n+1) - 1$.
Note that the formula in Corollary 10.2 is correct even in the special case where $n = 0$: The *empty binary tree* has height $h = \lg(n+1) - 1 = \lg(0+1) - 1 = \lg(1) - 1 = 0 - 1 = -1$.

The next corollary applies Corollary 10.1 together with the fact that the full binary tree of height h has more nodes than any other binary tree of height h.

Corollary 10.3 In any binary tree of height h,

$$h + 1 \leq n \leq 2^{h+1} - 1 \text{ and } \lfloor \lg n \rfloor \leq h \leq n-1$$

where n is the number of its nodes.

10.4 IDENTITY, EQUALITY, AND ISOMORPHISM

In a computer, two objects are *identical* if they occupy the same space in memory, so they have the same address. That meaning of equality is reflected in Java by the equality operator. If x and y are references to objects, then the condition (x == y) will be true only if x and y both refer to the same object.

However, the normal concept of equality in mathematics is that the two things have the same value. This distinction is handled in Java by the equals() method, defined in the Object class (see Section 3.4 on page 58) and thus inherited by every class. It is intended to be overridden in subclasses.

EXAMPLE 10.6 Testing Equality of Strings

```
public class Ex1006
{ static public void main(String[] args)
  { String x = new String("ABCDE");
    String y = new String("ABCDE");
    System.out.println("x = " + x);
    System.out.println("y = " + y);
    System.out.println("(x == y) = " + (x == y));
    System.out.println("x.equals(y) = " + x.equals(y));
  }
}
x = ABCDE
y = ABCDE
(x == y) = false
x.equals(y) = true
```

Here, the two objects x and y (or, more precisely, the two objects that are referenced by the reference variables x and y) are different objects, occupying different memory locations, so they are not identically equal: (x == y) evaluates to false. But they do both have the same value, so they are mathematically equal, and x.equals(y) evaluates to true.

The distinction between identical equality and mathematical equality exists in Java only for reference variables (i.e., only for objects). For all variables of primitive type, the equality operator tests for mathematical equality.

Data structures have both content and structure. So it is possible for two data structures to have equal contents (i.e., have the same contents) but organized differently. For example, two arrays could both contain the three numbers 22, 44, and 88, but in different orders.

EXAMPLE 10.7 Testing Equality of Arrays

```
import java.util.Arrays;
public class Testing
{ static public void main(String[] args)
  { int[] x = { 44, 22, 88 };
    int[] y = { 88, 44, 22 };
    System.out.println("Arrays.equals(x,y) = " + Arrays.equals(x,y));
    Arrays.sort(x);
    Arrays.sort(y);
    System.out.println("Arrays.equals(x,y) = " + Arrays.equals(x,y));
  }
}
```

```
Arrays.equals(x,y) = false
Arrays.equals(x,y) = true
```

We say that two data structures are *isomorphic* if they have the same structure; that is, if they have the same size and contain the same data, then the data can be rearranged to make the two structures equal. This will be possible if and only if there is a one-to-one correspondence between the nodes of the two structures that preserves adjacency.

The precise definition is:

> **Two structures *X* and *Y* are said to be *isomorphic* if there exists a function *f* that matches each element *x* of *X* with a unique element *y* = *f*(*x*) in *Y* so that every *y* in *Y* corresponds to a unique element *x* in *X*, and two elements x_1 and x_2 are adjacent in *X* if and only if $f(x_1)$ and $f(x_1)$ are adjacent in *Y*.**

A function *f* with the properties described in the definition is called an *isomorphism* between the two structures.

Notice that the definition of *isomorphism* does not require that the two structures contain the same data. Isomorphism is independent of content; it describes only the underlying structure.

With arrays, lists, and other linear data structures, the data can be rearranged (sorted) to make the two structures mathematically equal. But with nonlinear data structures, such as trees and graphs, it may not be possible. If two graphs have the same size and the same contents but are structured differently, there is no way that their contents can be rearranged to make them equal. They are nonisomorphic.

EXAMPLE 10.8 Isomorphic Trees

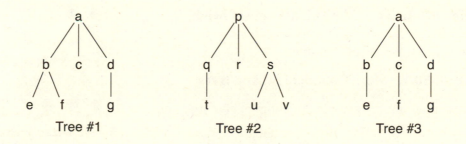

As unordered trees, Tree #1 and Tree #2 are isomorphic, but not equal.

However, Tree #3 is not isomorphic (and therefore, not equal) to either of the other two trees because it has only three leaves; the other two trees each have four leaves. That distinction leads fairly easily to a formal deduction that no isomorphism between Tree #1 and Tree #3.

As ordered trees, Tree #1 is not isomorphic to Tree #2 because their roots' leftmost subtrees have different sizes. The leftmost subtree in Tree #1 has three nodes (b, e, and f), while that of Tree #2 has only two nodes (q and t). Again, that distinction leads fairly easily to a formal deduction that no isomorphism between Tree #1 and Tree #2 can exist.

Binary trees are ordered trees; i.e., the order of the two children at each node is part of the structure of the binary tree.

EXAMPLE 10.9 Nonisomorphic Binary Trees

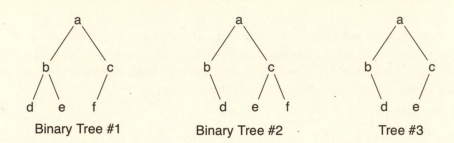

Here, Binary Tree #1 is not isomorphic to Binary Tree #2, for the same reason that the ordered trees in Example 10.8 are not isomorphic: The subtrees don't match, in order. However, as unordered trees, they would be isomorphic.

Even as unordered trees, neither of them is isomorphic to Tree #3, because it has only five nodes and the other trees have six.

10.5 COMPLETE BINARY TREES

A *complete binary tree* is either a full binary tree or one that is full except for a segment of missing leaves on the right side of the bottom level.

EXAMPLE 10.10 A Complete Binary Tree of Height 3

The tree shown at right is complete. The full binary tree below it was obtained by adding five leaves on the right at level 3.

Theorem 10.2 In a complete binary tree of height h,
$$h + 1 \le n \le 2^{h+1} - 1 \text{ and } h = \lfloor \lg n \rfloor$$
where n is the number of its nodes.

EXAMPLE 10.11 More Complete Binary Trees

Here are three more examples of complete binary trees:

Complete binary trees are important because they have a simple and natural implementation using ordinary arrays. The *natural mapping* (ses Section 12.2 on page 225) is actually defined for any binary tree: assign the number 1 to the root; for any node, if i is its number, then assign $2i$ to its left child and $2i+1$ to its right child (if they exist). This assigns a unique positive integer to each node. Then simply store the element at node `i` in `a[i]`, where `a[]` is an array.

Complete binary trees are important because of the simple way in which they can be stored in an array. This is achieved by assigning index numbers to the tree nodes by level, as shown in the next picture. The beauty in this natural mapping is in simple way that it allows the array indexes of the children and parent of a node to be computed from its index.

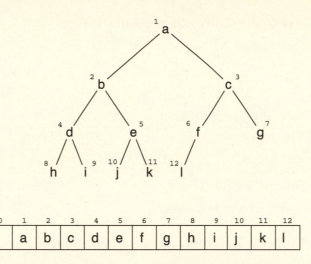

Algorithm 10.1 The Natural Mapping of a Complete Binary Tree into an Array

To navigate about a complete binary tree stored by its natural mapping in an array:

1. The parent of the node stored at location i is stored at location $i/2$.
2. The left child of the node stored at location i is stored at location $2i$.
3. The right child of the node stored at location i is stored at location $2i + 1$.

For example, node e is stored at index $i = 5$ in the array; its parent node b is stored at index $i/2 = 5/2 = 2$, its left child node j is stored at location $2i = 2 \cdot 5 = 10$, and its right child node k is stored at index $2i + 1 = 2 \cdot 5 + 1 = 11$.

The use of the adjective "complete" should now be clear: The defining property for complete binary trees is precisely the condition that guarantees that the natural mapping will store its nodes in an array with no gaps.

EXAMPLE 10.12 An Incomplete Binary Tree

Here is the binary tree from Example 10.1 on page 182:
It is not complete. The natural mapping of its nodes into an array leaves gaps:

0	1	2	3	4	5	6	7	8	9	10	11	12	13
	a	b	c	d	e	f		g	h	i			j

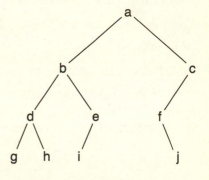

Warning: Some authors use the term "almost complete binary tree" for a complete binary tree and the term "complete binary tree" for a full binary tree.

10.6 BINARY TREE TRAVERSAL ALGORITHMS

The three traversal algorithms that are used for general trees (see Section 9.4 on page 172) apply to binary trees as well: the preorder traversal, the postorder traversal, and the level order traversal. In addition, binary trees support a fourth traversal algorithm: the inorder traversal. These four traversal algorithms are given next.

Algorithm 10.2   The Level Order Traversal of a Binary Tree

To traverse a nonempty binary tree:

1. Initialize a queue.

2. Enqueue the root.

3. Repeat steps 4–7 until the queue is empty.

4. Dequeue a node x from the queue.

5. Visit x.

6. Enqueue the left child of x if it exists.

7. Enqueue the right child of x if it exists.

EXAMPLE 10.13   The Level Order Traversal of a Binary Tree

Here is how the level order traversal looks on the full binary tree of height 3:

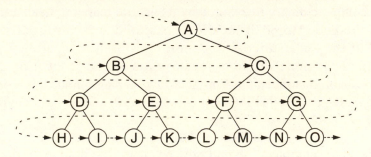

The nodes are visited in the order A, B, C, D, E, F, G, H, I, J, K, L, M, N, O.

Algorithm 10.3   The Preorder Traversal of a Binary Tree

To traverse a nonempty binary tree:

1. Visit the root.

2. If the left subtree is nonempty, do a preorder traversal on it.

3. If the right subtree is nonempty, do a preorder traversal on it.

EXAMPLE 10.14   The Preorder Traversal of a Binary Tree

This picture below shows the preorder traversal on the full binary tree of height 3.

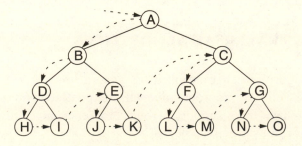

The nodes are visited in the order A, B, D, H, I, E, J, K, C, F, L, M, G, N, O.

Note that the preorder
traversal of a binary tree
can be obtained by cir-
cumnavigating the tree,
beginning at the root and
visiting each node the
first time it is encoun-
tered on the left:

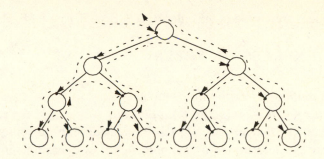

Algorithm 10.4   The Postorder Traversal of a Binary Tree

To traverse a nonempty binary tree:
1. If the left subtree is nonempty, do a postorder traversal on it.
2. If the right subtree is nonempty, do a postorder traversal on it.
3. Visit the root.

EXAMPLE 10.15   The Postorder Traversal of a Binary Tree

Here is how the postorder traversal looks on the full binary tree of height 3:

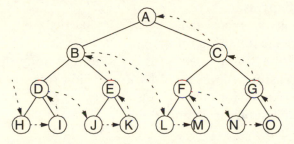

The nodes are visited in the order H, I, D, J, K, E, B, L, M, F, N, O, G, C, A.

The preorder traversal visits the root first and the postorder traversal visits the root last. This suggests a third alternative for binary trees: visit the root in between the traversals of the two subtrees. That is called the *inorder traversal*.

Algorithm 10.5   The Inorder Traversal of a Binary Tree

To traverse a nonempty binary tree:
1. If the left subtree is nonempty, do a preorder traversal on it.
2. Visit the root.
3. If the right subtree is nonempty, do a preorder traversal on it.

EXAMPLE 10.16   The Inorder Traversal of a Binary Tree

Here is how the preorder traversal looks on the full binary tree of height 3:

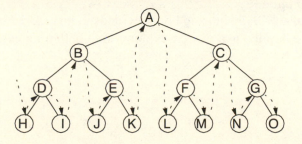

The nodes are visited in the order H, D, I, B, J, E, K, A, L, F, M, C, N, G, O.

10.7 EXPRESSION TREES

An *arithmetic expression* such as `(5 - x)*y + 6/(x + z)` is a combination of *arithmetic operators* (`+`, `-`, `*`, `/`, etc.), *operands* (`5`, `x`, `y`, `6`, `z`, etc.), and parentheses to override the precedence of operations. Each expression can be represented by a unique binary tree whose structure is determined by the precedence of operations in the expression. Such a tree is called an *expression tree*.

EXAMPLE 10.17 An Expression Tree

Here is the expression tree for the expression `(5 - x)*y + 6/(x + z)`:

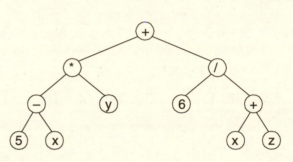

Here is a recursive algorithm for building an expression tree:

Algorithm 10.6 Build an Expression Tree
The expression tree for a given expression can be built recursively from the following rules:
1. The expression tree for a single operand is a single root node that contains it.
2. If E_1 and E_2 are expressions represented by expression trees T_1 and T_2, and if *op* is an operator, then the expression tree for the expression E_1 *op* E_2 is the tree with root node containing *op* and subtrees T_1 and T_2.

An expression has three representations, depending upon which traversal algorithm is used to traverse its tree. The preorder traversal produces the *prefix representation*, the inorder traversal produces the *infix representation*, and the postorder traversal produces the *postfix representation* of the expression. The postfix representation is also called *reverse Polish notation* or *RPN*. These were discussed in Section 6.2 on page 112.

EXAMPLE 10.18 The Three Representations of an Expression

The three representations for the expression in Example 10.17 are:

Prefix:	`+*-5xy/6+xz`
Infix:	`5-x*y+6/x+z`
Postfix (RPN):	`5x-y*6xz+/+`

Ordinary function syntax uses the prefix representation. The expression in Example 10.17 could be evaluated as
```
sum(product(difference(5, x), y), quotient(6, sum(x, z)))
```
Some scientific calculators use RPN, requiring both operands to be entered before the operator.

The next algorithm can be applied to a postfix expression to obtain its value.

Algorithm 10.7 Evaluating an Expression from Its Postfix Representation
To evaluate an expression represented in postfix, scan the representation from left to right:
1. Create a stack for operands.
2. Repeat steps 3–9 until the end of representation is reached.
3. Read the next token t from the representation.
4. If it is an operand, push its value onto the stack.
5. Otherwise, do steps 6–9:
6. Pop a from the stack.
7. Pop b from the stack.
8. Evaluate $c = a\ t\ b$.
9. Push c onto the stack.
10. Return the top element on the stack.

EXAMPLE 10.19 Evaluating an Expression from Its Postfix Representation

Evaluate the expression in Example 10.18 using 2 for x, 3 for y, and 1 for z:

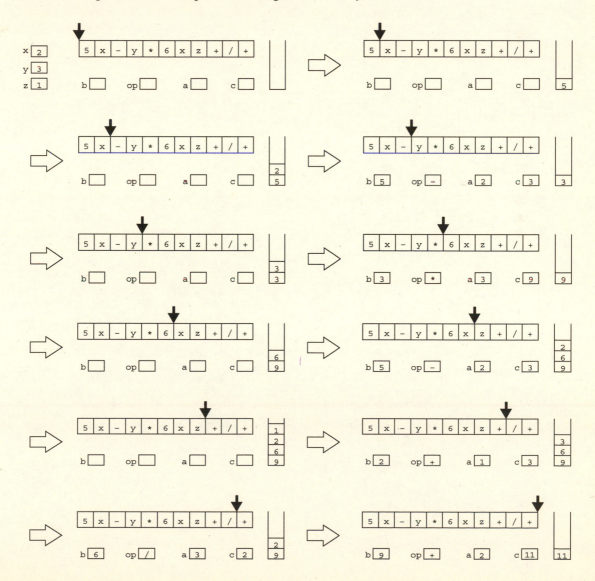

10.8 A `BinaryTree` CLASS

Here is a class for binary trees that directly implements the recursive definition for binary
trees. (See page 181.) By extending the `AbstractCollection` class (see Section 5.3 on page
95) it remains is consistent with the Java Collections Framework:

```java
import java.util.*;

public class BinaryTree extends java.util.AbstractCollection
{ protected Object root;
  protected BinaryTree left, right, parent;
  protected int size;

  public BinaryTree()
  {
  }

  public BinaryTree(Object root)
  { this.root = root;
    size = 1;
  }

  public BinaryTree(Object root, BinaryTree left, BinaryTree right)
  { this(root);
    if (left != null)
    { this.left = left;
      left.parent = this;
      size += left.size();
    }
    if (right != null)
    { this.right = right;
      right.parent = this;
      size += right.size();
    }
  }

  public boolean equals(Object object)
  { if (!(object instanceof BinaryTree)) return false;
    BinaryTree tree = (BinaryTree)object;
    return ( tree.root.equals(root)
          && tree.left.equals(left)
          && tree.right.equals(right)
          && tree.parent.equals(parent)
          && tree.size == size);
  }

  public int hashCode()
  { return root.hashCode() + left.hashCode() + right.hashCode() + size;
  }
```

```
    public Iterator iterator()
    { return new java.util.Iterator()   // anonymous inner class
      { private boolean rootDone;
        private java.util.Iterator lit, rit;   // child iterators
        public boolean hasNext()
        { return !rootDone || lit != null && lit.hasNext()
                           || rit != null && rit.hasNext();
        }
        public Object next()
        { if (rootDone)
          { if (lit != null && lit.hasNext()) return lit.next();
            if (rit != null && rit.hasNext()) return rit.next();
            return null;
          }
          if (left != null) lit = left.iterator();
          if (right != null) rit = right.iterator();
          rootDone = true;
          return root;
        }
        public void remove()
        { throw new UnsupportedOperationException();
        }
      };
    }
    public int size()
    { return size;
    }
  }
```

A BinaryTree object looks like this. It has five fields: an Object reference named root, an int field named size, and three BinaryTree references named left, right, and parent. The actual recursive definition for binary trees requires only the root, left, and right fields. The other two fields are included to simplify some of the code.

BinaryTree

The one-parameter constructor creates a singleton: i.e., a binary tree with a single node. The three-parameter constructor creates a binary tree recursively from two other binary trees, either of which may be null.

The java.util.AbstractCollection class requires the four methods that are defined here.

The equals(Object) method overrides the default version that is defined in the Object class. (See Section 3.4 on page 58.) For an Object to equal the BinaryTree object, it must be an instance of the BinaryTree class, and all of its fields must equal the corresponding five fields of the BinaryTree object.

The hashCode() method also overrides the default version that isn defined in the Object class. It simply returns an integer computed from the hash codes of its four member objects and its size field.

The iterator() method overrides the default (empty) version that is defined in the AbstractCollection class. Its job is to build an iterator object that can traverse the BinaryTree object. To do that, it creates its own anonymous inner Iterator class using the Java return new construct:

```
     return new Iterator()   // anonymous inner class
   { private boolean rootDone;
     private Iterator lit, rit;   // child iterators
     public boolean hasNext()   ...
     public Object next()   ...
     public void remove()   ..
   };
```

The body of this anonymous class is defined between the braces that immediately follow the invocation of the constructor `Iterator()`. Note that this block must be followed by a semicolon because it is actually the end of the `return` statement. The complete construct looks like a method definition; but it is not. It really is a complete class definition embedded within a `return` statement.

To return an `Iterator` object, this anonymous class must implement the `Iterator` interface. (See Section 5.5 on page 103.) This requires definitions for the three methods

```
     public boolean hasNext()   ...
     public Object next()   ...
     public void remove()   ..
```

This implementation is recursive. The `hasNext()` method invokes the `hasNext()` methods of iterators on the two subtrees, and the `next()` method invokes the `next()` methods of those two iterators, named `lit` and `rit`. The other local variable is a flag named `rootDone` that keeps track of whether the root object has been visited yet by the iterator.

The `hasNext()` method returns `true` unless all three parts of the tree have been visited: the root, the left subtree, and the right subtree. It does that by using the `lit` and `rit` iterators recursively.

The `next()` method also uses the `lit` and `rit` iterators recursively. If the root has already been visited, then the iterator visits the next node in the left subtree if there are any, and otherwise visits the next node in the right subtree if there are any. If the root has not yet been visited, then this must be the first call to the iterator on that particular subtree, so it initializes the `lit` and `rit` iterators, sets the `rootDone` flag, and returns the root.

The `remove()` method is not implemented because there is no simple way to remove an internal node from a binary tree.

EXAMPLE 10.20 Testing the `BinaryTree` Class

Here is a test driver for the `BinaryTree` class defined above:

```
   public class Ex1020
   { static public void main(String[] args)
     { BinaryTree e = new BinaryTree("E");
       BinaryTree g = new BinaryTree("G");
       BinaryTree h = new BinaryTree("H");
       BinaryTree i = new BinaryTree("I");
       BinaryTree d = new BinaryTree("D",null,g);
       BinaryTree f = new BinaryTree("F",h,i);
       BinaryTree b = new BinaryTree("B",d,e);
       BinaryTree c = new BinaryTree("C",f,null);
       BinaryTree tree = new BinaryTree("A",b,c);
       System.out.println("tree = " + tree);
     }
   }
tree = [A, B, D, G, E, C, F, H, I]
```

This program creates the binary tree drawn below and then indirectly invokes its `toString()` method that it inherits from the `AbstractCollections` class.

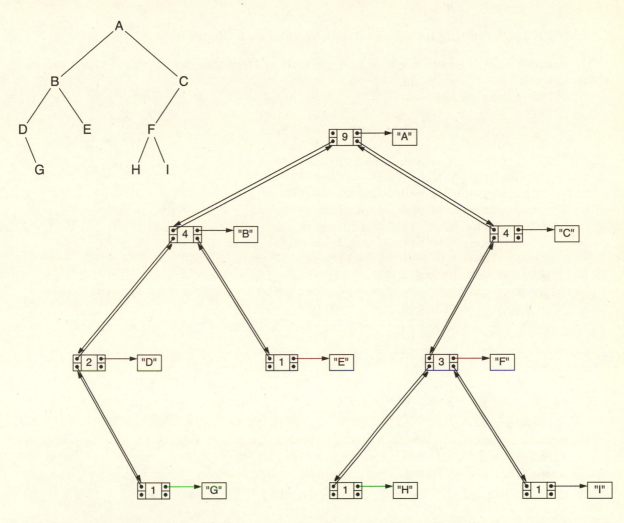

This picture shows two views of the same tree. The larger view shows all the details, representing each object reference with an arrow.

By extending the `AbstractCollection` class, the `BinaryTree` class automatically inherits the following methods that are defined by using the `iterator()` and `size()` methods:

```
public boolean          isEmpty()
public boolean          contains(Object object)
public Object[]         toArray()
public Object[]         toArray(Object[] objects)
public String           toString()
public boolean          add(Object object)
public boolean          addAll(Collection collection)
public void             clear()
public boolean          containsAll(Collection collection)
public boolean          remove(Object object)
public boolean          removeAll(Collection collection)
public boolean          retainAll(Collection collection)
```

However, the mutating methods will throw an `UnsupportedOperationException` exception because they invoke other methods that are not implemented, namely the `add()` and the `Iterator.remove()` methods.

EXAMPLE 10.21 Testing the `contains()` Method on a Binary Tree

This example builds the same tree as in Example 10.20 and then tests the `contains()` method on it and its subtrees:

```
public class Ex1020
{ static public void main(String[] args)
  { BinaryTree e = new BinaryTree("E");
    BinaryTree g = new BinaryTree("G");
    BinaryTree h = new BinaryTree("H");
    BinaryTree i = new BinaryTree("I");
    BinaryTree d = new BinaryTree("D",null,g);
    BinaryTree f = new BinaryTree("F",h,i);
    BinaryTree b = new BinaryTree("B",d,e);
    BinaryTree c = new BinaryTree("C",f,null);
    BinaryTree a = new BinaryTree("A",b,c);
    System.out.println("a = " + a);
    System.out.println("a.contains(\"H\") = " + a.contains("H"));
    System.out.println("b = " + b);
    System.out.println("b.contains(\"H\") = " + b.contains("H"));
    System.out.println("c = " + c);
    System.out.println("c.contains(\"H\") = " + c.contains("H"));
  }
}
```

```
a = [A, B, D, G, E, C, F, H, I]
a.contains("H") = true
b = [B, D, G, E]
b.contains("H") = false
c = [C, F, H, I]
c.contains("H") = true
```

The subtrees `b` and `c` are labeled on the diagram at right.

10.9 IMPLEMENTATIONS OF THE TRAVERSAL ALGORITHMS

The iterator that is returned by the `iterator()` method follows the preorder traversal algorithm (Algorithm 10.5 on page 189) to traverse the binary tree. The following modification of the `BinaryTree` class implements all four of the binary tree traversal algorithms:

```
public class BinaryTree extends java.util.AbstractCollection
{ private Object root;
  private BinaryTree left, right, parent;
  private int size;
  // Include the same code here as is in Section 10.8 on page 192

  abstract public class Iterator
  { protected boolean rootDone;
    protected Iterator lit, rit;  // child iterators
```

```
    public boolean hasNext()
    { return !rootDone || lit != null && lit.hasNext()
                       || rit != null && rit.hasNext();
    }
    abstract public Object next();
    public void remove()
    { throw new UnsupportedOperationException();
    }
}

public class PreOrder extends Iterator
{ public PreOrder()
    { if (left != null) lit = left.new PreOrder();
      if (right != null) rit = right.new PreOrder();
    }
    public Object next()
    { if (!rootDone)
      { rootDone = true;
        return root;
      }
      if (lit != null && lit.hasNext()) return lit.next();
      if (rit != null && rit.hasNext()) return rit.next();
      return null;
    }
}

public class InOrder extends Iterator
{ public InOrder()
    { if (left != null) lit = left.new InOrder();
      if (right != null) rit = right.new InOrder();
    }
    public Object next()
    { if (lit != null && lit.hasNext()) return lit.next();
      if (!rootDone)
      { rootDone = true;
        return root;
      }
      if (rit != null && rit.hasNext()) return rit.next();
      return null;
    }
}

public class PostOrder extends Iterator
{ public PostOrder()
    { if (left != null) lit = left.new PostOrder();
      if (right != null) rit = right.new PostOrder();
    }
    public Object next()
    { if (lit != null && lit.hasNext()) return lit.next();
      if (rit != null && rit.hasNext()) return rit.next();
      if (!rootDone)
      { rootDone = true;
```

```
            return root;
          }
          return null;
        }
      }

      public class LevelOrder extends Iterator
      { ArrayQueue queue = new ArrayQueue();
        public boolean hasNext()
        { return (!rootDone || !queue.isEmpty());
        }
        public Object next()
        { if (!rootDone)
          { if (left != null) queue.enqueue(left);
            if (right != null) queue.enqueue(right);
            rootDone = true;
            return root;
          }
          if (!queue.isEmpty())
          { BinaryTree tree = (BinaryTree)queue.dequeue();
            if (tree.left != null) queue.enqueue(tree.left);
            if (tree.right != null) queue.enqueue(tree.right);
            return tree.root;
          }
          return null;
        }
      }
    }
```

First we define an abstract inner class named `Iterator` , which will serve as a base class for all four of the concrete iterator classes. It declares the same three fields (`rootDone`, `rit`, and `lit`) as the anonymous iterator class defined previously. Note that, outside of the `BinaryTree` class there will be no name conflict between this `Iterator` class and the `java.util.Iterator` class because as an inner class this one must be referred to as `BinaryTree.Iterator`. (See Example 10.22.) We avoided a name conflict inside the `BinaryTree` class already by including the `java.util` package name as part of the `java.util.Iterator` class in the code previously.

The `hasNext()` and the `remove()` methods are implemented the same way in the abstract `Iterator` class as it was in the anonymous iterator class. But the `next()` method is declared `abstract` because each of the four traversal algorithms has a different implementation of it.

The `PreOrder` class defines the `lit` and `rit` iterators to be `PreOrder` iterators in its constructor to ensure that the recursive traversal follows the preorder traversal algorithm. That algorithm (Algorithm 10.3 on page 188) says to visit the root first, and then apply the same algorithm recursively to the left subtree and then to the right subtree. The three `if` statements do that:

```
    if (!rootDone)
    { rootDone = true;
      return root;
    }
    if (lit != null && lit.hasNext()) return lit.next();
    if (rit != null && rit.hasNext()) return rit.next();
```

The only differences between the `PreOrder`, `InOrder`, and `PostOrder` classes are their definitions of the recursive `rit` and `lit` iterators in the constructors and the order of those three if statements in the `next()` method. For the `InOrder` class, the order visits the root between the two recursive traversals. For the `PostOrder` class, the order visits the root after the two recursive traversals. ("Pre" means before, "in" means between, and "post" means after.)

The LevelOrder traversal class is significantly different from the other three. Instead of being recursive, it uses a queue.

EXAMPLE 10.22 Testing the Traversal Algorithms

```
public class Ex1022
{ static public void main(String[] args)
  { BinaryTree e = new BinaryTree("E");
    BinaryTree g = new BinaryTree("G");
    BinaryTree h = new BinaryTree("H");
    BinaryTree i = new BinaryTree("I");
    BinaryTree d = new BinaryTree("D",null,g);
    BinaryTree f = new BinaryTree("F",h,i);
    BinaryTree b = new BinaryTree("B",d,e);
    BinaryTree c = new BinaryTree("C",f,null);
    BinaryTree tree = new BinaryTree("A",b,c);
    System.out.println("tree = " + tree);
    BinaryTree.Iterator it;
    System.out.print("PreOrder Traversal:    ");
    for (it = tree.new PreOrder(); it.hasNext(); )
      System.out.print(it.next() + " ");
    System.out.print("\nInOrder Traversal:     ");
    for (it = tree.new InOrder(); it.hasNext(); )
      System.out.print(it.next() + " ");
    System.out.print("\nPostOrder Traversal:   ");
    for (it = tree.new PostOrder(); it.hasNext(); )
      System.out.print(it.next() + " ");
    System.out.print("\nLevelOrder Traversal: ");
    for (it = tree.new LevelOrder(); it.hasNext(); )
      System.out.print(it.next() + " ");
    System.out.println();
  }
}
tree = [A, B, D, G, E, C, F, H, I]
PreOrder Traversal:    A B D G E C F H I
InOrder Traversal:     D G B E A H F I C
PostOrder Traversal:   G D E B H I F C A
LevelOrder Traversal: A B C D E F G H I
```

10.10 FORESTS

A *forest* is a list of trees.

EXAMPLE 10.23 A Forest

Here is a forest that consists of three trees:

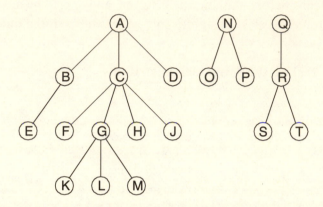

The following algorithm shows how a forest can be represented by a single binary tree.

Algorithm 10.8 The Natural Mapping of a Forest into a Binary Tree
1. Map the root of the first tree into the root of the binary tree.
2. If node X maps into X' and node Y is the first child of X, then map Y into the left child of X'.
3. If node X maps into X' and node Z is the sibling of X, then map Z into the right child of X'. The roots of the trees themselves are considered siblings.

EXAMPLE 10.24 Mapping a Forest into a Binary Tree

Here is the mapping of the forest shown in Example 10.23:

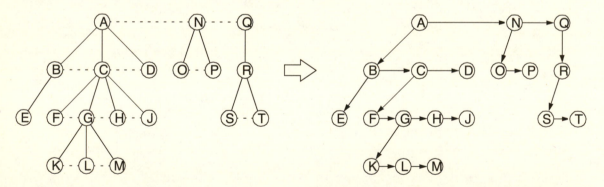

For example, in the original forest, C has oldest child F and next sibling D; so in the resulting binary tree, C has left child F and right child D.

Review Questions

10.1   How many leaf nodes does the full binary tree of height $h = 3$ have?

10.2   How many internal nodes does the full binary tree of height $h = 3$ have?

10.3   How many nodes does the full binary tree of height $h = 3$ have?

10.4   How many leaf nodes does a full binary tree of height $h = 9$ have?

10.5   How many internal nodes does a full binary tree of height $h = 9$ have?

10.6   How many nodes does a full binary tree of height $h = 9$ have?

10.7   What is the range of possible heights of a binary tree with $n = 100$ nodes?

10.8   Why is there no inorder traversal for general trees?

10.9   True or false:
   a. If all of its leaves are at the same level, then the binary tree is full.
   b. If the binary tree has n nodes and height h, then $h \geq \lfloor \lg n \rfloor$.
   c. A binary tree cannot have more than 2^d nodes at depth d.
   d. If every proper subtree of a binary tree is full, then the tree itself must also be full.

Problems

10.1   For each of these binary trees, draw the equivalent version that satisfies the second definition, namely that every internal node has two children:

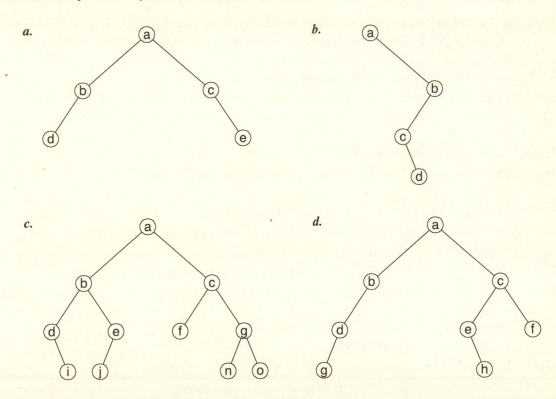

10.2   Give the order of visitation of the binary tree shown at right using
   a. the level order traversal
   b. the preorder traversal
   c. the inorder traversal
   d. the postorder traversal

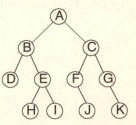

10.3   Give the order of visitation of the binary tree of size 10 shown in Example 10.1 on page 182
using
  a. the level order traversal
  b. the preorder traversal
  c. the inorder traversal
  d. the postorder traversal

10.4   Give the order of visitation of the
binary tree shown at right using
  a. the level order traversal
  b. the preorder traversal
  c. the inorder traversal
  d. the postorder traversal

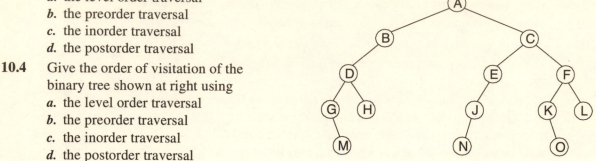

10.5   Show the array that is obtained by using the natural mapping (page 187) to store the binary
tree shown in Problem 10.1.

10.6   Show the array that is obtained by using the natural mapping to store the binary tree shown in
Example 10.1 on page 182.

10.7   Show the array that is obtained by using the natural mapping to store the binary tree shown in
Problem 10.4.

10.8   If the nodes of a binary tree are numbered according to their natural mapping, and the visit
operation prints the node's number, which traversal algorithm will print the numbers in
order?

10.9   Draw the expression tree for $a*(b + c)*(d*e + f)$.

10.10   Write the prefix and the postfix representations for the expression in Problem 10.8.

10.11   Draw the expression tree for each of the prefix expressions given in Problem 6.2 on page
117.

10.12   Draw the expression tree for each of the infix expressions given in Problem 6.4 on page 117.

10.13   Draw the expression tree for each of the postfix expressions given in Problem 6.6 on page
117.

10.14   Draw the expression tree for the expression $a*(b + c)*(d*e + f)$.

10.15   What are the bounds on the number n of nodes in a binary tree of height 4?

10.16   What are the bounds on the height h of a binary tree with 7 nodes?

10.17   What form does the highest binary tree have for a given number of nodes?

10.18   What form does the lowest binary tree (i.e., the least height) have for a given number of
nodes?

10.19   Verify the recursive definition of binary trees (page 181) for
the binary tree shown at right.

10.20   Draw all 42 binary trees of size $n = 5$.

10.21   How many different binary trees of size $n = 6$ are there?

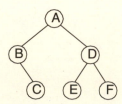

10.22   Derive a recurrence relation for the number $f(n)$ of binary trees
of size n.

10.23   Show that, for all $n \le 8$, the function $f(n)$ derived in Problem 10.22 produces the same
sequence as the following explicit formula

$$f(n) = \frac{\binom{2n}{n}}{n+1} = \frac{(2n)!}{n!(n+1)!} = \frac{(2n)(2n-1)(2n-2)\cdots(2n+3)(2n+2)}{(n)(n-1)(n-2)(n-3)\cdots(2)(1)}$$

For example,

$$f(4) = \frac{\binom{8}{4}}{5} = \frac{8!}{4!5!} = \frac{(8)(7)(6)}{(4)(3)(2)(1)} = \frac{(8)(7)}{4} = 14$$

10.24 Prove Corollary 10.3 on page 183.

10.25 Prove Theorem 10.2 on page 186.

10.26 Draw the forest that is represented by the binary tree shown on the right.

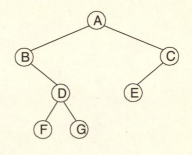

10.27 Derive an explicit formula for the number $f(h)$ of complete binary trees of height h.

10.28 Derive an explicit formula for the number $f(h)$ of full binary trees of height h.

10.29 Prove that every subtree of a full binary tree is also full.

10.30 Prove that every subtree of a complete binary tree is also complete.

Implement the each of the following methods for the `BinaryTree` class:

10.31   `public int leaves();`
     `// returns the number of leaves in this tree`

10.32   `public int height();`
     `// returns the height of this tree`

10.33   `public int level(Object object);`
     `// returns -1 if the given object is not in this tree;`
     `// otherwise, returns its level in this tree;`

10.34   `public void reflect();`
     `// swaps the children of each node in this tree`

10.35   `public void defoliate();`
     `// removes all the leaves from this tree`

Answers to Review Questions

10.1 The full binary tree of height 3 has $l = 2^3 = 8$ leaves.

10.2 The full binary tree of height 3 has $m = 2^3 - 1 = 7$ internal nodes.

10.3 The full binary tree of height 3 has $n = 2^{3+1} - 1 = 2^4 - 1 = 16 - 1 = 15$ nodes.

10.4 The full binary tree of height 9 has $l = 2^9 = 512$ leaves.

10.5 The full binary tree of height 9 has $m = 2^9 - 1 = 512 - 1 = 511$ internal nodes.

10.6 The full binary tree of height 9 has $n = 2^{9+1} - 1 = 2^{10} - 1 = 1024 - 1 = 1023$ nodes.

10.7 By Corollary 10.3, in any binary tree: $\lfloor \lg n \rfloor \le h \le n-1$. Thus in a binary tree with 100 nodes $\lfloor \lg 100 \rfloor \le h \le 100-1 = 99$. Since $\lfloor \lg 100 \rfloor = \lfloor (\log 100)/(\log 2) \rfloor = \lfloor 6.6 \rfloor = 6$, it follows that the height must be between 6 and 99, inclusive: $6 \le h \le 99$.

10.8 The inorder traversal algorithm for binary trees recursively visits the root in between traversing the left and right subtrees. This presumes the existence of exactly two (possibly empty) subtrees at every (nonempty) node. In general trees, a node may have any number of subtrees, so there is no simple algorithmic way to generalize the inorder traversal.

10.9   *a.* True
            b. True
            c. True
            d. False

Solutions to Problems

10.1   Drawing equivalent trees:

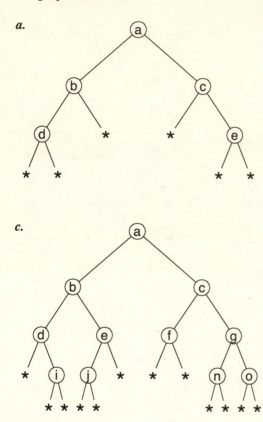

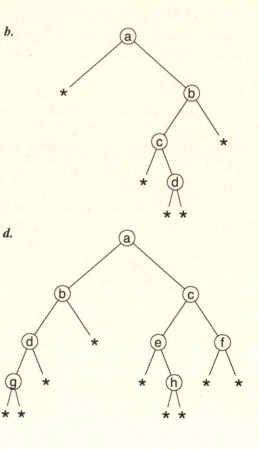

10.2   The order of visitation in the binary tree traversal:
    a. Level order: A, B, C, D, E, F, G, H, I, J, K
    b. Preorder: A, B, D, E, H, I, C, F, J, G, K
    c. Inorder: D, B, H, E, I, A, F, J, C, G, K
    d. Postorder: D, H, I, E, B, J, F, K, G, C, A

10.3   The order of visitation in the binary tree traversal:
    a. Level order traversal: A, B, C, D, E, F, H, I, J, M
    b. Preorder traversal: A, B, D, H, I, E, J, C, F, M
    c. Inorder traversal: H, D, I, B, J, E, A, F, M, C
    d. Postorder traversal: H, I, D, J, E, B, M, F, C, A

10.4   The order of visitation in the binary tree traversal:
    a. Level order traversal: A, B, C, D, E, F, G, H, J, K, L, M, N, O
    b. Preorder traversal: A, B, D, G, M, H, C, E, J, N, F, K, O, L
    c. Inorder traversal: G, M, D, H, B, A, N, J, E, C, K, O, F, L
    d. Postorder traversal: M, G, H, D, B, N, J, E, O, K, L, F, C, A

10.5   The picture below shows the natural mapping of the given binary tree.

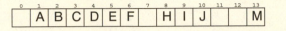

0	1	2	3	4	5	6	7	8	9	10	11	12	13	14	15
	A	B	C	D	E	F	G			H	I		J		K

10.6   The picture below shows the natural mapping of the binary tree shown in Example 10.1.

0	1	2	3	4	5	6	7	8	9	10	11	12	13
	A	B	C	D	E	F		H	I	J			M

10.7   The picture below shows the natural mapping of the given binary tree.

0	1	2	3	4	5	6	7	8	9	10	11	12	13	14	15	16	17	18	19	20	21	22	23	24	25	26	27	28	29
	A	B	C	D		E	F	G	H			J		K	L		M							N					O

10.8   The level order traversal will print the numbers from the natural mapping in order.

10.9   The expression tree for $a*(b + c)*(d*e + f)$ is:

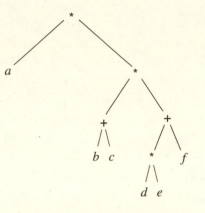

10.10   The prefix expression is $*a*+bc+*def$. The postfix expression is $*abc+de*f+**$.

10.11   The expression tree for the prefix expressions given in Problem 6.2 on page 117:

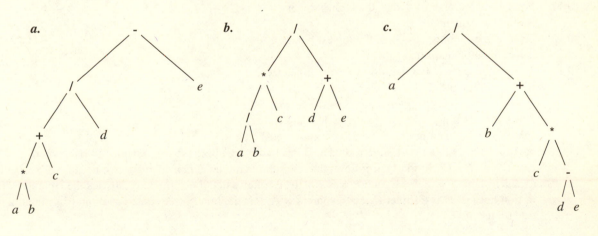

10.12   The expression tree for the prefix expressions given in Problem 6.4 on page 117:

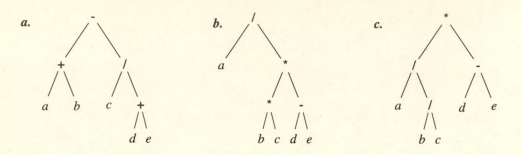

10.13   The expression tree for the prefix expressions given in Problem 6.6 on page 117:

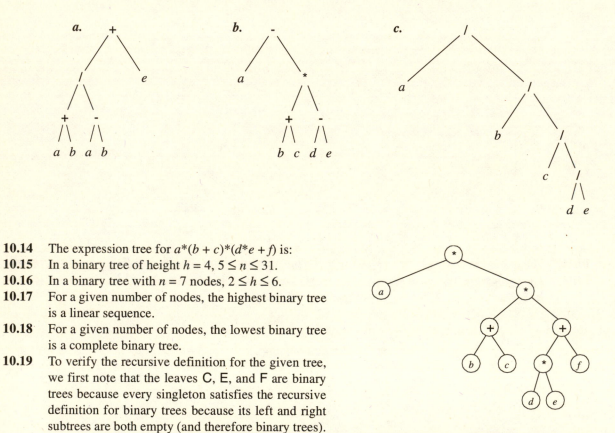

10.14   The expression tree for $a*(b + c)*(d*e + f)$ is:

10.15   In a binary tree of height $h = 4$, $5 \le n \le 31$.

10.16   In a binary tree with $n = 7$ nodes, $2 \le h \le 6$.

10.17   For a given number of nodes, the highest binary tree is a linear sequence.

10.18   For a given number of nodes, the lowest binary tree is a complete binary tree.

10.19   To verify the recursive definition for the given tree, we first note that the leaves C, E, and F are binary trees because every singleton satisfies the recursive definition for binary trees because its left and right subtrees are both empty (and therefore binary trees).

Next, it follows that the subtree rooted at B is a binary tree because it is a triplet (X,L,R) where $X =$ B, $L = \varnothing$, and $R =$ C. Similarly, it follows that the subtree rooted at D is a binary tree because it is a triplet (X,L,R) where $X =$ D, $L =$ E, and $R =$ F. Finally, it follows that the entire tree satisfies the recursive definition because it is a triplet (X,L,R) where $X =$ A, L is the binary tree rooted at B, and L is the binary tree rooted at D.

10.20   Here are the 42 different binary trees of size $n = 5$:

10.21   There are 132 different binary trees of size 6: $1 \cdot 42 + 1 \cdot 14 + 2 \cdot 5 + 5 \cdot 2 + 14 \cdot 1 + 42 \cdot 1 = 132$.

10.22   A nonempty binary tree consists of a root X, a left subtree L, and a right subtree R. Let n be the size of
the binary tree, let $n_L = |L| =$ the size of L, and $n_R = |R| =$ the size of R. Then $n = 1 + n_L + n_R$. So there
are only n different possible values for the pair (n_L, n_R): $(0, n{-}1)$, $(1, n{-}2)$, ..., $(n{-}1, 0)$. For example, if
$n = 6$ (as in Problem 10.21), the only possibilities are $(0,5)$, $(1,4)$, $(2,3)$, $(3,2)$, $(4,1)$, or $(5,0)$. In the $(0,
n{-}1)$ case, L is empty and $|R| = n{-}1$; there are $f(0) \cdot f(n{-}1)$ different binary trees in that case. In the $(1,
n{-}2)$ case, L is a singleton and $|R| = n{-}2$; there are $f(1) \cdot f(n{-}2)$ different binary trees in that case. The
same principle applies to each case. Therefore the total number of different binary trees of size n is

$$f(n) = 1 \cdot f(n{-}1) + 1 \cdot f(n{-}2) + 2 \cdot f(n{-}3) + 5 \cdot f(n{-}4) + 14 \cdot f(n{-}5) + \cdots + f(i{-}1) \cdot f(n{-}i) + \cdots + f(n{-}1) \cdot 1$$

In closed form, the formula is

$$f(n) = \sum_{i=1}^{n} f(i-1) \cdot f(n-i)$$

10.23   These are called the *Catalan numbers*:

n	$\binom{2n}{n}$	$n+1$	$\binom{2n}{n}/(n+1)$	$\sum f(i-1) \cdot f(n-i)$
0	1	1	1	1
1	2	2	1	$1 \cdot 1 = 1$
2	6	3	2	$1 \cdot 1 + 1 \cdot 1 = 2$
3	20	4	5	$1 \cdot 2 + 1 \cdot 1 + 2 \cdot 1 = 5$
4	70	5	14	$1 \cdot 5 + 1 \cdot 2 + 2 \cdot 1 + 5 \cdot 1 = 14$
5	252	6	42	$1 \cdot 14 + 1 \cdot 5 + 2 \cdot 2 + 5 \cdot 1 + 14 \cdot 1 = 42$
6	924	7	132	$1 \cdot 42 + 1 \cdot 14 + 2 \cdot 5 + 5 \cdot 2 + 14 \cdot 1 + 42 \cdot 1 = 132$
7	3432	8	429	$1 \cdot 132 + 1 \cdot 42 + 2 \cdot 14 + 5 \cdot 5 + 14 \cdot 2 + 42 \cdot 1 + 132 \cdot 1 = 429$

10.24 For a given height $h > 0$, the binary tree with the most nodes is the full binary tree. Corollary 10.2 states that that number is $n = 2^{h+1} - 1$. Therefore, in any binary tree of height h, the number n of nodes must satisfy $n \leq 2^{h+1} - 1$. The binary tree with the fewest nodes for a given height h is the one in which every internal node has only one child; that linear tree has $n = h + 1$ nodes because every node except the single leaf has exactly one child. Therefore, in any binary tree of height h, the number n of nodes must satisfy $n \geq h + 1$. The second pair of inequalities follows from the first by solving for h.

10.25 Let T be a complete tree of height h and size n. Let T_1 be the full subtree obtained by removing the bottom level of leaves from T, and let T_2 be the full supertree obtained by filling in the rest of the bottom level of leaves in T. Then T_1 has height $h - 1$ and T_2 has height h. Then, by Corollary 10.1 on page 183, $n_1 = |T_1| = 2^h - 1$ and $n_2 = |T_2| = 2^{h+1} - 1$. Now $n_1 < n \leq n_2$, so $2^h - 1 = n_1 < n \leq n_2 = 2^{h+1} - 1$, and so $2^h = n_1 + 1 \leq n \leq n_2 < n_2 + 1 = 2^{h+1}$. Thus $h \leq \lg n < h + 1$, so $h = \lfloor \lg n \rfloor$.

10.26 The forest that produced the given binary tree is obtained by reversing the natural map:

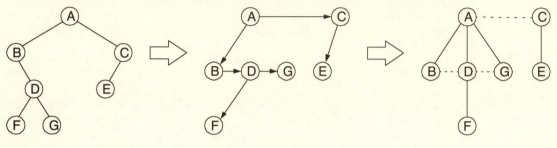

10.27 $f(h) = 1$

10.28 $f(h) = h$

10.29 **Theorem.** Every subtree of a full binary tree is also full.
Proof: Let T be a binary search tree, and let S be a subtree of T. Let x be any element in S, and let L and R be the left and right subtrees of x in S. Then, since S is a subtree of T, x is also an element of T and L and R are the left and right subtrees of x in T. Therefore, $y \leq x \leq z$ for every $y \in L$ and every $z \in R$ because T has the BST property. Therefore S too has the BST property.

10.30 **Theorem.** Every subtree of a complete binary tree is also complete.
Proof: Let T be a binary search tree, and let S be a subtree of T. Let x be any element in S, and let L and R be the left and right subtrees of x in S. Then, since S is a subtree of T, x is also an element of T and L and R are the left and right subtrees of x in T. Therefore, $y \leq x \leq z$ for every $y \in L$ and every $z \in R$ because T has the BST property. Therefore S too has the BST property.

10.31
```
public int leaves()
{ if (this == null) return 0;
  int leftLeaves = (left==null ? 0 : left.leaves());
  int rightLeaves = (right==null ? 0 : right.leaves());
  return leftLeaves + rightLeaves;
}
```

10.32
```
public int height()
{ if (this == null) return -1;
  int leftHeight = (left==null ? -1 : left.height());
  int rightHeight = (right==null ? -1 : right.height());
  return 1 + (leftHeight<rightHeight ? rightHeight : leftHeight);
}
```

10.33
```
public int level(Object object)
{ if (this == null) return -1;
  if (object == root) return 0;
  int leftLevel = (left==null ? -1 : left.level(object));
  int rightLevel = (right==null ? -1 : right.level(object));
  if (leftLevel<0 && rightLevel<0) return -1;
  return 1 + (leftLevel<rightLevel ? rightLevel : leftLevel);
}
```

10.34   ```
             public void reflect()
             { if (this == null) return;
               if (left != null) left.reflect();
               if (right != null) right.reflect();
               BinaryTree temp=left;
               left = right;
               right = temp;
             }
             ```

**10.35**    ```
             public void defoliate()
             { if (this == null) return;
               if (left == null && right == null)
               { root = null;
                 return;
               }
               if (left != null && left.left==null && left.right==null)
                 left = null;
               else left.defoliate();
               if (right != null && right.left==null && right.right==null)
                 right = null;
               else right.defoliate();
             }
             ```

Chapter 11

Search Trees

Tree structures are used to store data because their organization renders more efficient access to the data. A *search tree* is a tree that maintains its data in some sorted order.

11.1 MULTIWAY SEARCH TREES

Here is the recursive definition of a multiway search tree:

> A *multiway search tree of order m* **is either the empty set or a pair** (k, S), **where the first component is a sequence** $k = (k_1, k_2, ..., k_{n-1})$ **of** $n-1$ **keys and the second component is a sequence** $S = (S_0, S_1, S_2, ..., S_{n-1})$ **of** n **multiway search trees of order** m, **with** $2 \le n \le m$, **and** $s_0 \le k_1 \le s_1 \le ... \le k_{n-1} \le s_{n-1}$ **for each** $s_i \in S_i$.

This is similar to the recursive definition of a general tree. (See Section 9.1 on page 167.) A multiway search tree of order m can be regarded as a tree of order m in which the elements are sequences of keys with the ordering property described above.

EXAMPLE 11.1 A 5-Way Search Tree

Here is an m-way search tree with $m = 5$. It has three internal nodes of degree 5 (each containing four keys), three internal nodes of degree 4 (each containing 3 keys), four internal nodes of degree 3 (each containing two keys), and one internal node of degree 2 (containing 1 key).

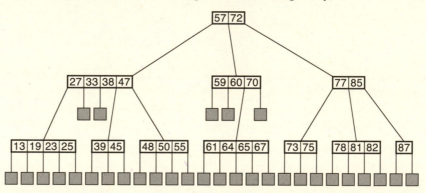

The root node has two keys and three children. All four keys in the first child are less than $k_1 = 57$. All three keys in the second child are between $k_1 = 57$ and $k_2 = 72$. Both keys in the third child are greater than $k_2 = 72$. In fact, all 13 keys in the first subtree are less than 57, all seven keys in the second subtree are between 57 and 72, and all eight keys in the third subtree are greater than 72.

An m-way search tree is called a search tree because it serves as a multilevel index for searching large lists. To search for a key value, begin at the root and proceed down the tree until the key is found or a leaf is reached. At each node, perform a binary search for the key. It it is not found in that node, the search will stop between two adjacent key values (with $k_0 = -\infty$ and $k_n = \infty$).

In that case, follow the link that is between those two keys to the next node. If we reach a leaf, then we know that the key is not in the tree.

For example, to search for key value 66, start at the root of the tree and then follow the middle link (because $57 \leq 66 < 72$) down to the middle 3-key node. Then follow its third link (because $60 \leq 66 < 70$) down to the bottom 4-key node. Then follow its third link (because $65 \leq 66 < 67$) down to that leaf node. Then conclude that the key 66 is not in the tree.

To insert a key into an *m*-way search tree, first apply the search algorithm. If the search ends at a leaf node, then the two bracketing keys of its parent node locate the correct position for the new key. So insert it in that internal node between those two bracketing keys. If that insertion gives the node *m* keys (thereby exceeding the limit of *m*–1 keys per node), then split the node into two nodes after moving its middle key up to its parent node. If that move gives the parent node *m* keys, repeat the splitting process. This process can iterate all the way back up to the root, if necessary. Splitting the root produces a new root, thereby increasing the height of the tree by one level.

EXAMPLE 11.2 Inserting into a 5-Way Tree

To insert 66 into the search tree of Example 11.1, first perform the search, as described above. This leads to the leaf node marked with an X here:

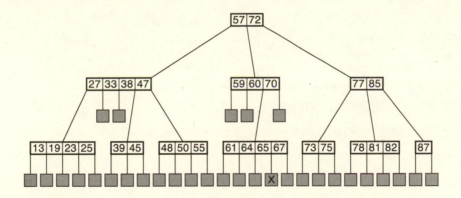

Insert the new key 66 in that last parent node between the bracketing keys 65 and 67:

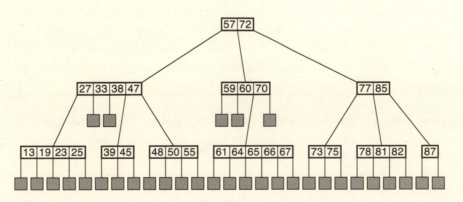

Now that node contains 5 keys, which violates the 4-key limit for a 5-way tree. So that node gets split, shifting its middle key 65 up to its parent node:

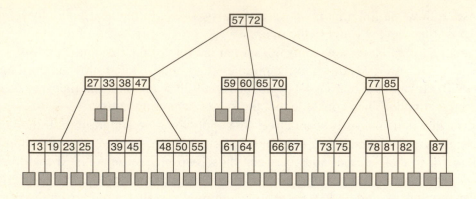

Node-splitting occurs relatively infrequently, especially if m is large. For example, if $m = 50$, then on average only 2% of the nodes would be full, so a bottom-level split would be required for only about 2% of the insertions. Furthermore, a second-from-bottom-level split (i.e., a double split) would be required for only about 2% of 2% of the insertions; i.e., with probability 0.0004. And the probability of a triple split would be 0.000008. So the chances of the root being split are very small. And since that is the only way that the tree can grow vertically, it tends to remain a very shallow, very broad tree, providing very fast search time.

11.2 B-TREES

A *B-tree of order m* is an m-way search tree that satisfies the following extra conditions:

1. The root has at least two children.

2. All other internal nodes have at least $\lceil m/2 \rceil$ children.

3. All leaf nodes are at the same level.

These conditions make the tree more balanced (and thus more efficient), and they simplify the insertion and deletion algorithms.

B-trees are used as indexes for large data sets stored on disk. In a relational database, data are organized in separate sequences of records, called tables. Each table could be stored as a sequential data file in which the records are numbered like the elements of an array. Or the database system might access the records directly by their disk addresses. Either way, each record is directly accessible on disk via some addressing scheme. So once we have the record's disk address, we can access it immediately (i.e., with a single disk read). So the "key" that is stored in the B-tree is actually a (key, address) pair containing the record's actual key value (e.g., a U.S. Social Security number for personnel records, or an ISBN for books) together with its disk address. In the outline that follows, only the key value will be shown, the accompanying disk address being understood to accompany it.

EXAMPLE 11.3 A B-Tree

Here is a B-tree of order 5 is shown at the top of the next page. Each of its internal nodes has 3, 4, or 5 children, and all the leaves are at level 3.

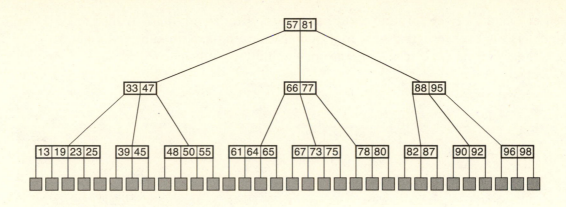

Algorithm 11.1 Searching in a B-Tree

To find a record with key k using a B-tree index of order m:

1. If the tree is empty, return `null`.
2. Let x be the root.
3. Repeat steps 4–6 until x is a leaf node.
4. Apply the Binary Search (Algorithm 2.2 on page 31) to node x for the key k_i, where $k_{i-1} < k \le k_i$ (regarding $k_0 = -\infty$ and $k_m = \infty$).
5. If $k_i = k$, retrieve the record from disk and return it.
6. Let x be the root of subtree S_i.
7. Return `null`.

Note how similar this process is to looking up a topic in the index of a book. Each page of the indes is labeled with a word or letter that represents the topics listed on that page. The page labels are analogous to the keys in the internal nodes of the search tree. The actual page number listed next to the topic in the book's index is analogous to the disk address of file name that leads you to the actual data. The last step of the search process is searching through that page in the book, or through that file on the disk. This analogy is closer if the book's index itself had an index. Each internal level of the multiway tree corresponds to another index level.

Algorithm 11.2 Inserting into a B-Tree

To insert a record with key k using a B-tree index of order m:

1. If the tree is empty, create a root node with two dummy leaves, insert k there, and return `true` (indicating that the insertion was successful).
2. Let x be the root.
3. Repeat steps 4–6 until x is a leaf node.
4. Apply the Binary Search (Algorithm 2.2 on page 31) to node x for the key k_i, where $k_{i-1} < k \le k_i$ (regarding $k_0 = -\infty$ and $k_m = \infty$).
5. If $k_i = k$, return `false` (indicating that the insertion was unsuccessful because a record with key k already exists, and keys should be unique).
6. Let x be the root of subtree S_i.
7. Add the record to disk.
8. Insert k (with the record's disk address) into x between k_{i-1} and k_i,.
9. Add a dummy leaf node to x.
10. If degree(x) = m, repeat steps 11–13 until degree(x) < m.
11. Let k_j be the middle key in node x.

12. Let u and v be the left and right halves of x after removing k_j from x.

13. If x is the root, create a new root node containing k_j with subtrees u and v.

14. Otherwise, insert k_j in x's parent node and attach subtrees u and v.

15. Return `true`.

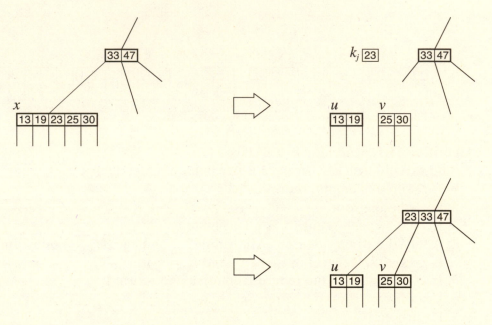

The deletion algorithm for B-trees is similar to the insertion algorithm.

All three algorithms run in time proportional to the height of the tree. From Corollary 9.1 on page 169 it follows that that height is proportional to $\log_m n$. From Theorem A.6 on page 336, it follows that that is proportional to $\lg n$. Thus we have:

Theorem 11.1 In a B-tree, searching, inserting, and deleting all run in $O(\lg n)$ time.

11.3 BINARY SEARCH TREES

A *binary search tree* is a binary tree whose elements include a *key field* of some ordinal type and which has the the following property: If k is the key value at any node, then $k \geq x$ for every key x in the node's left subtree and $k \leq y$ for every key y in the node's right subtree. This property, called the *BST property*, guarantees that an inorder traversal of the binary search tree will produce the elements in increasing order.

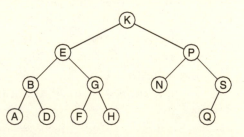

The BST property is applied for each insertion into the tree:

Algorithm 11.3 Inserting into a Binary Search Tree
To insert an element with key value k into a binary search tree:

1. If the tree is empty, insert the new element at the root. Then return.

2. Let p locate the root.

3. If k is less than the key stored at p and if the node at p has no left child, insert the

new element as the left child of p. Then return.

4. If k is less than the key stored at p and if the node at p has a left child, let p locate that left child of p. Then go back to step 3.

5. If the node at p has no right child, insert the new element as the right child of p. Then return.

6. Let p locate the right child of p. Then go back to step 3.

EXAMPLE 11.4 Inserting into a Binary Search Tree

Apply Algorithm 11.3 to insert an element with key M into the binary search tree shown on the previous page.

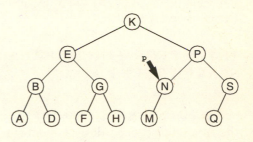

Step 1 starts the iterator p at the root K. Since M is greater than K (i.e., it follows it lexicographically) and node K has a right child, the algorithm proceeds to step 6, resetting the iterator p to node P, and then goes back to step 3. Next, since M is less than P (i.e., it precedes it lexicographically) and node P has a left child, the algorithm proceeds to step 4, resetting the iterator p to node N, and then goes back to step 3. Next, since M is also less than N but node N has no left child, the algorithm proceeds to step 5, inserts the new element as the left child of node N, and then returns.

EXAMPLE 11.5 Building a Binary Tree

The following sequence of pictures shows the binary search tree that is built by inserting the input sequence 44, 77, 55, 22, 99, 33, 88:

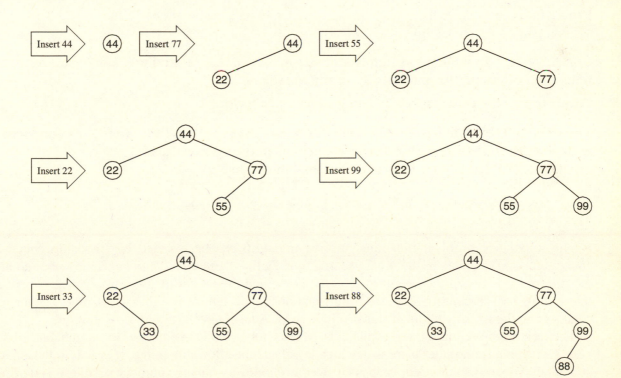

If a binary search tree is balanced, it allows for very efficient searching. As with the Binary Search, it takes $O(\lg n)$ steps to find an element in a balanced binary search tree. But without further restrictions, a binary search tree may grow to be very unbalanced. The worst case is when the elements are inserted in sorted order. In that case the tree degrades to a linear list, thereby making the search algorithm an $O(n)$ sequential search.

EXAMPLE 11.6 An Unbalanced Binary Search Tree

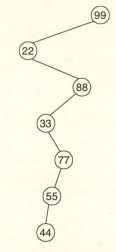

This is the same input data as in Example 11.5, but in a different order: 99, 22, 88, 33, 77, 55, 44. The resulting binary search tree is shown at right.

This shows that the same input in different order produces a different tree. But more important, it shows that it is not unlikely for the binary search tree to be linear, or nearly linear.

11.4 PERFORMANCE CHARACTERISTICS OF BINARY SEARCH TREES

Both the `insert()` and the `search()` functions begin at the root of the tree and proceed down toward the leaves, making one comparison at each level of the tree. Therefore the time required to execute either algorithm is proportional to $h + 1$, where h is the height of the tree. The `search()` function may terminate before reaching a leaf, but $h + 1$ is still an upper bound on the number of comparisons that it can make.

Theorem 11.2 In a binary search tree of size *n*, the `insert()` and the `search()` functions each require $O(\lg n)$ comparisons in the best case.

Proof: In the best case, the binary tree is completely balanced and nearly full, so by Theorem 11.3 on page 216, $h + 1 \approx \lg(n+1) = O(\lg n)$.

Corollary 11.1 In a binary search tree of size *n*, the `insert()` and the `search()` functions each require $O(n)$ comparisons in the worst case.

Proof: In the worst case the tree is linear, so $h + 1 = n = O(n)$.

Theorem 11.3 In a binary search tree of size *n*, the `insert()` and the `search()` functions each require $O(2\ln n) \approx O(1.39 \lg n)$ comparisons in the average case.

The proof of this result is beyond the scope of this outline.

11.5 AVL TREES

The imbalance problem illustrated in Example 11.6 can be avoided by imposing balance constraints on the nodes of the binary search tree. Define the *balance number* at any node to be the difference between the height of its left subtree and the height of its right subtree. An *AVL tree* is a binary search tree where the balance number at each node is either −1, 0, or 1. The name comes from the two inventors of this method: G. M. Adel'son-Velskii and Y. M. Landis.

The tree on the left at the top of the next page is not an AVL tree because it is imbalanced at node C. Its balance number there is 2, which is outside the allowable range. It is also imbalanced at node G. The tree on the right is an AVL tree because every balance number is either −1, 0 or 1.

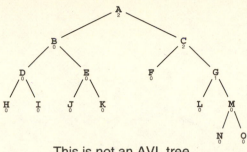

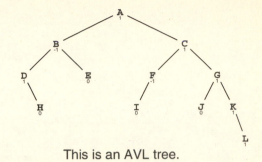

This is not an AVL tree.   This is an AVL tree.

AVL trees are closely tied to the Fibonacci numbers F_m. (See Section A.10 on page 342.)

Theorem 11.4 If an AVL tree has size n and height h, then $n \geq F_{h+2} - 1$.

Proof: Let T be an AVL tree of height h and size n. If $h = -1$ then $n = 0$ (i.e., the tree is empty) and $F_{h+2} - 1 = F_{(0)+2} - 1 = F_2 - 1 = 1 - 1 = 0 = n$. If $h = 0$ then $n = 1$ (i.e., the tree is a singleton) and $F_{h+2} - 1 = F_{(1)+2} - 1 = F_3 - 1 = 2 - 1 = 1 = n$. This establishes the basis for a recursive proof.

Now let $h > 1$ and assume (the inductive hypothesis) that the inequality is true for all AVL trees of height $< h$. Let T be an AVL tree of height h and size n. Then the balance number at the root of T must be either -1, 0, or 1. Let T_L and T_R be the left and right subtrees of T, and let h_L and h_R be their respective heights, and let n_L and n_R be their rtespective sizes. Then either $h_L = h - 1$ or $h_R = h - 1$, and both $h_L \geq h - 2$ and $h_R \geq h - 2$. So in either case, $F_{h_L} + F_{h_R} \geq F_{h-1} + F_{h-2} = F_h$. Thus, by the inductive hypothesis, $n = 1 + n_L + n_R \geq 1 + (F_{h_L + 2} - 1) + (F_{h_R + 2} - 1) \geq F_{h+2} - 1$.

Corollary 11.2 The height of an AVL tree is $O(1.44 \lg n)$.

Proof: By Corollary A.3 on page 343, $F_{h+2} = \Theta(\phi^{h+2}) = \Omega(\phi^h)$. So $n \geq F_{h+2} - 1 = \Omega(F_{h+2}) = \Omega(\phi^h)$; i.e., $n = \Omega(\phi^h)$. Thus $\phi^h = O(n)$, so $h = O(\log_\phi n) = O(1.44 \lg n)$.

Corollary 11.3 In an AVL tree, the run times for searches, insertions, and removals are not more than 44% slower than in a completely balanced tree.

11.6 An `AVLTree` CLASS

This class for AVL trees extends the `BinaryTree` class defined on Section 10.8 on page 192:

```
public class AVLTree extends BinaryTree
{ protected AVLTree left, right;
  protected int balance;
  protected java.util.Comparator comp;
  public AVLTree(java.util.Comparator comp){ this.comp = comp; }
  public AVLTree(Object root, java.util.Comparator comp)
  { this.root = root;
    this.comp = comp;
  }
  public boolean add(Object object)
  { AVLTree temp = attach(object);
    if (temp != this)
    { left = temp.left;
      right = temp.right;
      balance = temp.balance;
    }
```

```
      return true;
   }
public AVLTree attach(Object object)
{ if (root == null)  // tree is empty
   { root = object;
     return this;
   }
   if (comp.compare(object,root)<0)  // insert into left subtree
   { if (left == null)
     { left = new AVLTree(object,comp);
       ++size;
       --balance;
     }
     else
     { int lb = left.balance;
       left = left.attach(object);
       if (left.balance != lb && left.balance != 0) --balance;
     }
     if (balance < -1)
     { if (left.balance > 0) left = left.rotateLeft();
       return rotateRight();
     }
   }
   else  // insert into right subtree
   { if (right == null)
     { right = new AVLTree(object,comp);
       ++size;
       ++balance;
     }
     else
     { int rb = right.balance;
       right = right.attach(object);
       if (right.balance != rb && right.balance != 0) ++balance;
     }
     if (balance > 1)
     { if (right.balance < 0) right = right.rotateRight();
       return rotateLeft();
     }
   }
   return this;
}
private AVLTree rotateRight()  // see Problem 11.6 on page 220
private AVLTree rotateLeft()
{ AVLTree x = this, y = right, z = y.left;
   x.right = z;
   y.left = x;
   int xb = x.balance, yb = y.balance;
   if (yb < 1)
   { --x.balance;
     y.balance = ( xb>0 ? yb-1 : xb+yb-2 );
   }
   else if (yb < xb) { x.balance -= yb+1;  --y.balance; }
```

```
        else y.balance = xb-2;
        return y;
    }
}
```

EXAMPLE 11.7 Building an AVL Tree

Here are the insertions of G, M, T, D, and P into an empty AVL tree:

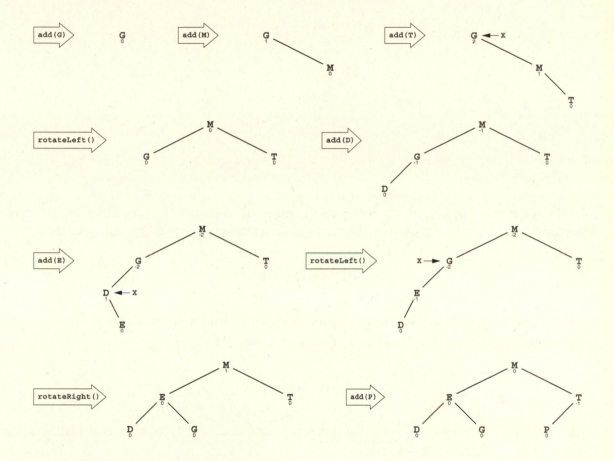

The first rotation occurs with the insertion of T. That increases the balance at the root to be 2 which violates the AVL constraint. The left rotation about the root x makes M become the parent of its prioir parent G.

The next rotation occurs after E in inserted. The right rotation at its parent D straightens out the dog leg G — D — E but leaves the balance at G at –2. That requires a second rotation in the opposite direction. Double rotations like this are required when the imbalance is at the top of a dog leg.

Note how efficient the rotations are. By making only local changes to references and balance numbers they restore the tree to nearly perfect balance.

EXAMPLE 11.8 Building an AVL Tree

The diagram at the top of the next page shows a later insertion into the same AVL tree, inserting W after U, V, and Z have been inserted.

This illustrates a double rotation where a nontrivial subtree gets shifted. The subtree containing U is shifted from parent V to parent T. Note that the BST property is maintained.

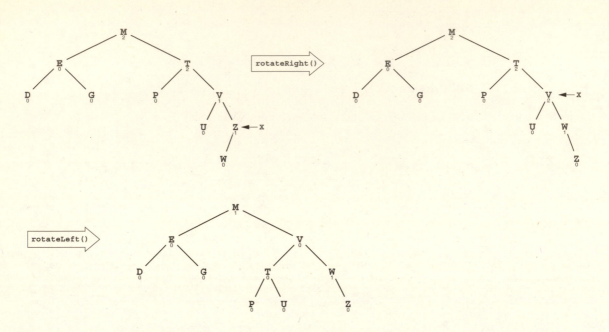

Although a bit complicated, the insertion algorithm for AVL trees is very efficient. The rotations that keep it balanced make only local canges to a few references and balance numbers.

Review Questions

11.1   What are the advantages and disadvantages of using a Binary Search tree?

11.2   What are the advantages and disadvantages of using an AVL tree?

Problems

11.1   Describe what happens in the 5-way tree shown in Example 11.1 on page 210 when a new record with key 16 is inserted.

11.2   Find two other orderings of the seven keys in Example 11.5 on page 215 that will produce the same binary search tree.

11.3   Describe a method for sorting arrays of objects using a binary search tree. Then determine the complexity of the algorithm.

11.4   Determine which of the binary trees shown at the top of the next page is a binary search tree.

11.5   Verify the following fact used in Corollary 11.2 on page 217:
$$\log_{\phi} n = 1.44 \lg n$$

11.6   Write the `rotateRight()` method for the `AVLTree` class.

11.7   Prove that every subtree of a binary search tree is also a binary search tree.

11.8   Prove that every subtree of an AVL tree is also an AVL tree.

11.9   Here are the U.S. Postal abbreviations of the first 10 states, in the order that they ratified the U.S. Constitution: DE, PA, NJ, GA, CT, MA, MD, SC, NH, VA. Show the AVL tree after the insertion of each of these strings.

a.
b.

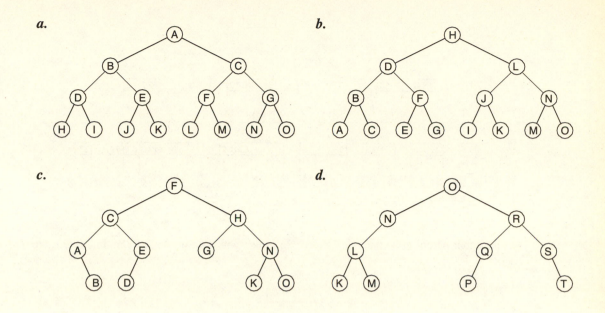

c.
d.

Answers to Review Questions

11.1   The disadvantage of a binary search tree is that it may become very unbalanced, in which case search-
         ing degenerates into an $O(n)$ algorithm. The advantage is the efficiency that a binary tree enjoys for
         insertions and deletions.

11.2   The advantage of an AVL tree is that it is always balanced, guaranteeing the $O(\lg n)$ speed of the
         Binary Search algorithm. The disadvantages the complex rotations used by the insertion and removal
         algorithms needed to maintain the tree's balance.

Solutions to Problems

11.1   To insert a new record with key 16 into the tree, the initial search would lead to the first leaf node:

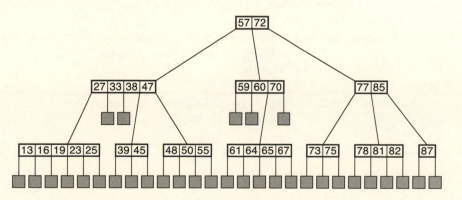

Since this is a 5-way search tree, that first leave node has overflowed, causing it to be split into two
leaf nodes and moving its middle key 19 up to its parent node:

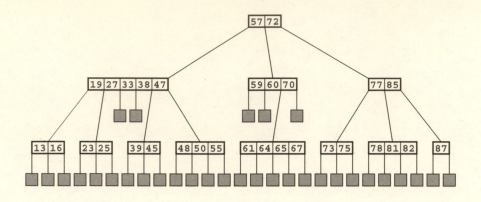

But now that parent node has overflowed. So it also gets split, moving its middle key up to its parent node:

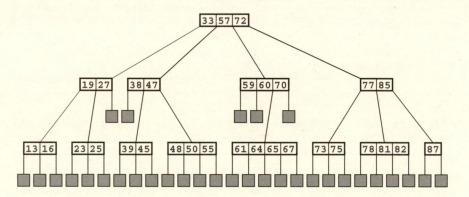

11.2   Two other ordering of the seven keys in Example 11.5 on page 215 that will produce the same BST:
 a. 44, 22, 33, 77, 55, 99, 88
 b. 44, 22, 77, 33, 55, 99, 88

11.3   An array of objects could be sorted by inserting their objects into a binary search tree and then using an inorder traversal to copy them back into the array. The BST property guarantees that the inorder traversal will visit the elements in order.

   If an AVL tree is used, then each insertion runs in $O(\lg n)$ time, so building the tree with n elements will require $O(n \lg n)$ time. The subsequent inorder traversal also has $O(n \lg n)$ complexity, so the entire algorithm sorts the array in $O(n \lg n)$ time.

11.4   All except *a* are binary search trees.

11.5 $\log_{\phi} n = (\log_{\phi} 2)(\lg n) = (\ln 2 \,/\, \ln \phi)(\lg n) = (0.693148/0.481212)(\lg n) = (1.4404)(\lg n) = 1.44 \lg n.$

11.6
```
private AVLTree rotateRight()
  { AVLTree x = this;
    AVLTree y = left;
    AVLTree z = y.left;
    x.left = z;
    y.left = x;
    int xb = x.balance;
    int yb = y.balance;
```

```
        if (yb > 1)
        { ++x.balance;
          y.balance = ( xb<0 ? yb+1 : xb+yb+2 );
        }
        else if (yb > xb)
        { x.balance += yb-1;
          ++y.balance;
        }
        else y.balance = xb+2;
        return y;
      }
```

11.7 **Theorem.** Every subtree of a binary search tree is a binary search tree.

Proof: Let T be a binary search tree, and let S be a subtree of T. Let x be any element in S, and let L and R be the left and right subtrees of x in S. Then, since S is a subtree of T, x is also an element of T, and L and R are the left and right subtrees of x in T. Therefore, $y \leq x \leq z$ for every $y \in L$ and every $z \in R$ because T has the BST property. Therefore S also has the BST property.

11.8 **Theorem.** Every subtree of an AVL tree is an AVL tree.

Proof: The proof that every subtree of a binary search tree is a binary search tree is given in Problem 11.7. If a S is a subtree of an AVL tree T, then every node is S is also in T. Therefore, the balance number at every node in S is –1, 0, or 1.

11.9 The solution is shown in the diagrams on this page and the next page.

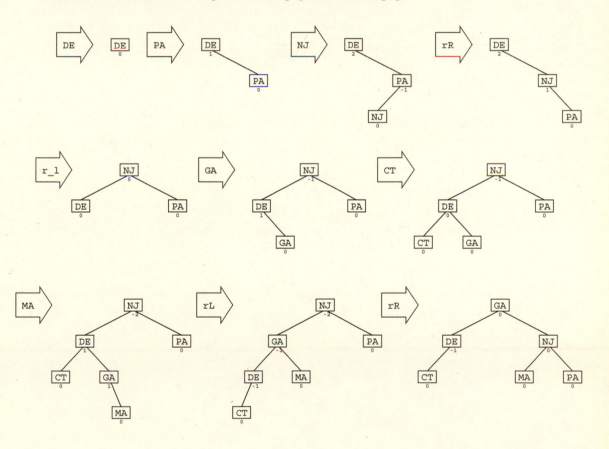

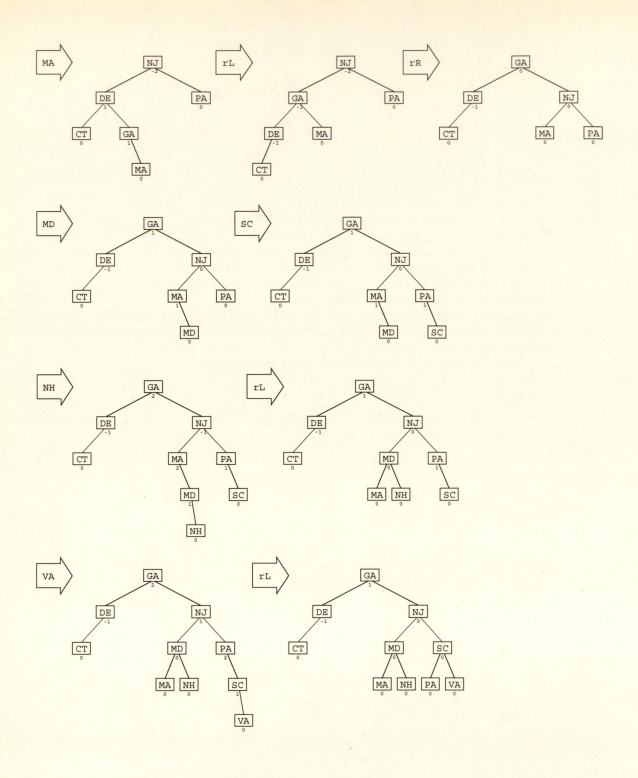

Chapter 12

Heaps and Priority Queues

12.1 HEAPS

A *heap* is a complete binary tree whose elements have keys that satisfy the following *heap property*: the keys along any path from root to leaf are nonincreasing. For example, the tree shown here is a heap because it is a complete binary tree and the elements along each of its root-to-leaf paths are nonincreasing:

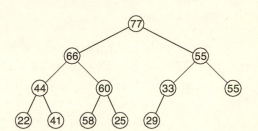

$$77 \geq 66 \geq 44 \geq 22;$$
$$77 \geq 66 \geq 44 \geq 41;$$
$$77 \geq 66 \geq 60 \geq 58;$$
$$77 \geq 66 \geq 60 \geq 25;$$
$$77 \geq 55 \geq 33 \geq 29;$$
$$77 \geq 55 \geq 55.$$

Note that heaps could represent family descendant trees because the heap property means that every parent is older than its children.

Heaps are used to implement priority queues (Section 12.7) and the Heap Sort algorithm (Section 13.8 on page 254).

12.2 THE NATURAL MAPPING

Every complete binary tree has a natural mapping into an array. (See Algorithm 10.1 on page 187.) For example, the heap shown above maps into the array

0	1	2	3	4	5	6	7	8	9	10	11	12
	77	66	55	44	60	33	55	22	41	58	25	29

shown here. The natural mapping is obtained from a level-order traversal of the tree. In the resulting array, the parent of the element at index i is at index $i/2$ and the children of that element are at indexes $2i$ and $2i+1$. For example, element 60 is at index $i = 5$, its parent is element 66 at index $i/2 = 2$, and its children are elements 58 and 25 at indexes $2i = 10$ and $2i + 1 = 11$.

The natural mapping between a complete binary tree and an array is a two-way correspondence. To map the array elements back into a complete binary tree, simply number the tree nodes consecutively in a level-order traversal beginning with number 1 at the root. Then copy the array element at index i into the tree node numbered i. If the resulting tree has the heap property, then we also say that the array has the *heap property*.

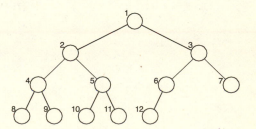

EXAMPLE 12.1 Determining Whether an Array has the Heap Property

To determine whether this array has the heap property, we first map it into a binary tree, then check each root-to-leaf path.

The path { 88, 66, 44, 51 } is *not* nonincreasing because 44 < 51. Hence, the tree does not have the heap property. Therefore, the array does not have the heap property.

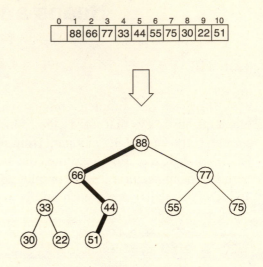

An array with the heap property is *partially ordered*. That means that most of the larger keys come before most of the smaller keys. More precisely, it means that every heap-path subarray is sorted in nonincreasing order, where a *heap-path subarray* is a subsequence of array elements in which each index number is half that of its successor. For example, { a[1], a[2], a[5], a[11], a[22], a[45], a[90], a[180] } would be a heap-path subarray of an array a[] of 200 elements. The Heap Sort algorithm (Algorithm 13.8 on page 255) exploits this fact to obtain a fast and efficient method for sorting arrays.

12.3 INSERTION INTO A HEAP

Elements are inserted into a heap next to its right-most leaf at the bottom level. Then the heap property is restored by percolating the new element up the tree until it is no longer "older" (i.e., its key is greater) than its parent. On each iteration, the child is swapped with its parent.

EXAMPLE 12.2 Inserting into a Heap

Here is how the key 75 would be inserted into the heap shown above:

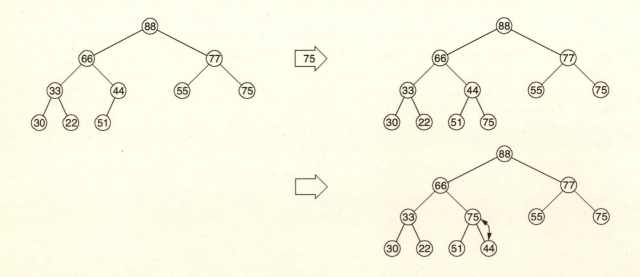

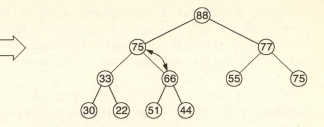

The element **75** is added to the tree as a new last leaf. Then it is swapped with its parent element **44** because 75 > 44. Then it is swapped with its parent element **66** because 75 > 66. Now the heap property has been restored because the new element **75** is less than its parent and greater than its children.

Note that the insertion affects only the nodes along a single root-to-leaf path.

12.4 REMOVAL FROM A HEAP

The heap removal algorithm always removes the root element from the tree. This is done by moving the last leaf element into the root element and then restoring the heap property by percolating the new root element down the tree until it is no longer "younger" (i.e., its key is less) than its children. On each iteration, the parent is swapped with the older of its two children.

EXAMPLE 12.3 Removing from a Heap

Here is how the root element (key **88**) would be removed from a heap:

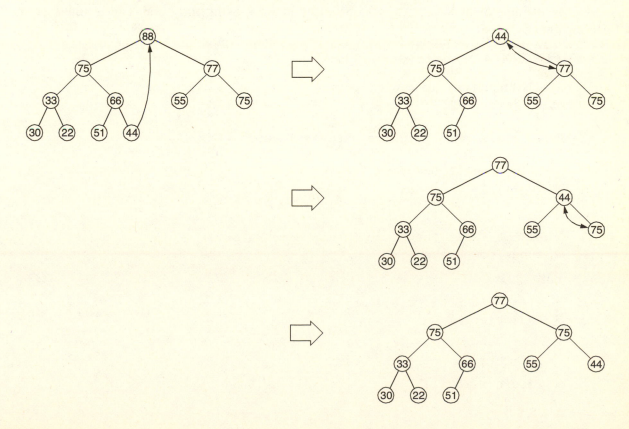

The last leaf (key 44) is removed and copied into the root, replacing the previous root (key 88), which is removed. Then, to restore the heap property, the element 44 is swapped with the larger of its two children (77). That step is repeated until the element 44 is no longer smaller than any of its children. In this case, the result is that 44 ends up as a leaf again.

Note that the removal affects only the nodes along a single root-to-leaf path. That gives us the following result from Theorem 10.2 on page 186:

Theorem 12.1 Insertions into and removals from a heap run in $O(\lg n)$ time.

12.5 A `PriorityQueue` CLASS

A *stack* is a LIFO container: the last one in comes out first. A *queue* is a "FIFO container: the first one in comes out first. A *priority queue* is a "BIFO container: the best one in comes out first. That means that each element is assigned a priority number, and the element with the highest priority comes out first.

Priority queues are widely used in computer systems. For example, if a printer is shared by several computers on a local area network, the print jobs that are queued to it would normally be held temporarily in a priority queue wherein smaller jobs are given higher priority over larger jobs.

Priority queues are usually implemented as heaps since the heap data structure always keeps the element with the largest key at the root and its insertion and removal operations are so efficient. (See Section 12.7 on page 231.) However, the Java Collections Framework provides another tree structure that is nearly as efficient: the `java.util.TreeSet` class. This makes it real easy to implement a `PriorityQueue` class in Java, using the `Comparator` interface as outlined next.

EXAMPLE 12.4 A `PriorityQueue` Class

Here is a class for priority queues of `Objects`:

```
import java.util.*;

public class PriorityQueue extends TreeSet
{
  public PriorityQueue()
  { super();
  }

  public PriorityQueue(Comparator comparator)
  { super(comparator);
  }

  public void push(Object object)
  { add(object);
  }

  public Object top()
  { return first();
  }
```

```
    public Object pop()
    { Object object = first();
      remove(object);
      return object;
    }
  }
```

This subclass exploits the functionality of the `TreeSet` class for efficient $O(\lg n)$ insertions and removals.

12.6 THE JAVA `Comparator` INTERFACE

A priority queue must be able to compare its elements according to their assigned priorities. This is done in the Java Collections Framework by means of a `Comparator` object.

EXAMPLE 12.5 A `Person` Class with Its Own `Comparator` Classes

Here is a `Person` class for representing people with known year of birth (`yob`) and year of death (`yod`). Its `toString()` method prints the person's entry in the format:

```
    Pascal(1623-1662)
```

The class has two constructors in case the person's year of death is not known (or has not yet occurred).

```
    public class Person
    { private String name;
      private int yob, yod;

      public Person(String name, int yob)
      { this.name = name;
        this.yob = yob;
      }

      public Person(String name, int yob, int yod)
      { this(name,yob);
        this.yod = yod;
      }

      public int getYob()
      { return yob;
      }

      public int getYod()
      { return yod;
      }

      public String toString()
      { return name + "(" + yob
                + (yod>0?"-"+yod:"") + ")";
      }
    }
```

Here is a `Comparator` class for the `Person` class. It compares instances of the `Person` class according to the person's year of birth.

```
class YobComparator implements java.util.Comparator
{ public int compare(Object o1, Object o2)
  { if (o1==null || !(o1 instanceof schaums.dswj.Person)) return -1;
    Person p1 = (Person)o1;
    if (o2==null || !(o2 instanceof Person)) return  1;
    Person p2 = (Person)o2;
    if (p1.getYob() < p2.getYob()) return -1;
    if (p1.getYob() > p2.getYob()) return  1;
    return 0;
  }
}
```

An instance of this class returns −1 if the first person's year of birth is earlier than the second person's, 1 if it is later, and 0 if it is the same year. This is the protocol that clients who use `Comparator` classes expect. Negative means "less than," 0 means "equal to," and positive means "greater than."

Note that the `Comparator` interface requires the signature to be

```
public int compare(Object o1, Object o2)
```

So any implementation should check the intrinsic class to which each argument belongs. That is handled by the `instanceof` operator. Also, the arguments have to be cast as `Person` objects here to access their `yob` fields.

EXAMPLE 12.6 Testing the `PriorityQueue` Class with a Comparator

```
public class Ex1206
{ static public void main(String[] args)
  { PriorityQueue yobQueue = new PriorityQueue(new YobComparator());
    yobQueue.push(new Person("Barrow",1630));
    yobQueue.push(new Person("Fermat",1601));
    yobQueue.push(new Person("Pascal",1623));
    yobQueue.push(new Person("Wallis",1616));
    System.out.println(yobQueue);
    while (!(yobQueue.isEmpty()))
      System.out.println("pop()=" + yobQueue.pop() + ": " + yobQueue);
  }
}
```
```
[Fermat(1601), Wallis(1616), Pascal(1623), Barrow(1630)]
pop()=Fermat(1601): [Wallis(1616), Pascal(1623), Barrow(1630)]
pop()=Wallis(1616): [Pascal(1623), Barrow(1630)]
pop()=Pascal(1623): [Barrow(1630)]
pop()=Barrow(1630): []
```

The program instantiates the `PriorityQueue` object `yobQueue`, binding a `YobComparator` to it. The `TreeSet` constructor that takes a `Comparator` argument handles the binding. Then it uses the `add()` method implemented by the `TreeSet` class to add four `Person` objects to the priority queue.

Next, it tests the `pop()` method repeatedly until the queue is empty. On each iteration it prints the entire contents of the priority queue, using the inherited `TreeSet.toString()` method which invokes the `Person.toString()` method.

The same `PriorityQueue` class can be used with different comparators simply by passing a different comparator object to its constructor.

EXAMPLE 12.7 Testing the `PriorityQueue` Class with a Different Comparator

```
public class Ex1207
{ static public void main(String[] args)
  { PriorityQueue yodQueue = new PriorityQueue(new YodComparator());
    yodQueue.add(new Person("Barrow",1630,1677));
    yodQueue.add(new Person("Fermat",1601,1665));
    yodQueue.add(new Person("Pascal",1623,1662));
    yodQueue.add(new Person("Wallis",1616,1703));
    System.out.println(yodQueue);
  }
}
class YodComparator implements java.util.Comparator
{ public int compare(Object o1, Object o2)
  { if (o1==null || !(o1 instanceof Person)) return -1;
    Person p1 = (Person)o1;
    if (o2==null || !(o2 instanceof Person)) return  1;
    Person p2 = (Person)o2;
    if (p1.yod<p2.yod) return -1;
    if (p1.yod>p2.yod) return  1;
    return 0;
  }
[Pascal(1623-1662), Fermat(1601-1665), Barrow(1630-1677), Wallis(1616-
1703)]
```

The `PriorityQueue` object class uses the methods of the `TreeSet` class to maintain the elements in a balances binary search tree. The `TreeSet.toString()` that it inherits returns a string representation of the elements in increasing order as determined by the comparator bound to it. The comparator used in Example 12.6 uses the `yob` field, so `Wallis(1616)` comes before `Pascal(1623)`. The comparator used in Example 12.7 uses the `yod` field, so `Wallis(1616-1703)` comes after `Pascal(1623-1662)`.

12.7 A DIRECT IMPLEMENTATION

The `PriorityQueue` class implementation in Section 12.5 on page 228 uses the Java Collections Framework, so instances of that class must store objects. Here is an implementation for primitive types:

EXAMPLE 12.8 An `IntPriorityQueueInterface` Interface

This requires five methods to implement a priority queue for integers:

```
public interface IntPriorityQueueInterface
{ public int top();
  public int pop();
  public void push(int x);
  public int size();
  public String toString();
}
```

EXAMPLE 12.9 An `IntPriorityQueue` Class

This class uses a heap to implement the interface defined in Example 12.8:

```java
public class IntPriorityQueue implements IntPriorityQueueInterface
{ private final int CAPACITY=16;
  private int capacity, size;
  private int[] ints;

  public IntPriorityQueue()
  { capacity = CAPACITY;
    ints = new int[capacity+1];
  }

  public IntPriorityQueue(int capacity)
  { this.capacity = capacity;
    ints = new int[capacity+1];
  }

  public int top()
  { return ints[1];
  }

  public int pop()
  { int x = ints[1];
    ints[1] = ints[size--];
    heapifyDown();
    return x;
  }

  public void push(int x)
  { if (size==capacity) resize();
    ints[++size] = x;
    heapifyUp();
  }

  public int size()
  { return size;
  }

  public String toString()
  { if (size==0) return "[]";
    String string = "[" + ints[1];
    for (int i=2; i<=size; i++)
      string += "," + ints[i];
    return string + "]";
  }

  private void heapifyUp()
  { for (int j=size, i; j>0; j = i)
    { i = j/2;
      if (ints[j]<ints[i]) swap(ints,i,j);
    }
  }
```

```
    private void heapifyDown()
    { for (int i=1, j; i<=size/2; i = j)
      { j = 2*i;
        if (j<size && ints[j]>ints[j+1]) ++j;
        if (ints[j]<ints[i]) swap(ints,i,j);
      }
    }

    private void resize()
    { int[] temp = new int[capacity+1];
      for (int i=1; i<=capacity; i++)
        temp[i] = ints[i];
      capacity *= 2;
      ints = new int[capacity+1];
      for (int i=1; i<=size; i++)
        ints[i] = temp[i];
    }

    private void swap(int[] a, int i, int j)
    { int tmp=a[i];
      a[i] = a[j];
      a[j] = tmp;
    }
  }
```

This implementation uses an array to store the priority queue as a heap. The the `size` field stores the number of elements in the priority queue. They are stored in `ints[1..size]`; i.e., the implementation uses 1-based indexing (instead of 0-based indexing) to simplify the heap operations. This is the natural mapping. (See Algorithm 10.1 on page 187 and Section 12.2 on page 225.)

To allow for efficient growth, this implementation uses *capacity doubling protocol*. That is, it uses a separate field, named `capacity`, to determine the actual size of the `ints[]` array. Since we're using 1-based indexing, that actual size will always be `capacity+1`. The `capacity` field is initialized with the constant `CAPACITY`, which in this example is chosen to be 16 but could be any positive integer. So the `ints[]` array starts out at actual size 17. This accommodates up to 16 elements in the priority queue. If `push()` is called when `size == capacity`, the `private resize()` method is called to double the `capacity` of the heap.

The implementation of `push()` follows the algorithm outlined in Section 12.3 on page 226 and the implementation of `pop()` follows the algorithm outlined in Section 12.4. These use the `private heapifyUp()` and `heapifyDown()` methods, respectively.

EXAMPLE 12.10 Testing the `IntPriorityQueue` Class

This program tests the `IntPriorityQueue` class implemented in Example 12.9:

```
public class Ex1210
{ public static void main(String[] args)
  { IntPriorityQueue queue = new IntPriorityQueue();
    queue.push(50);
    queue.push(95);
    queue.push(70);
    queue.push(30);
    queue.push(90);
    queue.push(25);
    queue.push(55);
```

```
        queue.push(35);
        queue.push(80);
        queue.push(60);
        queue.push(40);
        queue.push(20);
        queue.push(10);
        queue.push(75);
        queue.push(45);
        queue.push(65);
        System.out.println(queue.size() + ": " + queue);
        queue.push(85);
        System.out.println(queue.size() + ": " + queue);
        queue.pop();
        System.out.println(queue.size() + ": " + queue);
        while(queue.size()>0)
           System.out.println("queue.pop() = " + queue.pop());
        System.out.println(queue.size() + ": " + queue);
     }
   }
```

```
16:  [10,35,20,50,40,25,45,65,80,90,60,70,30,75,55,95]
17:  [10,35,20,50,40,25,45,65,80,90,60,70,30,75,55,95,85]
16:  [20,35,25,50,40,30,45,65,80,90,60,70,85,75,55,95]
queue.pop() = 20
queue.pop() = 25
queue.pop() = 30
queue.pop() = 35
queue.pop() = 40
queue.pop() = 45
queue.pop() = 50
queue.pop() = 55
queue.pop() = 60
queue.pop() = 65
queue.pop() = 70
queue.pop() = 75
queue.pop() = 80
queue.pop() = 85
queue.pop() = 90
queue.pop() = 95
0: []
```

After instantiating `queue` as an `IntPriorityQueue` object, this program calls its `push()` method to insert 17 elements into the priority queue. The `println()` method invokes the `IntPriority-Queue`'s `toString()` method to print the elements in the order in which they are stored in the `ints[]` array. For example, the first line of output

```
16:  [10,35,20,50,40,25,45,65,80,90,60,70,30,75,55,95]
```

reports that the queue has 16 elements and then prints `ints[1..16]`. From this output, the heap property can be checked. For example, the root-to-leaf path `ints[1,2,4,8,16]` is the nondecreasing sequence `[10,35,50,65,95]`, and the root-to-leaf path `ints[1,3,6,13]` is the nondecreasing sequence `[10,20,25,70]`. (See Problem 12.7 on page 236 for a complete trace.)

The second line of output shows that the `private resize()` method is working correctly. The last call to the `push()` method

```
        queue.push(85);
```

attempts an insertion when the `ints[]` array is full (`size == capacity`). So `push()` calls `resize()` to double the capacity of the `ints[]` array before doing the insertion.

The next operation calls `pop()` to remove one element from the priority queue. It removes the element that has the highest priority (the smallest integer), which is the element 10. Since the priority queue is implemented as a heap, this smallest element is at the root of the heap, which is at index 1 in the `ints[]` array. The removal algorithm (see Section 12.4 on page 227) moves the last element into the root and then performs the `heapifyDown()` operation to restore the heap property. This pushes the element 85 back down the heap transforming the root-to-leaf path `ints[1,3,6,13]` from `[85,20,25,30]` into `[20,25,30,85]`.

Finally, a `while` loop is used to remove all the other elements from the priority queue, calling `pop()` 16 times. Note that the elements are popped in increasing order: 20, 25, 30, 35, ..., 95.

The output from Example 12.10 suggests an efficient way to sort a sequence: push the data onto a priority queue and then pop them out. If the priority queue is implemented with a heap, then each call to `pop()` runs in $O(\lg n)$ time. So popping all n elements will run in $O(n \lg n)$ time. The n insertions run in $O(n)$ time, so the entire sorting process runs in $O(n \lg n)$ time. This algorithm is called the Heap Sort. (See Section 13.8 on page 254.)

Review Questions

12.1 What are the two main applications of heaps?

12.2 How efficient are insertions into and removals from a heap?

12.3 Why is a priority queue called a BIFO container?

12.4 What is the difference between a queue and a priority queue?

12.5 Why are heaps used to implement priority queues?

12.6 In the natural mapping of a binary tree into an array `a[]`, why do we start at `a[1]` instead of `a[0]`?

12.7 The implementation of the `IntPriorityQueue` class rebuilds the storage array, doubling its capacity, when `push()` is invoked and the array is full. Would it make sense then also to rebuild the array, halving its capacity, when `pop()` is invoked and the array is only half full?

Problems

12.1 Determine which of the following binary trees is a heap.

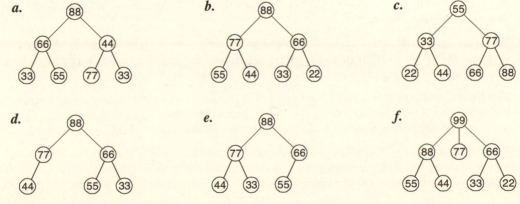

12.2 Determine which of the following arrays have the heap property.

a.

0	1	2	3	4	5	6	7
	88	66	44	33	55	77	33

b.

0	1	2	3	4	5	6	7
	88	77	66	55	44	33	22

c.

0	1	2	3	4	5	6	7
	88	44	77	22	33	55	66

d.

0	1	2	3	4	5	6	7
	88	77	55	44		33	22

e.

0	1	2	3	4	5	6	7
	88	66	77	22	33	44	55

f.

0	1	2	3	4	5	6	7
	88	77	22	33	44	55	66

12.3 Show the heap after inserting each of these keys in this order: 44, 66, 33, 88, 77, 55, 22.

12.4 Show the array obtained from the natural map of each of the heaps obtained in Problem 12.3.

12.5 Prove that every subtree of a heap is a heap.

12.6 Add and test the following method to the `IntPriorityQueue` class in Example 12.9 on page 232:

```
public boolean isHeap()

// returns true if and only if ints[] satisfies the heap property
```

12.7 Trace through the execution of the program in Example 12.10 on page 233, showing the heap both as a binary tree and as an array, after each change.

12.8 Revise the client/server simulation in Example 7.7 on page 130 using a priority queue instead of an ordinary queue. Define a `Comparator` class for the `Client` class so that shorter print jobs will have higher priority.

Answers to Review Questions

12.1 Heaps are used to implement priority queues and to implement the Heap Sort (see Algorithm 13.8 on page 255).

12.2 Insertions into and removals from a heap are very efficient; they run in $O(\lg n)$.

12.3 A priority queue is a "best-in-first-out" container; i.e., the element with the highest priority comes out first.

12.4 Elements are removed from a queue in the same order in which they are inserted: first-in-first-out. Elements in a priority queue must have an ordinal key field which determines the priority order in which they are to be removed.

12.5 Heaps are used to implement priority queues because they allow $O(\lg n)$ insertions and removals. This is because both the `push()` and the `pop()` functions are implemented by traversing a root-to-leaf path through the heap. Such paths are no longer than the height of the tree which is at most $\lg n$.

12.6 The natural mapping starts at `a[1]` instead of `a[0]` to facilitate navigation up and down the heap (tree). By numbering the root 1 and continuing sequentially with a level order traversal, the number of the parent of any node numbered k will be $k/2$, and the numbers of its child nodes will be $2k$ and $2k+1$.

12.7 Rebuilding the `IntPriorityQueue`'s array when `push()` is invoked and the array is full is necessary. Halving its capacity, when `pop()` is invoked and the array is only half full is not necessary. It could save some storage, but the savings is not worth the consequent extra runtime and complexity.

Solutions to Problems

12.1   Which binary trees are heaps:

    a. This is not a heap because the root-to-leaf path { 88, 44, 77 } is not nonincreasing (44 < 77).

    b. This is a heap.

    c. This is not a heap because the root-to-leaf path { 55, 33, 44 } is not nonincreasing (33 < 44) and the root-to-leaf path { 55, 77, 88 } is not nonincreasing (55 < 77 < 88).

    d. This is not a heap because the binary tree is not complete.

    e. This is a heap.

    f. This is not a heap because the tree is not binary.

12.2   Which arrays have the heap property:

    a. This array does not have the heap property because the root-to-leaf path { a[1], a[3], a[6] } = { 88, 44, 77 } is not nonincreasing (44 < 77).

    b. This array does have the heap property.

    c. This array does have the heap property.

    d. This array does not have the heap property because its data elements are not contiguous: it does not represent a complete binary tree.

    e. This array does have the heap property.

    f. This array does not have the heap property because the root-to-leaf path { a[1], a[3], a[6] } = { 88, 22, 55 } is not nonincreasing (22 < 55) and the root-to-leaf path { a[1], a[3], a[7] } = { 88, 22, 66 } is not nonincreasing (22 < 66).

12.3   Inserting the keys 44, 66, 33, 88, 77, 55, 22 into a heap:

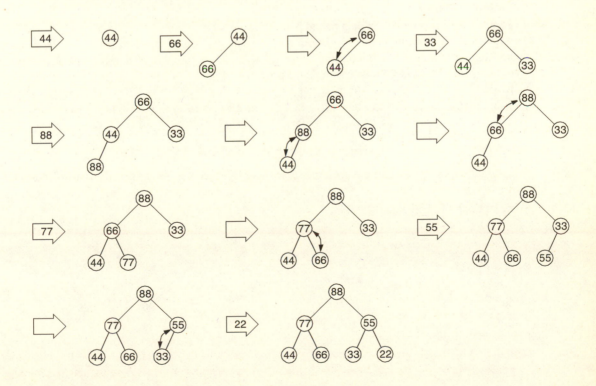

12.4   The arrays for the heaps in Problem 12.3:

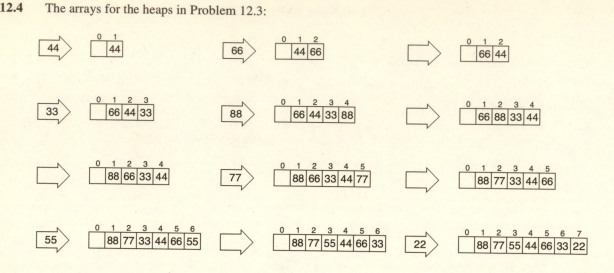

12.5   **Theorem.** Every subtree of a heap is also a heap.
Proof: Let T be a heap, and let S be a subtree of T. By definition, T is a complete binary tree with the heap property. Therefore by the theorem in the solution, S is also a complete binary tree. Let x be the root of S, and let p be any root-to-leaf path in S. Then x is an element of T since S is a subtree of T, and there is a unique path q in T from x to the root of T. Also, p is a path in T that connects x to a leaf of T since S is a subtree of T. Let q^{-1} represent the reverse of the path q, and let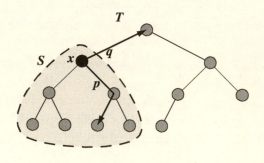

$q^{-1}p$ represent the concatenation of q^{-1} with p in T. Then $q^{-1}p$ is a root-to-leaf path in T. Hence the elements along $q^{-1}p$ must be nonincreasing because T has the heap property. Therefore the elements along p are nonincreasing. Thus S also has the heap property.

12.6

```
public boolean isHeap()
{ for (int leaf=size/2+1; leaf<=size; leaf++)
    for (int j=leaf, i; j>0; j = i)
    { i = j/2;
      if (ints[j]<ints[i]) return false;
    }
  return true;
}
```

12.7   Trace of Example 12.10 on page 233:

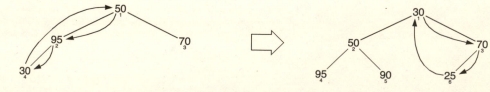

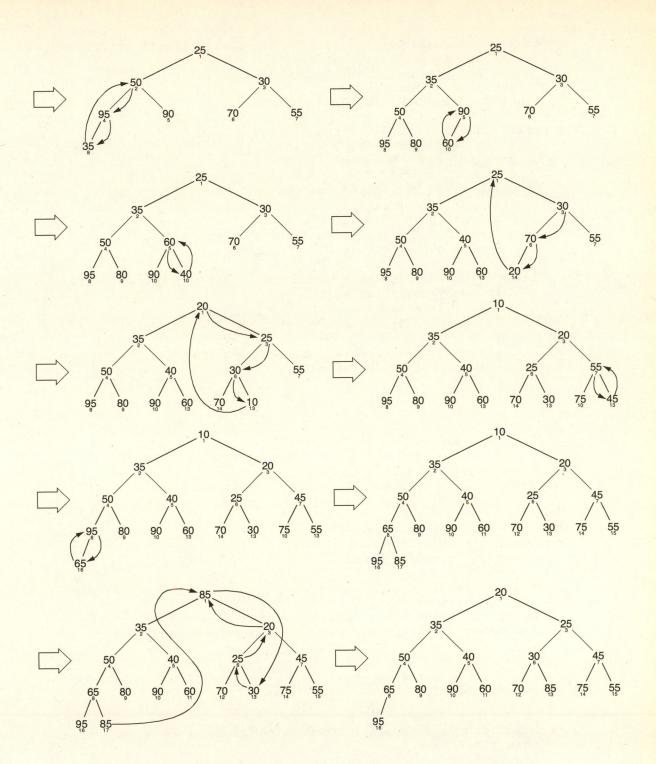

12.8   Revision of the client/server simulation:

```
public class Pr1208
{ private static final int NUMBER_OF_SERVERS = 4;
  private static final double MEAN_INTERARRIVAL_TIME = 5.0;
  private static final int DURATION = 200;
```

```
  private static Server[] servers = new Server[NUMBER_OF_SERVERS];
  private static PriorityQueue clients
    = new PriorityQueue(new ClientComparator());
  private static Random random
   = new Random(MEAN_INTERARRIVAL_TIME);

  public static void main(String[] args)
  { for (int i=0; i<NUMBER_OF_SERVERS; i++)
      servers[i] = new Server();
   int timeOfNextArrival = random.intNextExponential();
   for (int t=0; t<DURATION; t++)
   { if (t == timeOfNextArrival)  // new arrival
     { clients.push(new Client(t));
       timeOfNextArrival += random.intNextExponential();
       System.out.println(t + "\t" + clients);
     }
     for (int i=0; i<NUMBER_OF_SERVERS; i++)  // process servers
       if (servers[i].isFree())
       { if(!clients.isEmpty())
           servers[i].beginServing((Client)clients.pop(),t);
       }
       else if (t == servers[i].getTimeServiceEnds())
         servers[i].endServing(t);
   }
  }
}

public class Server
{ private static Random randomMeanServiceRate
    = new Random(1.00,0.20);
  private static char nextId = 'A';
  private Random randomServiceRate;
  private char id;
  private double meanServiceRate, serviceRate;
  private Client client;
  private int timeServiceEnds;

  public Server()
  { id = (char)nextId++;
    meanServiceRate = randomMeanServiceRate.nextGaussian();
    randomServiceRate = new Random(meanServiceRate,0.10);
  }

  public Client getClient()
  { return client;
  }

  public void beginServing(Client client, int time)
  { this.client = client;
    serviceRate = randomServiceRate.nextGaussian();
    client.beginService(this,time);
    int serviceTime
      = (int)Math.ceil(client.getJobSize()/serviceRate);
    timeServiceEnds = time + serviceTime;
    System.out.println(time + "\t" + id + " starts serving "
                          + client);
  }
```

```
    public void endServing(int time)
    { client.endService(time);
      System.out.println(time + "\t" + id + " finishes serving "
                              + client);
      this.client = null;
    }

    public int getTimeServiceEnds()
    { return timeServiceEnds;
    }

    public boolean isFree()
    { return client == null;
    }

    public String toString()
    { int percentMeanServiceRate
            = (int)Math.round(100*meanServiceRate);
      int percentServiceRate = (int)Math.round(100*serviceRate);
      return id + "(" + percentMeanServiceRate + "%,"
              + percentServiceRate + "%)";
    }
}

public class ClientComparator implements java.util.Comparator
{ public int compare(Object o1, Object o2)
  { if (o1==null || !(o1 instanceof schaums.dswj.Client))
      return -1;
    Client c1 = (Client)o1;
    if (o2==null || !(o2 instanceof Client)) return  1;
    Client c2 = (Client)o2;
    if (c1.getJobSize() < c2.getJobSize()) return -1;
    if (c1.getJobSize() > c2.getJobSize()) return  1;
    return 0;
  }
}

public class Client
{ public static final int MEAN_JOB_SIZE = 20;
  private static Random randomJobSize = new Random(MEAN_JOB_SIZE);
  private static int nextId = 0;
  private int id, jobSize, tArrived, tBegan, tEnded;
  private Server server;

  public Client(int time)
  { id = ++nextId;
    jobSize = randomJobSize.intNextExponential();
    tArrived = time;
    System.out.println(time + "\t" + this + " arrives");
  }

  public double getJobSize()
  { return jobSize;
  }
```

```java
  public int getWaitTime()
  { return tBegan - tArrived;
  }

  public int getServiceTime()
  { return tEnded - tBegan;
  }

  public void beginService(Server server, int time)
  { this.server = server;
    tBegan = time;
  }

  public void endService(int time)
  { tEnded = time;
    server = null;
  }

  public String toString()
  { return "#" + id + "(" + (int)Math.round(jobSize) + ")";
  }

  private static void print(int job, int time, double size)
  { System.out.println("Job #" + job + " arrives at time " + time
      + " with " + (int)Math.round(size) + " pages.");
  }

  private static void printBegins(Server server, int job, int time)
  { System.out.println("Printer " + server + " begins Job #" + job
      + " at time " + time + ".");
  }

  private static void printEnds(Server server, int job, int time)
  { System.out.println("Printer " + server + " ends Job #" + job
      + " at time " + time + ".");
  }
}
```

Chapter 13

Sorting

We saw in Chapter 2 that searching through an array is far more efficient if its elements are sorted first. That fact is obvious to anyone who has ever looked up a number in a phone book or a word in a dictionary. This chapter summarizes 10 of the most widely used algorithms for sorting a linear data structure such as an array or list.

All of the sorting algorithms are implemented using the same Java signature

```
public static void sort(int[] a)
```

for sorting an array of integers. This can easily be modified to sort an array of any other primitive type or an array of objects that implement the `Comparable` interface. See the exercises for sorting lists and other structures.

The pseudocode and the Java code include preconditions, postconditions, and loop invariants. These are used to prove that the algorithms are correct and to analyze their complexity.

The exchange sorts use the following general method:

```
private static void swap(int[] a, int i, int j)
{ // PRECONDITIONS: 0 <= i < a.length; 0 <= j < a.length;
  // POSTCONDITION: a[i] and a[j] are interchanged;
  if (i == j) return;
  int temp=a[j];
  a[j] = a[i];
  a[i] = temp;
}
```

This method simply swaps the *i*th and *j*th elements of the array.

In the pseudocode we use the notation $s = \{s_0, s_1, \ldots, s_{n-1}\}$ for a sequence of n elements. The notation $\{s_p..s_q\}$ denotes the subsequence $\{s_p, s_{p+1}, \ldots, s_q\}$ of elements from s_p to s_q. In Java code comments, we represent the subsequence by `s[p..q]`. For example, $\{s_3..s_7\}$ and `s[3..7]` would denote the subsequence $\{s_3, s_4, s_5, s_6, s_7\}$.

Unless otherwise noted, "sorted" will always mean that the elements of the sequence are in non decreasing order: $s_0 \leq s_1 \leq s_2 \leq \cdots \leq s_{n-1}$.

13.1 THE JAVA `Arrays.sort()` METHOD

The standard Java class library defines a `sort()` method in the `java.util.Arrays` class. It actually defines 18 overloaded versions of the method, four for arrays of objects, and two for arrays of each primitive type except `boolean`. The signatures for the two `sort()` methods for arrays of `int`s are

```
public static void sort(int[] a)
public static void sort(int[] a, int p, int q)
```

The first of these sorts the entire array. The second sorts the subarray `a[p..q]`.

EXAMPLE 13.1 Using the `Arrays.sort()` Method

```java
public static void main(String[] args)
{ int[] a = { 77, 44, 99, 66, 33, 55, 88, 22 };
  print(a);
  java.util.Arrays.sort(a);
  print(a);
}

private static void print(int[] a)
{ for (int i=0; i<a.length; i++)
    System.out.print(a[i]+" ");
  System.out.println();
}
```

```
77 44 99 66 33 55 88 22
22 33 44 55 66 77 88 99
```

The `Arrays.sort()` method implements the Quick Sort. (See Algorithm 13.6 on page 252.)

13.2 THE BUBBLE SORT

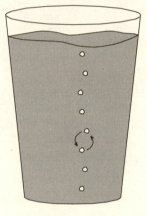

The *Bubble Sort* makes $n-1$ passes through a sequence of n elements. On each pass it compares adjacent elements in pairs, from left to right, and swaps each pair that is out of order. This gradually moves the larger elements to the right. It is called the "bubble" sort because if the elements are visualized in a vertical column then each pass appears to "bubble up" the next largest element by bouncing it off smaller elements, much like the rising bubbles in a carbonated beverage.

Algorithm 13.1 The Bubble Sort

(Precondition: $s = \{s_0, s_1, s_2, \ldots, s_{n-1}\}$ is a sequence of n ordinal values.)
(Postcondition: the entire sequence s is sorted.)
1. Do steps 2–4 for $i = n-1$ down to 1.
2. Do step 3 for $j = 1$ to i.
3. If the two elements s_{j-1} and s_j, are out of order, swap them.
4. (Invariants: the subsequence $\{s_i..s_{n-1}\}$ is sorted, and $s_i = \max\{s_0..s_i\}$.)

EXAMPLE 13.2 The Bubble Sort

```java
public static void sort(int[] a)
{ // POSTCONDITION: a[0] <= a[1] <= ... <= a[a.length-1];
  for (int i=a.length-1; i>0; i--)              // step 1
    for (int j=1; j<=i; j++)                     // step 2
      if (a[j-1]>a[j]) swap(a,j-1,j);            // step 3
    // INVARIANTS: a[i] <= a[i+1] <= ... <= a[a.length-1];
    //             a[i] >= a[j] for all j < i;
}
```

EXAMPLE 13.3 Tracing the Bubble Sort

Here is a trace of the Bubble Sort on the array {77, 44, 99, 66, 33, 55, 88, 22}:

a[0]	a[1]	a[2]	a[3]	a[4]	a[5]	a[6]	a[7]
77	44	99	66	33	55	88	22
44	77						
		66	99				
			33	99			
				55	99		
					88	99	
						22	**99**
	66	77					99
		33	77				99
			55	77			99
					22	**88**	99
	33	66				88	99
		55	66			88	99
				22	**77**	88	99
33	44				77	88	99
			22	**66**	77	88	99
		22	**55**	66	77	88	99
	22	**44**	55	66	77	88	99
22	**33**	44	55	66	77	88	99

Theorem 13.1 The Bubble Sort is correct.

See the solution to Problem 13.14 on page 270 for a proof of this theorem.

Theorem 13.2 The Bubble Sort runs in $O(n^2)$ time.

See the solution to Problem 13.15 on page 270 for a proof of this theorem.

13.3 THE SELECTION SORT

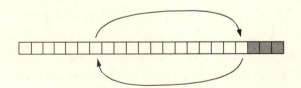

The *Selection Sort* is similar to the Bubble Sort. It makes the $n-1$ passes through a sequence of n elements, each time moving the largest of the remaining unsorted elements into its correct position. But it is more efficient than the Bubble Sort because it doesn't move any elements in the process of finding the largest. It makes only one swap on each pass after it has found the largest. It is called the Selection Sort because on each pass it selects the largest of the remaining unsorted elements and puts it in its correct position.

Algorithm 13.2 The Selection Sort

(Precondition: $s = \{s_0, s_1, s_2, \ldots, s_{n-1}\}$ is a sequence of n ordinal values.)
(Postcondition: the entire sequence s is sorted.)
1. Do steps 2–4 for $i = n-1$ down to 1.
2. Locate the index j of the largest element among $\{s_0..s_i\}$.
3. Swap s_i and s_j.
4. (Invariants: the subsequence $\{s_i..s_{n-1}\}$ is sorted, and $s_i = \max\{s_0..s_i\}$.)

EXAMPLE 13.4 The Selection Sort

```
public static void sort(int[] a)
{ // POSTCONDITION: a[0] <= a[1] <= ... <= a[a.length-1];
  for (int i=a.length-1; i>0; i--)                      // step 1
  { int j=0;                                            // step 2
    for (int k=1; k<=i; k++)
      if (a[k] > a[j]) j = k;
    // INVARIANT: a[j] >= a[k] for all k <= i;
    swap(a,i,j);                                        // step 3
    // INVARIANTS: a[i] >= a[k] for all k <= i;
    //             a[i] <= a[i+1] <= ... <= a[a.length-1];
  }
}
```

EXAMPLE 13.5 Tracing the Selection Sort

Here is a trace of the Selection Sort on the array {77, 44, 99, 66, 33, 55, 88, 22}:

a[0]	a[1]	a[2]	a[3]	a[4]	a[5]	a[6]	a[7]
77	44	99	66	33	55	88	22
							99
						88	99
55					77	88	99
			33	66	77	88	99
33			55	66	77	88	99
	22	44	55	66	77	88	99
22	33	44	55	66	77	88	99

Theorem 13.3 The Selection Sort is correct.
See the solution to Problem 13.19 on page 271 for a proof of this theorem.

Theorem 13.4 The Selection Sort runs in $O(n^2)$ time.
See the solution to Problem 13.20 on page 272 for a proof of this theorem.

Note that even though the Bubble Sort and the Selection Sort have the same complexity function, the latter runs quite a bit faster. That fact is suggested by the two traces: The Bubble Sort made 18 swaps while the Selection Sort made only seven. The Selection Sort has the advantage of swapping elements that are far apart, so it makes one swap where the Bubble Sort could require several. (See Exercise 11.8.)

13.4 THE INSERTION SORT

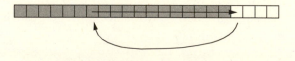

Like the two previous algorithms, the *Insertion Sort* makes $n-1$ passes through a sequence of n elements. On each pass it inserts the next element into the subarray on its left, thereby leaving that subarray sorted. When the last element is "inserted" this way, the entire array is sorted.

Algorithm 13.3 The Insertion Sort
(Precondition: $s = \{s_0, s_1, s_2, \ldots, s_{n-1}\}$ is a sequence of n ordinal values.)

(Postcondition: the entire sequence s is sorted.)
1. Do steps 2–4 for $i = 1$ up to $n - 1$.
2. Hold the element s_i in a temporary space.
3. Locate the least index j for which $s_j >= s_i$.
4. Shift the subsequence $\{s_j..s_{i-1}\}$ up one position to $\{s_{j+1}..s_i\}$.
5. Copy the held value of s_i into s_j.
6. (Invariant: the subsequence $\{s_0..s_i\}$ is sorted.)

EXAMPLE 13.6 The Insertion Sort

```
public static void sort(int[] a)
{ // POSTCONDITION: a[0] <= a[1] <= ... <= a[a.length-1];
  for (int i=1; i<a.length; i++)                          // step 1
  { int temp=a[i], j;                                     // step 2
    for (j=i; j>0 && a[j-1]>temp; j--)                    // step 3
      a[j] = a[j-1];                                      // step 4
    a[j] = temp;                                          // step 5
    // INVARIANT: a[0] <= a[1] <= ... <= a[i];
  }
}
```

EXAMPLE 13.7 Tracing the Insertion Sort

Here is a trace of the Insertion Sort on the array $\{77, 44, 99, 66, 33, 55, 88, 22\}$:

a[0]	a[1]	a[2]	a[3]	a[4]	a[5]	a[6]	a[7]
77	44	99	66	33	55	88	22
44	77						
	66	77	99				
33	44	66	77	99			
	55	66	77	99			
					88	99	
22	33	44	55	66	77	88	99

Theorem 13.5 The Insertion Sort is correct.
See the solution to Problem 13.23 on page 272 for a proof of this theorem.

Theorem 13.6 The Insertion Sort runs in $O(n^2)$ time.
See the solution to Problem 13.24 on page 272 for a proof of this theorem.

Theorem 13.7 The Insertion Sort runs in $O(n)$ time on a sorted sequence.
See the solution to Problem 13.25 on page 273 for a proof of this theorem.

13.5 THE SHELL SORT

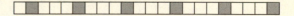

Theorem 13.7 suggests that if the
sequence is nearly sorted, then the Insertion
Sort will run nearly in $O(n)$ time. That is true. The *Shell Sort* exploits that fact to obtain an
algorithm that in general runs in better than $O(n^{1.5})$ time. It applies the Insertion Sort repeatedly
to skip-subsequences such as $\{s_0, s_3, s_6, s_9, \ldots, s_{n-2}\}$ and $\{s_1, s_4, s_7, s_{10}, \ldots, s_{n-1}\}$. These are two of
the three skip-3-subsequences.

Algorithm 13.4 The Shell Sort

(Precondition: $s = \{s_0, s_1, s_2, \ldots, s_{n-1}\}$ is a sequence of n ordinal values.)

(Postcondition: the entire sequence s is sorted.)

1. Set $d = 1$;
2. Repeat step 3 until $9d > n$;
3. Set $d = 3d + 1$;
4. Do steps 5–6 until $d = 0$;
5. Apply the Insertion Sort to each of the d skip-d-subsequences of s;
6. Set $d = d/3$;

EXAMPLE 13.8 The Shell Sort

Suppose s has $n = 200$ elements. Then the loop at step 2 would iterate three times, increasing d from 1 to $d = 4$, 13, and 40.

The first iteration of the loop at step 4 would apply the Insertion Sort to each of the 40 skip-40-subsequences $\{s_0, s_{40}, s_{80}, s_{120}, s_{160}\}$, $\{s_1, s_{41}, s_{81}, s_{121}, s_{161}\}$, $\{s_2, s_{42}, s_{82}, s_{122}, s_{162}\}$, ..., $\{s_{39}, s_{79}, s_{119}, s_{159}, s_{199}\}$. Then step 6 would reduce d to 13, and then the second iteration of the loop at step 4 would apply the Insertion Sort to each of the thirteen skip-13-subsequences $\{s_0, s_{13}, s_{26}, s_{39}, s_{52}, s_{65}, \ldots, s_{194}\}$, $\{s_1, s_{14}, s_{27}, s_{40}, s_{53}, s_{66}, \ldots, s_{195}\}$, ..., $\{s_{12}, s_{25}, s_{38}, s_{51}, s_{64}, s_{77}, \ldots, s_{193}\}$. Then step 6 would reduce d to 4, and the third iteration of the loop at step 4 would apply the Insertion Sort to each of the four skip-4-subsequences $\{s_0, s_4, s_8, s_{12}, \ldots, s_{196}\}$, $\{s_1, s_5, s_9, s_{13}, \ldots, s_{197}\}$, $\{s_2, s_6, s_{10}, s_{14}, \ldots, s_{198}\}$, and $\{s_3, s_7, s_{11}, s_{15}, \ldots, s_{199}\}$. Then step 6 would reduce d to 1, and, and the fourth iteration of the loop at step 4 would apply the Insertion Sort to the entire sequence. This entire process would apply the Insertion Sort 58 times: 40 times to subsequences of size $n_1 = 5$, 13 times to subsequences of size $n_2 = 15$, 4 times to subsequences of size $n_3 = 50$, and once to the entire sequence of size $n_4 = n = 200$.

At first glance, the repeated use of the Insertion Sort within the Shell Sort would seem to take longer than simply applying the Insertion Sort directly just once to the entire sequence. Indeed, a direct calculation of the total number of comparisons required in Example 13.8, using the complexity function n^2, yields

$$40(n_1{}^2) + 13(n_2{}^2) + 4(n_3{}^2) + 1(n_4{}^2) = 40(5^2) + 13(15^2) + 4(50^2) + 1(200^2) = 53{,}925$$

which is quite a bit worse than the single

$$n^2 = 200^2 = 40{,}000$$

But after the first iteration of step 4, the subsequent subsequences are nearly sorted. So the actual number of comparisons needed there will be closer to n. So the actual number of comparisons would be more like

$$40(n_1{}^2) + 13(n_2) + 4(n_3) + 1(n_4) = 40(5^2) + 13(15) + 4(50) + 1(200) = 1{,}595$$

which is quite a bit better than 40,000.

Theorem 13.8 The Shell Sort runs in $O(n^{1.5})$ time.

Note that, for $n = 200$, $n^{1.5} = 200^{1.5} = 2{,}829$, which is a lot better than $n^2 = 200^2 = 40{,}000$.

EXAMPLE 13.9 The Shell Sort

```
public static void sort(int[] a)
{ int d=1, j, n=a.length;                        // step 1
  while (9*d<n)                                   // step 2
    d = 3*d + 1;                                  // step 3
```

```
   while (d>0)                                              // step 4
   { for (int i=d; i<n; i++)                                // step 5
     { int temp=a[i];
       j=i;
       while (j>=d && a[j-d]>temp)
       { a[j] = a[j-d];
         j -= d;
       }
       a[j] = temp;
     }
     d /= 3;                                                // step 6
   }
 }
```

13.6 THE MERGE SORT

The *Merge Sort* applies the divide-and-conquer strategy to sort a sequence. First it subdivides the sequence into subsequences of singletons. Then it successively merges the subsequences pairwise until a single

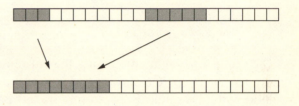

sequence is reformed. Each merge preserves order, so each merged subsequence is sorted. When the final merge is finished, the complete sequence is sorted.

Although it can be implemented iteratively, the Merge Sort is naturally recursive: split the sequence in two, sort each half, and then merge them back together preserving their order. The basis occurs when the subsequence contains only a single element.

Algorithm 13.5 The Merge Sort

(Precondition: $s = \{s_0, s_1, s_2, \ldots, s_{n-1}\}$ is a sequence of n ordinal values.)

(Postcondition: the entire sequence s is sorted.)

1. If $n > 1$, do steps 2–5.
2. Split s into two subsequences: $a = \{s_0..s_{m-1}\}$ and $b = \{s_m..s_{n-1}\}$, where $m = n/2$.
3. Sort a.
4. Sort b.
5. Reform s by merging a and b, preserving order.

EXAMPLE 13.10 The Merge Sort

```
public static void sort(int[] a)
{ // POSTCONDITION: a[0] <= a[1] <= ... <= a[a.length-1];
  if (n>1) sort(a,0,a.length);                             // step 1
}
public static void sort(int[] a, int k, int n)
{ // PRECONDITIONS: 2 <= n <= k+n <= a.length;
  // POSTCONDITION: a[k] <= a[k+1] <= ... <= a[k+n-1];
  if (n<2) return;
  sort(a,k,n/2);                                           // steps 2 & 3
  sort(a,k+n/2,n-n/2);                                     // step 4
  merge(a,k,n);                                            // step 5
}
```

```
public static void merge(int[] a, int k, int n)
{ // PRECONDITIONS: 1 <= n <= k+n <= a.length;
  //                a[k] <= a[k+1] <= ... <= a[k+n/2-1];
  //                a[k+n/2] <= ... <= a[k+n-1];
  // POSTCONDITION: a[k] <= a[k+1] <= ... <= a[k+n-1];
  int[] temp = new int[n];
  int i=0, lo=k, hi=k+n/2;
  while (lo<k+n/2 && hi<k+n)
    temp[i++] = ( a[lo]<=a[hi] ? a[lo++] : a[hi++] );
    // INVARIANT: temp[0..i] is sorted
  while (lo<k+n/2)
    temp[i++] = a[lo++];
    // INVARIANT: temp[0..i] is sorted
  while (hi<k+n)
    temp[i++] = a[hi++];
    // INVARIANT: temp[0..i] is sorted
  for (i=0; i<n; i++)
    a[k+i] = temp[i];
}
```

The main sort() method sorts the entire array by invoking the overloaded sort() method with parameters for the starting index k and the length n of the subarray. That three-parameter method sorts the subarray by sorting its left half and its right half separately and then merging them together.

The merge() method merges the two halves s[k..m-1] and s[m..k+n-1] into a temporary array, where m is the middle index m = k + n/2. The first while loop copies one element on each iteration; it copies the smaller of the two elements a[lo] and a[hi]. The post increment operator automatically advances the index of the copied element. When all the elements of one half have been copied, the first while loop stops and then one of the other two while loops copies the remaining elements into temp[]. Finally, all the elements are copied back into a[].

EXAMPLE 13.11 Tracing the Merge Sort

Here is a trace of the Merge Sort on the array {77, 44, 99, 66, 33, 55, 88, 22}:

a[0]	a[1]	a[2]	a[3]	a[4]	a[5]	a[6]	a[7]
77	44	99	66	33	55	88	22
44	77						
		66	99				
	66	77					
						22	44
22	33	44	44	55	66	77	88

The diagram on the top right of the next page shows how the subarrays are subdivided and then recombined.

Theorem 13.9 The Merge Sort runs in $O(n \lg n)$ time.

Proof: In general, the Merge Sort works by repeatedly dividing the array in half until the pieces are singletons, and then it merges the pieces pairwise until a single piece remains. This is illustrated by the diagram below. The number of iterations in the first part equals the number of times n can be halved: that is $\lg n - 1$. In terms of the number and sizes of the pieces, the second part of the process reverses the first. So the second part also has $\lg n - 1$ steps. So the entire algorithm has $O(\lg n)$ steps. Each step compares all n elements. So the total number of comparisons is $O(n \lg n)$.

Theorem 13.10 The Merge Sort is correct.

Proof: The proof follows from the preconditions and post-conditions given in the code. In the main `sort()` method, the array is already sorted if its length is 0 or 1. Otherwise, the postcondition of the three-parameter `sort()` method guarantees that the array will be sorted after that method returns because the entire array is passed to it. That post-condition is the same as the postcondition of the `merge()` method, which is invoked last, so it remains to verify that the `merge()` method's postcondion will be true.

The `merge()` method's postcondion follows from its three loop invariants because when those loops have finished, the `temp[]` array is sorted and that is copied back into `a[]` in the same order. So it remains to verify the three loop invariants.

Suppose that in one of the three `while` loops some element y got copied into `temp[]` and is less than some previously copied element x. Then x must have been copied from the other half array because 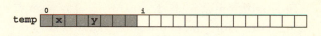 both halves were already sorted and x was copied before y. Thus it must have occurred in the first `while` loop. Without loss of generality, we may assume that y was in the first half and x was in the second half. Now if y < x, then since the half array was already sorted, all the elements from `a[k]` to y must also be less than x. But the assignment

        temp[i++] = (a[lo]<=a[hi] ? a[lo++] : a[hi++]);

always copies the smaller element first, so it must have copied all the elements from `a[k]` to y into `temp[]` before copying x. This contradicts the supposition, thereby verifying the loop invariant.

By using the *divide and conquer* strategy the Merge Sort obtains an $O(n \lg n)$ run time, a significant improvement over the $O(n^2)$ times spent by the previous sorting algorithms. The strategy is

1. Split the sequence into two subsequences.
2. Sort each subsequence separately.
3. Merge the two subsequences back together.

The Merge Sort does the first step in the simplest balanced way possible: it splits the sequence at its middle. If the first step is done in other ways, we obtain different sorting algorithms. The divide and conquer strategy is also used in the Binary Search (Algorithm 2.2 on page 31).

The simplest unbalanced way to split the sequence is to put all but the last element in the first subsequence, leaving only the last element in the second subsequence. This produces the recursive version of the Insertion Sort. (See Problem 13.22 on page 266.)

Another unbalanced way to split the sequence is to put the largest element alone in the second subsequence, leaving all the other elements in the first subsequence. This produces the recursive version of the Selection Sort. (See Problem 13.18 on page 265.) Not that this makes the merge step 3 trivial: merely append the largest element to the end of the first subsequence.

A fourth way to split the sequence is to partition it so that every element in the first subsequence is less than every the element in the second subsequence. This condition of course is true in the previous case that led to the recursive Selection Sort. However, if we can obtain this property together with having the two subsequences the same size, then we obtain a new $O(n \lg n)$ algorithm, called the Quick Sort.

13.7 THE QUICK SORT

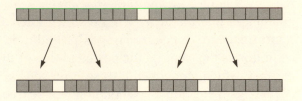

The Quick Sort is like the Merge Sort: It is recursive, it requires an auxiliary function with several loops, and it runs in $O(n \lg n)$ time. But in most cases it is quicker than the Merge Sort.

The Quick Sort works by partitioning the array into two pieces separated by a single element x that is greater than or equal to every element in the left piece and less than or equal to every element in the right piece. This guarantees that the single element x, called the *pivot* element, is in its correct position. Then the algorithm proceeds, applying the same method to the two pieces separately. This is naturally recursive, and very quick.

Algorithm 13.6 The Quick Sort
(Precondition: $s = \{s_0, s_1, s_2, \ldots, s_{n-1}\}$ is a sequence of n ordinal values.)
(Postcondition: the entire sequence s is sorted.)
1. If $n > 1$, do steps 2–5.
2. Apply the Quick Partition (Algorithm 13.7) to s, obtaining the pivot element s_i.
3. (Invariant: the pivot element s_i is in its correct sorted position.)
4. Apply the Quick Sort to $a = \{s_0, s_1, \ldots, s_{i-1}\}$.
5. Apply the Quick Sort to $b = \{s_{i+1}, s_{i+2}, \ldots, s_{n-1}\}$.

Algorithm 13.7 The Quick Partition
(Precondition: $s = \{s_k, s_{k+1}, s_{k+2}, \ldots, s_{k+n-1}\}$ is a sequence of n ordinal values.)
(Postcondition: $k \le j < n$ and $s_p \le s_j \le s_q$ for $k \le p < j < q < k+n$.)
1. Set $x = s_k$ (the *pivot* element).
2. Set $i = k$ and $j = k + n$.
3. Repeat steps 4–7 while $i < j$.
4. Repeat incrementing i while $s_i < x$.
5. Repeat decrementing j while $s_j > x$.
6. Swap s_i with s_j.
7. (Invariant: $s_p \le x \le s_q$ for $k \le p < i$ and for $j < q < k+n$.)
8. Swap s_k with s_j.
9. (Invariant: $s_p \le s_j \le s_q$ for $k \le p < j < q < k+n$.)

EXAMPLE 13.12 The Quick Sort

```
public static void sort(int[] a)
{ // POSTCONDITION: a[0] <= a[1] <= ... <= a[a.length-1];
  if (a.length>1) sort(a,0,a.length);                    // step Q.S.1
}

public static void sort(int[] a, int k, int n)
{ // PRECONDITIONS: 0 <= k <= k+n <= a.length;
```

```
// POSTCONDITION: a[k] <= a[k+1] <= ... <= a[k+n-1];
if (n<2) return;
int pivot = a[k];                                      // step Q.P.1
int i = k;
int j = k+n;
while (i < j)                                          // step Q.P.3
{ while (i+1<k+n && a[++i]<pivot) ;                    // step Q.P.4
  while (a[--j]>pivot) ;                               // step Q.P.5
  if (i < j) swap(a,i,j);                              // step Q.P.6
  // INVARIANT: a[p]<=pivot<=a[q] for k<=p=<i<j=<q<k+n  // step Q.P.7
}

swap(a,k,j);                                           // step Q.P.8
// INVARIANT: a[p]<=a[j]<=a[q] for k<p<j<q<k+n         // step Q.P.9
sort(a,k,j-k);                                         // step Q.S.4
sort(a,j+1,k+n-j-1);                                   // step Q.S.5
}
```

EXAMPLE 13.13 Tracing the Quick Sort

Here is a trace of the Quick Sort on the array {77, 44, 99, 66, 33, 55, 88, 22}:

a[0]	a[1]	a[2]	a[3]	a[4]	a[5]	a[6]	a[7]
77	44	99	66	33	55	88	22
		22					99
55					77		
			33	66	77		
33			55		77	88	
	22	44	55		77	88	
22	33		55		77	88	99
22	33	44	55	66	77	88	99

Algorithm 13.7 selects the pivot element to be the last element in the sequence. The algorithm works just as well if it is selected to be the first element, or the middle element. Slightly better performance is obtained by selecting the median of those three elements.

The Java `Arrays.sort()` method implements the Quick Sort, selecting the pivot as the median of the three elements $\{s_0, s_{n/2}, s_{n-1}\}$ when $n \leq 40$, and the median of 9 equally spaced elements when $n > 40$. It also switches to the Insertion Sort (Algorithm 13.3 on page 246) when $n < 7$.

Theorem 13.11 The Quick Sort runs in $O(n \lg n)$ time in the best case.

Proof: The best case is when the sequence values are uniformly randomly distributed so that each call to the Quick Partition algorithm will result in balanced split of the sequence. In that case, each recursive call to the Quick Sort algorithm divides the sequence into two subsequences of nearly equal length. As with the Binary Search (Algorithm 2.2 on page 31) and the Merge Sort (Algorithm 13.5 on page 249), this repeated subdivision takes $\lg n$ steps to get down to size 1 subsequences, as illustrated in the diagram on the next page. So there are $O(\lg n)$ calls made to the Quick Partition algorithm which runs in $O(n)$ time, so the total running time for the Quick Sort algorithm is $O(n \lg n)$.

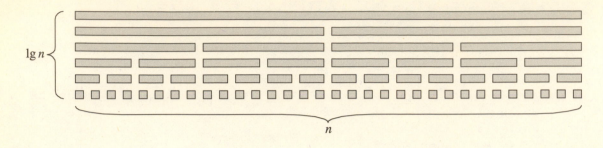

Theorem 13.12 The Quick Sort runs in $O(n^2)$ time in the worst case.

Proof: The worst case is when the sequence is already sorted (or sorted in reverse order). In that case, the Quick Partition algorithm will always select the last element (or the first element, if the sequence is sorted in reverse order), resulting in the most unbalanced split possible: one piece has $n-2$ elements and the other piece has 1 element. Repeated division of this type will occur $O(n)$ times before bother pieces get down to size 1. So there are $O(n)$ calls made to the Quick Partition algorithm which runs in $O(n)$ time, so the total running time for the Quick Sort algorithm is $O(n^2)$.

Note that in the worst case, the Quick Sort reverts to the Selection Sort (Algorithm 13.2 on page 245) because each call to Quick Partition amounts to selecting out the largest element from the subsequence passed to it. So actually, Theorem 13.12 a corollary to Theorem 13.4 on page 246.

Theorem 13.13 The Quick Sort runs in $O(n \lg n)$ time in the average case.

The proof of this fact is beyond the scope of this outline.

Theorem 13.14 The Quick Sort is correct.

Proof: The invariant inside the `while` loop proof claims that all the elements to the left of `a[i]` are less than or equal to the `pivot` element, and all the elements to the right of `a[j]` are greater than or equal to the `pivot`. This is true because every element to the left of `a[i]` that is greater than the `pivot` was swapped with some element to the right of `a[j]` that is less than the `pivot`, and conversely (every element to the right of `a[j]` that is less than the `pivot` was swapped with some element to the left of `a[i]` that is greater than the `pivot`. When that loop terminates, $j \leq i$, so at that point all the elements that are greater than the `pivot` have been moved to the right of `a[i]`, and all the elements that are less than the `pivot` have been moved to the left of `a[i]`. This is the invariant in step 7 of the Quick Partition algorithm. So after the swap in step 8, all the elements that are greater than the `a[i]` are to the right of `a[i]`, and all the elements that are less than the `a[i]` are to the left of `a[i]`. This is the invariant in step 7 of the Quick Partition algorithm, which is the same as the invariant in step 3 of the Quick Sort algorithm. So then sorting the left segment and the right segment independently will render the entire sequence sorted.

13.8 THE HEAP SORT

A heap is by definition partially sorted, because each linear string from root to leaf is sorted. (See Chapter 12.) This leads to an efficient general sorting algorithm called the *Heap Sort*. As with all sorting algorithms, it applies to an array (or `vector`). But the underlying heap structure (a binary tree) that the array represents is used to define this algorithm.

Like the Merge Sort and the Quick Sort, the Heap Sort uses an auxiliary function that is called from the `sort()` function. And also like the Merge Sort and the Quick Sort, the Heap Sort has complexity function $O(n \lg n)$. But unlike the Merge Sort and the Quick Sort, the Heap Sort is not recursive.

The Heap Sort essentially loads n elements into a heap and then unloads them. By Theorem 12.1 on page 228, each element takes $O(\lg n)$ time to load and $O(\lg n)$ time to unload, so the entire process on n element runs in $O(n \lg n)$ time.

Algorithm 13.8 The Heap Sort

(Precondition: $s = \{s_0, s_1, s_2, \ldots, s_{n-1}\}$ is a sequence of n ordinal values.)
(Postcondition: the entire sequence s is sorted.)
1. Do steps 2–3 for $i = n/2 - 1$ down to 0.
2. Apply the Heapify Algorithm to the subsequence $\{s_i, s_{i+1}, \ldots, s_{n-1}\}$.
3. (Invariant: every root-to-leaf path in s is non increasing.)
4. Do steps 5–7 for $i = n - 1$ down to 1.
5. Swap s_i with s_0.
6. (Invariant: the subsequence $\{s_i, s_{i+1}, \ldots, s_{n-1}\}$ is sorted.)
7. Apply the Heapify Algorithm to the subsequence $\{s_0, s_1, \ldots, s_{i-1}\}$.

Algorithm 13.9 The Heapify

(Preconditions: $ss = \{s_i, s_{i+1}, \ldots, s_{j-1}\}$ is a subsequence of $j - i$ ordinal values with $0 \le i < j \le n$, and both subsequences $\{s_{i+1}, \ldots, s_{j-1}\}$ and $\{s_{i+2}, \ldots, s_{j-1}\}$ has the heap property.)
(Postcondition: ss itself has the heap property.)
1. Let $t = s_{2i+1}$.
2. Let $s_k = \max\{s_{2i+1}, s_{2i+2}\}$, so $k = 2i+1$ or $2i+2$, the index of the larger child.
3. If $t < s_k$, do steps 4–6.
4. Set $s_i = s_k$.
5. Set $i = k$.
6. If $i < n/2$ and $s_i < \max\{s_{2i+1}, s_{2i+2}\}$, repeat steps 1–4.
7. Set $s_k = t$.

There are two aspects to these algorithms that distinguish them from the methods of Chapter 12. The heaps here are in the reverse order, so each root-to-leaf path is nonincreasing. And these algorithms use 0-based indexing. The reverse order guarantees that Heapify will always leave the largest element at the root of the subsequence. Using 0-base indexing instead of 1-based indexing renders the `sort()` method consistent with all the other `sort()` methods at the expense of making the code a little more complicated.

EXAMPLE 13.14 The Heap Sort

```
public static void sort(int[] a)
{ // POSTCONDITION: a[0] <= a[1] <= ... <= a[a.length-1];
  for (int i=a.length/2-1; i>=0; i--)                      // step 1
    heapify(a,i,n);                                        // step 2
  for (int i=a.length-1; i>0; i--)                         // step 4
  { swap(a,0,i);                                           // step 5
    heapify(a,0,i);                                        // step 7
  }
}
```

```
private static void heapify(int[] a, int i, int j)
{ int tmp=a[i], k;                                              // step 1
  while (2*i+1<j)
  { k=2*i+1;
    if (k+1<j && a[k+1] > a[k]) ++k;    // a[k] is the larger child
    if (tmp>=a[k]) break;                                       // step 3
    a[i] = a[k];                                                // step 4
    i = k;                                                      // step 5
  }
  a[k] = tmp;                                                   // step 7
}
```

Note that the heapify() method here is equivalent to the heapifyDown() method in Example 12.9 on page 232

EXAMPLE 13.15 Tracing the Heap Sort

Here is a trace of the Heap Sort on the array {77, 44, 99, 66, 33, 55, 88, 22, 44}:

a[0]	a[1]	a[2]	a[3]	a[4]	a[5]	a[6]	a[7]	a[8]
77	44	99	66	33	55	88	22	44
	66		44					
99	66	88	44	33	55	77	22	44
44								99
88	66	77	44	33	55	44	22	
22							88	
77	66	55	44	33	22	44		
44						77		
66	44	55	44	33	22			
22					66			
55	44	22	44	33				
33				55				
44	44	22	33					
33			44					
44	33	22						
22		44						
33	22							
22	33							

Each shaded area shows the result of a call to heapify(). It happens once in step 2 and then $n-2$ more times in step 7.

The sort() function first converts the array so that its underlying complete binary tree is transformed into a heap. This is done by applying the heapify() function to each nontrivial subtree. The nontrivial subtrees (i.e., those having more than one element) are the subtrees that are rooted above the leaf level. In the array, the leaves are stored at positions a[n/2] through a[n]. So the first for loop in the sort() function applies the heapify() function to elements a[n/2-1] back through a[0] (which is the root of the underlying tree). The result is an array whose corresponding tree has the heap property, illustrated at the top of the next page.

Now the main (second) for loop progresses through n-1 iterations. Each iteration does two things: it swaps the root element with element a[i], and then it applies the heapify() function to the subtree of elements a[0:i-1]. That subtree consists of the part of the array that is still unsorted. Before

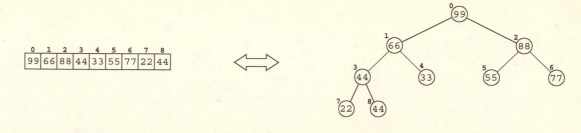

the `swap()` executes on each iteration, the subarray `a[0:i]` has the heap property, so `a[i]` is the largest element in that subarray. That means that the `swap()` puts element `a[i]` in its correct position.

The first seven iterations of the main `for` loop have the effect shown by the seven pictures on the next two pages. The array (and its corresponding imaginary binary tree) is partitioned into two parts: The first part is the subarray `a[0:i-1]` that has the heap property, and the second part is the remaining `a[i:n-1]` whose elements are in their correct positions. The second part is shaded in each of the seven pictures below. Each iteration of the main `for` loop decrements the size of the first part and increments the size of the second part. So when the loop has finished, the first part is empty and the second (sorted) part constitutes the entire array. This analysis verifies that the Heap Sort works:

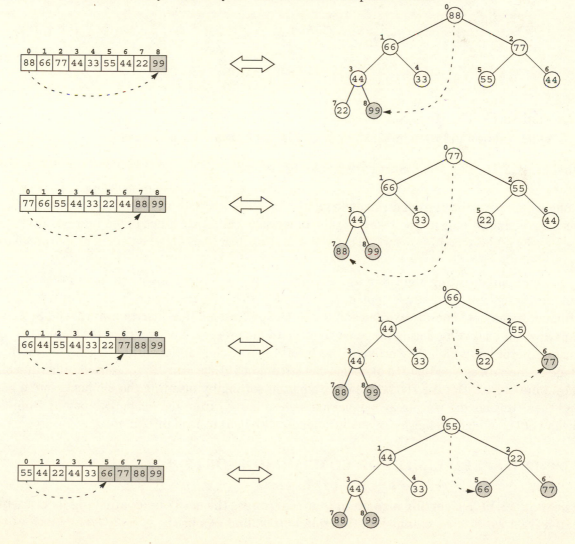

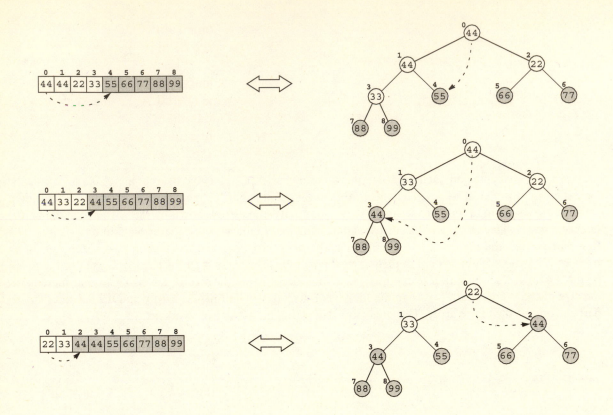

Theorem 13.15 The Heap Sort is correct.

See the solution to Problem 13.31 on page 274 for a proof of this theorem.

Theorem 13.16 The Heap Sort runs in $O(n \lg n)$ time.

Proof: Each call to the `heapify()` function takes at most $\lg n$ steps because it iterates only along a path from the current element down to a leaf. The longest such path for a complete binary tree of n elements is $\lg n$. The `heapify()` function is called $n/2$ times in the first `for` loop, and $n-1$ times in the second `for` loop. That comes to less than $(3n/2) \lg n$, which is proportional to $n \lg n$.

If we regard a sorting algorithm as a stream process wherein elements stream into an array in random order and then stream out in sorted order, then the Heap Sort can be regarded as an efficient mean between the extremes of the Selection Sort and the Insertion Sort. The Selection Sort does all its sorting during the removal stage of the process, having stored the elements in the unsorted order in which they arrived. The Insertion Sort does all its sorting during the insertion stage of the process, so that the elements can stream out of the array in the sorted order in which they were stored. But the Heap Sort does a partial sorting by inserting the elements into a heap and then finishes the sorting as the elements are removed from the heap. The payoff from this mean between the extremes is greater efficiency: $O(n \lg n)$ instead of $O(n^2)$.

13.9 THE SPEED LIMIT FOR COMPARISON SORTS

Theorem 13.17 No sorting algorithm that rearranges the array by comparing its elements can have a worst-case complexity function better than $O(n \lg n)$.

Proof: Consider the decision tree that covers all possible outcomes of the algorithm on an array of size n. Since the algorithm rearranges the array by comparing its elements, each node in the decision tree represents a condition of the form `(a[i] < a[j])`. Each such condition has two possible outcomes (`true` or `false`), so the decision tree is a binary tree. And since the tree must cover all possible arrangements, it must have at least $n!$ leaves. Therefore, by Corollary 10.3 on page 203, the height of the decision tree must be at least $\lg(n!)$. In the worst case, the number of comparisons that the algorithm makes is the same as the height of the decision tree. Therefore, the algorithm's worst-case complexity function must be $O(\lg(n!))$.

Now by Stirling's Formula (Theorem B.11 on page 281),

$$n! \approx \sqrt{2n\pi}\left(\frac{n}{e}\right)^n$$

so

$$\log(n!) \approx \log\left(\sqrt{2n\pi}\left(\frac{n}{e}\right)^n\right) \approx \log(n^n) = n\log n$$

(Here, "log" means the binary logarithm $\lg = \log_2$.) Therefore, the algorithm's worst-case complexity function must be $O(n\lg n)$.

Theorem 13.17 applies only to comparison sorts. A *comparison sort* is an algorithm that sorts elements by comparing their values and then change their relative positions according to the outcomes of those comparisons. All the sorting algorithms outlined previously are comparison sorts. But in addition to comparisons sorts, there are several other kinds of sorting algorithms.

13.10 THE RADIX SORT

The *Radix Sort assumes* that the sequence's element type is a lexicographic array of constant size; i.e., either a character string type or an integer type. Let r be the array element's *radix* (e.g., $r = 26$ for ASCII character strings, $r = 10$ for decimal integers, $r = 2$ for bit strings), and let w be the constant width of the lexicographic array. For example, for United States Social Security numbers, $d = 10$ and $w = 9$.

EXAMPLE 13.16 Sorting Books by Their ISBNs

Every book published since the 1970s has been assigned a unique International Standard Book Number. These are usually printed at the bottom of the back cover of the book. For example, the ISBN for this book is 0071361286. (ISBNs are usually hyphenated, like this: 0-07-136128-6, to distinguish the four separate fields that make up the code.) The last digit is a check digit, computed from the other nine digits. Since it can be any of the 10 numeric digits or the letter X, we have that the radix $r = 11$ while the number of digits $d = 10$.

Algorithm 13.10 The Radix Sort

(Precondition: $s = \{s_0, s_1, s_2, \ldots, s_{n-1}\}$ is a sequence of n integers or character strings with radix r and width w.)

(Postcondition: the sequence s is sorted lexicographically.)

1. Repeat steps 2–4 for $d = 0$ up to $w - 1$.

2. Apply a stable sorting algorithm to the sequence s, sorting only on digit number d.

A sorting algorithm is said to be *stable* if it preserves the relative order of elements with equal keys. For example, the Insertion Sort is stable

EXAMPLE 13.17 Sorting ISBNs with the Radix Sort

Here are the first three iterations of the Radix Sort applied to a sequence of 12 ISBNs:

```
0070308373      0071353461      0071342109      0071342109
0071353461      0070308373      8838650527      007052713X
0071342109      0071353453      0830636528      0071361286
0071353453      0070308683      007052713X      0070308373
0070308683      8838650454      0071353453      0071353453
0071361286      9742080585      8838650454      8838650454
007052713X      0071361286      0071353461      0071353461
0830636528      8838650527      0070308373      0830628479
0830628479      0830636528      0830628479      8838650527
8838650527      0830628479      0070308683      0830636528
```

Note how the stability is needed to conserve the work done by previous iterations. For example, after the first iteration, `8838650527` precedes `0830636528` because $7 < 8$. Both of these keys have the same value 2 in their second least significant digit (digit number $d = 1$). So on the second iteration, which sorts only on digit number 1, these two keys evaluate as being equal. But they should retain their previous relative order because $27 < 28$. Stability guarantees that they do.

The columns that have been processed are shaded. So after the third iteration, the right-most 3-digit subsequences are sorted: $109 < 13X < 286 < 373 < 453$, etc. (Note that X stands for the value 10. So `13x` numerically means $130 + 10 = 140$.)

After the other seven iterations have finished, the sequence will end up this way:

```
0830628479
0830636528
0070308373
0070308683
007052713X
0071353461
0071342109
0071353453
0071361286
8838650454
```

EXAMPLE 13.18 The Radix Sort

This method assumes that the constants `RADIX` has `WIDTH` have been defined. For example, for arrays of `int`s:

```java
public static final int RADIX=10;
public static final int WIDTH=10;

public static void sort(int[] a)
{ // POSTCONDITION: a[0] <= a[1] <= ... <= a[a.length-1];
  for (int d=0; d<WIDTH; d++)                                 // step 1
    sort(a,d);                                                // step 2
}

private static void sort(int[] a, int d)
{ // POSTCONDITION: a[] is sorted stably on digit d;
  int[] c = new int[RADIX];
  for (int i=0; i<a.length; i++)
    ++c[digit(d,a[i])];  // tally the values in a[]
  for (int j=1; j<RADIX; j++)
    c[j] += c[j-1];  // c[j] == num elts in a[] that are <= j
  int[] tmp = new int[a.length];
  for (int i=a.length-1; i>=0; i--)
    tmp[--c[digit(d,a[i])]] = a[i];
  for (int i=0; i<a.length; i++)
  a[i] = tmp[i];
}
```

```
private static int digit(int d, int x)
{ // e.g., digit(3,1234567890) returns 7;
   return x/(int)Math.pow(10,d)%RADIX;
}
```

The secondary sorting method is called a *counting sort* or *tally sort*.

Theorem 13.18 The Radix Sort runs in $O(n)$ time.

Proof: The algorithm has WIDTH iterations, and processes all n elements on each iteration three times. Thus the running time is proportional to WIDTH*n, and is a constant.

Although $O(n)$ is theoretically better than $O(n \lg n)$, the Radix Sort is rarely faster than the $O(n \lg n)$ sorting algorithms (Merge Sort, Quick Sort, and Heap Sort). That is because it has a lot of overhead extracting digits and copying arrays.

13.11 THE BUCKET SORT

The *Bucket Sort* is another distribution sort. It distributes the elements into "buckets" according to some coarse grain criterion and then applies another sorting algorithm to each bucket. It is similar to the Quick Sort in that all the elements in bucket i are greater than or equal all the elements in bucket $i-1$ and less than or equal to all the elements in bucket $i+1$. Whereas Quick Sort partitions the sequence into two buckets, the Bucket Sort partitions the sequence into n buckets.

Algorithm 13.11 The Bucket Sort

(Precondition: $s = \{s_0, s_1, s_2, \ldots, s_{n-1}\}$ is a sequence of n ordinal values with know minimum value min and maximum value max.)

(Postcondition: the sequence s is sorted.)

1. Initialize an array of n buckets (collections).
2. Repeat step 3 for each s_i in the sequence.
3. Insert s_i into bucket j, where $j = \lfloor rn \rfloor$, $r = (s_i - \text{min})/(\text{max} + 1 - \text{min})$.
4. Sort each bucket.
5. Repeat step 6 for j from 0 to $n-1$.
6. Add the elements of bucket j sequentially back into s.

EXAMPLE 13.19 Sorting U. S. Social Security Numbers with the Bucket Sort.

Suppose you have 1,000 9-digit identification numbers. Set up 1,000 arrays of type int and then distribute the numbers using the formula $j = \lfloor rn \rfloor$, $r = (s_i - \text{min})/(\text{max} + 1 - \text{min}) = (s_i - 0)/(10^9 + 1 - 0)$ $\cong s_i/10^9$. So for example, the identification number 666666666 would be inserted into bucket number j where $j = \lfloor rn \rfloor = \lfloor (666666666/10^9)(10^3) \rfloor = \lfloor 666.666666 \rfloor = 666$. Similarly, identification number 123456789 would be inserted into bucket number 123, and identification number 666543210 would be inserted into bucket 666.

Then each bucket would be sorted. Note that the number of elements in each bucket will average 1, so the choice of sorting algorithm will not affect the running time.

Finally, the elements are copied back into *s*, starting with bucket number 0:

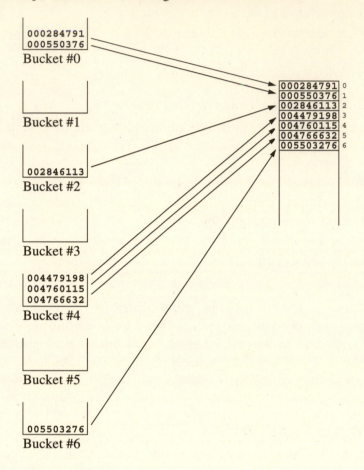

EXAMPLE 13.20 The Bucket Sort

```
public static void sort(int[] a)
{ // POSTCONDITION: a[0] <= a[1] <= ... <= a[a.length-1];
  int min=minimum(a);
  int max=maximum(a);
  int n=a.length;
  Bucket[] bucket = new Bucket[n];                        // step 1
  for (int j=0; j<n; j++)
    bucket[j] = new Bucket();
  for (int i=0; i<n; i++)                                 // step 2
  { int j = n*(a[i]-min)/(max+1-min);
    bucket[j].add(a[j]);                                  // step 3
  }
  int i=0;
  for (int j=0; j<n; j++)
  { Bucket bucketj=bucket[j];
    bucketj.sort();                                       // step 4
    for (int k=0; k<bucketj.size(); k++)                  // step 5
      a[i++] = bucketj.get(k);
  }
}
```

This program requires the implementation of the following interface:

```
public interface Bucket
{ public void add(int x);   // appends x to end of bucket
  public int get(int k);    // returns element k from bucket
  public int size();        // returns the number of elements
}
```

It also requires the two local methods:

```
public int minimum(int[] a);  // returns the smallest value in a[]
public int maximum(int[] a);  // returns the largest value in a[]
```

Theorem 13.19 The Bucket Sort runs in $O(n)$ time.

Proof: The algorithm has three parallel loops, each iterating n times. The last loop has an inner loop, but it averages only 1 iteration. The `minimum()` and `maximum()` methods also requires n steps each. Hence the number of steps executed is proportional to $5n$.

Like the Radix Sort, the $O(n)$ Bucket Sort is in practice much slower than the $O(n \lg n)$ sorting algorithms because of substantial overhead costs.

Review Questions

13.1 Why is the Bubble Sort so slow?

13.2 The proof to Theorem 13.2 on page 245 concludes that the Bubble Sort makes $n(n-1)/2$ comparisons. How does it follow that its complexity function is $O(n^2)$?

13.3 Why are the $O(n)$ sorting algorithms (Radix Sort and Bucket Sort) slower than the $O(n \lg n)$ sorting algorithms (Merge Sort, Quick Sort, and Heap Sort)?

13.4 The Merge Sort applies the general method, known as *divide and conquer*, to sort an array. It divides the array into pieces and applies itself recursively to each piece. What other sorting algorithm(s) use this method?

13.5 Which sorting algorithms work as well on linked lists as on arrays?

13.6 Which sorting algorithms have a different worst case complexity than their average case?

13.7 Which sorting algorithms have a different best case complexity than their average case?

13.8 Why is the nonrecursive version of a recursive sorting algorithm usually more efficient?

13.9 How is the Quick Sort like the Merge Sort?

13.10 Under what circumstances would the Merge Sort be preferred over the other two $O(n \lg n)$ sorting algorithms?

13.11 Under what circumstances is the Quick Sort like the Selection Sort?

13.12 Under what circumstances would the Quick Sort be preferred over the other two $O(n \lg n)$ sorting algorithms?

13.13 How is the Heap Sort similar to the Selection Sort and the Insertion Sort?

13.14 Which algorithm does the Java API use to implement its `java.util.Arrays.sort()` methods?

13.15 A sorting algorithm is said to be *stable* if it preserves the order of equal elements. Which of the sorting algorithms are not stable?

13.16 Which of the nine sorting algorithms outlined in this chapter require extra array space?

13.17 Which of the nine sorting algorithms outlined in this chapter would work best on an external file of records?

13.18 The Merge Sort is *parallelizable*. That means that parts of it can be performed simultaneously, independent of each other, provided that the computer has multiple processors that can run in parallel. This works for the Merge Sort because several different parts of the array can be subdivided or merged independently of other parts. Which of the other sorting algorithms described in this chapter are parallelizable?

13.19 Imagine a website that has a Java applet for each sorting algorithm that shows how the algorithm works by displaying an animation of a test run on an array `a[]` of 256 random numbers in the range 0.0 to 1.0. The animation shows on each iteration of the algorithm's main loop a two-dimensional plot of 256 points (x, y), one for each element in the array, where $x =$ `i+1` and $y =$ `a[i]`. Each plot shown below shows the progress half-way through the sort for one of the following algorithms:

Selection Sort
Insertion Sort
Merge Sort
Quick Sort
Heap Sort
Radix Sort

Match each plot with the sorting algorithm that produced it:

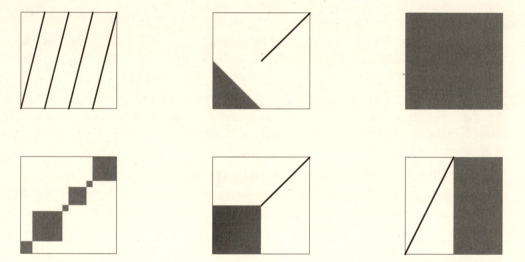

Problems

13.1 If an $O(n^2)$ algorithm (e.g., the Bubble Sort, the Selection Sort, or the Insertion Sort) takes 3.1 milliseconds to run on an array of 200 elements, how long would you expect it to take to run on a similar array of:
a. 400 elements?
b. 40,000 elements?

13.2 If an $O(n \lg n)$ algorithm (e.g., the Merge Sort, the Quick Sort, or the Heap Sort) takes 3.1 milliseconds to run on an array of 200 elements, how long would you expect it to take to run on a similar array of 40,000 elements?

13.3   The Insertion Sort runs in linear time on an array that is already sorted. How does it do on an array that is sorted in reverse order?

13.4   How does the Bubble Sort perform on:
a. an array that is already sorted?
b. an array that is sorted in reverse order?

13.5   How does the Selection Sort perform on:
a. an array that is already sorted?
b. an array that is sorted in reverse order?

13.6   How does the Merge Sort perform on:
a. an array that is already sorted?
b. an array that is sorted in reverse order?

13.7   How does the Quick Sort perform on:
a. an array that is already sorted?
b. an array that is sorted in reverse order?

13.8   How does the Heap Sort perform on:
a. an array that is already sorted?
b. an array that is sorted in reverse order?

13.9   The Bubble Sort, the Selection Sort, and the Insertion Sort are all $O(n^2)$ algorithms. Which is the fastest, and which is the slowest among them?

13.10 The Merge Sort, the Quick Sort, and the Heap Sort are all $O(n \lg n)$ algorithms. Which is the fastest, and which is the slowest among them?

13.11 Trace by hand the sorting of this array
```
int a[] = { 44, 77, 55, 99, 66, 33, 22, 88, 77 }
```
by each of the following algorithms:
a. The Bubble Sort
b. The Selection Sort
c. The Insertion Sort
d. The Merge Sort
e. The Quick Sort
f. The Heap Sort

13.12 Modify the Bubble Sort so that it sorts the array in nonincreasing order.

13.13 Modify the Bubble Sort so that it is "smart" enough to terminate as soon as the array is sorted.

13.14 Prove Theorem 13.1 on page 245.

13.15 Prove Theorem 13.2 on page 245.

13.16 The *Shaker Sort* is the same as the Bubble Sort except that it alternates "bubbling" up and down the array. Implement the Shaker Sort, and determine whether it is more efficient than the straight Insertion Sort.

13.17 Modify the Selection Sort (Algorithm 13.2 on page 245) so that it uses the smallest element of $\{s_i..s_{n-1}\}$ in step 2.

13.18 Rewrite the Selection Sort recursively.

13.19 Prove Theorem 13.3 on page 246.

13.20 Prove Theorem 13.4 on page 246.

13.21 Modify the Insertion Sort so that it sorts the array indirectly. This requires a separate *index array* whose values are the indexes of the actual data elements. The indirect sort rearranges the index array, leaving the data array unchanged.

13.22   Rewrite the Insertion Sort recursively.

13.23   Prove Theorem 13.5 on page 247.

13.24   Prove Theorem 13.6 on page 247.

13.25   Prove Theorem 13.7 on page 247.

13.26   Modify the Quick Sort so that it selects its pivot as the last element instead of the first element of the subsequence.

13.27   Modify the Quick Sort so that it selects its pivot as the median of the first, middle, and last elements.

13.28   Modify the Quick Sort so that it reverts to the Insertion Sort when the array size is below 8.

13.29   Since the Heap Sort runs in $O(n \lg n)$ time, why isn't it always preferred over the Quick Sort, which runs in $O(n^2)$ in the worst case?

13.30   Since the Heap Sort runs in $O(n \lg n)$ time and requires no extra array space, why isn't it always preferred over the Merge Sort, which requires duplicate array space?

13.31   Prove Theorem 13.15 on page 258.

13.32   Here is the *Las Vegas Sort*, as applied to sorting a deck of cards:

      1. Randomly shuffle the cards.

      2. If the deck is not sorted, repeat step 1.

Derive the complexity function for this sorting algorithm.

Answers to Review Questions

13.1   The Bubble Sort is so slow because it operates only locally. Each element moves only one position at a time. For example, the element 99 in Example 13.1 on page 244 is moved by six separate calls to the `swap()` function to be put into its correct position at `a[8]`.

13.2   The jump from $n(n-1)/2$ to $O(n^2)$ is justified as follows:

    a. For large values of n (e.g., $n > 1000$), $n(n-1)/2$ is nearly the same as $n^2/2$.

    b. A complexity function is used only for comparisons. For example, how much longer will it take to sort an array that is twice as large? For that analysis, proportional functions are equivalent. And since $n^2/2$ is proportional to n^2, we can drop the (1/2) factor and simplify our conclusion with $O(n^2)$.

13.3   The $O(n)$ sorting algorithms (Radix Sort and Bucket Sort) are slower than the $O(n \lg n)$ sorting algorithms (Merge Sort, Quick Sort, and Heap Sort) because, although their running time is proportional to n, the constant of proportionality is large due to large overhead. For both the Radix Sort and the Bucket Sort, each iteration requires copying all the elements into a list of queues or arrays and then copying them back.

13.4   The Merge Sort, Quick Sort, and Bucket Sort all use the divide-and-conquer strategy.

13.5   The Bubble Sort, Selection Sort, Insertion Sort, Merge Sort, and Quick Sort work as well on linked lists as on arrays.

13.6   The Quick Sort and Bucket Sort are significantly slower in the worst case.

13.7   The Insertion Sort, Shell Sort, and Radix Sort are significantly faster in the best case.

13.8   Recursion carries the overhead of many recursive method invocations.

13.9   The Quick Sort implements the divide-and-conquer strategy: first it performs its $O(\lg n)$ partitioning of the sequence, and then it recursively sorts each of the two pieces independently. The Merge Sort implements the divide-and-conquer strategy but in the reverse order: it makes its two recursive calls first before performing its $O(\lg n)$ merge. Both algorithms do $O(n)$ amount of work $O(\lg n)$ times thus obtaining $O(n \lg n)$ complexity.

13.10   The Merge Sort is best for sorting linked lists and external files.

13.11   The Quick Sort reverts to the Selection Sort in the worst case, when the sequence is already sorted.

13.12   The Quick Sort is best for sorting large arrays of primitive types.

13.13   The Selection Sort can be seen as a sort-on-output process: Insert the elements into an array as they are given, and then repeatedly select out the next largest element. The Selection Sort can be seen as a sort-on-input process: Repeatedly insert each element into its correct ordered position in an array, and then remove them in their array order. So the Selection Sort inserts the elements into the array in $O(n)$ time and removes them in $O(n^2)$, while the Insertion Sort inserts the elements into the array in $O(n^2)$ time and removes them in $O(n)$. Both result in an $O(n^2)$ algorithm.

The heap Sort can be seen as a partial-sort-on-input-and-partial-sort-on-output process: Insert the elements into an array maintaining the (partially-sorted) heap property, and then repeatedly select the first (which is the smallest) element and restore the heap property. Both the insertion process and the removal process have the same $O(n \lg n)$ running time, resulting in a total $O(n \lg n)$ running time.

13.14   The Java API uses the Merge Sort to implement its `Arrays.sort()` methods for arrays of objects, and it uses the Quick Sort to implement its `Arrays.sort()` methods for arrays of primitive types.

13.15   The Shell Sort, Quick Sort, and Heap Sort are unstable.

13.16   The Merge Sort, Radix Sort, and Bucket Sort require extra array storage.

13.17   The Bubble Sort, Selection Sort, Insertion Sort, Merge Sort, and Quick Sort work as well on external files of records.

13.18   The Shell Sort, Merge Sort, Quick Sort, and Bucket Sort all would run significantly faster on a parallel computer.

13.19   Matching algorithms with graphical output:

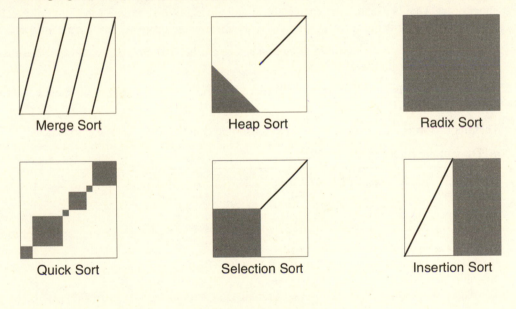

| Merge Sort | Heap Sort | Radix Sort |
| Quick Sort | Selection Sort | Insertion Sort |

Solutions to Problems

13.1   The $O(n^2)$ algorithm should take:

a. 12.4 milliseconds (4 times as long) to run on the 400-element array;

b. 124 seconds (40,000 times as long) to run on the 40,000-element array. That's about 2 minutes. This answer can be computed algebraically as follows. The running time t is proportional to n^2, so there is some constant c for which $t = c \cdot n^2$. If it takes $t = 3.1$ milliseconds to sort $n = 200$ elements, then (3.1 milliseconds) $= c \cdot (200 \text{ elements})^2$, so $c = (3.1 \text{ milliseconds})/(200 \text{ elements})^2 = 0.0000775$ milliseconds/element^2. Then, for $n = 40,000$, $t = c \cdot n^2 = (0.0000775 \text{ milliseconds/element}^2) \cdot (40,000 \text{ elements})^2 = 124,000$ milliseconds $= 124$ seconds.

13.2   The $O(n \lg n)$ algorithm should take 1.24 seconds (400 times as long) to run on the 40,000-element array. This answer can be computed algebraically. The running time t is proportional to $n \lg n$, so there is some constant c for which $t = c \cdot n \lg n$. If it takes $t = 3.1$ milliseconds to sort $n = 200$ elements, then $(3.1) = c \cdot (200) \lg(200)$, so $c = (3.1 \text{ milliseconds})/(200 \cdot \lg(200)) = 0.0155/\lg(200)$. Then, for $n = 40,000$, $t = c \cdot n \lg n = (0.0155/\lg(200))(40,000 \cdot \lg(40,000)) = 620 \cdot (\lg(40,000)/\lg(200))$. Now $40,000 = 200^2$, so $\lg(40,000) = \lg(200^2) = 2 \cdot \lg 200$. Thus, $\lg(40,000)/\lg(200) = 2$, so $t = 620 \cdot 2$ milliseconds = 1240 milliseconds = 1.24 s.

13.3   The Insertion Sort has its worst performance on an array that is sorted in reverse order, because each new element inserted requires all of the elements on its left to be shifted one position to the right.

13.4   The Bubble Sort, as implemented in Algorithm 13.1 on page 244, is *insensitive to input*. That means that it will execute the same number $n(n-1)/2$ of comparisons regardless of the original order of the elements in the array. So it doesn't matter whether the array is already sorted or whether it is sorted in reverse order; it is still very slow.

13.5   The Selection Sort is also insensitive to input: It takes about the same amount of time to sort arrays of the same size, regardless of their initial order.

13.6   The Merge Sort is also insensitive to input: It takes about the same amount of time to sort arrays of the same size, regardless of their initial order.

13.7   The Quick Sort is quite sensitive to input. As implemented in Algorithm 13.6 on page 252, the Quick Sort will degrade into an $O(n^2)$ algorithm in the special cases where the array is initially sorted in either order. That is because the pivot element will always be an extreme value within its subarray, so the partitioning splits the subarray very unevenly, thereby requiring n steps instead of $\lg n$.

13.8   The Heap Sort is a little sensitive to input, but not much. The `heapify()` function may require fewer than $\lg n$ iterations.

13.9   The Bubble Sort is slower than the Selection Sort, and the Insertion Sort (in most cases) is a little faster.

13.10   The Merge Sort is slower than the Heap Sort, and the Quick Sort (in most cases) is faster.

13.11   *a.* Trace of the Bubble Sort:

a[0]	a[1]	a[2]	a[3]	a[4]	a[5]	a[6]	a[7]	a[8]
44	77	55	99	66	33	22	88	77
	55	77						
			66	99				
				33	99			
					22	99		
						88	99	
							77	99
		66	77					
			33	77				
				22	77			
						77	88	
		33	66					
			22	66				
	33	55						
		22	55					
33	44							
	22	44						
22	33							

b. Trace of the Selection Sort:

a[0]	a[1]	a[2]	a[3]	a[4]	a[5]	a[6]	a[7]	a[8]
44	77	55	99	66	33	22	88	77
22						44		
	33				77			
		44				55		
			55			99		
						77		99

c. Trace of the Insertion Sort:

a[0]	a[1]	a[2]	a[3]	a[4]	a[5]	a[6]	a[7]	a[8]
44	77	55	99	66	33	22	88	77
	55	77						
		66	77	99				
33	44	55	66	77	99			
22	33	44	55	66	77	99		
						88	99	
						77	88	99

d. Trace of the Merge Sort:

a[0]	a[1]	a[2]	a[3]	a[4]	a[5]	a[6]	a[7]	a[8]
44	77	55	99	66	33	22	88	77
44	55	77	99					
				33	66			
							77	88
				22	33	66	77	88
22	33	44	55	66	77	77	88	99

e. Trace of the Quick Sort:

a[0]	a[1]	a[2]	a[3]	a[4]	a[5]	a[6]	a[7]	a[8]
44	77	55	99	66	33	22	88	77
			22			99		
						77		99
22			44					
	33				77			
		44	55					

f. Trace of the Heap Sort:

a[0]	a[1]	a[2]	a[3]	a[4]	a[5]	a[6]	a[7]	a[8]
44	77	55	99	66	33	22	88	77
	99		77					
			88				77	
99	44							
	88		44					
			77				44	
77								99

a[0]	a[1]	a[2]	a[3]	a[4]	a[5]	a[6]	a[7]	a[8]
88	77							
44							88	
77	44							
	77		44					
22						77		
77	22							
	66			22				
33					77			
66	33							
	44		33					
22				66				
55		22						
		33	22					
22			55					
44	22							
33		44						
22	33							

13.12 A modified Bubble Sort to sort in nonincreasing order:

```
public static void sort(int[] a)
{ for (int i=a.length-1; i>0; i--)
    for (int j=1; j<=i; j++)
      if (a[j-1]<a[j]) swap(a,j-1,j);
}
```

13.13 A smart Bubble Sort:

```
public static void sort(int[] a)
{ boolean sorted=false;
  for (int i=a.length-1; i>0; i--)
  { for (int j=1; j<=i; j++)
    { sorted = true;
      if (a[j-1] > a[j])
      { swap(a,j-1,j);
        sorted = false;
      }
    }
    if (sorted) return;
  }
}
```

13.14 Proof that the Bubble Sort is correct:

The loop invariant can be used to prove that the Bubble Sort does indeed sort the array. After the first iteration of the main i loop, the largest element must have moved to the last position. Wherever it began, it had to be moved step-by-step all the way to the right, because on each comparison the larger element is moved right. For the same reason, the second largest element must have been moved to the second-from-last position in the second iteration of the main i loop. So the two largest elements are in the correct locations. This reasoning verifies that the loop invariant is true at the end of every iteration of the main i loop. But then, after the last iteration, the n-1 largest elements must be in their correct locations. That forces the nth largest (i.e., the smallest) element also to be in its correct location, so the array must be sorted.

13.15 Proof that the Bubble Sort runs in $O(n^2)$ time:

The complexity function $O(n^2)$ means that, for large values of n, the number of loop iterations tends to be proportional to n^2. That means that, if one large array is twice the size of another, it should take about four times as long to sort. The inner j loop iterates $n-1$ times on the first iteration of the outside i loop, $n-2$ times on the second iteration of the i loop, $n-3$ times on the third iteration of the i loop, etc. For example, when $n = 7$, there are 6 comparisons made on the first iteration of the i loop, 5 comparisons made on the second iteration of the i loop, 4 comparisons made on the third iteration of the i loop, etc., so the total number of comparisons is $6 + 5 + 4 + 3 + 2 + 1 = 21$. In general, the total number of comparisons will be $(n-1) + (n-2) + (n-3) + \cdots + 3 + 2 + 1$. This sum is $n(n-1)/2$. (See Theorem B.8 on page 778.) For large values of n, that expression is nearly $n^2/2$ which is proportional to n^2.

13.16 The Shaker Sort:

```
public static void sort(int[] a)
{ for (int i=a.length; i>0; i -= 2)
  { for (int j=1; j<i; j++)
      if (a[j-1] > a[j]) swap(a,j-1,j);
    for (int j=i-2; j>0; j--)
      if (a[j-1] > a[j]) swap(a,j-1,j);
  }
}
```

13.17 A modifies Selection Sort that uses the smallest element of each subsequence:

```
public static void sort(int[] a)
{ for (int i=0; i<a.length-1; i++)
  { int j=i;
    for (int k=i+1; k<a.length; k++)
      if (a[k] < a[j]) j = k;
    swap(a,i,j);
  }
}
```

13.18 A recursive Selection Sort:

```
public static void sort(int[] a)
{ sort(a,a.length);
}
public static void sort(int[] a, int n)
{ if (n<2) return;
  int j=0;
  for (int k=1; k<n; k++)
    if (a[k] > a[j]) j = k;
  swap(a,n-1,j);
  sort(a,n-1);
}
```

13.19 Proof that the Selection Sort is correct:

The last loop invariant proves correctness. So, like the proof for the Bubble Sort, we need only verify the loop invariants.

On the first iteration of the main loop (step 1), a[i] is the last element in the array, so the index k of the inner loop run through every element after a[0]. The value of the index j begins at 0 and then changes each time k finds a larger element. Since j is always reset to the index of the larger element, a[j] will be the largest element of the array when the inner loop finishes. This verifies the first loop invariant. On each successive iteration of the outer loop, the index k runs through the remaining unsorted segment of the array, so for the same reason, a[j] will be the largest element of that remaining segment when the inner loop finishes. This verifies that the first loop invariant is true on every iteration of the outer loop.

Since swap(a,i,j) simply interchanges a[i] with a[j], the second loop invariant follows from the first.

The third loop invariant follows from the second and by mathematical induction. During the first iteration of the main loop, the inner loop finds a[j] to be the largest element in the array. The swap(a,i,j) puts that largest element in the last location a[i], so a[i] must be >= all the a[j]. Prior to the ith iteration of the main loop, we have by the inductive hypothesis that the subarray a[i+1..n-1] is sorted and all the values in the subarray a[0..i] are smaller than a[i+1]. Then after the ith iteration, a[i] is one of those smaller elements, so a[i] <= a[i+1] <= ... <= a[n-1].

13.20 Proof that the Selection Sort runs in $O(n^2)$ time:

Again, the proof is essentially the same as that for the corresponding theorem for the Bubble Sort. On the first iteration of the outer i loop, the inner j loop iterates $n-1$ times. On the second, it iterates $n-2$ times. This progression continues, giving a total of $(n-1)+(n-2)+\cdots+2+1 = n(n-1)/2$.

13.21 Testing an indirect Insertion Sort:

```
public static void main(String[] args)
{ int[] a = { 77, 44, 99, 66, 33, 55, 88, 22 };
  int[] index = {0,1,2,3,4,5,6,7};
  print(a,index);
  sort(a,index);
  print(a,index);
}
public static void sort(int[] a, int[] index)
{ for (int i=1; i<a.length; i++)
  { int temp=index[i], j;
    for (j=i; j>0 && a[index[j-1]]>temp; j--)
      index[j] = index[j-1];
    index[j] = temp;
  }
}
private static void print(int[] a, int[] index)
{ for (int i=0; i<a.length; i++)
    System.out.print(a[index[i]]+" ");
  System.out.println();
}
```

13.22 A recursive Insertion Sort:

```
public static void sort(int[] a)
{ sort(a,a.length);
}
public static void sort(int[] a, int n)
{ if (n<2) return;
  sort(a,n-1);
  int temp=a[n-1], j;
  for (j=n-1; j>0 && a[j-1]>temp; j--)
    a[j] = a[j-1];
  a[j] = temp;
}
```

13.23 Proof that the Insertion Sort is correct:

On the first iteration of the main loop, a[1] is compared with a[0] and interchanged if necessary. So a[0] <= a[1] after the first iteration. If we assume that the loop invariant is true prior to some kth iteration, then it must also be true after that iteration because during it a[k] is inserted between the elements that are less than or equal to it and those that are greater. It follows by mathematical induction that the loop invariant is true for all k.

13.24 Proof that the Insertion Sort runs in $O(n^2)$ time:

The proof is similar to that for the corresponding theorems for the Bubble Sort and the Selection Sort. On the first iteration of the outer i loop, the inner j loop iterates once. On the second, it iterates once or twice, depending upon whether a[1] > a[2]. On the third iteration, the inner j loop iterates at most three times, again depending upon how many of the elements on the left of a[3] are greater than a[3]. This pattern continues, so that on the kth iteration of the outer loop, the inner loop iterates at most k times. Thus the maximum total number of iterations is: $1 + 2 + \cdots + (n-1)$ $= n(n-1)/2$.

13.25 Proof that the Insertion Sort runs in $O(n)$ time when the sequence is already sorted:

In this case, the inner loop will iterate only once for each iteration of the outer loop. So the total number of iterations of the inner loop is: $1 + 1 + 1 + \cdots + 1 + 1 = n-1$.

13.26 The Quick Sort pivoting on the last element:

```
public static void sort(int[] a)
{ if (a.length>1) sort(a,0,a.length);
}

public static void sort(int[] a, int k, int n)
{ if (n<2) return;
  int pivot = a[k+n-1];
  int i = k-1;
  int j = k+n-1;
  while (i < j)
  { while (a[++i]<pivot) ;
    while (j>0 && a[--j]>pivot) ;
    if (i < j) swap(a,i,j);
  }
  swap(a,i,k+n-1);
  sort(a,k,i-k);
  sort(a,i+1,k+n-i-1);
}
```

13.27 The Quick Sort with the pivot set to be the median of three elements:

```
private static void setMedian(int[] a, int i, int j, int k)
{ // POSTCONDITION: either a[i] <= a[j] <= a[k]
  //                    or a[k] <= a[j] <= a[i]
  //    i.e., a[j] is the median of {a[i],a[j],a[k]}
  if (a[i] <= a[k] && a[k] <= a[j]) swap(a,j,k);
  else if (a[j] <= a[i] && a[i] <= a[k]) swap(a,j,i);
  else if (a[j] <= a[k] && a[k] <= a[i]) swap(a,j,k);
  else if (a[k] <= a[i] && a[i] <= a[j]) swap(a,j,i);
}

public static void sort(int[] a)
{ if (a.length>1) sort(a,0,a.length);
}

public static void sort(int[] a, int k, int n)
{ // PRECONDITIONS: 0 <= k <= k+n <= a.length;
  if (n<2) return;
  setMedian(a,k+n/2,k,k+n-1);  // a[k] = median
  int pivot = a[k];
  int i = k;
  int j = k+n;
  while (i < j)
  { while (i+1<k+n && a[++i]<pivot) ;
    while (a[--j]>pivot) ;
    if (i < j) swap(a,i,j);
  }
  swap(a,k,j);
  sort(a,k,j-k);
  sort(a,j+1,k+n-j-1);
}
```

13.28 The Quick Sort with reversion to the Insertion Sort when $n < 8$:

```java
public static void sort(int[] a)
{ if (a.length>1) sort(a,0,a.length);
}


public static void sort(int[] a, int k, int n)
{ // PRECONDITIONS: 0 <= k <= k+n <= a.length;
  if (n<2) return;
  if (n<8)
  { insertionSort(a,k,n);
    return;
  }
  int pivot = a[k];
  int i = k;
  int j = k+n;
  while (i < j)
  { while (i+1<k+n && a[++i]<pivot) ;
    while (a[--j]>pivot) ;
    if (i < j) swap(a,i,j);
  }
  swap(a,k,j);
  sort(a,k,j-k);
  sort(a,j+1,k+n-j-1);
}


public static void insertionSort(int[] a, int k, int n)
{ // POSTCONDITION: a[k] <= a[k+1] <= ... <= a[n-1];
  for (int i=k+1; i<n; i++)
  { int temp=a[i], j;
    for (j=i; j>k && a[j-1]>temp; j--)
      a[j] = a[j-1];
    a[j] = temp;
  }
}
```

13.29 The Heap Sort is not always preferred over the Quick Sort because it is slower in the average case.

13.30 The Heap Sort is not always preferred over the Merge Sort because it is not stable.

13.31 Proof that the Heap Sort is correct:

The postcondition of the Heapify establishes the loop invariant in step 3. That guarantees that the root s_0 is the maximum element of the subsequence. Step 5 inserts that maximum at the end of the subsequence. So when the loop at step 4 is finished, the sequence will be sorted.

The Heapify algorithm restores the heap property to the complete segment ss by applying the `heapifyDown()` method from its root.

13.32 The *Las Vegas Sort* has complexity $O(n^n)$.

There are $n!$ different permutations of a deck of n cards. Shuffling them is equivalent to selecting a permutation at random. Only one of the $n!$ permutations is correct; i.e., leaves the cards in order. So the expected number of random shuffles required before the correct one occurs is $n!$. Then each permutation takes $n-1$ comparisons to see if it is the correct one. So the total complexity is $O(n\,n!)$. Finally, by Stirling's Formula (Corollary A.2 on page 342), $O(n\,n!) = O(n^n)$.

Chapter 14

Tables

A *table* (also called a *map*, a *lookup table*, an *associative array*, or a *dictionary*) is a container that allows direct access by any index type. It works like an array or vector except that the index variable need not be an integer. A good analogy is a dictionary; the index variable is the word being looked up, and the element that it indexes is its dictionary definition.

A table is a sequence of pairs. The first component of the pair is called the *key*. It serves as the index into the table, generalizing the subscript integer used in arrays. The second component is called the *value* of its key component. It contains the information being looked up. In the dictionary example, the key is the word being looked up, and the value is that word's definition (and everything else listed for that word).

A table is also called a map because we think of the keys being mapped into their values, like a mathematical function: *f(key)* = *value*. Tables are also called an associative arrays because they can be implemented using two parallel arrays; the keys in one array and the values in the other.

14.1 THE JAVA `Map` INTERFACE

```
Object
  └─ AbstractMap · · · · · · · · · Map
       ├─ HashMap
       ├─ TreeMap · · · · · · · · · · ─┴─ SortedMap
       └─ WeakHashMap
```

The `Map` interface is defined in the `java.util` package like this:

```java
public interface Map
{ int size();
  boolean isEmpty();
  boolean containsKey(Object key);
  boolean containsValue(Object value);
  Object get(Object key);
  Object put(Object key, Object value);
  Object remove(Object key);
  void putAll(Map map);
  void clear();
  public Set keySet();
  public Collection values();
  public Set entrySet();
  public interface Entry
  { Object getKey();
    Object getValue();
    Object setValue(Object value);
    boolean equals(Object o);
    int hashCode();
  }
  boolean equals(Object o);
  int hashCode();
}
```

14.2 THE `HashMap` CLASS

As the class hierarchy on the previous page shows, Java defines four implementations of its Map interface: the `AbstractMap` class, the `HashMap` class, the `TreeMap` class, and the `WeakHashMap` class.

EXAMPLE 14.1 A German-English Dictionary

This program uses the `HashMap` class to build a German-English dictionary:

```
public class Ex1401
{ public static void main(String[] args)
  { Map map = new HashMap();
    map.put("Tag","day");
    map.put("Hut","hat");
    map.put("Uhr","clock");
    map.put("Rad","wheel");
    map.put("Ohr","ear");
    map.put("Tor","gate");
    System.out.println("map=" + map);
    System.out.println("map.size()=" + map.size());
    System.out.println("map.keySet()=" + map.keySet());
    System.out.println("map.values()=" + map.values());
    System.out.println("map.get(\"Uhr\")=" + map.get("Uhr"));
    System.out.println("map.remove(\"Rad\")=" + map.remove("Rad"));
    System.out.println("map.get(\"Rad\")=" + map.get("Rad"));
    System.out.println("map=" + map);
    System.out.println("map.size()=" + map.size());
  }
}
```

```
map={Rad=wheel, Uhr=clock, Ohr=ear, Tor=gate, Hut=hat, Tag=day}
map.size()=6
map.keySet()=[Rad, Uhr, Ohr, Tor, Hut, Tag]
map.values()=[wheel, clock, ear, gate, hat, day]
map.get("Uhr")=clock
map.remove("Rad")=wheel
map.get("Rad")=null
map={Uhr=clock, Ohr=ear, Tor=gate, Hut=hat, Tag=day}
map.size()=5
```

The `put()` method inserts key/value pairs into the table. For example,

```
        map.put("Tag","day");
```

inserts the key/value pair (`"Tag"`,`"day"`), where `"Tag"` is the key and `"day"` is the value.

The first call to `println()` invokes the `HashMap.toString()` method, printing the entire `map` object. The second call to `println()` invokes the `HashMap.size()` method, showing that the `map` object has six key/value elements. The next call to `println()` invokes the `HashMap.keySet()` method, which returns a `Set` object containing all the keys (the six German words). The next call to `println()` invokes the `HashMap.values()` method, which returns a `Collection` object containing all the values (the six English words). The next call to `println()` invokes the `HashMap.get()` method, which returns the value for a given key. This call returns the value object `"clock"` for the key object `"Uhr"`.The next call to `println()` invokes the `HashMap.remove()` method, which deletes the (`"Rad"`,`"wheel"`) pair, which is confirmed by the next call: `map.get("Rad")` returns `null`, indicating that there is no key/value pair in `map` whose key is `"Rad"`. The last two lines prints the entire `map` again and its size, revealing that the (`"Rad"`,`"wheel"`) pair has indeed been deleted.

The order in which the key/value pairs were stored in the `HashMap` object in Example 14.1 seems to be random and unrelated to the order in which the pairs were inserted. The next example verifies this.

EXAMPLE 14.2 Java `HashMap` Objects are Hash Tables

This program creates two independent `HashMap` objects and loads them with the same key/value pairs but in different orders:

```
public class Ex1402
{ public static void main(String[] args)
  { Map map1 = new HashMap();
    map1.put("Tor","gate");
    map1.put("Rad","wheel");
    map1.put("Tag","day");
    map1.put("Uhr","clock");
    map1.put("Hut","hat");
    map1.put("Ohr","ear");
    System.out.println("map1=" + map1);
    Map map2 = new HashMap();
    map2.put("Rad","wheel");
    map2.put("Uhr","clock");
    map2.put("Ohr","ear");
    map2.put("Tag","day");
    map2.put("Tor","gate");
    map2.put("Hut","hat");
    System.out.println("map2=" + map2);
  }
map1={Rad=wheel, Uhr=clock, Ohr=ear, Tor=gate, Hut=hat, Tag=day}
map2={Rad=wheel, Uhr=clock, Ohr=ear, Tor=gate, Hut=hat, Tag=day}
```

The order in which the key/value pairs are stored in the `HashMap` table is reflected by the output from the `toString()` method. That stored order is same in both tables, independent of the order in which they were inserted. Note that it is also the same stored order in the `HashMap` table in Example 14.1.

14.3 JAVA HASH CODES

The order in which the key/value pairs are stored in a `HashMap` table depends only upon the capacity of the table and the values of objects' the hash codes. Recall (c.f., Section 3.4 on page 58) that every object in Java is given an intrinsic *hash code*, which is computed from the actual hard data stored in the object. The `Object.hashCode()` method returns that code for each object.

EXAMPLE 14.3 Hash Codes of Some String Objects

This program prints the intrinsic hash codes of the `String` objects stored in the previous programs:

```
public class Ex1403
{ public static void main(String[] args)
  { printHashCode("Rad");
    printHashCode("Uhr");
    printHashCode("Ohr");
    printHashCode("Tor");
    printHashCode("Hut");
```

```
            printHashCode("Tag");
        }
        private static void printHashCode(String word)
        { System.out.println(word+": "+word.hashCode());
        }
    }
Rad: 81909
Uhr: 85023
Ohr: 79257
Tor: 84279
Hut: 72935
Tag: 83834
```

The fact that all six codes are relatively close 5-digits integers reflects the fact that these `String` objects all have length 3.

14.4 HASH TABLES

A *hash table* is a table that uses a special function to compute the location of data values from their key values instead of storing the keys in the table. The special function is called the *hash function* for the table. Since the lookup time is independent of the size of the table, hash tables have very faster access time.

Java defined a `Hashtable` class in its java.util package. But it has essentially been upgraded to the `HashMap` class. That is, a `HashMap` table can do everything that a `Hashtable` object can do. Moreover, the `HashMap` class is more consistent with rest of the Java Collections Framework.

A general hash table looks like the one pictured here: an array of Objects indexed by their hash values. This requires that the range of the hash function match the range of index values in the array. This is almost always managed by simply using the remainder operator modulo the size of the array:

0	
1	
2	Ohr
3	Rad
4	Uhr
5	Hut
6	Tag
7	
8	Tor
9	
10	

EXAMPLE 14.4 Mapping Keys into a Hash Table of Size 11

This program prints hash code values for `String` objects to be stored in a hash table of size 11:

```
    public class Ex1404
    { private static final int MASK = 0x7FFFFFFF; // 2^32-1
      private static final int CAPACITY = 11;

      public static void main(String[] args)
      { printHash("Rad");
        printHash("Uhr");
        printHash("Ohr");
        printHash("Tor");
        printHash("Hut");
        printHash("Tag");
      }

      private static void printHash(String word)
      { System.out.println("hash(" + word + ") = " + hash(word));
      }
```

```
    private static int hash(Object object)
    { return (object.hashCode() & MASK) % CAPACITY;
    }
}
hash(Rad) = 3
hash(Uhr) = 4
hash(Ohr) = 2
hash(Tor) = 8
hash(Hut) = 5
hash(Tag) = 3
```

The hash function values are computed by the statement

```
        return (object.hashCode() & MASK) % CAPACITY;
```

where CAPACITY is 11 and MASK is 2147483647, expressed in hexadecimal as 0x7FFFFFFF. The operation   n & MASK simply removes the sign from whatever integer n has. This is the right thing to do in Java before using the remainder operator to compute an array index because (unlike C++) Java may give a negative result to m % CAPACITY if m is negative. So the resulting value returned by the hash() function in this example is guarantees to be in the range 0 to 10.

The first five strings hash into index values 3, 4, 2, 8, and 5, so they would be stored in those locations in the hash table. But the sixth string ("Tag") also hashes to 3, causing a collision with "Rad", which would already be stored in component 3. The most common algorithm to apply when such collisions occur is to simply put the new item in the next available component. That would be component 6 in this example, since "Uhr" would already be in component 4 and "Hut" would already be in component 5. This "collision resolution" algorithm is called *linear probing*.

The HashMap class uses a hash function just like the one in Example 14.4 to implement its accessor methods: containsKey(), get(), put(), remove(), and entrySet(). Its sets the hash table size at 101 initially. With that knowledge, we can see why the six strings in the previous examples were stored in the order indicated.

EXAMPLE 14.5 Mapping Keys into a Hash Table of Size 101

This program is identical to the one in Example 14.4 except that the hash table CAPACITY is 101 instead of 11:

```
public class Ex1405
{ private static final int MASK = 0x7FFFFFFF; // 2^32-1
  private static final int CAPACITY = 101;

  public static void main(String[] args)
  { printHash("Rad");
    printHash("Uhr");
    printHash("Ohr");
    printHash("Tor");
    printHash("Hut");
    printHash("Tag");
  }

  private static void printHash(String word)
  { System.out.println("hash(" + word + ") = " + hash(word));
  }
```

```
      private static int hash(Object object)
      { return (object.hashCode() & MASK) % CAPACITY;
      }
}
hash(Rad)  = 99
hash(Uhr)  = 82
hash(Ohr)  = 73
hash(Tor)  = 45
hash(Hut)  = 13
hash(Tag)  = 4
```

The result is that the items are stored in reverse order from which they are accessed.

14.5 HASH TABLE PERFORMANCE

A hash table of size 101 that contain six elements will perform very well. It is very unlikely to have any collisions, so the access functions are immediate: the run in time $O(1)$. This is *direct access*, just like an array.

But a hash table of size 101 that contains 100 elements is likely to perform very poorly because there will have been many collisions in the process of storing its elements. For example, if the string `"Lob"` had 60 collisions before a free component were found for it, then each time it is accessed, it will take 60 "probes" to find it. That kind of performance is close to $O(n)$; i.e., not much better than a linked list.

The solution to the problem described here is to prevent the hash table from becoming too full. This is done by resizing it whenever it reaches a threshold size.

The measure of fullness depends upon two parameters: the *size* of the hash table is the actual number of elements in the table; the *capacity* of the table is the number of components that it has. The ratio of these two parameters is called the *load factor*. In the first example cited in this section, the size was 6 and the capacity was 101, resulting in a load factor of 6/101 = 5.94%. In the second example, the size was 100, resulting in a load factor of 100/101 = 99.01%.

The `HashMap` class automatically resizes its hash table when the load factor reaches a specific *threshold* value. This threshold value can be set when the hash table is created, using the constructor

```
      public HashMap(int initialCapacity, float loadFactor)
```

which also allows the initial capacity to be set. If you use a constructor that does not take one or the other of these two arguments, then the default values of capacity 101 and load threshold 75% will be used.

14.6 COLLISION RESOLUTION ALGORITHMS

The collision resolution algorithm used in the previous examples is called *linear probing*. When a new item hashes to a table component that is already in use, the algorithm specifies to increment the index until an empty component is found. This may require a "wraparound" back to the beginning of the hashtable.

EXAMPLE 14.6 Linear Probing

This program extends the program in Example 14.4. It keeps track of which table components are used and the load factor after each hashing.

```java
public class Ex1406
{ private static final int MASK = 0x7FFFFFFF; // 2^32-1
  private static final int CAPACITY = 11;
  private static int size=0;
  private static boolean[] used = new boolean[CAPACITY];

  public static void main(String[] args)
  { printHash("Rad");
    printHash("Uhr");
    printHash("Ohr");
    printHash("Tor");
    printHash("Hut");
    printHash("Tag");
    printHash("Eis");
    printHash("Ast");
    printHash("Zug");
    printHash("Hof");
    printHash("Mal");
  }

  private static void printHash(String word)
  { System.out.println("hash(" + word + ") = " + hash(word)
            + ", load = " + 100*size/CAPACITY + "%");
  }

  private static int hash(Object object)
  { ++size;
    int h = (object.hashCode() & MASK) % CAPACITY;
    while (used[h])
    { System.out.print(h + ", ");
      h = (h+1)%CAPACITY;
    }
    used[h] = true;
    return h;
  }
}
```

```
hash(Rad) = 3, load = 9%
hash(Uhr) = 4, load = 18%
hash(Ohr) = 2, load = 27%
hash(Tor) = 8, load = 36%
hash(Hut) = 5, load = 45%
3, 4, 5, hash(Tag) = 6, load = 54%
5, 6, hash(Eis) = 7, load = 63%
3, 4, 5, 6, 7, 8, hash(Ast) = 9, load = 72%
9, hash(Zug) = 10, load = 81%
3, 4, 5, 6, 7, 8, 9, 10, hash(Hof) = 0, load = 90%
2, 3, 4, 5, 6, 7, 8, 9, 10, 0, hash(Mal) = 1, load = 100%
```

The size field contains the number of items hashed into the table. The used[] array flags, which components are occupied in the table. The printHash() method prints the hash table index and the resulting load factor as a percent. When linear probing kicks in, each successive index number probe is printed.

As seen in Example 14.4, the collision occurs with the insertion of "Tag". This program shows that it had three collisions (at index numbers 3, 4, and 5) before finding a free hash location at index 6. After that insertion, the table is 54% full.

Every item after that also collides. And, of course, as the table fills up, the number of collisions becomes more frequent. The last item, "Hut", has 10 collisions. That mean that thereafter, every time this item is accesses it will have to search every one of the 11 items before it is found, clearly an $O(n)$ process.

Another collision resolution algorithm that usually performs better than linear probing is called *quadratic probing*. This algorithm jumps over items in its probing, with the result that the used components are more uniformly distributed with fewer large clusters. That improves performance because the resulting probe chains are shorter.

Notice the index "wraparound" on the insertion of "Mal": 2, 3, 4, 5, 6, 7, 8, 9, 10, 0, 1.

EXAMPLE 14.7 Quadratic Probing

This program is the same as the program in Example 14.6 except for the modified hash() function shown here.

```
private static int hash(Object object)
{ ++size;
  int h = (object.hashCode() & MASK) % CAPACITY;
  if (used[h])
  { int h0=h;
    int jump=1;
    while (used[h])
    { System.out.print(h + ", ");
      h = (h0+jump*jump)%CAPACITY;   // squared increment
      ++jump;
    }
  }
  used[h] = true;
  return h;
}
```

```
hash(Rad) = 3, load = 9%
hash(Uhr) = 4, load = 18%
hash(Ohr) = 2, load = 27%
hash(Tor) = 8, load = 36%
hash(Hut) = 5, load = 45%
3, 4, hash(Tag) = 7, load = 54%
5, hash(Eis) = 6, load = 63%
3, 4, 7, hash(Ast) = 1, load = 72%
hash(Zug) = 9, load = 81%
```

The essential difference here is in the successive index number probes computed within the while loop when a collision occurs. Instead of searching linearly, it uses a squared increment. For example, when the insertion of "Ast" collides at index 3, linear probing continued probing at indexes 4, 5, 6, 7, 8, and 9 (in Example 14.6). But with quadratic probing, only indexes 3, 4, 7, and 1 (= 12 mod 11) are probed, using successive jumps of 1, 4, and 9 (1^2, 2^2, and 3^2.). Linear probing required 50% more probes.

The price that the Quadratic Probing algorithm pays for its improved performance is that it is more likely to result in an infinite loop. That happens in Example 14.7 with the next insertion.

The string "Hof" hashes initially to index 3. After eight collisions, the Linear Probing algorithm found a free cell at index 0 (= 11 mod 11). But the probe sequence used on this item by the Quadratic Probing algorithm is the same as for "Ast": 3, 4, 7, 1, 8, 6, 6, 8 1, 7, 4, 3, 4, ... This is computed from the unmodulated quadratic sequence 3, 4, 7, 12, 19, 28, 39, 52, 67, 84, 103, 124, 147, ... This continues indefinitely, probing only the six indexes 3, 4, 7, 1, 8, and 6, all of which have already been used. So even though the table is only 81% full, the insertion fails. That can't happen with linear probing.

14.7 SEPARATE CHAINING

Instead of devising a more effective collision resolution algorithm, we can avoid collisions altogether by allowing more than one item per table component. This method is called *separate chaining*, because is uses linked lists ("chains") to hold the multiple items. In this context, the table components are usually called "buckets."

EXAMPLE 14.8 Separate Chaining

Here is how part of a definition for a `HashTable` class might look, using separate chaining:

```
public class HashTable
{ private static final int MASK = 0x7FFFFFFF; // 2^32-1
  private static int capacity=101;
  private static int size=0;
  private static float load=0.75F;
  private static LinkedList[] buckets;

  HashTable()
  { buckets = new LinkedList[capacity];
    for (int i=0; i<capacity; i++)
      buckets[i] = new LinkedList();
  }

  HashTable(int capacity, float load)
  { this();
    this.capacity = capacity;
    this.load = load;
  }

  Object put(Object key, Object value);
  { int h=hash(key);
    LinkedList bucket=buckets[h];
    Object oldValue=null;
    for (ListIterator it = bucket.iterator(); it.hasNext(); )
    { Map.Entry entry = it.next();
      if (entry.getKey().equals(key)) break;
    }
    if (entry.getKey().equals(key)) oldValue = entry.setValue(value);
    else bucket.add(new Entry(key,value));
    return oldValue;
  }

  // more methods...
}
```

Note that `put()` serves two different purposes. If the table already has an entry with the given key, it only changes the value of that entry. Otherwise, it adds a new entry with that key/value pair.

The `java.util.HashMap` class uses separate chaining in a way that is similar to Example 14.8 on page 283.

14.8 APPLICATIONS

Tables are widely used in systems programming. Moreover, they are the primary building blocks of relational databases.

Here is an example in applications programming.

EXAMPLE 14.9 A Concordance

A *concordance* is a list of words that appear in a text document along with the numbers of the lines on which the words appear. It is just like an index of a book except that it lists line numbers instead of page numbers. Concordances are useful for analyzing documents to find word frequencies and associations that are not evident from reading the document directly.

This program builds a concordance for a text file. The run here uses this particular text taken from Shakespeare's play *Julius Caesar*. The first part of the resulting concordance is shown on the right.

Shakespeare.txt

```
Friends, Romans, countrymen, lend me your ears!
I come to bury Caesar, not to praise him.
The evil that men do lives after them,
The good is oft interred with their bones;
So let it be with Caesar.  The noble Brutus
Hath told you Caesar was ambitious;
If it were so, it was a grievous fault;
And grievously hath Caesar answer'd it.
Here, under leave of Brutus and the rest, --
For Brutus is an honourable man;
So are they all, all honourable men.
Come I to speak in Caesar's funeral.
He was my friend, faithful and just to me.
But Brutus says he was ambitious;
And Brutus is an honourable man.
He hath brought many captives home to Rome.
Whose ransoms did the general coffers fill:
Did this in Caesar seem ambitious?
When that the poor have cried, Caesar hath wept;
Ambition should be made of sterner stuff.
Yet Brutus says he was ambitious;
And Brutus is an honourable man.
You all did see that on the Lupercal
I thrice presented him with a kingly crown,
Which he did thrice refuse: was this ambition?
Yet Brutus says he was ambitious;
And, sure, is an honourable man.
I speak not to disprove what Brutus spoke,
But here I am to speak what I do know.
You all did love him once, not without cause.
What cause withholds you, then, to mourn for him?
O judgement! thou art fled to brutish beasts,
And men have lost their reason!
```

Ex1409.out

```
STUFF=20
THE=3, 4, 5, 9, 17, 19, 23
GRIEVOUS=7
GRIEVOUSLY=8
WHOSE=17
REASON=33
AND=8, 9, 13, 15, 22, 27, 33
FAULT=7
KINGLY=24
COUNTRYMEN=1
MOURN=31
FRIENDS=1
GOOD=4
LEAVE=9
ROME=16
CROWN=24
SHOULD=20
INTERRED=4
WEPT=19
FOR=10, 31
FRIEND=13
BUT=14, 29
BRUTUS=5, 9, 10, 14, 15, 21, 22, 26, 28
MAN=10, 15, 22, 27
CAUSE=30, 31
SURE=27
PRESENTED=24
YOU=6, 23, 30, 31
SEE=23
BONES=4
LIVES=3
REFUSE=25
HERE=9, 29
```

This output is obtained by obtaining a `Set` "view" of the concordance and then iterating through the set, printing one element per line. Each element is a `Map.Entry` object whose `Key` is the word from the text (in all upper case letters) and whose Value is the listing of line numbers where the word was found. For example, the word "man" was found on lines 10, 15, 22, and 27. Line 10 is

        For Brutus is an honourable man;

Here is the complete program:

```
import java.io.*;
import java.util.*;
```

```
public class Ex1409
{ private static HashMap concordance;
  private static File file;
  private static FileReader reader;
  private static BufferedReader in;

  public static void main(String[] args)
  { new Ex1409("Shakespeare.txt");
    load();
    dump();
  }
  Ex1409(String filename)
  { try
    { concordance = new HashMap();
      file = new File(filename);
      reader = new FileReader(file);
      in = new BufferedReader(reader);
    }
    catch(Exception e) { System.out.println(e); }
  }

  private static void load()
  { String line=null;
    StringTokenizer parser=null;
    int lineNumber=0;
    try
    { while ((line=in.readLine()) != null)
      { ++lineNumber;
        parser = new StringTokenizer(line,",.;:()-!?' ");
        while (parser.hasMoreTokens())
        { String word = parser.nextToken().toUpperCase();
          String listing = (String)concordance.get(word);
          if (listing==null) listing = "" + lineNumber;
          else listing += ", " + lineNumber;
          concordance.put(word,listing);
        }
      }
    }
    catch(Exception e) { System.out.println(e); }
  }

  private static void dump()
  { Set set = concordance.entrySet();
    for (Iterator it=set.iterator(); it.hasNext(); )
      System.out.println(it.next());
  }
}
```

The main() method instantiates the Ex1409 class, passing the string "Shakespeare.txt" to its constructor. The constructor instantiates the HashMap class, creating the concordance object. It also instantiates the input file reader object in.

Then `main()` calls `load()`, which loads the concordance from the text file. This method uses the `StringTokenizer` object `parser` to parse the text, extracting each word with its `nextToken()` method. It keeps track of the line numbers with the `lineNumber` counter, which is incremented each time a new line is read. Each iteration of the outer `while` loop reads one line; each iteration of the inner `while` loop reads one word. The statement

```
String listing = (String)concordance.get(word);
```

looks for the word as a key in the concordance. If found, it assigns the corresponding value to the `listing` string. Otherwise, listing will be `null`. If `null`, then listing is assigned a string containing the line number; otherwise, the line number is concatenated to the existing listing. In either case, the statement

```
concordance.put(word,listing);
```

then puts the new listing into the hash table, either as a new entry or as an updated entry.

Note that the `parser` object is created by the constructor call

```
parser = new StringTokenizer(line,",.;:()-!? ");
```

This uses the two-argument constructor for the `StringTokenizer` class, the second argument being a string that contains all the characters to be used as delimiters. By listing the comma `','`, the period `'.'`, the semicolon `';'`, etc., we are able to exclude these characters from the words being stored.

Finally, `main()` calls `dump()`, which prints the concordance. Since the HashMap class has no direct way of being traversed (see Section 14.1 on page 275), we have to dump the concordance into a `Set` object first. This gives us a different "view" of the hash table: a set whose elements are the table entries. Then, since the `Set` interface provides an `iterator()` method, we can easily traverse it with a for loop, accessing each entry sequentially. The iterator's `next()` method returns an entry as an `Object` whose intrinsic type is `Map.Entry`. (Note on page page 275 that `Entry` is an inner interface of `Map`.) So when it is passed to the `println()` method, its `Map.Entry.toString()` method is invoked, producing an output sting like this:

```
BRUTUS=5, 9, 10, 14, 15, 21, 22, 26, 28
```

The equals sign `'='` separates the entry's key from its value. The key here is the string `"BRUTUS"` and its value is the string `"5, 9, 10, 14, 15, 21, 22, 26, 28"`.

Concordances are used for analyzing text. This example shows that Shakespeare's scene is more about Brutus than anything else. It reveals nine references to "Brutus" (more than to "Caesar") and the homonymous use of the word "brutish."

The output from the program in Example 14.9 demonstrates a critical feature of hash tables: their contents are not ordered. To obtained an alphabetized printout of the concordance, we would have to sort it.

14.9 THE `TreeMap` CLASS

The `TreeMap` class extends the `AbstractMap` class and implements the `SortedMap` interface. (See Section 14.1 on page 275. It is called a "tree map" because it is a binary search tree instead of a hash table. But it is still a map with key/value entries. As a tree structure, it loses its $O(1)$ access time but it has the advantage of being ordered.

EXAMPLE 14.10 An Ordered Concordance

This program is the same as the program in Example 14.9 except that the class name `HashMap` has been replaced by `TableMap` in the constructor:

```
Ex1410(String filename)
{ try
    { concordance = new TableMap();
      file = new File(filename);
```

```
            reader = new FileReader(file);
            in = new BufferedReader(reader);
        }
        catch(Exception e) { System.out.println(e); }
    }
```
The result is that the concordance is stored as an ordered binary search tree, so its output is sorted:

```
A=7, 24
AFTER=3
ALL=11, 11, 23, 30
AM=29
AMBITION=20, 25
AMBITIOUS=6, 14, 18, 21, 26
AN=10, 15, 22, 27
AND=8, 9, 13, 15, 22, 27, 33
ANSWER=8
ARE=11
ART=32
BE=5, 20
BEASTS=32
BONES=4
BROUGHT=16
BRUTISH=32
BRUTUS=5, 9, 10, 14, 15, 21, 22, 26, 28
BURY=2
BUT=14, 29
CAESAR=2, 5, 6, 8, 12, 18, 19
CAPTIVES=16
CAUSE=30, 31
COFFERS=17
COME=2, 12
COUNTRYMEN=1
CRIED=19
CROWN=24
D=8
DID=17, 18, 23, 25, 30
DISPROVE=28
DO=3, 29
EARS=1
EVIL=3
FAITHFUL=13
FAULT=7
FILL=17
FLED=32
FOR=10, 31
FRIEND=13
FRIENDS=1
FUNERAL=12
GENERAL=17
GOOD=4
GRIEVOUS=7
GRIEVOUSLY=8
HATH=6, 8, 16, 19
HAVE=19, 33
HE=13, 14, 16, 21, 25, 26
HERE=9, 29
HIM=2, 24, 30, 31
```

Besides demonstrating the fundamental dichotomy between linear time unordered hash tables and quadratic time ordered binary search trees, Example 14.10 also reveals the excellent design and efficiency of the Java Collections Framework. Since both the `HashMap` and the `TreeMap` classes implement the same `Map` interface, we can replace one with the other by changing only the name of the constructor called to create the map.

Review Questions

14.1 What is the difference between a table and a vector?

14.2 Why is a table also called a map?

14.3 Why is a table also called a associative array?

14.4 Why is a table also called a dictionary?

14.5 What is a concordance?

14.6 What is a hash table?

14.7 What is the difference between the Java `Hashtable` class and the Java `HashMap` class?

14.8 The first two examples showed that the order of insertion into a hash table is irrelevant if there are no collisions. What if there are?

14.9 What are the advantages and disadvantages of quadratic probing compared to linear probing?

14.10 What are the advantages and disadvantages of using a `HashMap` compared to a `TreeMap`?

Problems

14.1 Run a program similar to the one in Example 14.1 on page 276 to insert the following 16 entries into the German-English dictionary:

```
map.put("Ast","gate");
map.put("Eis","ice");
map.put("Hof","court, yard, farm");
map.put("Hut","hat");
map.put("Lob","praise");
map.put("Mal","mark, signal");
map.put("Mut","courage");
map.put("Ohr","ear");
map.put("Ost","east");
map.put("Rad","wheel");
map.put("Rat","advice, counsel");
map.put("Tag","day");
map.put("Tor","gate");
map.put("Uhr","clock");
map.put("Wal","whale");
map.put("Zug","procession, train");
```

CommonWords.txt

```
A
AFTER
ALL
AM
AN
AND
ARE
BE
BROUGHT
BUT
COME
DID
DO
FOR
HATH
HAVE
HE
HERE
HIM
I
IF
IN
IS
IT
LET
MADE
MANY
O
OF
ON
```

14.2 Modify the `Concordance` class so that it filters out common words (pronouns, adverbs, etc.) whose listing would not contribute to new insights into the document. Store the common words in a separate file. The file named `CommonWords.txt` would look like the list on the right.

14.3   Modify the program in Example 14.1 on page 276 so that it stores the words in alphabetical order. Have it load the same data as in Problem 14.1 above and then print the table's contents in alphabetical order.

14.4   Implement a `FrequencyTable` class for producing a list of words together with their frequency of occurrence in a given text file.

Answers to Review Questions

14.1   A vector provides direct access to its elements by means of its integer index. A table provides direct access to its elements by means of a key field, which can be of any ordinal type: `int`, `double`, `string`, etc.

14.2   A table is also called a map because, like a mathematical function, it maps each key value into a unique element.

14.3   A table is also called an associative array because it acts like an array (see Answer 14.1) in which each key value is associated with its unique element. Like a mathematical function, it maps each key value into a unique element.

14.4   A table is also called a dictionary because it is used the same way as an ordinary natural language dictionary: to look up elements, as one would look up words in a dictionary.

14.5   A *concordance* is a list of words that appear in a text document along with the numbers of the lines on which the words appear. (See page 284.)

14.6   A *hash table* is a table that uses a special function to compute the location of data values from their key values instead of storing the keys in the table. (See page 278.)

14.7   Not much. The Java `Hashtable` class has generally been superseded by the Java `HashMap` class, which conforms a little better to the Java Collections Framework.

14.8   If there are collisions, then the order of insertion is relevant.

14.9   Quadratic probing generally results in fewer collisions because the probes jump over gaps in the index range. But unlike linear probing, quadratic probing can cause infinite loops even when the table is not full.

14.10   A `HashMap` object is a hash table implemented with separate chaining and a default load threshold of 75%, so it provides nearly $O(1)$ access time for insertions, deletions, and searches. A `TreeMap` object is a balanced binary search tree implemented as a red-black tree, so it provides nearly $O(\lg n)$ access time for insertions, deletions, and searches. So a `HashMap` is faster, but a `TreeMap` is ordered.

Solutions to Problems

14.1   Inserting 16 entries into the German-English dictionary:

```
import java.util.*;
public class Testing
{ public static void main(String[] args)
    { Map map = new HashMap(11);
      map.put("Ast","gate");
      map.put("Eis","ice");
      map.put("Hof","court, yard, farm");
      map.put("Hut","hat");
      map.put("Lob","praise");
      map.put("Mal","mark, signal");
      map.put("Mut","courage");
      map.put("Ohr","ear");
      map.put("Ost","east");
```

```
      map.put("Rad","wheel");
      map.put("Rat","advice, counsel");
      map.put("Tag","day");
      map.put("Tor","gate");
      map.put("Uhr","clock");
      map.put("Wal","whale");
      map.put("Zug","procession, train");
      System.out.println("map=" + map);
      System.out.println("map.keySet()=" + map.keySet());
      System.out.println("map.size()=" + map.size());
    }
  }
```

14.2   A Concordance that filters out common words:

```
      import java.io.*;
      import java.util.*;
      public class Pr1403
      { private static Map concordance;
        private static Set words;
        private static File file;
        private static FileReader reader;
        private static BufferedReader in;
        public static void main(String[] args)
        { loadSet("CommonWords.txt");
          dumpSet();
          loadMap("Shakespeare.txt");
          dumpMap();
        }
        private static void loadSet(String filename)
        { try
          { words = new HashSet();
            file = new File(filename);
            reader = new FileReader(file);
            in = new BufferedReader(reader);
            String line=null;
            StringTokenizer parser=null;
            while ((line=in.readLine()) != null)
            { parser = new StringTokenizer(line,",.;:()-!?' ");
              String word = parser.nextToken().toUpperCase();
              words.add(word);
            }
          }
          catch(Exception e) { System.out.println(e); }
        }
        private static void dumpSet()
        { for (Iterator it=words.iterator(); it.hasNext(); )
            System.out.println(it.next());
        }
        private static void loadMap(String filename)
        { try
          { concordance = new TreeMap();
            file = new File(filename);
            reader = new FileReader(file);
            in = new BufferedReader(reader);
            String line=null;
            StringTokenizer parser=null;
            int lineNumber=0;
```

```
            while ((line=in.readLine()) != null)
            { ++lineNumber;
              parser = new StringTokenizer(line,",.;:()-!?' ");
              while (parser.hasMoreTokens())
              { String word = parser.nextToken().toUpperCase();
                if (!words.contains(word))
                { String listing = (String)concordance.get(word);
                  if (listing==null) listing = "" + lineNumber;
                  else listing += ", " + lineNumber;
                  concordance.put(word,listing);
                }
              }
            }
          }
          catch(Exception e) { System.out.println(e); }
        }

        private static void dumpMap()
        { Set set = concordance.entrySet();
          for (Iterator it=set.iterator(); it.hasNext(); )
            System.out.println(it.next());
        }
      }
```

14.3   A sorted German-English dictionary:

```
        import java.util.*;
        public class Pr1202
        { private static Map map;
          public static void main(String[] args)
          { map = new TreeMap();
            load();
            dump();
          }
          private static void load()
          { map.put("Ast","gate");
            map.put("Eis","ice");
            map.put("Hof","court, yard, farm");
            map.put("Hut","hat");
            map.put("Lob","praise");
            map.put("Mal","mark, signal");
            map.put("Mut","courage");
            map.put("Ohr","ear");
            map.put("Ost","east");
            map.put("Rad","wheel");
            map.put("Rat","advice, counsel");
            map.put("Tag","day");
            map.put("Tor","gate");
            map.put("Uhr","clock");
            map.put("Wal","whale");
            map.put("Zug","procession, train");
          }
          private static void dump()
          { Set set = map.entrySet();
            for (Iterator it=set.iterator(); it.hasNext(); )
              System.out.println(it.next());
          }
        }
```

14.4 A frequency table:

```java
import java.io.*;
import java.util.*;
public class Pr1404
{ private static Map concordance;
  private static File file;
  private static FileReader reader;
  private static BufferedReader in;
  public static void main(String[] args)
  { loadMap("Shakespeare.txt");
    dumpMap();
  }
  private static void loadMap(String filename)
  { try
    { concordance = new TreeMap();
      file = new File(filename);
      reader = new FileReader(file);
      in = new BufferedReader(reader);
      String line=null;
      StringTokenizer parser=null;
      int lineNumber=0;
      while ((line=in.readLine()) != null)
      { ++lineNumber;
        parser = new StringTokenizer(line,",.;:()-!?' ");
        while (parser.hasMoreTokens())
        { String word = parser.nextToken().toUpperCase();
          String frequency = (String)concordance.get(word);
          if (frequency==null) frequency = "1";
          else
          { int n=Integer.parseInt(frequency);
            ++n;
            frequency = "" + n;
          }
          concordance.put(word,frequency);
        }
      }
    }
    catch(Exception e) { System.out.println(e); }
  }
  private static void dumpMap()
  { Set set = concordance.entrySet();
    for (Iterator it=set.iterator(); it.hasNext(); )
      System.out.println(it.next());
  }
}
```

Chapter 15

Sets

15.1 MATHEMATICAL SETS

A *set* is a collection of unique elements. The *size* of a set is the number of its elements. The unique set of size 0 is called the *empty set*, denoted by $\varnothing$.

In mathematics, sets are denoted either by listing their elements like this:

$$A = \{44, 77, 22\}$$

or by indicating a pattern, like this:

$$B = \{2, 4, 6, 8, 10, 12, \ldots\}$$

or by specifying a condition, like this:

$$C = \{n \in \mathbf{Z} \mid n \text{ is even}\} = \{n \in \mathbf{Z} : n \text{ is even}\}$$

The symbol represents the set of all integers:

$$\mathbf{Z} = \{0, 1, -1, 2, -2, 3, -3, \ldots\}$$

Both the pipe symbol "|" and the colon ":" are pronounced "such that." So the definition of the set C above is pronounced "the set of all integers n such that n is even," which of course means simply the set of all even integers.

The three primary operations on sets are union, intersection, and relative complement (also called subtraction). The *union* of sets A and B is denoted by $A \cup B$ and defined by

$$A \cup B = \{x : x \in A \text{ or } x \in B\}$$

The *intersection* of sets A and B is denoted by $A \cap B$ and defined by

$$A \cap B = \{x : x \in A \text{ and } x \in B\}$$

The *relative complement* of set B in set A is denoted by $A - B$ and defined by

$$A - B = \{x : x \in A \text{ but } (x \notin B)\}$$

The primary relational operator on sets is the subset operator: A is a *subset* of B if and only if every element of A is also an element of B. This condition is denoted by $A \subseteq B$. Note that every set is a subset of itself, and the empty set is a subset of every set.

EXAMPLE 15.1 Set-Theoretic Operations

Let $A = \{1, 2, 3, 4, 5\}$ and $B = \{4, 5, 6, 7\}$. Then $A \cup B = \{1, 2, 3, 4, 5, 6, 7\}$, $A \cap B = \{4, 5\}$, and $A - B = \{1, 2, 3\}$.

Let $C = \{2, 3, 4\}$. Then C is a subset of A, but not of B.

15.2 THE JAVA `Set` INTERFACE

The Java Collections Framework (see Section 5.1 on page 94) implementation of set data structures is parallel to its implementation of table data structures. (See Chapter 14.) The framework includes the following classes and interfaces

The `java.util.Set` interface is a subinterface of the `Collection` interface, inheriting these methods:

```
public boolean   add(Object);
public boolean   addAll(Collection);
public void      clear();
public boolean   contains(Object);
public boolean   containsAll(Collection);
public boolean   equals(Object);
public int       hashCode();
public boolean   isEmpty();
public Iterator  iterator();
public boolean   remove(Object);
public boolean   removeAll(Collection);
public boolean   retainAll(Collection);
public int       size();
public Object[]  toArray();
public Object[]  toArray(Object[]);
```

No other methods are added to the `Set` interface.

15.3 THE JAVA `AbstractSet` CLASS

The `java.util.AbstractSet` class is a partial implementation of the `Set` interface. Like other abstract classes in the Collections Framework, it is designed to reduce the effort required to build a complete class. It implements most of the methods required by the `Set` interface:

```
public abstract class AbstractSet extends AbstractCollection
                                   implements Set
{ protected                AbstractSet() { }
  public          boolean  add(Object);
```

```
    public            boolean   addAll(Collection);
    public            void      clear();
    public            boolean   contains(Object);
    public            boolean   containsAll(Collection);
    public            boolean   equals(Object);
    public            int       hashCode();
    public            boolean   isEmpty();
    public abstract Iterator    iterator();
    public            boolean   remove(Object);
    public            boolean   removeAll(Collection);
    public            boolean   retainAll(Collection);
    public abstract int         size();
    public            Object[]  toArray();
    public            Object[]  toArray(Object[]);
}
```

15.4 THE JAVA `HashSet` CLASS

The Java `HashSet` class is essentially the same as the Java `HashMap` class except that its objects are single-component set elements instead of double-component map key/value pairs. Like the `HashMap` class, the `HashSet` class uses the objects' intrinsic `hashCode()` values to store them in a hash table. So access to its elements (by its `add()`, `contains()`, and `remove()` methods) runs in nearly constant time (i.e., the algorithms have $O(1)$ complexity).

The class is defined in the `java.util` package like this:

```
public class HashSet extends AbstractSet implements Set
{ public HashSet();
  public HashSet(Collection collection);
  public HashSet(int capacity, float threshold);
  public HashSet(int capacity);
  public Iterator iterator();
  public int size();
  public boolean isEmpty();
  public boolean contains(Object object);
  public boolean add(Object object);
  public boolean remove(Object object);
  public void clear();
  public Object clone();
}
```

EXAMPLE 15.2 A `HashSet` of Strings

This program creates a `HashSet` named countries, loads it with seven strings, and then uses an iterator to traverse the hash table to print its contents.

```
import java.util.*;
public class Ex1502
{ public static void main(String[] args)
  { Set countries = new HashSet();
    load(countries);
    dump(countries);
  }
```

```
    private static void load(Set set)
    { set.add("Cuba");
      set.add("Iran");
      set.add("Iraq");
      set.add("Laos");
      set.add("Oman");
      set.add("Peru");
      set.add("Togo");
    }
    private static void dump(Set set)
    { for (Iterator it=set.iterator(); it.hasNext(); )
        System.out.println(it.next());
      System.out.println("set.size() = " + set.size());
    }
}
```

```
Peru
Oman
Iraq
Iran
Cuba
Togo
Laos
set.size() = 7
```

Note that the order of the element in the hash table has been "hashed" (randomized). The actual indexes of the elements is computed by the private hash function which uses the remainder modulo 101 if the string's `Object.hashCode()`, which is computed from the Unicode values of its characters.

EXAMPLE 15.3 Modifying a `HashSet` of Strings

This program illustrates the `add()`, `contains()`, and `remove()` methods for `HashSet` sets. It uses the same data as in Example 15.2:

```
import java.util.*;
public class Ex1502
{ public static void main(String[] args)
  { Set countries = new HashSet();
    load(countries);
    report(countries,"Iraq");
    System.out.println("countries.remove(\"Iraq\") = "
                        + countries.remove("Iraq"));
    report(countries,"Iraq");
    report(countries,"Fiji");
    System.out.println("countries.remove(\"Fiji\") = "
                        + countries.remove("Fiji"));
    System.out.println("countries.add(\"Fiji\") = "
                        + countries.add("Fiji"));
    report(countries,"Fiji");
    System.out.println("countries.add(\"Fiji\") = "
                        + countries.add("Fiji"));
    report(countries,"Fiji");
  }
```

```
        private static void report(Set set, String string)
        { System.out.println("\t\t" + set.size() + " elements: " + set);
          System.out.println("\t\tset.contains(" + string + ") = "
                              + set.contains(string));
        }
        private static void load(Set set)
        { set.add("Cuba");
          set.add("Iran");
          set.add("Iraq");
          set.add("Laos");
          set.add("Oman");
          set.add("Peru");
          set.add("Togo");
        }
    }
```

```
                7 elements: [Peru, Oman, Iraq, Iran, Cuba, Togo, Laos]
                set.contains(Iraq) = true
countries.remove("Iraq") = true
                6 elements: [Peru, Oman, Iran, Cuba, Togo, Laos]
                set.contains(Iraq) = false
                6 elements: [Peru, Oman, Iran, Cuba, Togo, Laos]
                set.contains(Fiji) = false
countries.remove("Fiji") = false
countries.add("Fiji") = true
                7 elements: [Peru, Fiji, Oman, Iran, Cuba, Togo, Laos]
                set.contains(Fiji) = true
countries.add("Fiji") = false
                7 elements: [Peru, Fiji, Oman, Iran, Cuba, Togo, Laos]
                set.contains(Fiji) = true
```

The `remove()` method reports whether it is successful. So the call `countries.remove("Fiji")` returns `false` because at that point `"Fiji"` was not an element of the set. The `add()` method also reports whether it is successful. So access to its elements (by its `add()`, `contains()`, and `remove()` methods) runs in *logarithmic time* (i.e., the algorithms have $O(\lg n)$ complexity).

15.5 THE JAVA `TreeSet` CLASS

The Java `TreeSet` class is essentially the same as the Java `TreeMap` class except that its objects are single-component set elements instead of double-component map key/value pairs. Like the `TreeMap` class, the `TreeSet` class stores its objects in a balanced binary search tree (a red-black tree). So access to its elements (by its `add()`, `contains()`, and `remove()` methods) runs in logarithmic time (i.e., the algorithms have $O(\lg n)$ complexity).

The class is defined in the `java.util` package like this:

```
    public class TreeSet extends AbstractSet implements Set
    { public TreeSet();
      public TreeSet(Collection collection);
      public TreeSet(SortedSet set);
      public TreeSet(Comparator comparator);
      public Iterator iterator();
      public int size();
      public boolean isEmpty();
      public boolean contains(Object object);
```

```
        public boolean add(Object object);
        public boolean remove(Object object);
        public void clear();
        public Object clone();
        public Comparator comparator();
        public Object first();
        public Object last();
        public SortedSet subSet(Object start, Object stop);
        public SortedSet headSet(Object stop);
        public SortedSet tailSet(Object start);
    }
```

This includes the same methods that the `HashSet` class implements. The extra methods are required by the `SortedSet` interface. These include the last five methods listed here, which return the first element, the last element, and three kinds of subset segments.

The `HashSet` class uses its elements' `equals()` method to search for given elements. That is sufficient, since order is irrelevant in a hash table. But order is important in search trees, so the `TreeSet` class uses either its elements' `compareTo()` method or a `Comparator` object instead of its elements' `equals()` method. If the fourth constructor listed above is invoked, then the `Comparator` object passed to is used. (See Section 12.6 on page 230.)

EXAMPLE 15.4 Using a `TreeSet` of Strings

This program illustrates the `first()`, `last()`, `headSet()`, `subSet()`, and `tailSet()` methods for `TreeSet` sets.:

```
    import java.util.*;
    public class Ex1504
    { public static void main(String[] args)
        { SortedSet countries = new TreeSet();
        load(countries);
        System.out.println(countries);
        System.out.println("countries.first() = " + countries.first());
        System.out.println("countries.last()  = " + countries.last());
        String s1="Fiji";
        String s2="Laos";
        System.out.println("countries.headSet(" + s1 + ") = "
                        + countries.headSet(s1));
        System.out.println("countries.subSet(" + s1 + "," + s2 + ") = "
                        + countries.subSet(s1,s2));
        System.out.println("countries.tailSet(" + s2 + ") = "
                        + countries.tailSet(s2));
    }
    private static void load(Set set)
    { set.add("Laos");
        set.add("Cuba");
        set.add("Iraq");
        set.add("Togo");
        set.add("Iran");
        set.add("Oman");
        set.add("Chad");
        set.add("Peru");
        set.add("Guam");
```

```
        set.add("Fiji");
    }
}
```

<pre style="background:#ccc">
[Chad, Cuba, Fiji, Guam, Iran, Iraq, Laos, Oman, Peru, Togo]
countries.first() = Chad
countries.last() = Togo
countries.headSet(Fiji) = [Chad, Cuba]
countries.subSet(Fiji,Laos) = [Fiji, Guam, Iran, Iraq]
countries.tailSet(Laos) = [Laos, Oman, Peru, Togo]
</pre>

Note that, as usual, whenever a range of elements is specified, the start element is the first one in the segment, and the stop element is the one after the last one in the segment. For example, the call `countries.subSet("Fiji","Laos")` returns the segment that begins with `"Fiji"` and ends with `"Iraq"`, which comes just before `"Laos"`.

Review Questions

15.1   What happens when you try to `add()` an element to a set that already contains it?

15.2   What happens when you try to `remove()` an element from a set when it is not in the set?

15.3   What are the advantages and disadvantages of using a `HashSet` compared to a `TreeSet`?

Problems

15.1   Implement the following set-theoretic operation for `TreeSet` objects:
```
public static Set union(Set a, Set b)
// returns a new set that contains every element of set a,
// every element of set b, and no others
```

15.2   Implement the following set-theoretic operation for `TreeSet` objects:
```
public static Set intersection(Set a, Set b)
// returns a new set that contains only those elements
// that are in both set a and set b
```

15.3   Implement the following set-theoretic operation for `TreeSet` objects:
```
public static Set complement(Set a, Set b)
// returns a new set that contains only those elements
// that are in set a and not in set b
```

15.4   Implement the following set-theoretic operation for `TreeSet` objects:
```
public static isSubset(Set a, Set b)
// returns true if and only if every element of set a
// is also an element of set b
```

Answers to Review Questions

15.1   An attempt to `add()` a duplicate element to a set will return `false` without changing the set. (See Example 15.3 on page 296.)

15.2   An attempt to `remove()` a nonexistent element from a set will return `false` without changing the set. (See Example 15.3 on page 296.)

15.3   A `HashSet` object is a hash table implemented with separate chaining and a default load threshold of 75%, so it provides nearly $O(1)$ access time for insertions, deletions, and searches. A `TreeSet` object is a balanced binary search tree implemented as a red-black tree, so it provides $O(\lg n)$ access time for insertions, deletions, and searches. So a `HashSet` is faster but a `TreeSet` is ordered.

Solutions to Problems

15.1   The union operation for `TreeSet` objects:

```
public static Set union(Set a, Set b)
{ Set c = new TreeSet(a);
  for (Iterator it=b.iterator(); it.hasNext(); )
    c.add(it.next());
  return c;
}
```

15.2   The intersection operation for `TreeSet` objects:

```
public static Set intersection(Set a, Set b)
{ Set c = new TreeSet(a);
  for (Iterator it=a.iterator(); it.hasNext(); )
  { String x=(String)it.next();
    if (!b.contains(x)) c.remove(x);
  }
  return c;
}
```

15.3   The relative complement operation for `TreeSet` objects:

```
public static Set complement(Set a, Set b)
{ Set c = new TreeSet(a);
  for (Iterator it=b.iterator(); it.hasNext(); )
    c.remove(it.next());
  return c;
}
```

15.4   The subset operation for `TreeSet` objects:

```
public static boolean isSubset(Set a, Set b)
{ for (Iterator it=a.iterator(); it.hasNext(); )
    if (!b.contains(it.next())) return false;
  return true;
```

Chapter 16

Graphs

16.1 SIMPLE GRAPHS

A (*simple*) *graph* is a pair $G = (V, E)$, where V and E are finite sets and every element of E is a two-element subset of V (i.e., an unordered pair of distinct elements of V). The elements of V are called *vertices* (or *nodes*), and the elements of E are called *edges* (or *arcs*). If $e \in E$ then $e = \{a, b\}$ for some $a, b \in V$. In this case, we can denote e more simply as $e = ab = ba$. We say that the edge e *connects* the two vertices a and b, that e is *incident with* a and b, that a and b are *incident upon* e, that a and b are the *terminal points* or *endpoints* of the edge e, and that a and b are *adjacent*.

The *size* of a graph is the number of elements in its vertex set.

EXAMPLE 16.1 A Simple Graph

The picture here shows a simple graph (V, E) of size 4. Its vertex set $V = \{a, b, c, d\}$ and its edge set $E = \{ab, ac, ad, bd, cd\}$. This graph has four vertices and five edges.

Note that by definition an edge is a set with exactly two elements. This prevents the possibility of a loop being an edge because a loop involves only one vertex. So the definition for simple graphs excludes the possibility of loops.

Also note that since E is a set, an edge cannot be listed more than once. (Sets do not allow repeated members.) So the definition for simple graphs excludes the possibility of multiple edges.

General (not necessarily simple) graphs do allow loops and multiple edges; simple graphs do not.

16.2 GRAPH TERMINOLOGY

If $G = (V, E)$ is a graph and $G' = (V', E')$ where $V' \subseteq V$ and $E' \subseteq E$, then G' is called a *subgraph* of G. If $V' = V$, then G' is called a *spanning subgraph* of G.

Every graph is a spanning subgraph of itself.

EXAMPLE 16.2 Subgraphs

The graph $G_1 = (V_1, E_1)$ with vertex set $V_1 = \{a, b, d\}$ and its edge set $E_1 = \{ad, bd\}$ is a nonspanning subgraph of the graph in Example 16.1. This subgraph has size 3.

The graph $G_2 = (V_2, E_2)$ with vertex set $V_2 = \{a, b, c, d\}$ and its edge set $E_2 = \{ab, ac, cd\}$ is a spanning subgraph of the graph in Example 16.1. This subgraph has size 4.

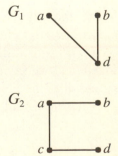

The *degree* (or *valence*) of a vertex is the number of edges that are incident upon it. For example, in the graph in Example 16.1, vertex a has degree 3 and vertex b has degree 2. But in the subgraph in Example 16.2, vertices a and b both have degree 1.

An *isolated point* is a vertex of degree 0.

Theorem 16.1 The sum of the degrees of the vertices of a graph with m edges is $2m$.
Proof: Each edge contributes 1 to the degree of each of the two vertices that determine it. So the total contribution if m edges is $2m$.

A *complete graph* is a simple graph in which every pair of vertices is connected by an edge. For a given number n of vertices, there is only one complete graph of that size, so we refer to the complete graph on a given vertex set.

EXAMPLE 16.3 The Complete Graph on a Set of Four Vertices

Here is the complete graph on the set $V = \{a, b, c, d\}$. Its edge set E is
$E = \{ab, ac, ad, bc, bd, cd\}$.

Note that the graphs in the previous examples are subgraphs of this one.

Theorem 16.2 The number of edges in the complete graph on n vertices is $n(n-1)/2$.
Proof: There are n vertices, and for each of them there are $n-1$ other vertices to which it could be adjacent. So there are $n(n-1)$ ordered pairs of vertices. Therefore there are $n(n-1)/2$ unordered pairs because each unordered pair could be ordered in two ways. For example, the unordered pair $\{a, b\}$ can be ordered as either (a, b) or (b, a).

For example, the number of edges in the complete graph on the 4-vertex set in Example 16.3 is $n(n-1)/2 = 4(4-1)/2 = 6$.

Corollary 16.1 The number of edges in any graph on n vertices is $m \leq n(n-1)/2$.

16.3 PATHS AND CYCLES

A *walk from vertex a to vertex b* in a graph is a sequence of edges $(a_0a_1, a_1a_2, ..., a_{k-1}a_k)$ where $a_0 = a$ and $a_k = b$; i.e., a sequence of edges $(e_1, e_2, ..., e_k)$ where if edge e_i connects some vertex to vertex a_i then the next edge e_{i+1} connects that vertex a_i to some other vertex, thereby forming a chain of connected vertices from a to b. The *length* of a walk is the number k of edges that form the walk.

Although a walk is a sequence of edges, it naturally induces a sequence of adjacent vertices which the edges connect. So we may denote the walk $(a_0a_1, a_1a_2, ..., a_{k-1}a_k)$ more simply by $a_0a_1a_2...a_{k-1}a_k$ as long as each pair (a_{i-1}, a_i) is a valid edge in the graph.

If $p = a_0a_1a_2...a_{k-1}a_k$ is a walk in a graph, then we refer to p as a walk *from a_0 to a_k* (or *from a_k to a_0*), and we say that p *connects* a_0 to a_k and that a_0 and a_k are *connected* by p. We also refer to a_0 and a_k as the *terminal points* or the *endpoints* of the walk.

A *path* is a walk all whose vertices are distinct.

EXAMPLE 16.4 Graph Paths

In the graph shown here, *abcfde* is a path of length 5. It is, more formally, the path (*ab*, *bc*, *cf*, *fd*, *de*).

The walk *abefdbc* of length 6 is not a path because vertex *b* appears twice. The walk *abefa* of length 4 is also not a path.

The sequence *abf* is not a walk because *bf* is not an edge. And the sequence *abb* is not a walk because *bb* is not an edge.

Finally, *aba* is a walk of length 2, and *ab* is a walk of length 1.

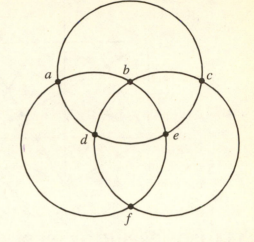

A graph is said to be *connected* if every pair of its vertices are connected by some path. A graph that is not connected is called *disconnected*.

All the graphs shown above are connected.

EXAMPLE 16.5 A Disconnected Graph

Here is a graph of size 12 that is not connected.

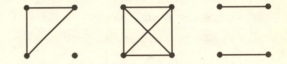

A *connected component* of a graph is a subgraph that is maximally connected; i.e., a connected subgraph with the property that any larger subgraph that contains it is disconnected.

The graph in Example 16.5 has 5 connected components, of sizes 3, 1, 4, 2, and 2.

Theorem 16.3 Every graph is a union of a unique set of connected components.

A walk is *closed* if its two endpoints are the same vertex. A *cycle* is a closed walk of length at least 3 all of whose interior vertices are distinct.

EXAMPLE 16.6 Graph Cycles

In the graph shown in Example 16.4, the walk *abefa* is a cycle.
The walk *abedbcfa* is not a cycle because it is not a path: it has the duplicate internal vertex *b*.
The path *abef* is not a cycle because it is not closed.
And the walk *aba* is not a cycle because its length is only 2.

A graph is said to be *acyclic* if it contains no cycles.
Among the graphs shown above, only the ones in Example 16.2 on page 301 are acyclic.
An acyclic graph is also called a *free forest*, and a connected acyclic graph is also called a *free tree*. Note that a tree (see Chapter 9) is the same as a free tree in which one node has been designated as the root. So in the context of graph theory, a tree is called a *rooted tree*, which is defined to be a connected acyclic graph with one distinguished node.
A *spanning tree* of a graph is a connected acyclic spanning subgraph.

EXAMPLE 16.7 Spanning Trees

The graph shown next is a spanning tree of the graph on its left.

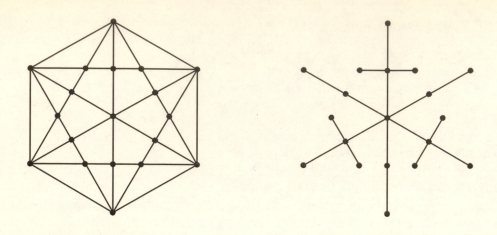

16.4 ISOMORPHIC GRAPHS

An *isomorphism* between two graphs $G = (V, E)$ and $G' = (V', E')$ is a function f that assigns to each vertex x in V some vertex $y = f(x)$ in V' so that the following three conditions are satisfied:

1. f is *one-to-one*: each x in V gets assigned a different $y = f(x)$ in V'.

2. f is *onto*: every y in V' gets assigned to some x in V.

3. f *preserves adjacency*: if $\{x_1, x_2\}$ is an edge in E, then $\{f(x_1), f(x_2)\}$ is an edge in E'.

Two graphs are said to be *isomorphic* if there is an isomorphism from one to the other. The word "isomorphic" means "same form." When applied to graphs, it means that they have the same mathematical (topological) structure. Graphically, two graphs are isomorphic if one can be twisted around to for the same shape as the other without breaking any of the edge connections.

EXAMPLE 16.8 Isomorphic Graphs

The follow two graphs are isomorphic:

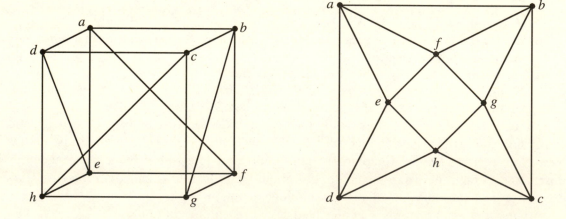

The isomorphism is indicated by the labeling of the vertices.

It can be verified that if vertex x_1 is adjacent to vertex x_2 in one graph, then the corresponding vertices are adjacent in the other graph. For example, vertex a is adjacent to vertices b, d, e, and f (but not c, g, or h) in both graphs.

To prove that two graphs are isomorphic (by definition) it is necessary to find an isomorphism between them. This is equivalent to labeling both graphs with the same set of labels so that adjacency applies equally to both labelings. Finding such an isomorphism by chance is unlikely because there are $n!$ different possibilities. For example, there are $8! = 40,320$ different possible ways to assign the 8 labels to the 8 vertices of each graph in Example 16.8. The following algorithm is more efficient:

1. Arbitrarily label the vertices of one graph. (Assume here that the positive integers are used for labels).
2. Find a vertex on the second graph that has the same degree as vertex 1 on the first graph, and number that vertex 1 also.
3. Label the vertices that are adjacent to the new vertex 1 with the same numbers that correspond to the vertices that are adjacent to the other vertex 1.
4. Repeat step 3 for each of the other newly labeled vertices.

If at some point in the process, step 3 is not possible, then backtrack and try a different labeling. If no amount of backtracking seems to help, try proving that the two graphs are not isomorphic.

To prove that two graphs are not isomorphic (by definition) would require showing that every one of the possible $n!$ different labelings fails to preserve adjacency. That is impractical. The following theorem makes it much easier to prove that two graphs are not isomorphic.

Theorem 16.4 Isomorphism Tests for Graphs

All of the following conditions are necessary for two graphs to be isomorphic:

1. They must have the same number of vertices.
2. They must have the same number of edges.
3. They must have the same number of connected components.
4. They must have the same number of vertices of each degree.
5. They must have the same number of cycles of each length.

EXAMPLE 16.9 Proving that Two Graphs are Not Isomorphic

Here are three graphs, to be compared with the two isomorphic graphs in Example 16.8 on page 304:

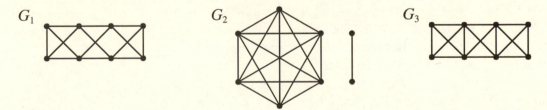

Each of these graphs has 8 vertices, so each could be isomorphic to those two graphs.

Graph G_1 is not isomorphic to those two graphs because it has only 14 edges. The graphs in Example 16.8 each have 16 edges. Condition 2 of Theorem 16.5 says that isomorphic graphs must have the same number of edges.

Graph G_2 does have 16 edges. But it is not isomorphic to the two graphs in Example 16.8 because it has 2 connected components. Each of the two graphs in Example 16.8 has only 1 connected component. Condition 3 of Theorem 16.5 says that isomorphic graphs must have the same number of connected components.

Graph G_3 has 16 edges and only 1 connected component. But it is still not isomorphic to the two graphs in Example 16.8 because it has some vertices of degree 3 (and some of degree 5). All the vertices of the two graphs in Example 16.8 have degree 4. Condition 4 of Theorem 16.5 says that isomorphic graphs must have the same number of vertices of each degree.

Note that in Example 16.9 we really only have to compare each graph with one of the two graphs in Example 16.8, not both of them.

Theorem 16.5 Graph Isomorphism Is an Equivalence Relation
The isomorphism relation among graphs satisfies the three properties of an equivalence relation:
1. Every graph is isomorphic to itself.
2. If G_1 is isomorphic to G_2 then G_2 is isomorphic to G_1.
3. If G_1 is isomorphic to G_2 and G_2 is isomorphic to G_3, then G_1 is isomorphic to G_3.

Corollary 16.2
If G_1 is isomorphic to G_2 and some other graph G is not isomorphic to G_1, then G is also not isomorphic to G_2.

16.5 THE ADJACENCY MATRIX FOR A GRAPH

An *adjacency matrix* for a graph (V, E) is a two-dimensional boolean array
```
boolean[][] a;
```
obtained by ordering the vertices $V = \{v_0, v_1, ..., v_{n-1}\}$ and then assigning `true` to `a[i][j]` if and only if vertex v_i is adjacent to vertex v_j.

EXAMPLE 16.10 An Adjacency Matrix

Here is the adjacency matrix for the graph in Example 16.1 on page 301.

	a	b	c	d
a	F	T	T	T
b	T	F	F	T
c	T	F	F	T
d	T	T	T	F

Note the following facts about adjacency matrices:
1. The matrix is *symmetric*; i.e., `a[i][j]==a[j][i]` will be true for all i and j.
2. The number of `true` entries is twice the number of edges.
3. Different orderings of the vertex set V will result in different adjacency matrices for the same graph.

Adjacency matrices are often expressed with 0s and 1s instead of `true`s and `false`s. In that form, the adjacency matrix for Example 16.10 would be the one shown here:

	a	b	c	d
a	0	1	1	1
b	1	0	0	1
c	1	0	0	1
d	1	1	1	0

16.6 THE INCIDENCE MATRIX FOR A GRAPH

An *incidence matrix* for a graph (V, E) is a two-dimensional array
```
int[][] a;
```
obtained by ordering the vertices $V = \{v_0, v_1, ..., v_{n-1}\}$ and the edges $E = \{e_0, e_1, ..., e_{m-1}\}$ and then assigning 1 to `a[i][j]` if vertex v_i is incident upon edge e_j and 0 otherwise.

EXAMPLE 16.11 An Incidence Matrix

Here is the incidence matrix for the graph in Example 16.1 on page 301.

The first row indicates that vertex *a* is incident upon edges 1, 2, and 3; the second row indicates that vertex *b* is incident upon edges 1 and 4; etc.

a	1	1	1	0	0
b	1	0	0	1	0
c	0	1	0	0	1
d	0	0	1	1	1

Note that, no matter how many vertices and edges a graph has, there will always be exactly two 1s in each column of any incidence matrix. Why? (See Question 16.6 on page 320.)

16.7 THE ADJACENCY LIST FOR A GRAPH

An *adjacency list* (or *adjacency structure*) for a graph (*V, E*) is a list that contains one element for each vertex in the graph and in which each vertex list element contains a list of the vertices that are adjacent to its vertex. The secondary list for each vertex is called its *edge list*.

EXAMPLE 16.12 An Adjacency List

Here is the adjacency list for the graph in Example 16.1 on page 301.

The edge list for vertex *a* has three element, one for each of the three edges that are incident with *a*; the edge list for vertex *b* has two element, one for each of the two edges that are incident with *b*; etc.

Note that each edge list element corresponds to a unique `true` entry in the graph's corresponding incidence matrix. For example, the three elements in the edge list for vertex *c* correspond to the three `trues` in the third row (the row for vertex *c*) in the incidence matrix in Example 16.11 above. The collection of all edge list nodes has the same array form as the incidence matrix.

The diagram in Example 16.12 is rather complex. Although it truly represents the pointers (i.e., references) that would be stored in the edge lists, authors often simplify the representation by listing the referenced vertex directly instead of the indirect references, like this:

Note that the edge lists are not ordered; i.e., their order is irrelevant.

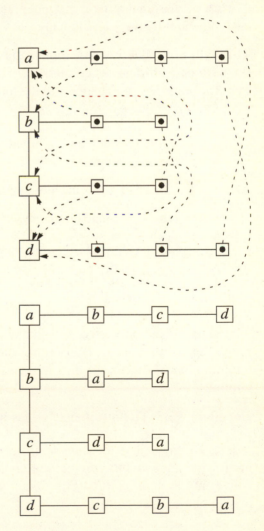

16.8 DIGRAPHS

A *digraph* (or *directed graph*) is a pair $G = (V, E)$, where V is a finite set and E is a set of ordered pairs of elements of V. As with (undirected) graphs, the elements of V are called *vertices* (or *nodes*) and the elements of E are called *edges* (or *arcs*). If $e \in E$ then $e = (a, b)$ for some a, $b \in V$. In this case, we can denote e more simply as $e = ab$. We say that the edge e *emanates from* (or is *incident from*) vertex a and *terminates at* (or is *incident to*) vertex b. The *outdegree* of a vertex is the number of edges that emanate from it. The *indegree* of a vertex is the number of edges that terminate at it.

Note that, unlike the graph definition, the digraph definition naturally allows an edge to terminate at the same vertex from which it emanates. Such an edge is called a *loop*. A *simple digraph* is a digraph that has no loops.

EXAMPLE 16.13 A Digraph

Here is a digraph with vertex set $V = \{a, b, c, d\}$ and edge set $E = \{ab, ad, bd, ca, dc\}$.

Vertex a has outdegree 2 and indegree 1. Vertices b and c each have outdegree 1 and indegree 1. Vertex d has outdegree 1 and indegree 2.

Theorem 16.6 If G is a digraph with m edges, then the sum of all outdegrees equals m and the sum of all indegrees equals m.
Proof: Each edge contributes 1 to the total of all outdegrees and 1 to the total of all indegrees. So each total must be m.

The *complete digraph* a the digraph that has a (directed) edge from every vertex to every other vertex.

EXAMPLE 16.14 The Complete Digraph on Six Vertices.

The graph shown at right is the complete digraph on 6 vertices. It has 15 double directed edges, so the total number of (one-way) edges is 30, which is $n(n-1) = 6(6-1) = 6(5) = 30$.

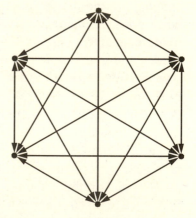

Theorem 16.7 The number of edges in the complete digraph on n vertices is $n(n-1)$.
Proof: By Theorem 16.2 on page 302, there are $n(n-1)/2$ undirected edges on the corresponding complete undirected graph. That makes $n(n-1)/2$ double directed edges, so the total number of (one-way) directed edges must be twice that number.

Corollary 16.3 The number of edges in any digraph on n vertices is $m \leq n(n-1)$.

Every digraph has an *embedded graph*, obtained by converting each directed edge into an undirected edge and then removing duplicate edges and loops. Mathematically, this amounts to converting each ordered pair (x, y) of vertices in E into the set $\{x, y\}$ and then removing all sets of size one (i.e., singletons).

EXAMPLE 16.15 The Embedded Graph of a Digraph

The embedded graph of the digraph in Example 16.13 is the graph in Example 16.1.

An *adjacency matrix* for a digraph (V, E) is a two-dimensional boolean array
```
boolean[][] a;
```
obtained by ordering the vertices $V = \{v_0, v_1, ..., v_{n-1}\}$ and then assigning `true` to `a[i][j]` if and only if there exists an edge emanating from vertex v_i and terminating at vertex v_j.

EXAMPLE 16.16 An Adjacency Matrix for a Digraph

Here is the adjacency matrix for the graph in Example 16.13.

	a	b	c	d
a	F	T	F	T
b	F	F	F	T
c	T	F	F	F
d	F	F	T	F

Note that the number of `true` entries in an adjacency matrix for a digraph is equal to the number of edges. Also, as with undirected graphs, different orderings of the vertex set V will result in different adjacency matrices for the same digraph.

An *incidence matrix* for a digraph (V, E) is a two-dimensional integer array
```
int[][] a;
```
obtained by ordering the vertices $V = \{v_0, v_1, ..., v_{n-1}\}$ and the edges $E = \{e_0, e_1, ..., e_{m-1}\}$ and then assigning 1 to `a[i][j]` and -1 to `a[j][i]` if there exists an edge emanating from vertex v_i and terminating at vertex v_j, and assigning 0 everywhere else.

EXAMPLE 16.17 An Incidence Matrix for a Digraph

Here is an incidence matrix for the digraph in Example 16.13.

The first row indicates that two edges emanate from vertex a and one edge terminates there.

The last 1 is in the row for vertex d and the last column. The only other nonzero entry in that column is the -1 in the row for vertex c, meaning that this edge emanates from vertex d and terminates at vertex c.

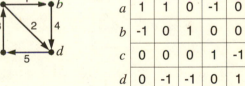

a	1	1	0	-1	0
b	-1	0	1	0	0
c	0	0	0	1	-1
d	0	-1	-1	0	1

An *adjacency list* for a digraph (V, E) is a list that contains one element for each vertex in the graph and in which each vertex list element contains a list of the edges that emanate from that vertex. This is the same as the adjacency list for a graph, except that the links are not duplicated unless there are edges going both ways between a pair of vertices.

EXAMPLE 16.18 An Adjacency List for a Digraph

Here is the adjacency list for the digraph in Example 16.13. The edge list for vertex a has two elements, one for each of the two edges that emanate from a: ab and ad.

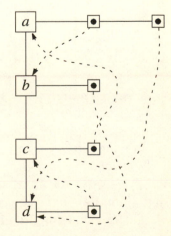

16.9 PATHS IN A DIGRAPH

A *walk from vertex a to vertex b* in a digraph is a sequence of edges $(a_0a_1,\ a_1a_2,\ ...,\ a_{k-1}a_k)$ where $a_0 = a$ and $a_k = b$. As with undirected paths in an undirected graphs, directed paths are usually abbreviated by their vertex string: $p = a_0a_1a_2...a_{k-1}a_k$. Either way, we say that the path *emanates from* (or *starts at*) vertex *a* and *terminates at* (or *ends at*) vertex *b*.

A walk is *closed* if it terminates at the same vertex from which it emanates. A *path* is a walk with all distinct vertices. A *cycle* is a closed walk with all interval vertices distinct.

EXAMPLE 16.19 Directed Paths

In the digraph of Example 16.13, *adcabdc* is a walk of length 6 which is not closed. The walk *abdcacda* is closed, but it is not a cycle because *d* (and *c*) are repeated internal vertices. The walk *dcab* is a path, which is not closed. The walk *cabdc* is a cycle of length 4, and the walk *dcad* is a cycle of length 3.

Note that different cycles may traverse the same vertices. For example, *adca* and *cadc* are different cycles in the digraph in Example 16.13.

A digraph is *strongly connected* if there is a path between every pair of vertices. A digraph is *weakly connected* if its embedded graph is connected. A digraph that is not weakly connected is said to be *disconnected*.

EXAMPLE 16.20 Strongly Connected and Weakly Connected Digraphs

Digraph G_1 is strongly connected (and therefore also weakly connected). Digraph G_2 is weakly connected, but not strongly connected because there is no path that terminates at vertex *x*. Digraph G_3 is disconnected.

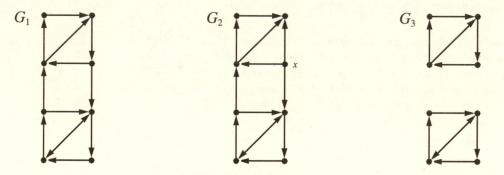

16.10 WEIGHTED DIGRAPHS AND GRAPHS

A *weighted digraph* is a pair (V, w) where V is a finite set of vertices and w is a function that assigns to each pair (x, y) of vertices either a positive integer or ∞ (infinity). The function w is called the *weight function*, and its value $w(x, y)$ can be interpreted as the cost (or time or distance) for moving directly from x to y. The value $w(x, y) = \infty$ indicates that there is no edge from x to y.

A *weighted graph* is a weighted digraph (V, w) whose weight function w is symmetric; i.e., $w(y,x) = w(x,y)$ for all $x, y \in V$. Just as every digraph has an embedded graph, every weighted digraph has an *embedded weighted graph* (V, w) and an embedded (unweighted) digraph. The weight function for the embedded weighted graph can be defined as $w'(x, y) = \min\{w(x,y),$

$w(y,x)$}, where w is the weight function of the weighted digraph. The vertex set for the embedded digraph can be defined as $E = \{ (x,y) : w(x,y) < \infty \}$.

The properties described above for digraphs and graphs apply to weighted digraphs and weighted graphs. In addition there are some extended properties that depend upon the underlying weight function in the obvious manner. For example, the *weighted path length* is the sum of the weights of the edges along the path. And the *shortest distance* from x to y would be the minimum weighted path length among all the paths from x to y.

EXAMPLE 16.21 A Weighted Digraph and Its Embedded Structures

Here is a weighted digraph together with its embedded weighted graph, its embedded digraph, and its embedded graph. The weights are shown on the edges.

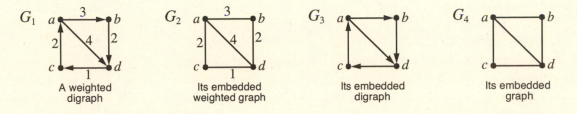

| G_1 A weighted digraph | G_2 Its embedded weighted graph | G_3 Its embedded digraph | G_4 Its embedded graph |

In graph G_1 the weighted path length of the path $cabd$ is $|cabd| = 2 + 3 + 2 = 7$, and the shortest distance from c to d is 6 (along the path cad). But in graph G_2 that shortest distance is 1 (along the path cd).

Note that graph G_3 is the same as in Example 16.13 on page 308, and graph G_4 is the same as in Example 16.1 on page 301.

Here are the adjacency matrix, the incidence matrix, and the adjacency list for graph G_1:

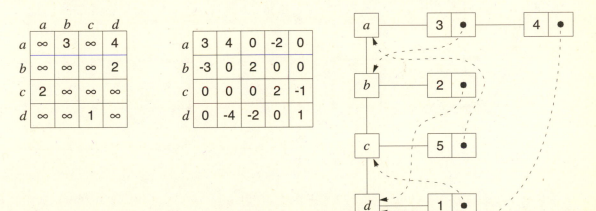

	a	b	c	d
a	∞	3	∞	4
b	∞	∞	∞	2
c	2	∞	∞	∞
d	∞	∞	1	∞

a	3	4	0	-2	0
b	-3	0	2	0	0
c	0	0	0	2	-1
d	0	-4	-2	0	1

16.11 EULER AND HAMILTONIAN PATHS AND CYCLES

An *euler path* in a graph is a walk that includes each edge exactly once. An *euler cycle* is a closed walk that includes each edge exactly once. An *eulerian* graph is a graph that has an euler cycle.

Note that euler paths and cycles need not have distinct vertices, so they are not strict paths.

EXAMPLE 16.22 Euler Paths and Cycles

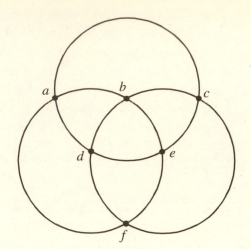

In the graph on the right, the closed walk *acedabefdbcfa* is an euler cycle. So this is an eulerian graph.

Note that every vertex in this graph has degree 4, and its 12 edges are partitioned into three circles. As the following theorem reports, each of these two properties will always guarantee that the graph is eulerian.

Theorem 16.8 Eulerian Graphs

If *G* is a connected graph, then the following conditions are equivalent:

1. *G* is eulerian.
2. Every vertex has even degree.
3. The set of all edges of *G* can be partitioned into cycles.

A *hamiltonian path* in a graph is a path that includes each vertex exactly once. A *hamiltonian cycle* is a cycle that includes each vertex exactly once. A *hamiltonian graph* is a graph that has a hamiltonian cycle.

Unfortunately, there is no simple characterization like Theorem 16.8 for hamiltonian graphs. In fact, the problem of finding such a simple characterization is one of the big unsolved problems in computer science.

EXAMPLE 16.23 Hamiltonian Graphs

The graph on the left is hamiltonian. The graph on the right is not; it has a hamiltonian path, but no hamiltonian cycle.

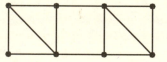   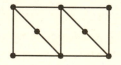

16.12 DIJKSTRA'S ALGORITHM

Dijkstra's Algorithm finds the shortest path from one vertex v_0 to each other vertex in a digraph. When it has finished, the length of the shortest distance from v_0 to v is stored in the vertex v, and the shortest path from v_0 to v is recorded in the back pointers of v and the other vertices along that path. (See Example 16.24.) The algorithm uses a priority queue, initializing it with all the vertices and then dequeueing one vertex on each iteration.

Algorithm 16.1 Dijkstra's Shortest Paths Algorithm

(Precondition: $G = (V,w)$ is a weighted graph with initial vertex v_0.)

(Postcondition: each vertex v in V stores the shortest distance from v_0 to v and a back reference to the preceding vertex along that shortest path.)

1. Initialize the distance field to 0 for v_0 and to ∞ for each of the other vertices.

2. Enqueue all the vertices into a priority queue Q with highest priority being the lowest distance field value.
3. Repeat steps 4–10 until Q is empty.
4. (Invariant: the distance and back reference fields of every vertex that is not in Q are correct.)
5. Dequeue the highest priority vertex into x.
6. Do steps 7–10 for each vertex y that is adjacent to x and in the priority queue.
7. Let s be the sum of the x's distance field plus the weight of the edge from x to y.
8. If s is less than y's distance field, do steps 9–10; otherwise go back to Step 3.
9. Assign s to y's distance field.
10. Assign x to y's back reference field.

EXAMPLE 16.24 Tracing Dijkstra's Algorithm

Here is a trace of Algorithm 16.1 on a graph with 8 vertices. On each iteration, the vertices that are still in the priority queue are shaded and vertex x is labeled. The distance fields for each vertex are shown adjacent to the vertex, and the back pointers are drawn as arrows.

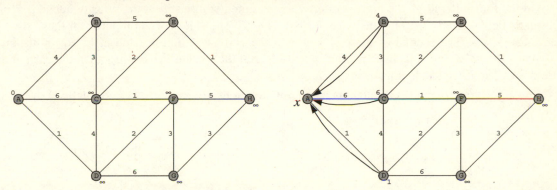

On the first iteration, the highest priority vertex is $x = A$, because its distance field is 0 and all the others are infinity. Steps 7–10 iterate 3 times, once for each of A's neighbors $y = B$, C, and D. The values of s computed for these are $0 + 4 = 4$, $0 + 6 = 6$, and $0 + 1 = 1$. Each of these is less than the current (infinite) value of the corresponding distance field, so all three of those values are assigned and the back pointers for all three neighbors are set to point to A.

On the second iteration, the highest priority vertex among those still in the priority queue is $x = D$ with distance field 1. Steps 7–10 iterate three times again, once for each of D's unvisited neighbors $y = B$, F, and G. The values of s computed for these are $1 + 4 = 5$, $1 + 2 = 3$, and $1 + 6 = 7$. Each of these is less than the current value of the corresponding distance field, so all of those values are assigned and the back pointers are set to D. Note how this changes the distance field and point in vertex B.

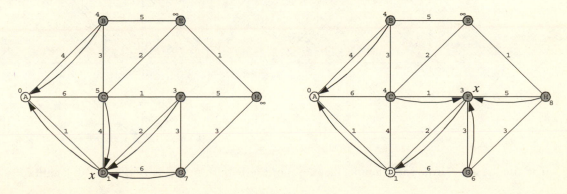

On the third iteration, the highest priority vertex among those still in the priority queue is x = F with distance field 3. Steps 7–10 iterate three times again, once for each of F's unvisited neighbors y = C, G, and H. The values of s computed for these are $3 + 1 = 4$, $3 + 3 = 6$, and $3 + 5 = 8$. Each of these is less than the current value, so all of them are assigned and the back pointers are set to F. Note how this changes the distance field and point in vertex B again.

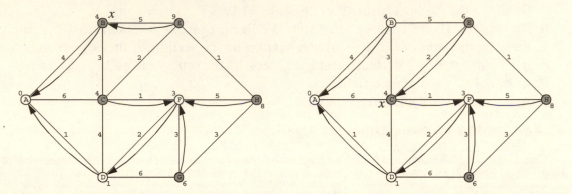

On the fourth iteration, the highest priority vertex among those still in the priority queue is x = B with distance field 4. Steps 7–10 iterate twice, for y = C and E. The values of s computed for these are $4 + 3 = 7$ and $4 + 5 = 9$. The second of these is less than the current (infinite) value at E, so its distance field assigned the value 9 and its back pointer is set to B. But the s value 7 is not less than the current distance field for C, so its fields do not change.

The algorithm progresses through its remaining iterations, for x = C, E, G, and finally H the same way:

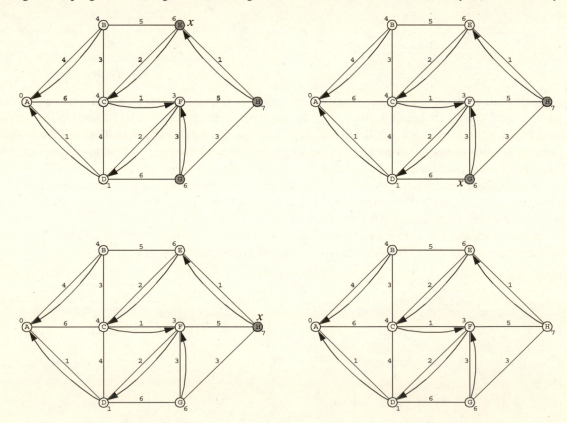

The final result shows, for example, that the shortest path fro A to E is ADFCE with length 6.

EXAMPLE 16.25 A Java Implementation of Dijkstra's Algorithm

Here is a Java implementation of Algorithm 16.1. It defines a `Network` class whose instances represent weighted digraphs.

```java
public class Network
{ Vertex start;

  private class Vertex
  { Object object;
    Edge edges;
    Vertex nextVertex;
    boolean done;
    int dist;
    Vertex back;
  }

  private class Edge
  { Vertex to;
    int weight;
    Edge nextEdge;
  }

  public Network()
  { if (start != null)
    { start.dist = 0;
      for (Vertex p = start.nextVertex; p != null; p = p.nextVertex)
        p.dist = Integer.MAX_VALUE;  // infinity
    }
  }

  public void findShortestPaths()
  { // implements Dijkstra's Algorithm:
    for (Vertex v = start; v != null; v = closestVertex())
    { for (Edge e = v.edges; e != null; e = e.nextEdge)
      { Vertex w = e.to;
        if (!w.done && v.dist+e.weight < w.dist)
        { w.dist = v.dist+e.weight;
          w.back = v;
        }
      }
      v.done = true;
    }
  }

  private Vertex closestVertex()
  { // returns the vertex with minimal dist among those not done:
    Vertex v = null;
    int minDist = Integer.MAX_VALUE;
    for (Vertex w = start; w != null; w = nextVertex)
      if (!w.done && w.dist < minDist) { v = w; minDist = w.dist; }
    return v;
  }
}
```

In this implementation, we have used a simple search method `closestVertex()` instead of a priority queue. This is less efficient, running in $O(n)$ time instead of the $O(\lg n)$ time that a priority queue would use.

16.13 GRAPH TRAVERSAL ALGORITHMS

The paths produced by Dijkstra's Algorithm produce a *minimal spanning tree* for the graph. That is a spanning tree whose total weighted length is minimal for the graph; i.e., no other spanning tree has a smaller total length. The spanning tree is formed in a breadth-first manner, by considering the vertices that are adjacent to the current vertex on each iteration. This is one of two general ways to traverse a graph.

The *Breadth-First Search* algorithm is essentially the same as Dijkstra's algorithm without regard to the distance fields.

Algorithm 16.2 The Breadth-First Search (BFS) Algorithm
  (Preconditions: $G = (V,E)$ is a graph or digraph with initial vertex v_0; each vertex has a boolean visited field initialized to false; T is an empty set of edges; L is an empty list of vertices.)
  (Postcondition: L lists the vertices in BFS order, and T is a BFS spanning tree for G.)
  1. Initialize an empty queue Q for temporary storage of vertices.
  2. Enqueue v_0 into Q.
  3. Repeat steps 4–6 while Q is not empty.
  4. Dequeue Q into x.
  5. Add x to L.
  6. Do step 7 for each vertex y that is adjacent to x.
  7. If y has not been visited, do steps 8–9.
  8. Add the edge xy to T.
  9. Enqueue y into Q.

EXAMPLE 16.26 Tracing the BFS Algorithm

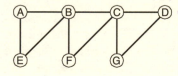

Here is a trace of Algorithm 16.2 on the graph shown here:
The start vertex $v_0 = $ A.

Q	x	L	y	T
A	A	A	B	AB
B			E	AB, AE
B, E	B		C	AB, AE, BC
E, C		A, B	F	AB, AE, BC, BF
E, C, F	E	A, B, E		
C, F	C	A, B, E, C	D	AB, AE, BC, BF, CD
F, D			G	AB, AE, BC, BF, CD, CG
F, D, G	F	A, B, E, C, F		
D, G	D	A, B, E, C, F, D		
G	G	A, B, E, C, F, D, G		

The resulting BFS order of visitation is returned in the list L = (A, B, E, C, F, D, G), and the resulting BFS spanning tree is returned in the set $T = \{AB, AE, BC, BF, CD, CD\}$.

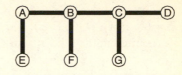

The *Depth-First Search* algorithm uses a stack instead of a queue.

Algorithm 16.3 The Depth-First Search (DFS) Algorithm

(Preconditions: $G = (V,E)$ is a graph or digraph with initial vertex v_0; each vertex has a boolean visited field initialized to false; T is an empty set of edges; L is an empty list of vertices.)

(Postcondition: L lists the vertices in DFS order, and T is a DFS spanning tree for G.)

1. Initialize an empty stack S for temporary storage of vertices.
2. Add v_0 to L.
3. Push v_0 onto S.
4. Mark v_0 visited.
5. Repeat steps 6–8 while S is not empty.
6. Let x be the top element on S.
7. If x has any adjacent unvisited vertices, do steps 9–13.
8. Otherwise, pop the stack S and go back to step 5.
9. Let y be an unvisited vertex that is adjacent to x.
10. Add the edge xy to T.
11. Add y to L.
12. Push y onto S.
13. Mark y visited.

EXAMPLE 16.27 Tracing the DFS Algorithm

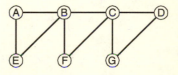

Here is a trace of Algorithm 16.3 on the same graph as in Example 16.26. The start vertex $v_0 = $ A.

L	S	x	y	T
A	A	A	B	AB
A, B	A, B	B	C	AB, BC
A, B, C	A, B, C	C	D	AB, BC, CD
A, B, C, D	A, B, C, D	D	G	AB, BC, CD, DG
A, B, C, D, G	A, B, C, D, G	G		
	A, B, C, D	D		
	A, B, C	C	F	AB, BC, CD, DG, CF
A, B, C, D, G, F	A, B, C, F	F		
	A, B, C	C		
	A, B	B	E	AB, BC, CD, DG, CF, BE
A, B, C, D, G, F, E	A, B, E	E		
	A, B	B		
	A	A		

The resulting DFS order of visitation is returned in the list
L = (A, B, C, D, G, F, E), and the resulting DFS spanning tree
is returned in the set T = {AB, BC, CD, DG, CF, BE}.

Since the Depth-First Traversal uses a stack, it has a
natural recursive version:

Algorithm 16.4 The Recursive Depth-First Search (DFS) Algorithm
(Preconditions: $G = (V,E)$ is a graph or digraph with initial vertex x; each vertex has a boolean
visited field initialized to false; T is a global set of edges; L is a global list of vertices.)
(Postcondition: L lists the vertices in DFS order, and T is a DFS spanning tree for G.)
1. Mark x visited.
2. Add x to L.
3. Repeat steps 4–5 for each unvisited vertex y that is adjacent to v.
4. Add the edge xy to T.
5. Apply the DFS algorithm to the subgraph with initial vertex y.

EXAMPLE 16.28 Tracing the Recursive DFS Algorithm

Here is a trace of Algorithm 16.4 on the same graph as in
Example 16.26. The start vertex v_0 = A.

L	x	y	T
A	A	B	AB
A, B	B	C	AB, BC
A, B, C	C	D	AB, BC, CD
A, B, C, D	D	G	AB, BC, CD, DG
A, B, C, D, G	G		
	D		
	C	F	AB, BC, CD, DG, CF
A, B, C, D, G, F	F		
	C		
	B	E	AB, BC, CD, DG, CF, BE
A, B, C, D, G, F, E	E		
	B		
	A		

The result, of course, is the same as in Example 16.27. The only real difference is that the explicit stack
S has been replaced by the system stack that keeps track of the recursive calls.

EXAMPLE 16.29 Implementing the Graph Traversal Algorithms

Here is a Java implementation of the two traversal algorithms for the Network class introduced in
Example 16.25 on page 315:

```
   public class Network
   { Vertex start;

     private class Vertex
     { Object object;
       Edge edges;
       Vertex nextVertex;
       boolean visited;
     }

     private class Edge
     { Vertex to;
       int weight;
       Edge nextEdge;
     }

     public static void visit(Vertex x)
     { System.out.println(x.object);
     }

     public void breadthFirstSearch()
     { if (start == null) return;
       Vector queue = new Vector();
       visit(start);
       start.visited = true;
       queue.addElement(start);
       while (!queue.isEmpty())
       { Vertex v = queue.firstElement();
         queue.removeElementAt(0);
         for (Edge e = v.edges; e != null; e = e.nextEdge)
         { Vertex w = e.to;
           if (!w.visited)
           { visit(w);
             w.visited = true;
             queue.addElement(w);
           }
         }
       }
     }

     public void depthFirstSearch()
     { if (start != null) depthFirstSearch(start);
     }

     public void depthFirstSearch(Vertex x)
     { visit(x);
       x.visited = true;
       for (Edge e = x.edges; e != null; e = e.nextEdge)
       { Vertex w = e.to;
         if (!w.visited) depthFirstSearch(w);
       }
     }
   }
```

This uses the recursive version of the Depth-First Search. That requires the depthFirstSearch() method with zero parameters to start the recursive depthFirstSearch() method.

Review Questions

16.1   What is the difference between a graph and a simple graph?

16.2   In an undirected graph, can an edge itself be a path?

16.3   What is the difference between connected vertices and adjacent vertices?

16.4   Using only the definition of graph isomorphism, is it easier to prove that two graphs are isomorphic or to prove that two graphs are not isomorphic? Why?

16.5   Are the five conditions in Theorem 16.4 sufficient for two graphs to be isomorphic?

16.6   Why is it that the natural definition for a simple graph prohibits loops while the natural definition for a digraph allows them?

16.7   True or false:
   a. If a graph has n vertices and $n(n-1)/2$ edges, then it must be a complete graph.
   b. The length of a path must be less than the size of the graph.
   c. The length of a cycle must equal the number of distinct vertices it has.
   d. If the incidence matrix for a graph has n rows and $n(n-1)/2$ columns, then the graph must be a complete graph.
   e. In an incidence matrix for a digraph, the sum of the entries in each row equals the indegree for that vertex.
   f. The sum of all the entries in an incidence matrix for a graph is $2|E|$.
   g. The sum of all the entries in an incidence matrix for a digraph is always 0.

16.8   A graph (V, E) is called *dense* if $|E| = \Theta(|V|^2)$, and it is called *sparse* if $|E| = O(|V|)$.
   a. Which of the three representations (adjacency matrix, incidence matrix, or adjacency list) would be best for a dense graph?
   b. Which representation would be best for a sparse graph?

Problems

16.1   Find each of the following properties for this graph:
   a. its size n
   b. its vertex set V
   c. its edge set E
   d. the degree $d(x)$ of each vertex x
   e. a path of length 3
   f. a path of length 5
   g. a cycle of length 4
   h. a spanning tree
   i. its adjacency matrix
   j. its incidence matrix
   k. its adjacency list

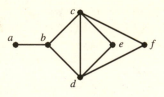

16.2   Find each of the following properties for this digraph:
   a. its size n
   b. its vertex set V
   c. its edge set E
   d. the indegree $id(x)$ of each vertex x
   e. the outdegree $od(x)$ of each vertex x

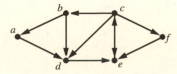

      f. a path of length 3

      g. a path of length 5

      h. a cycle of length 4

      i. its adjacency matrix

      j. its incidence matrix

      k. its adjacency list

16.3   Draw the complete graph on *n* vertices for *n* = 2, 3, 4, 5, and 6.

16.4   Determine whether the graph G_1 below is either eulerian or hamiltonian:

G_1

G_2

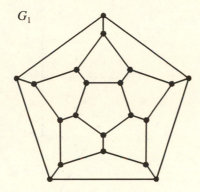
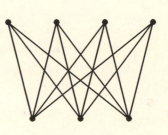

16.5   Determine whether the graph G_2 above is either eulerian or hamiltonian:

16.6   For each of the following subgraphs of the graph in Example 16.7 on page 303, tell whether it is connected, acyclic, and/or spanning. (Graphs *a – b* are shown below; graphs *c – l* are shown on the next two pages.).

      a.   *b.*

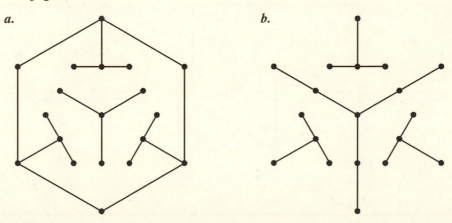

16.7   Find two nonisomorphic graphs for which all five conditions of Theorem 16.4 on page 305 are true.

16.8   Prove Corollary 16.2 on page 306.

16.9   Describe the adjacency matrix for the complete graph on *n* vertices.

16.10   Describe the incidence matrix for the complete graph on *n* vertices.

c.

d.

e.

f.

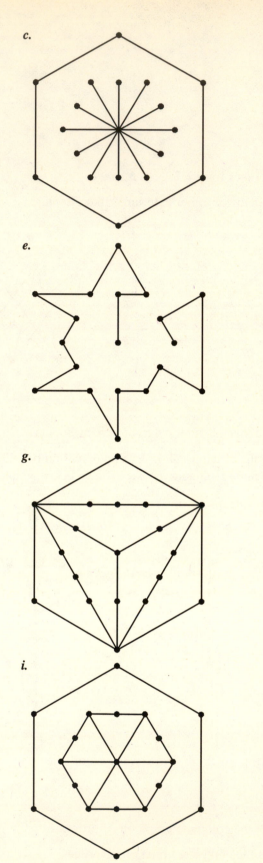

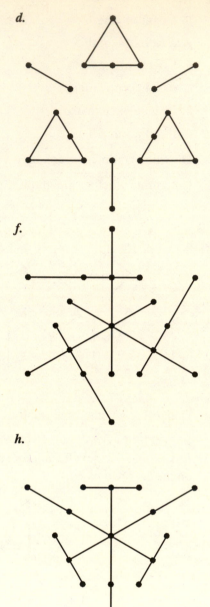

g.

h.

i.

j.

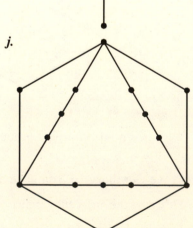

k.   **l.**

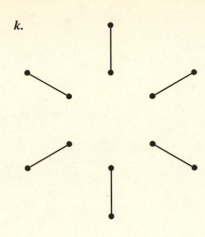   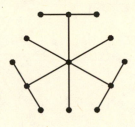

16.11   Let G_1 be the graph represented by this adjacency list:

    a. Draw G_1.

    b. Is G_1 a directed graph?

    c. Is G_1 strongly connected?

    d. Is G_1 weakly connected?

    e. Is G_1 acyclic?

    f. Give the adjacency matrix for G_1.

A	F	
B	C	
C	B	
D	A	B
E	C	D
F	E	

16.12   Let G_1 be the graph whose adjacency matrix is shown below:

    a. Draw G_1.

    b. Is G_1 a directed graph?

    c. Is G_1 strongly connected?

    d. Is G_1 weakly connected?

    e. Is G_1 acyclic?

    f. Give the adjacency matrix for G_1.

$$\begin{bmatrix} 0 & 1 & 0 & 1 & 0 \\ 1 & 0 & 1 & 0 & 1 \\ 0 & 1 & 0 & 1 & 0 \\ 1 & 1 & 1 & 0 & 1 \\ 0 & 1 & 1 & 0 & 1 \end{bmatrix}$$

G_2

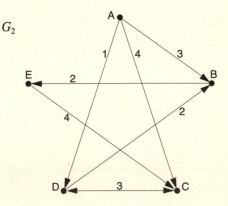

16.13   Consider the weighted digraph G_2 shown above:

    a. Draw the adjacency matrix for this graph.

    b. Draw the adjacency list for this graph.

    c. Is this graph connected? Justify your answer.

    d. Is this graph acyclic? Justify your answer.

16.14 Determine which of the following graphs are isomorphic. Note that all seven graphs have size 10:

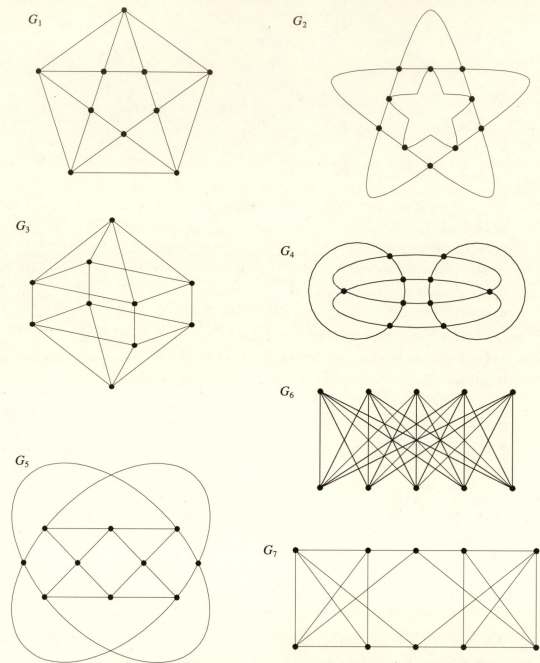

16.15 Let G_1 and G_2 be the graphs shown below. (G_1 is the graph from Example 16.22 on page 312.)

a. Determine whether G_2 and G_3 are isomorphic. Justify your conclusion.

b. Either find an Euler cycle for G_2 or explain why it has none.

c. Either find a Hamiltonian cycle for G_2 or explain why it has none.

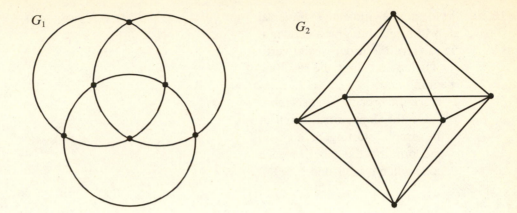

16.16   A *wheel graph* on n vertices is a graph of size $n+1$ consisting
        of a n-cycle in which each of the n vertices is also adjacent to
        a single common center vertex. For example, the graph shown
        here is the wheel graph on 6 vertices. Describe:

        a. the adjacency matrix of a wheel graph on n vertices

        b. the incidence matrix of a wheel graph on n vertices

        c. the adjacency list of a wheel graph on n vertices

16.17   Trace Dijkstra's Algorithm (Algorithm 16.1 on page 312) on the graph G_8 below, showing
        the shortest path and its distance from node A to every other node.

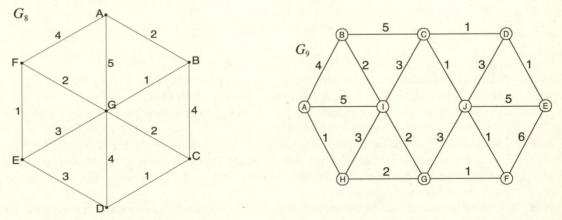

16.18   Trace Dijkstra's Algorithm (Algorithm 16.1 on page 312) on the graph G_9 above, showing
        the shortest path and its distance from node A to every other node.

16.19   There are four standard algorithms for traversing binary trees: the preorder traversal, the
        inorder traversal, the postorder traversal. and the level-order traversal. If a binary tree is
        regarded as a connected acyclic graph, which tree traversal results from a:

        a. depth-first search

        b. breadth-first search

16.20 Perform the indicated traversal algorithm on this graph shown at right. Give the order of the vertices visited and show the resulting spanning tree:

a. Trace the breadth-first search.

b. Trace the depth-first search of the graph, starting at node A and printing the label of each node when it is visited.

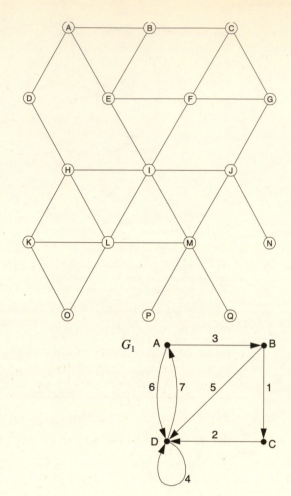

16.21 For the weighted digraph G_1 shown here:

a. Draw the adjacency matrix.

b. Draw the incidence matrix.

c. Draw the adjacency list.

Answers to Review Questions

16.1 A graph is simple if it has no loops or repeated edges.

16.2 No: In an undirected graph, an edge cannot be a path because an edge is a set of two elements (i.e., an unordered pair) while a path is a sequence (i.e., an ordered list of vertices).

16.3 Two vertices are connected if there is a path from one to the other. Two vertices are adjacent if they form an edge.

16.4 Using only the definition of graph isomorphism, it is easier to prove that two graphs are isomorphic because it only requires finding an isomorphism and verifying that it is one. Proving from the definition that two graphs are not isomorphic would require verifying that every one of the $n!$ one-to-one functions is not an isomorphism.

16.5 No: The five conditions of are not sufficient for two graphs to be isomorphic. It is possible for all five conditions to be true for two nonisomorphic graphs. (See Problem 16.7.)

16.6 The reason that the natural definition for a graph prohibits loops is that an edge in a graph is a two-element set and that requires the two elements to be different. In the natural definition for a digraph, an edge is an ordered pair and that allows both components to be the same.

16.7 *a.* True
    b. True
    c. True
    d. True
    e. False
    f. True
    g. True

16.8   The adjacency matrix is best for a dense graph because it is compact and provides fast direct access. The adjacency list is best for a sparse graph because it allows easy insertion and deletion of edges.

Solutions to Problems

16.1   *a.* $n = 6$.
  b. $V = \{a, b, c, d, e, f\}$.
  c. $E = \{ab, bc, bd, cd, ce, de, cf, df\}$.
  d. $d(a) = 1, d(b) = 3, d(e) = d(f) = 2, d(c) = d(d) = 4$.
  e. The path *abcd* has length 3.
  f. The path *abcfde* has length 5.
  g. The cycle *bcedb* has length 4.
  h. A spanning tree is shown at right.
  i. Its adjacency matrix is shown below.
  j. Its incidence matrix is shown below.
  k. Its adjacency list is shown below.

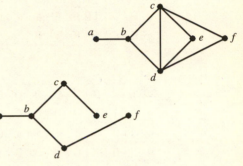
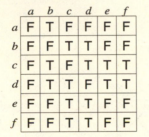

	a	b	c	d	e	f
a	F	T	F	F	F	F
b	F	F	T	T	F	F
c	F	T	F	T	T	T
d	F	T	T	F	T	T
e	F	F	T	T	F	F
f	F	F	T	T	F	F

a	1	0	0	0	0	0	0	0
b	1	1	1	0	0	0	0	0
c	0	1	0	1	1	1	0	0
d	0	0	1	1	0	0	1	1
e	0	0	0	0	1	0	1	0
f	0	0	0	0	0	1	0	1

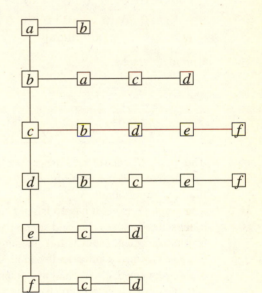

16.2   *a.* $n = 6$.
  b. $V = \{a, b, c, d, e, f\}$.
  c. $E = \{ad, ba, bd, cb, cd, ce, cf, de, ec, fe\}$.
  d. $id(a) = id(b) = id(c) = id(f) = 1, id(d) = id(e) = 3$.
  e. $od(a) = od(d) = od(e) = od(f) = 1, od(b) = 2, od(c) = 4$.
  f. The path *adec* has length 3.
  g. The path *fecbad* has length 5.
  h. The cycle *adcba* has length 4.
  i. A spanning tree is shown at right.
  j. Its adjacency matrix is shown below.
  k. Its incidence matrix is shown below.

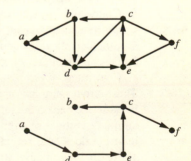

l. its adjacency list is shown below.

	a	b	c	d	e	f
a	F	F	F	T	F	F
b	T	F	F	T	F	F
c	F	T	F	T	T	T
d	F	F	F	F	T	F
e	F	F	T	F	F	F
f	F	F	F	F	T	F

a	1	-1	0	0	0	0	0	0	0	0
b	0	1	1	-1	0	0	0	0	0	0
c	0	0	0	1	1	1	1	0	-1	0
d	-1	0	-1	0	-1	0	0	1	0	0
e	0	0	0	0	0	-1	0	-1	1	-1
f	0	0	0	0	0	0	-1	0	0	1

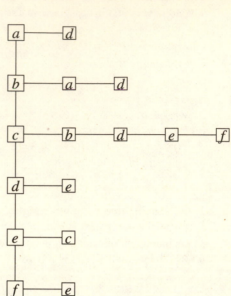

16.3 Complete graphs:

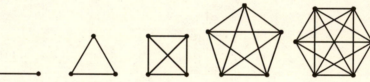

16.4 The graph G_1 cannot be eulerian because it has vertices of odd degree. But the hamiltonian cycle shown here verifies that it is hamiltonian:

16.5 The graph G_2 is neither eulerian nor hamiltonian

16.6 *a.* Disconnected, cyclic, and spanning.
   b. Disconnected, acyclic, and spanning.
   c. Disconnected, cyclic, and spanning.
   d. Disconnected, cyclic, and not spanning.
   e. Connected, acyclic, and spanning.
   f. Connected, acyclic, and spanning.
   g. Connected, cyclic, and spanning.
   h. Connected, acyclic, and not spanning.
   i. Disconnected, cyclic, and spanning.
   j. Connected, cyclic, and not spanning.
   k. Disconnected, acyclic, and not spanning.
   l. Connected, acyclic, and not spanning.

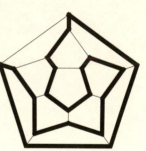

16.7 These two graphs are not isomorphic because the one on the left has a 4-cycle containing 2 vertices of degree 2 and the one on the right does not. Yet, all five conditions of Theorem 16.4 on page 305 are satisfied.

16.8 Assume that G_1 is isomorphic to G_2 and that G is not isomorphic to G_1. By part 1 of Theorem 16.5 on page 306, G_2 is also not isomorphic to G_1. If G were isomorphic to G_2, then by part 3 of Theorem 16.5, G would also have to be isomorphic to G_1. Thus, since G is not isomorphic to G_1, it cannot be isomorphic to G_2 either.

16.9   The adjacency matrix for the complete graph on n vertices is an n-by-m boolean matrix with `false` value at each entry on the diagonal and `true` value at every other entry.

16.10   The incidence matrix M_n for the complete graph on n vertices is the following matrix:

Its has n rows and $n(n-1)/2$ columns (see Theorem 16.2 on page 302).

If $n = 2$, it is the 2-by-1 matrix containing `true` in both entries.

If $n > 2$, it is the matrix A concatenated horizontally with the matrix obtained from M_{n-1} by placing one row of all `false` values on top of it.

$$\mathsf{M}_2 = \begin{bmatrix} 1 \\ 1 \end{bmatrix}$$

$$\mathsf{M}_3 = \begin{bmatrix} 1 & 1 & 0 \\ 1 & 0 & 1 \\ 0 & 1 & 1 \end{bmatrix}$$

$$\mathsf{M}_4 = \begin{bmatrix} 1 & 1 & 1 & 0 & 0 & 0 \\ 1 & 0 & 0 & 1 & 1 & 0 \\ 0 & 1 & 0 & 1 & 0 & 1 \\ 0 & 0 & 1 & 0 & 1 & 1 \end{bmatrix}$$

$$\mathsf{M}_5 = \begin{bmatrix} 1 & 1 & 1 & 1 & 0 & 0 & 0 & 0 & 0 & 0 \\ 1 & 0 & 0 & 0 & 1 & 1 & 1 & 0 & 0 & 0 \\ 0 & 1 & 0 & 0 & 1 & 0 & 0 & 1 & 1 & 0 \\ 0 & 0 & 1 & 0 & 0 & 1 & 0 & 1 & 0 & 1 \\ 0 & 0 & 0 & 1 & 0 & 0 & 1 & 0 & 1 & 1 \end{bmatrix}$$

16.11   *a.* The digraph G_1 is shown below at right.

        b. Yes, this is a digraph: It has at least one one-way edge.

        c. No, the digraph is not strongly connected: there is no path from C to D.

        d. Yes, the digraph is weakly connected: its embedded (undirected) graph is connected.

        e. No, the digraph is not acyclic: It contains the cycle AFEDA.

        f. Its adjacency matrix is:

$$\begin{bmatrix} 0 & 0 & 0 & 0 & 0 & 1 \\ 0 & 0 & 1 & 0 & 0 & 0 \\ 0 & 1 & 0 & 0 & 0 & 0 \\ 1 & 1 & 0 & 0 & 0 & 0 \\ 0 & 0 & 1 & 1 & 0 & 0 \\ 0 & 0 & 0 & 0 & 1 & 0 \end{bmatrix}$$

G_1

16.12   *a.* The digraph G_1 is shown below at right.

        b. No, this is not a simple digraph because it has a loop.

        c. Yes it is a digraph: Its adjacency matrix is not symmetric.

        d. Yes, this digraph is strongly connected.

        e. Yes, this digraph is weakly connected.

        f. No, the digraph is not acyclic: It contains the cycle ADB.

16.13	For the given graph, the adjacency matrix and the adjacency list are:

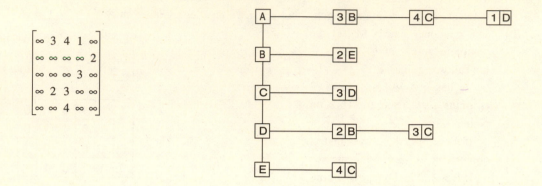

$$\begin{bmatrix} \infty & 3 & 4 & 1 & \infty \\ \infty & \infty & \infty & \infty & 2 \\ \infty & \infty & \infty & 3 & \infty \\ \infty & 2 & 3 & \infty & \infty \\ \infty & \infty & 4 & \infty & \infty \end{bmatrix}$$

The graph is not connected because there is no path from B to A. The graph is not acyclic because it contains the cycle BECDB.

16.14	Among the seven graphs:

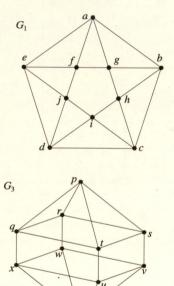

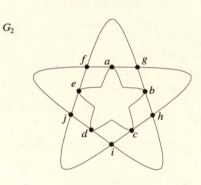

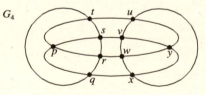

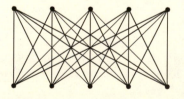

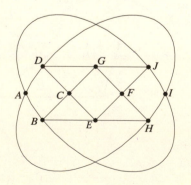

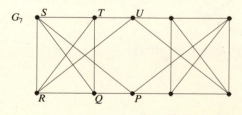

G_1 is isomorphic to G_2 : the isomorphism is shown by the vertex labels *a–j* shown above.

G_3 is isomorphic to G_4 : the isomorphism is shown by the vertex labels *p–y* shown above.

G_6 cannot be isomorphic to any of the other graphs because it has 25 edges and all the others have 20.

G_3 (and thus also G_4) cannot be isomorphic to any of the other graphs because it has a pyramid of four adjacent 3-cycles (*pqr, prs, pst,* and *ptq*) and none of the other graphs (except G_6) does.

G_6 cannot be isomorphic to any of the other graphs because it has a chain of three adjacent 4-cycles (*ABCD, CEFG,* and *FHIJ*) and none of the other graphs (except G_6) does.

Similarly, G_7 cannot be isomorphic to any of the other graphs because it has a chain of four adjacent 3-cycles (*PQS, QSR, SRT,* and *RTU*) and none of the other graphs (except G_6) does.

16.15   *a.* The two graphs are isomorphic. The bijection is defined by the vertex labels shown below:

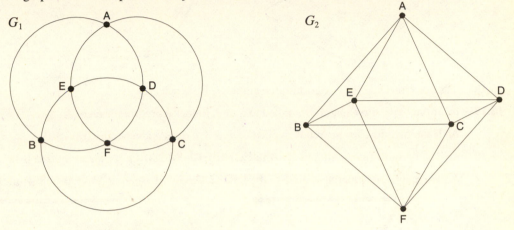

   b. An euler cycle for G_2 is ABCDEBFCADFEA.

   c. A hamiltonian cycle for G_2 is ABCDFEA.

16.16   *a.* The adjacency matrix for a wheel graph looks like matrix *A* shown at the bottom of the next page.

   b. The incidence matrix for a wheel graph looks like matrix *B* shown at the bottom of the next page (for the case *n* = 4). In general, it will have *n* 1s followed by *n* 0s on the first row. Below that will lie the identity matrix (all 1s on the diagonal and 0s elsewhere) followed by the square matrix with 1s on the diagonal and the subdiagonal. Compare this with the recursive solution to Problem 16.10 on page 321.

   c. The adjacency list for a wheel graph looks like the list shown below. The edge list for the first vertex (the central vertex) has *n* edge nodes, one for every other vertex. Every other edge list has three edge nodes: one pointing to the central vertex (labeled *a* in the example below) and one to each of its neighbors.

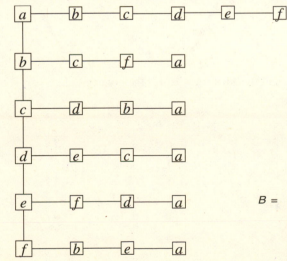

$$A = \begin{bmatrix} F & T & T & T & T & T \\ T & F & T & F & F & F \\ T & T & F & T & F & F \\ T & F & T & F & T & F \\ T & F & F & T & F & T \\ T & F & F & F & T & F \end{bmatrix}$$

$$B = \begin{bmatrix} 1 & 1 & 1 & 1 & 0 & 0 & 0 & 0 \\ 1 & 0 & 0 & 0 & 1 & 0 & 0 & 1 \\ 0 & 1 & 0 & 0 & 1 & 1 & 0 & 0 \\ 0 & 0 & 1 & 0 & 0 & 1 & 1 & 0 \\ 0 & 0 & 0 & 0 & 0 & 0 & 1 & 1 \end{bmatrix}$$

16.17 The trace of Dijkstra's Algorithm on graph G_8 is shown below:

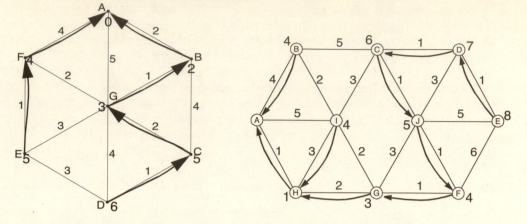

16.18 The trace of Dijkstra's Algorithm on graph G_8 is shown above:

16.19 *a.* If the depth-first search is applied to a tree, it does a preorder traversal.

     b. If the breadth-first search is applied to a tree, it does a level-order traversal.

16.20 *a.* The breadth-first search visits ABDECHFIGKLJMONPQ; its spanning tree is below on the left.

     b. The depth-first search visits ABCFEIHDKLMJGN; its spanning tree is below on the right.

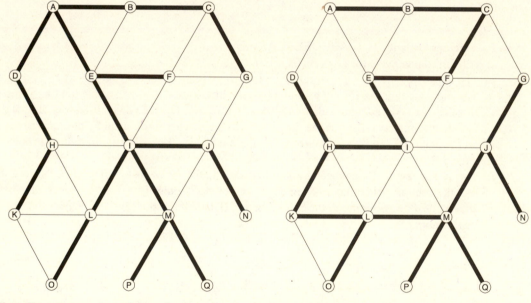

16.21 The adjacency matrix and the adjacency list for the given graph:

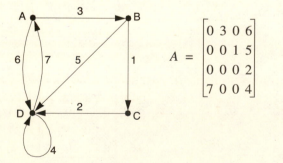

$$A = \begin{bmatrix} 0 & 3 & 0 & 6 \\ 0 & 0 & 1 & 5 \\ 0 & 0 & 0 & 2 \\ 7 & 0 & 0 & 4 \end{bmatrix}$$

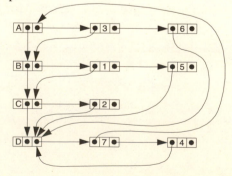

Appendix A

Essential Mathematics

As a science, computer science depends upon fundamental theoretical principles that are derived and applied using mathematics. This appendix summarizes those mathematical topics that are needed for the study of data structures.

A.1 THE FLOOR AND CEILING FUNCTION

The floor and ceiling functions return the nearest integer for a given real number. The *floor* of x, denoted by $\lfloor x \rfloor$, is the greatest integer that is not greater than x. The *ceiling*

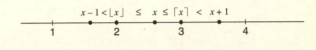

of x, denoted by $\lceil x \rceil$, is the smallest integer that is not smaller than x. Another way to put it is that the floor and ceiling of x are the nearest integers on the left and on the right of x, respectively.

EXAMPLE A.1 The Floor and Ceiling Functions

If $x = 2.71828$, then $\lfloor x \rfloor = 2$ and $\lceil x \rceil = 3$.

Let **Z** be the set of all integers and let **R** be the set of all real numbers. Then the floor and ceiling functions map **R** into **Z**; i.e., each returns an integer for a decimal number input. In the following discussion, we also let **N** be the set of all natural numbers: $\mathbf{N} = \{ n \in \mathbf{Z} \mid n \geq 1 \} = \{ 1, 2, 3, \ldots \}$.

Theorem A.1

The floor and ceiling functions have the following properties, for all real numbers x:

    a. $\lfloor x \rfloor = \max\{ m \in \mathbf{Z} \mid m \leq x \}$, and $\lceil x \rceil = \min\{ n \in \mathbf{Z} \mid n \geq x \}$.
    b. $\lfloor x \rfloor \leq x < \lfloor x \rfloor + 1$, and $\lceil x \rceil - 1 < x \leq \lceil x \rceil$.
    c. $x - 1 < \lfloor x \rfloor \leq x \leq \lceil x \rceil < x + 1$.
    d. If $n \in \mathbf{Z}$ and $n \leq x < n + 1$, then $n = \lfloor x \rfloor$. If $n \in \mathbf{Z}$ and $n - 1 < x \leq n$, then $n = \lceil x \rceil$.
    e. If $x \in \mathbf{Z}$, then $\lfloor x \rfloor = x = \lceil x \rceil$.
    f. If $x \notin \mathbf{Z}$, then $\lfloor x \rfloor < x < \lceil x \rceil$.
    g. $\lfloor -x \rfloor = -\lceil x \rceil$ and $\lceil -x \rceil = -\lfloor x \rfloor$.
    h. $\lfloor x + 1 \rfloor = \lfloor x \rfloor + 1$ and $\lceil x + 1 \rceil = \lceil x \rceil + 1$.
See Problem A.2 on page 347 for the proofs.

A.2 LOGARITHMS

The *base b logarithm* of a number x is the exponent on b that produces the value x. For example, the base 10 logarithm of 1000 is 3 because $10^3 = 1000$. This is written $\log_{10} 1000 = 3$.

Social scientists usually use base 10 and write log x for $\log_{10} x$; this is called the *common logarithm*. Physical scientists and mathematicians usually use base $e = 2.718281828459045$ and write ln$x$ for $\log_e x$; this is called the *natural logarithm*. Computer scientists usually use base 2 and write lg x for $\log_2 x$; this is called the *binary logarithm*.

As mathematical functions, logarithms are the inverses of exponential functions:

$$y = \log_b x \Leftrightarrow b^y = x$$

For example, $\log_2 256 = 8$ because $2^8 = 256$. This equivalence may be taken as the definition of the logarithm for any base b.

The following properties of logarithms follow directly from the above definition.

Theorem A.2 The Laws of Logarithms

    a. $\log_b(b^y) = y$

    b. $b^{\log_b x} = x$

    c. $\log_b uv = \log_b u + \log_b v$

    d. $\log_b u/v = \log_b u - \log_b v$

    e. $\log_b u^v = v \log_b u$

    f. $\log_b x = (\log_c x)/(\log_c b) = (\log_b c)(\log_c x)$

See Problem A.3 on page 347 for the proofs.

EXAMPLE A.2 Applying the Laws of Logarithms

$\log_2 256 = \log_2(2^8) = 8$

$\log_2 1000 = (\log_{10} 1000)/(\log_{10} 2) = 3/0.30103 = 9.966$

$\log_2 1{,}000{,}000{,}000{,}000 = \log_2 1000^4 = 4(\log_2 1000) = 4(9.966) = 39.86$

Theorem A.3

The binary logarithm has the following properties:

    a. If $p \in \mathbf{Z}$ and $2^p < n < 2^{p+1}$, then $p = \lfloor \lg n \rfloor$ and $p + 1 = \lceil \lg n \rceil$.

    b. If $n \in \mathbf{N}$, then $\lceil \lg(n + 1) \rceil = \lfloor \lg n \rfloor + 1$.

See Problem A.4 on page 347 for the proofs.

The integer $\lfloor \lg n \rfloor$ is called the *integral binary logarithm* of n. This is essentially the number of times that n can be divided by 2 before reaching 1. For example, the integral binary logarithm of 1000 is 9 because 1000 can be split in half 9 times: 500, 250, 125, 62, 31, 15, 7, 3, 1.

EXAMPLE A.3 Testing the Integral Binary Logarithm

```
public class ExA01
{ public static void main(String[] args)
  { System.out.println("iLg(1)   = " + iLg(1));
    System.out.println("iLg(2)   = " + iLg(2));
    System.out.println("iLg(3)   = " + iLg(3));
    System.out.println("iLg(4)   = " + iLg(4));
    System.out.println("iLg(10)  = " + iLg(10));
    System.out.println("iLg(100)  = " + iLg(100));
    System.out.println("iLg(1000)  = " + iLg(1000));
    System.out.println("iLg(10000)  = " + iLg(10000));
  }
```

```
    public static int iLg(int n)
{ int count=0;
  while (n > 1)
  { n /= 2;
    ++count;
  }
  return count;
}
}
iLg(1) = 0
iLg(2) = 1
iLg(3) = 1
iLg(4) = 2
iLg(10) = 3
iLg(100) = 6
iLg(1000) = 9
iLg(10000) = 13
```

A.3 COMPLEXITY CLASSES

In computer science, algorithms are classified by their complexity functions. These are functions that describe the algorithms' running times relative to the sizes of the problems that they solve. For example, the Bubble Sort (Algorithm 13.1 on page 244) has complexity $O(n^2)$ because if you use it to sort an array that is twice as long, it will take 4 times as long to run: $(2n)^2 = 4n^2$. The symbol $O()$ stands for "order" and $O(n^2)$ is pronounced "order n-squared."

The "big Oh" notation can be defined precisely in terms of limits. If f and g are nondecreasing functions on the set positive integers, let $L(f, g)$ denote the limit

$$L(f, g) = \lim_{n \to \infty} \frac{f(n)}{g(n)}$$

This constant could be 0, any positive number, or infinite. For example, if $f(n) = n^2$ and $g(n) = \sqrt{n}$, then $L(f, g) = \infty$ because $n^2/\sqrt{n} = n^{3/2} \to \infty$. With this notation, we can define all five standard complexity classes:

$o(g) = \{ f \in M \mid L(f, g) = 0 \}$

$O(g) = \{ f \in M \mid 0 \le L(f, g) < \infty \}$

$\Theta(g) = \{ f \in M \mid 0 < L(f, g) < \infty \}$

$\Omega(g) = \{ f \in M \mid 0 < L(f, g) \le \infty \}$

$\omega(g) = \{ f \in M \mid L(f, g) = \infty \}$

Here, M is the set of all positive monotonically increasing functions on the positive integers.

Theorem A.4

The three sets $o(g)$, $\Theta(g)$, and $\omega(g)$ partition M; i.e., every function in M is in one and only one of these three sets.

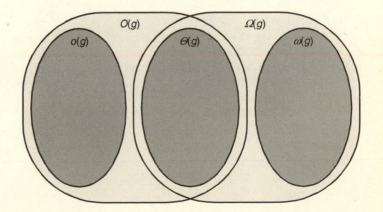

Theorem A.5

$$O(g) = o(g) \cup \Theta(g)$$

$$\Theta(g) = O(g) \cap \Omega(g)$$

$$\Omega(g) = \Theta(g) \cup \omega(g)$$

The diagram above shows the relationships among the five complexity classes.

Note that, although the five complexity classes are sets of functions, it is traditional to write $f(n) = O(g(n))$ instead of the more precise $f \in O(g)$, and $f(n) \neq O(g(n))$ instead of $f \notin O(g)$.

EXAMPLE A.4 Complexity Classes

$n \lg n = O(n^2)$ but $n \lg n \neq \Theta(n^2)$ because $(n \lg n)/(n^2) = (\lg n)/n \to 0$
$n \lg n = \Theta(n \lg n)$ because $(n \lg n)/(n \log n) = (\log_2 n)/(\log_{10} n) = \log_{10} 2$, which is a positive constant
$n \lg n = \Omega(\sqrt{n})$ but $n \lg n \neq O(\sqrt{n})$ because $(n \lg n)/(\sqrt{n}) = \sqrt{n} \lg n \to \infty$

Theorem A.6 For any base $b > 1$, $\log_b n = O(\lg n)$.

Proof: By **Theorem A.2(f)**, $\log_b n = c \lg n$, where $c = 1/\lg b = \log_b 2$.

Note that the limit $L(f, g)$ may not exist. In that case, we let $L(f, g)$ represent the set of all limits of subsequences of the sequence $f(n)/g(n)$. Then the inequalities for $L(f, g)$ are interpreted as being required for every element of that set.

EXAMPLE A.5 An Oscillating Ratio

Let $f(n) = 2^n$, and $g(n) = 4^{\lfloor n/2 \rfloor}$. The the sequence $\{f(n)/g(n)\} = \{1, 2, 1, 2, 1, 2, 1, 2, 1, 2, ...\}$ which has no (unique) limit, so the symbol would represent the set $\{1, 2\}$. Since every element x in that set (i.e., both $x = 1$ and $x = 2$) satisfies the inequalities $0 < x < \infty$, it follows that $f = \Theta(g)$ (and $g = \Theta(f)$).

A.4 THE FIRST PRINCIPLE OF MATHEMATICAL INDUCTION

The First Principle of Mathematical Induction, also called "weak induction," is often used to prove formulas about the natural numbers.

Theorem A.7 (The First Principle of Mathematical Induction)

If $\{P(1), P(2), P(3), P(4), . . . \}$ is a sequence of statements with the following two properties, then all of the statements are true:

1. $P(1)$ is true.
2. Any one of the statements can be deduced from its predecessor.

EXAMPLE A.6 Using Weak Induction

Prove the inequality $2^n \leq (n + 1)!$ for all $n \geq 1$.
The formula asserts the following sequence of statements:

$P(1)$: $2^1 \leq 2!$
$P(2)$: $2^2 \leq 3!$
$P(3)$: $2^3 \leq 4!$
$P(4)$: $2^4 \leq 5!$
etc.

These first four statements are obviously true, because:

$$2^1 = 2 \le 2 = 2!$$
$$2^2 = 4 \le 6 = 3!$$
$$2^3 = 8 \le 24 = 4!$$
$$2^4 = 16 \le 120 = 5!$$

Any one of the other formulas could also be verified directly this way. But they can't all be verified this way because there are infinitely many of them.

Part 1 of Theorem A.7 requires that $P(1)$ be verified. This was done in the preceding paragraph. Part 2 of the theorem requires the deduction of $P(n)$ from $P(n-1)$. So assume that $P(n-1)$ is true for some $n > 1$. That means we are assuming that $2^{n-1} \le n!$ is true for some n. Then to deduce $P(n)$ from that assumption, look for some relationship between $P(n-1)$ and $P(n)$; that is, try to relate the two formulas:

$$P(n-1): \quad 2^{n-1} \le n!$$
$$P(n): \quad 2^n \le (n+1)!$$

The statement $P(n)$ can be rewritten as:

$$P(n): \quad (2)(2^{n-1}) \le (n+1)(n!)$$

Now the progress from $P(n-1)$ to $P(n)$ is apparent: the left side of the inequality increases by a factor of 2 while the right side increases by a factor of $n+1$. So as long as $n+1 > 2$, the increase on the left is less than the increase on the right. And we know that $n+1 > 2$ because $n > 1$. Thus we have the implication:

$$2^{n-1} \le n! \quad \Rightarrow \quad 2^n \le (n+1)!$$

i.e., $\quad P(n-1) \quad \Rightarrow \quad P(n)$

This is the requirement of part 2 of Theorem A.7 on page 336. Thus we can conclude that $P(n)$ is true for all $n \ge 1$.

Part 1 of Theorem A.7 is called the *basis* of the proof and part 2 is called the *inductive step*. The assumption in part 2 that $P(n)$ is true for some n is called the *inductive hypothesis*.

A.5 THE SECOND PRINCIPLE OF MATHEMATICAL INDUCTION

The Second Principle of Mathematical Induction, also called "strong induction," is nearly the same as the First Principle. The only difference is in the inductive step (part 2).

Theorem A.8 The Second Principle of Mathematical Induction

If $\{P(1), P(2), P(3), P(4), \ldots \}$ is a sequence of statements with the following two properties, then all of the statements are true:

1. $P(1)$ is true.
2. Any one of the statements can be deduced from *all* of its predecessors.

The inductive step (part 2) means that $P(n)$ can be deduced from the assumption that all of its preceding statements $\{P(1), P(2), P(3), \ldots, P(n-1)\}$ are true.

EXAMPLE A.7 Proof of the Fundamental Theorem of Arithmetic

Theorem A.9 The Fundamental Theorem of Arithmetic

Every positive integer has a unique representation as a product of powers of prime numbers:

$$p_1^{n_1} \cdot p_2^{n_2} \cdot p_3^{n_3} \cdots p_k^{n_k}$$

where $p_1, p_2, p_3, \ldots$ are the prime numbers: $p_1 = 2, p_2 = 3, p_3 = 5$, etc., and each n_j is a nonnegative integer.

For example, the positive integer 23,115,456 has the unique representation $2^6 3^4 5^0 7^3 11^0 13^1$.

The proof applies the Second Principle of Mathematical Induction to the sequence of statements:

$P(1)$ = "1 has a unique representation as a product of prime numbers."

$P(2)$ = "2 has a unique representation as a product of prime numbers."

$P(3)$ = "3 has a unique representation as a product of prime numbers."

$P(4)$ = "4 has a unique representation as a product of prime numbers."

etc.

These first four statements are true because:

$1 = 2^0$

$2 = 2^1$

$3 = 3^1$

$4 = 2^2$

The first of these statements verifies the basis of the induction. To verify the inductive step, we assume that all the statements $\{P(1), P(2), P(3), \ldots, P(n-1)\}$ are true for some $n > 1$.

If n has a prime factor, call it p and let $m = n/p$. Then m is a positive integer that is less than n, so by the inductive hypothesis, $P(m)$ must be true; i.e., m has a unique representation as a product of prime powers. But then so does n, because $n = p \cdot m$. Thus $P(n)$ is true in this case.

If n has no prime factors, then it must be a prime number itself, so it certainly does have a unique representation as a product of prime powers: $n = n^1$. Thus $P(n)$ is true in this case.

The proof is complete because we have deduced $P(n)$ from $\{P(1), P(2), P(3), \ldots, P(n-1)\}$.

A.6 GEOMETRIC SERIES

A *geometric series* is a sum in which each term is the same multiple of its previous term. For example, $10 + 30 + 90 + 270 + 810 + 2430 + \cdots$ is a geometric series because each term is 3 times the size of its predecessor. The multiplier 3 is called the *common ratio* of the series.

Theorem A.10 Sum of a Finite Geometric Series

$$a + ar + ar^2 + ar^3 + \cdots + ar^{n-1} = \frac{a(1 - r^n)}{1 - r}$$

Here, a is the first term of the series, r is the common ratio, and n is the number of terms in the sum.

EXAMPLE A.8 Finding the Sum of a Finite Geometric Series

$10 + 30 + 90 + 270 + 810 + 2430 = 10(1 - 3^6)/(1 - 3) = 10(1 - 729)/(-2) = 10(-728)/(-2) = 3640$

Theorem A.11 The Sum of an Infinite Geometric Series

$$a + ar + ar^2 + ar^3 + \cdots = \frac{a}{1 - r}$$

This formula is valid only for $-1 < r < 1$.

EXAMPLE A.9 Finding the Sum of an Infinite Geometric Series

$6 + 3 + 3/2 + 3/4 + 3/8 + \cdots = 6/(1 - 1/2) = 6/(1/2) = 12$

A.7 SUMMATION FORMULAS

Theorem A.12 Sum of the First n Positive Integers

$$1 + 2 + 3 + \cdots + n = \frac{n(n+1)}{2}$$

Note that the parameter n equals the number of terms in the sum.

An easy way to remember this useful formula is to remember this picture. It shows two triangles of dots, one white and one gray. The two triangles have the same number of dots, namely $S = 1 + 2 + 3 + \ldots + n$. Together, they form a rectangle n dots wide and $(n + 1)$ dots high. So the total number of dots is $n(n + 1)$, which is twice the size of the sum S.

EXAMPLE A.10 Finding the Sum of an Arithmetic Sequence

$$1 + 2 + 3 + 4 + 5 + 6 + 7 + 8 = 8(9)/2 = 36$$

Theorem A.13 Sum of the First n Squares

$$1^2 + 2^2 + 3^2 + \cdots + n^2 = \frac{n(n+1)(2n+1)}{6}$$

Note that the sum is an integer even though the right-hand side appears to be a fraction.

EXAMPLE A.11 Finding a Sum of Squares

$$1 + 4 + 9 + 16 + 25 + 36 + 49 = 7(8)(15)/6 = 140$$

A.8 HARMONIC NUMBERS

The *harmonic numbers* are defined by the formula:

$$H_n = \sum_{k=1}^{n} \frac{1}{k} = 1 + \frac{1}{2} + \frac{1}{3} + \frac{1}{4} + \frac{1}{5} + \cdots + \frac{1}{n}$$

n	H_n
1	1.000000
2	1.500000
3	1.83333᠉
4	2.083333
5	2.283333
6	2.450000

The first six harmonic numbers are shown in the table on the right.

The harmonic sequence grows very slowly. But as the next theorem and its corollary show, the sequence does continue to grow without bound.

Theorem A.14 The Harmonic Sequence is Asymptotically Logarithmic

The limit $\lim_{n \to \infty} (H_n - \ln n)$ is a positive constant.

Corollary A.1

The harmonic numbers grow logarithmically: $H_n = \Theta(\ln n)$

The next example provides empirical evidence that Theorem A.14 is true.

EXAMPLE A.12 Euler's Constant

To test the conjecture that the limit $\lim_{n \to \infty} (H_n - \ln n)$ is a positive constant, we run the following program that prints the values of $H_n - \ln n$ for all values of n that are powers of 2 less than 10,000,000:

```java
public class ExA10
{ public static void main(String[] args)
  { double hn=0.0;                 // harmonic numbers
    int pow2=1;                     // powers of 2
    for (int n=1; n<1e7; n++)
    { hn += 1.0/n;                  // the nth harmonic number
      if (n==pow2)                  // print only for powers of 2
      { double ln=Math.log(n);      // natural logarithm of n
        double difn = hn - ln;      // approaches Euler's constant
        System.out.println(n+"\t"+hn+"\t"+ln+"\t"+difn);
        pow2 *= 2;
      }
    }
  }
}
```

1	1.0	0.0	1.0
2	1.5	0.6931471805599453	0.8068528194400547
4	2.083333333333333	1.3862943611198906	0.697038972213
8	2.7178571428571425	2.0794415416798357	0.638415601177
16	3.3807289932289937	2.772588722239781	0.608140270989
32	4.05849519543652	3.4657359027997265	0.592759292636
64	4.7438909037057675	4.1588830833596715	0.585007820346
128	5.433147092589174	4.852030263919617	0.581116828669
256	6.124344962817281	5.545177444479562	0.579167518337
512	6.81651653454972	6.238324625039508	0.578191909510
1024	7.509175672278132	6.931471805599453	0.577703866678
2048	8.202078771817716	7.6246189861593985	0.577459785658
4096	8.89510389696629	8.317766166719343	0.577337730246
8192	9.588190046095265	9.010913347279288	0.577276698815
16384	10.281306710008463	9.704060527839234	0.577246182169
32768	10.974438632012168	10.39720770839918	0.577230923612
65536	11.667578183235785	11.090354888959125	0.577223294276
131072	12.360721549112862	11.78350206951907	0.577219479593
262144	13.053866822328144	12.476649250079015	0.577217572249
524288	13.747013049214582	13.16979643063896	0.577216618575
1048576	14.440159752936799	13.862943611198906	0.577216141737
2097152	15.133306695078193	14.556090791758852	0.577215903319
4194304	15.826453756428641	15.249237972318797	0.577215784109
8388608	16.51960087738358	15.94238515287874	0.577215724504

As n increases, the difference $H_n - \ln n$ approaches the constant 0.5772157. This number is known as *Euler's constant* and is usually denoted by the Greek letter gamma:

$$\gamma = \lim_{n \to \infty} (H_n - \ln n) = 0.5772157 \cdots$$

It remains an open question whether γ is a rational number.

A.9 STIRLING'S FORMULA

The factorial function occurs frequently in computer science analysis. In that context, the analysis concerns the magnitude of expressions involving $n!$ as n grows large. But these values are difficult to obtain directly because they are so large. For example, $70! > 10^{100}$. *Stirling's formula* provides a convenient method for approximating large factorials:

Theorem A.15 Stirling's Formula

$$1 < \frac{n!}{\sqrt{2n\pi}}\left(\frac{e}{n}\right)^n < 1 + \frac{1}{2n}$$

Here, e and π are the mathematical constants $e = 2.71828$ and $\pi = 3.14159$.

The following program shows that these tighter bounds apply:

$$\sqrt{2n\pi}\left(\frac{n}{e}\right)^n \le n! \le \sqrt{2n\pi}\left(\frac{n}{e}\right)^{n+1/(12n)}$$

EXAMPLE A.13 Stirling's Approximation

```
public class ExA12
{ public static void main(String[] args)
  { final double E=Math.E;                         // e = 2.71828
    final double PI=Math.PI;                        // pi = 3.14159
    final double INF=Double.POSITIVE_INFINITY;      // = 1.8E308
    double f=3628800.0;                             // 10! = 3,628,800
    int n=10;
    while (f != INF)
    { double s = Math.sqrt(2*n*PI)*Math.pow(n/E,n);
      double ss = Math.sqrt(2*n*PI)*Math.pow(n/E,n+1.0/(12*n));
      System.out.println(n+"\t"+s+"\t"+f+"\t"+ss);
      for (int i=n+1; i<=n+10; i++)
        f *= i;
      n += 10;
    }
  }
}
```

```
10      3598695.6187410373      3628800.0             3637971.7959937225
20      2.4227768467611351E18   2.43290200817664E18   2.4430176532620851E18
30      2.6451709592296516E32   2.6525285981219103E32 2.6628732015735442E32
40      8.142172644946236E47    8.159152832478977E47  8.187911721520889E47
50      3.036344593938168E64    3.0414093201713376E64 3.0511169215892805E64
60      8.3094383149767E81      8.320987112741392E81  8.345226643189724E81
70      1.1964320047337557E100  1.19785716699696989E100 1.2010678721362897E100
80      7.14949447318118E118    7.156945704626378E118 7.174726163602993E118
90      1.4843409438918685E138  1.485715964481607E138 1.4891588486241144E138
100     9.32484762526942E157    9.3326215443944E157   9.352904468745705E157
110     1.587042784164154E178   1.5882455415227421E178 1.5914981328581203E178
120     6.68485904870404E198    6.895029134491124E198 6.702464725447769E198
130     6.462711405582573E219   6.46685548922047E219  6.4787535645487E219
140     1.3454001771051692E241  1.346201247571752E241 1.3485604820896678E241
150     5.7102107404794024E262  5.7133839564458505E262 5.7294802133358916E262
160     4.712268693324974E284   4.714723635992059E284 4.7222810411380736E284
170     7.25385893454291E306    7.257415615307994E306 7.268579978559315E306
```

Note that Stirling's approximation is accurate to within 1%, and that this relative accuracy improves as n increases. For example, for $n = 100$, $n! = 9.3326(10^{178})$ and Stirling's approximation is $9.3248(10^{178})$. That's an absolute error of $0.0078(10^{178})$, which is a relative error of 0.08%.

Corollary A.2 $n! = o(n^n)$.

Proof: By Stirling's formula, the ratio

$$\frac{n!}{n^n} \leq \sqrt{2n\pi}\left(\frac{n}{e}\right)^{1/(12n)}\left(\frac{1}{e}\right)^n$$

The limit of the expression on the right is 0.

A.10 THE FIBONACCI NUMBERS

The *Fibonacci numbers* are 1, 1, 2, 3, 5, 8, 13, 21, 34, 55, ... Each number after the second is the sum of the two preceding numbers:

$$F_n = \begin{cases} 0, \text{ if } n = 0 \\ 1, \text{ if } n = 1 \\ F_{n-1} + F_{n-2}, \text{ if } n > 1 \end{cases}$$

n	F_n
0	0
1	1
2	1
3	2
4	3
5	5
6	8
7	13
8	21
9	34
10	55

A.11 THE GOLDEN MEAN

The *golden mean* (also called the *golden ratio*) is the mathematical constant

$$\phi = \frac{1 + \sqrt{5}}{2} \approx 1.618$$

It originated as the solution to the following ancient Greek problem: determine the point C on a line segment AB so that $AB/AC = AC/CB$. This intermediate point was called the *golden section*.

A ——————————— C ————— B

Theorem A.16 The Golden Mean
If C is the golden section of AB, then $AB/AC = \phi$.

The proof (see Problem A.11) finds ϕ to be one of the roots of the quadratic equation $x^2 = x + 1$. The other root $\psi = (1 - \sqrt{5})/2 = -0.618$ is called the *conjugate golden mean*. It and ϕ have the following peculiar properties:

Theorem A.17 Some Properties of the Golden Mean
If $\phi = (1 + \sqrt{5})/2$ and $\psi = (1 - \sqrt{5})/2$, then

a. $\phi^2 = \phi + 1$
b. $\psi^2 = \psi + 1$
c. $1/\phi = \phi - 1$
d. $1/\psi = \psi - 1$
e. $\phi + \psi = 1$
f. $\phi - \psi = \sqrt{5}$

The golden mean is tied to the Fibonacci numbers, and thus to computer science, by the following result.

Theorem A.18 The Explicit Formula for the Fibonacci Numbers

$$F_n = \frac{\phi^n - \psi^n}{\sqrt{5}}$$

The formula in Theorem A.18 is remarkable because, although ϕ, ψ, and $\sqrt{5}$ are all irrational numbers, the Fibonacci numbers are positive integers.

Corollary A.3

The Fibonacci Function is Asymptotically Exponential: $F_n = \Theta(\phi^n)$.

A.12 THE EUCLIDEAN ALGORITHM

The *Euclidean Algorithm* computes the greatest common multiple of two positive integers. For example, the gcd of 494 and 130 is 26 because the divisors of 494 are {1, 2, 13, 19, **26**, 38, 247, 494} and the divisors of 130 are {1, 2, 5, 10, 13, **26**, 130}.

Algorithm A.1 The Euclidean Algorithm

The iterative version is:

```
public static long gcd(long a, long b)
{ while (b>0)
   { long r=a%b;
     a = b;
     b = r;
     // INVARIANT: gcd(a,b) is constant
   }
   return a;
}
```

The recursive version is:

```
public static long gcd(long a, long b)
{ if (b==0) return a;
   // INVARIANT: gcd(a,b) is constant
   return gcd(b,a%b);
}
```

For example, this trace shows why `gcd(494,130)` returns `26`:

The following analysis depends upon this result from number theory:

Theorem A.19 If $a > b > 0$ and $r = a \% b > 0$ and $d \mid b$, then $d \mid a \Leftrightarrow d \mid r$.

Here, the symbol "|" means "d divides b" and the symbol "$a \% b$" means "the remainder from the division of a by b".

Corollary A.4 If $a > b > 0$ and $r = a \% b > 0$, then $(d \mid a) \wedge (d \mid b) \Leftrightarrow (d \mid b) \wedge (d \mid r)$.

Corollary A.5 If $a > b > 0$ and $r = a \% b > 0$, then $\gcd(a, b) = \gcd(b, r)$.

For example, $\gcd(494,130) = \gcd(130,104) = \gcd(104,26) = \gcd(26,0) = 26$.

Theorem A.20 The Euclidean Algorithm is correct.

The loop invariant is Q_k: $\gcd(a_k, b_k) = \gcd(a,b)$, where a_k and b_k are the values of a and b on the kth iteration.

Theorem A.21 The Euclidean Algorithm runs in logarithmic time.

Specifically, the Euclidean Algorithm executes at most $\log_\varphi n$ divisions, where φ is the golden mean and $n = \max\{a, b\}$.

A.13 THE CATALAN NUMBERS

The *Catalan numbers* are defined recursively by:

$$C(n) = \begin{cases} 1, \text{ if } n = 0 \\ C(0)C(n-1) + C(1)C(n-2) + C(2)C(n-3) + \cdots + C(n-1)C(0), \text{ if } n > 0 \end{cases}$$

The first 10 Catalan numbers are shown here. This sequence is similar to the Fibonacci sequence: It is defined recursively and it grows exponentially.

EXAMPLE A.14 Implementation of the Catalan Function

```
public static long cat(int n)
{ if (n < 2) return 1;
  long sum=cat(n-1);
 for (int i=1; i<n-1; i++)
   sum += cat(i)*cat(n-1-i);
 return sum;
}
```

n	$C(n)$
0	1
1	1
2	2
3	5
4	14
5	42
6	132
7	429
8	1430
9	4862

The Catalan sequence was discovered by applying the Second Principle of Mathematical Induction to the following problem.

EXAMPLE A.15 Counting the Triangulations of a Polygon

A *polygon* is a plane region bounded by noncrossing line segments. A *convex polygon* is a polygon any two points of which have their connecting line segment contained within the polygon, so its boundary has no dents.

Here are some convex polygons.

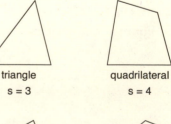

triangle
s = 3

quadrilateral
s = 4

pentagon
s = 5

hexagon
s = 6

A *triangulation* of a convex polygon is a subdivision of the polygon into triangles, all of whose corners are also corners of the polygon. A triangulation of an *s*-sided polygon is simply a set a $s-3$ nonintersecting diagonals. Here are four different triangulations of the hexagon:

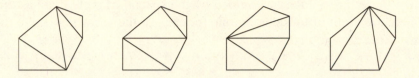

The following pictures show that there are two triangulations of a quadrilateral, five triangulations of a pentagon, and 14 triangulations of a hexagon. From this data we can infer the following.

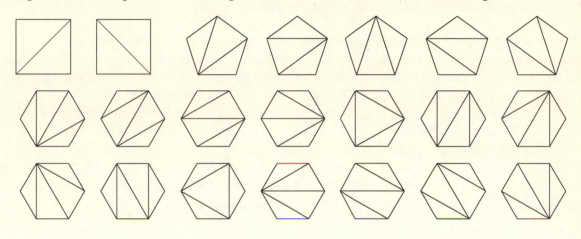

Theorem A.22

The number of triangulations of a polygon with $n+2$ sides is the *n*th Catalan number $C(n)$.

Proof: If we let $f(s)$ be the number of triangulations of a polygon with s sides, then we have to prove that $f(n+2) = C(n)$ for all $n \geq 1$. We use strong induction.

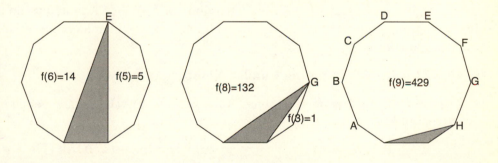

The basis is the statement $f(3) = C(1) = 1$; this is verified by the fact that there is exactly one triangulation of a triangle: itself.

For the inductive step, assume that for some $n > 1$, $f(k+2) = C(k)$ for all $k < n$. We don't know what n is, but suppose $n = 8$. The we would have to show that $f(10) = C(8)$; i.e., that a decagon has 1430 different triangulations. The top figure at right shows a decagon with one triangle partitioning it into two other pieces: a hexagon and a pentagon. By our inductive hypothesis, we know that there are $f(6) = C(4) = 14$ different ways to triangulate the hexagon, and there are $f(5) = C(3) = 5$ different ways to triangulate the pentagon. Hence there are $C(4) \cdot C(3) = 14 \cdot 5 = 70$ different ways to triangulate this decagon so that the shaded triangle is part of the triangulation. Similarly, the second figure shows that there are $f(8) \cdot f(5) = C(4) \cdot C(3) = 132 \cdot 1 = 132$ different ways to triangulate the decagon so that that shaded triangle is part of the triangulation. And the bottom figure shows that there are $f(9) = C(7) = 429$ different ways to triangulate the decagon so that that shaded triangle is part of the triangulation. All $f(10)$ triangulations are partitioned into distinct cases like these three, each determined by the special triangle that has the same base as the decagon. There are eight of these cases, one for each of the vertices A–H. So the total number of triangulations of the decagon is

$$f(10) = f(9) + f(3) \cdot f(8) + f(4) \cdot f(7) + f(5) \cdot f(6) + f(6) \cdot f(5) + f(7) \cdot f(4) + f(8) \cdot f(3) + f(9)$$

Since $f(s) = C(n-2)$ and $C(0) = 1$,

$$f(10) = C(7) + C(1) \cdot C(6) + C(2) \cdot C(5) + C(3) \cdot C(4) + C(4) \cdot C(3) + C(5) \cdot C(2) + C(6) \cdot C(1) + C(7)$$
$$= C(8).$$

The same argument shows that $f(n+2) = C(n)$ for any n.

The technique used in the proof of Theorem A.22 is called *divide-and-conquer*. It is widely used in computer science. The main idea is that, once you have analyzed a problem for all sizes smaller than n, you can analyze the problem for size n by splitting it into two parts and applying your previous analysis to each part. Then the analysis of the complete problem reduces to an analysis of how it relates to the two smaller problems. The divide and conquer strategy is also used in the Binary Search (Algorithm 2.2 on page 31), the Merge Sort (Algorithm 13.5 on page 249), and the Quick Sort (Algorithm 13.6 on page 252).

The formula that defines the Catalan numbers is *recursive*: you cannot use it to obtain the value of $C(n)$ unless you already have obtained the values of $C(k)$ for all $k < n$. In contrast, the next formula is more practical, providing an explicit formula.

Theorem A.23 Theorem

$$C(n) = \frac{(2n)!}{n!(n+1)!} = \frac{(2n)(2n-1)(2n-2)\cdots(n+2)}{(n)(n-1)(n-2)\cdots(2)}$$

In words, this formula says to form the fraction $(2n)/(n)$; then repeatedly add factors in pairs, one in the numerator and one in the denominator, each 1 less than its predecessor, until the factor in the denominator is 2.

EXAMPLE A.16 Computing Catalan Numbers Directly

The following application of Theorem A.23 confirms the value 4862 given in the table on Example A.13 on page 341:

$$C(9) = \frac{(18)(17)(16)(15)(14)(13)(12)(11)}{(9)(8)(7)(6)(5)(4)(3)(2)} = (17)(13)(11)(2) = 4862$$

Since $n = 9$ here, there are 8 factors in the numerator and 8 in the denominator.

Note that all the factors in the denominator cancel.

Theorem A.24 The Number of Binary Trees of Size n

The number of distinct binary trees of size n is the nth Catalan number $C(n)$.

Proof: Let $f(n)$ be the number of distinct binary trees of size n. Then $f(0) = 1 = C(0)$ because there is exactly 1 binary tree of size 0: the empty tree. The pictures at right shows that $f(1) = 1 = C(1)$, $f(2) = 2 = C(2)$, and $f(3) = 5 = C(3)$. This verifies the basis of a proof by strong induction (Theorem A.8 on page 337).

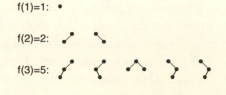

Now assume that for some $n > 0$, $f(k) = C(k)$ for all $k < n$. Let T be a binary tree of size n. As in the proof of Theorem A.22, we apply the divide and conquer strategy. Let T_L and T_R be the left and right subtrees of T. Let n_L and n_R be the sizes of T_L and T_R respectively. Then since n_L and n_R are both less than n, we can apply the inductive hypothesis: $f(n_L) = C(n_L)$ and $f(n_R) = C(n_R)$. Now $n = 1 + n_L + n_R$ because each node in T must be either the root or in T_L or in T_R. So $n_R = n - 1 - n_L$. And n_L could be any number k in the range $0 \le k \le n-1$. So all the binary trees of size n are partitioned into n classes, one for each value of $n_L = k$ for $0 \le k \le n-1$.

The picture at right shows two binary trees of size $n = 8$, one for the case where $n_L = 3$ and one for the case where $n_L = 5$. For the case where $n_L = k$ there are $C(n_L)$ different possible binary trees for T_L and $C(n_R)$ different possible binary trees for T_R, so the total number for that case is $C(n_L) \cdot C(n_R) = C(k) \cdot C(n - 1 - n)$. Hence the total number of binary trees is

$$f(n) = C(0) \cdot C(n-1) + C(1) \cdot C(n-2) + C(2) \cdot C(n-3) + \cdots + C(n-1) \cdot C(0) = C(n).$$
This shows that $f(n) = C(n)$ for all n.

Review Questions

A.1　A function $f()$ is called *idempotent* if $f(f(x)) = f(x)$ for all x in the domain of $f()$. Explain why the floor and ceiling functions are idempotent.

A.2　What is a logarithm?

A.3　What is the difference between the weak induction and strong induction?

A.4　How can you decide when to use strong induction?

A.5　What is Euler's constant?

A.6　What makes Stirling's Formula useful?

A.7　Which is more useful, the recursive definition of the Fibonacci numbers (Example 4.5 on page 74) or its explicit formula (Theorem A.18 on page 343)?

Problems

A.1　Sketch the graphs of
    a. $y = \lfloor x \rfloor$
    b. $y = \lceil x \rceil$
    c. $y = \lceil x \rceil - x$
    d. $y = \lceil x \rceil - \lfloor x \rfloor$

A.2　Prove Theorem A.1 on page 333.

A.3　Prove Theorem A.2 on page 334.

A.4　Prove Theorem A.3 on page 334.

A.5　True of false:
    a. $f = o(g) \iff g = \omega(f)$
    b. $f = O(g) \iff g = \Omega(f)$
    c. $f = \Theta(g) \iff g = \Theta(f)$
    d. $f = O(g) \implies f = \Theta(g)$
    e. $f = \Theta(g) \implies f = \Omega(g)$

   f. $f = \Theta(h) \wedge g = \Theta(h) \Rightarrow f + g = \Theta(h)$

   g. $f = \Theta(h) \wedge g = \Theta(h) \Rightarrow fg = \Theta(h)$

   h. $n^2 = O(n \lg n)$

   i. $n^2 = \Theta(n \lg n)$

   j. $n^2 = \Omega(n \lg n)$

   k. $\lg n = \omega(n)$

   l. $\lg n = o(n)$

A.6   Prove Theorem A.4 on page 335.

A.7   Prove Theorem A.5 on page 336.

A.8   Prove Theorem A.10 on page 338.

A.9   Prove Theorem A.11 on page 338.

A.10 Prove Theorem A.12 on page 339.

A.11 Prove Theorem A.16 on page 342.

A.12 Prove Theorem A.17 on page 342.

A.13 Prove Theorem A.18 on page 343.

A.14 Prove Corollary A.3 on page 343.

A.15 Run a program that tests the formula in Theorem A.18 on page 343 by comparing the values obtained from it with those obtained from the recursive definition of the Fibonacci numbers.

A.16 Prove Theorem A.19 on page 343.

A.17 Prove Corollary A.4 on page 344.

A.18 Prove Corollary A.5 on page 344.

A.19 Prove Theorem A.20 on page 344.

A.20 Prove Theorem A.21 on page 344.

Answers to Review Questions

A.1   The floor and ceiling functions are idempotent because they return integer values, and according to Theorem A.1*e*, the floor or ceiling of an integer is itself.

A.2   A *logarithm* is an exponent. It is the exponent on the given base that produces the given value.

A.3   The First Principle of Mathematical Induction ("weak" induction) allows the inductive hypothesis that assumes that the proposition $P(n)$ is true for some single value of n. The Second Principle of Mathematical Induction ("strong" induction) allows the inductive hypothesis that assumes that all the propositions $P(k)$ are true for all k less than or equal to some value of n.

A.4   Use weak induction (the First Principle) when the proposition $P(n)$ can be directly related to its predecessor $P(n-1)$. Use strong induction (the Second Principle) when the proposition $P(n)$ depends upon $P(k)$ for $k < n-1$.

A.5   *Euler's constant* is the limit of the difference $(1 + 1/2 + 1/3 + ... + 1/n) - \ln n$. Its value is approximately 0.5772.

A.6   Stirling's formula is a useful method for approximating $n!$ for large n (e.g., $n > 20$).

A.7   The recursive definition of the Fibonacci numbers (Example 4.5 on page 74) is useless for $n > 20$ because the number of recursive calls grows exponentially. The explicit formula (Theorem A.18 on page 343) is a very useful alternative for $n < 1475$.

Solutions to Problems

A.1   The graphs of (*a*) $y = \lfloor x \rfloor$, (*b*) $y = \lceil x \rceil$, (*c*) $y = \lceil x \rceil - x$, and (*c*) $y = \lceil x \rceil - \lfloor x \rfloor$:

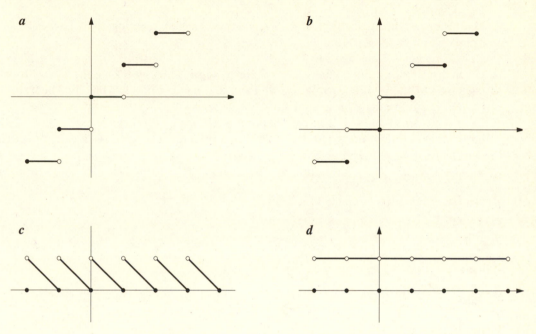

A.2   Proof of Theorem A.1 on page 333:

a. The relationships $\lfloor x \rfloor = \max\{m \in \mathbf{Z} \mid m \le x\}$, and $\lceil x \rceil = \min\{n \in \mathbf{Z} \mid n \ge x\}$ are merely restatements of the definitions of $\lfloor x \rfloor$ and $\lceil x \rceil$.

b. Let $m = \lfloor x \rfloor$ and $n = \lceil x \rceil$. Then by definition, $m \le x < m + 1$ and $n - 1 < x \le n$. Then $x - 1 < m$ and $n < x + 1$. Thus $x - 1 < m \le x \le n < x + 1$.

c. The inequalities $x - 1 < \lfloor x \rfloor \le x \le \lceil x \rceil < x + 1$ merely summarize those in **b** above.

d. Let $n \in \mathbf{Z}$ such that $n \le x < n + 1$, and let $A = \{m \in \mathbf{Z} \mid m \le x\}$. Then $n \in A$ and $\lfloor x \rfloor = \max A$, so $n \le \lfloor x \rfloor$. Now if $n < \lfloor x \rfloor$, then $n + 1 \le \lfloor x \rfloor$ (since both n and $\lfloor x \rfloor$ are integers). But $n + 1 \le \lfloor x \rfloor$, by hypothesis. Therefore $n = \lfloor x \rfloor$. The proof of the second part is analogous.

e. Assume that $x \in \mathbf{Z}$ (i.e., x is an integer). Then let $n = x$ in **d** above: $x \le x < x + 1$ so $x = \lfloor x \rfloor$, and $x - 1 < x \le x$ so $x = \lceil x \rceil$.

f. Assume that $x \notin \mathbf{Z}$ (i.e., x is not an integer). Let $u = x - \lfloor x \rfloor$ and $v = \lceil x \rceil - x$. Then, by **c**, $u \ge 0$ and $v \ge 0$. Also by **c**, $x - 1 < \lfloor x \rfloor = x - u$ and $v + x = \lceil x \rceil < x + 1$, so $u < 1$ and $v < 1$. Thus $0 \le u < 1$ and $0 \le v < 1$. But u and v cannot be integers because if either were, then so would x because $x = \lfloor x \rfloor + u = \lceil x \rceil - v$. Therefore, $0 < u < 1$ and $0 < v < 1$, so $x = \lfloor x \rfloor + u > \lfloor x \rfloor$ and $x = \lceil x \rceil - v < \lceil x \rceil$.

g. Let $n = -\lfloor -x \rfloor$. Then $(-n) = \lfloor (-x) \rfloor$ so by **c**, $(-x) - 1 < (-n) \le (-x)$, so $x \le n < x + 1$, so $x \le n$ and $n - 1 < x$, so $n - 1 < x \le n$. Thus by **d**, $n = \lceil x \rceil$. Thus $-\lfloor -x \rfloor = \lceil x \rceil$, so $\lfloor -x \rfloor = -\lceil x \rceil$.
The second identity follows from the first by replacing x with $-x$.

h. Let $n = \lfloor x + 1 \rfloor$. Then by **c**, $(x + 1) - 1 < n \le (x + 1)$, so $x - 1 < n - 1 \le x$ and $x = (x + 1) - 1 < n$. Thus $n - 1 \le x < n$; i.e., $(n - 1) \le x < (n - 1) + 1$. Thus by **d**, $(n - 1) = \lfloor -x \rfloor$, so $\lfloor x + 1 \rfloor = n = \lfloor x \rfloor + 1$. The proof of the second identity is similar.

A.3   Proof of Theorem A.2 on page 334:

a. Let $x = b^y$. Then by definition, $\log_b(b^y) = \log_b(x) = y$.

b. Let $y = \log_b x$. Then by definition, $b^{\log_b x} = b^y = x$.

c. Let $y = \log_b u$ and $z = \log_b v$. Then by definition, $u = b^y$ and $v = b^z$, so $uv = (b^y)(b^z) = b^{y+z}$, so $\log_b(uv) = y + z = \log_b u + \log_b v$.

d. By Law *c* above, $\log_b v + \log_b u/v = \log_b(v\, u/v) = \log_b u$, so $\log_b u/v = \log_b u + \log_b u$.

e. Let $y = \log_b u$. Then by definition, $u = b^y$, so $u^v = (b^y)^v = b^{vy}$. Then by definition, $\log_b(u^v) = vy = v \log_b u$.

f. Let $y = \log_b x$. Then by definition, $x = b^y$, so $\log_c x = \log_c(b^y) = y \log_c b$, by Law *e* above. Thus $\log_b x = y = (\log_c x)/(\log_c b)$.

A.4   Proof of Theorem A.3 on page 334:

a. Given that $2^p < n < 2^{p+1}$, where $n, p \in \mathbf{Z}$, let $x = \lg n$. Then by taking the binary logarithm of each part of the double inequality, we have that $p < x < p + 1$. Thus by Theorem A.1*d*, $p = \lfloor x \rfloor = \lfloor \lg n \rfloor$. Similarly, $(p + 1) - 1 < x < (p + 1)$, so $p + 1 = \lceil \lg n \rceil$.

b. Let $x = \lg(n+1)$ and $y = \lg n$. By Theorem A.1*c*, $y < \lfloor y \rfloor + 1$, so $n = 2^y < 2^{\lfloor y \rfloor + 1}$. But now both sides of this inequality $n < 2^{\lfloor y \rfloor + 1}$ are integers, so $n + 1 \le 2^{\lfloor y \rfloor + 1}$. Thus $x = \lg(n+1) \le \lfloor y \rfloor + 1$. But also, $x = \lg(n+1) > = \lg n = y \ge \lfloor y \rfloor$, so $m - 1 < x \le m$, where $m = \lfloor y \rfloor + 1 = \lfloor \lg n \rfloor + 1$. Therefore, by Theorem A.1*d*, $\lceil x \rceil = m$; i.e., $\lceil \lg(n+1) \rceil = \lfloor \lg n \rfloor + 1$.

A.5   *a.* True

b. True

c. True

d. False

e. True

f. True

g. False

h. False

i. False

j. True

k. False

l. True

A.6   Proof of Theorem A.4 on page 335:

For given functions f and g in M, the expression $L(f,g)$ is either 0, positive, or infinite. These three mutually exclusive cases determine whether f is in $o(g)$, $\Theta(g)$, or $\omega(g)$, respectively.

A.7   Proof of Theorem A.5 on page 336:

$$O(g) = \{\, f \in M \mid 0 \le L(f, g) < \infty \,\}$$

$$= \{\, f \in M \mid L(f, g) = 0 \text{ or } 0 < L(f, g) < \infty \,\}$$

$$= \{\, f \in M \mid L(f, g) = 0 \,\} \cup \{\, f \in M \mid 0 < L(f, g) < \infty \,\}$$

$$= o(g) \cup \Theta(g)$$

$$\Theta(g) = \{\, f \in M \mid 0 < L(f, g) < \infty \,\}$$

$$= \{\, f \in M \mid L(f, g) > 0 \text{ and } L(f, g) < \infty \,\}$$

$$= \{\, f \in M \mid L(f, g) > 0 \,\} \cap \{\, f \in M \mid L(f, g) < \infty \,\}$$

$$= \Omega(g) \cap O(g)$$

$$\Omega(g) = \{\, f \in M \mid 0 < L(f, g) \le \infty \,\}$$

$$= \{\, f \in M \mid 0 < L(f, g) < \infty \text{ or } L(f, g) = \infty \,\}$$

$$= \{\, f \in M \mid 0 < L(f, g) < \infty \,\} \cup \{\, f \in M \mid L(f, g) = \infty \,\}$$

$$= \Theta(g) \cup \omega(g)$$

A.8   Proof of Theorem A.10 on page 338:

Let $S = a + ar + ar^2 + ar^3 + \cdots + ar^{n-1}$. Then $rS = ar + ar^2 + ar^3 + ar^4 + \cdots + ar^n$, so $S - rS = a - ar^n$, $(1 - r)S = a(1 - r^n)$, and thus $S = a(1 - r^n)/(1 - r)$.

A.9   Proof of Theorem A.11 on page 338:

If $-1 < r < 1$, then as n increases without bound, r^n shrinks down to zero. Letting $r^n = 0$ in the formula in Theorem A.10 yields Theorem A.11.

A.10   Proof of Theorem A.12 on page 339:

Let $S = 1 + 2 + 3 + \cdots + n$. Then $S = n + \cdots + 3 + 2 + 1$ also. Add these two equations, summing the $2n$ terms on the right pairwise: $(1 + n)$, $(2 + (n-1))$, etc. There are n pairs, and each pair has the same sum of $n + 1$. So the total sum on the right is $n(n + 1)$. Then, since the sum on the left is $2S$, the correct value of S must be $n(n + 1)/2$.

A.11   Proof of Theorem A.16 on page 342:

If $r = AC/CB$, then $r = AC/CB = AB/AC = (AC + CB)/AC = 1 + CB/AC = 1 + 1/r$, so $r^2 = r + 1$. Completing the square produces $(r - 1/2)^2 = r^2 - r + 1/4 = (r + 1) - r + 1/4 = 5/4$, so $r - 1/2 = \pm\sqrt{5/4}$ and $r = (1 \pm \sqrt{5})/2$. The decimal forms of these two roots are

$r_1 = (1 + \sqrt{5})/2 = \phi = 1.6180339887498948482045868343656 \cdots$

$r_2 = (1 - \sqrt{5})/2 = \psi = -0.6180339887498948482045868343656 \cdots$

Since the golden mean ϕ is the only positive solution, it must be the correct ratio.

A.12   Proof of Theorem A.17 on page 342:

a. $\phi^2 = \phi + 1$ because ϕ is a solution to the equation $x^2 = x + 1$.

b. $\psi^2 = \psi + 1$ because ψ is a solution to the equation $x^2 = x + 1$.

c. $1/\phi = \phi - 1$ because $1 = \phi^2 - \phi$.

d. $1/\psi = \psi - 1$ because $1 = \psi^2 - \psi$.

e. $\phi + \psi = (1 + \sqrt{5})/2 + (1 - \sqrt{5})/2 = 1$.

f. $\phi - \psi = (1 + \sqrt{5})/2 - (1 - \sqrt{5})/2 = 2(\sqrt{5}/2) = \sqrt{5}$.

A.13   Proof of Theorem A.18 on page 343:

$$F_0 = \frac{\phi^0 - \psi^0}{\sqrt{5}} = \frac{1 - 1}{\sqrt{5}} = \frac{0}{\sqrt{5}} = 0$$

$$F_1 = \frac{\phi^1 - \psi^1}{\sqrt{5}} = \frac{\phi - \psi}{\sqrt{5}} = \frac{\sqrt{5}}{\sqrt{5}} = 1$$

$$F_{n+1} = \frac{\phi^{n+1} - \psi^{n+1}}{\sqrt{5}} = \frac{(\phi^n + \phi^{n-1}) - (\psi^n + \psi^{n-1})}{\sqrt{5}}$$

$$= \frac{\phi^n + \psi^n}{\sqrt{5}} + \frac{\phi^{n-1} + \psi^{n-1}}{\sqrt{5}}$$

$$= F_n + F_{n-1}, \text{ by the inductive hypothesis.}$$

A.14   Proof of Corollary A.3 on page 343:

Since $-1 < \psi < 0$, high powers of ψ are negligible; therefore, $F_n = k\phi^n$, where $k = 1/\sqrt{5}$.

A.15   Program to test the explicit formula for Fibonacci numbers (Theorem A.18 on page 343):

```
public class PrA15
{ public static void main(String[] args)
  { final double SQRT5 = Math.sqrt(5.0);
    final double PHI = (1 + SQRT5)/2;
    final double PSI = (1 - SQRT5)/2;
    long f0, f1=0, f2=1;
    for (int n=2; n<32; n++)
    { f0 = f1;
      f1 = f2;
      f2 = f1 + f0;
```

```
    float fn = (float)((Math.pow(PHI,n)-Math.pow(PSI,n))/SQRT5);
    System.out.println(f2+"\t"+fn);
    }
  }
}
```

A.16   Proof of Theorem A.19 on page 343:

Assume that $a > b > 0$ and $r = a\%b > 0$ and $d \mid b$. Then $a = qb + r$ for some $q \in \mathbf{N}$, and $b = kd$ for some $k \in \mathbf{N}$. Thus $a = qb + r = qkd + r$. Then $d \mid a \Rightarrow a = md$, for some $m \in \mathbf{N} \Rightarrow md = a = qkd + r \Rightarrow r = md - qkd = (m - qk)d \Rightarrow d \mid r$. Similarly, $d \mid r \Rightarrow r = nd$, for some $n \in \mathbf{N} \Rightarrow a = qkd + r = qkd + nd = (qkd + n)d \Rightarrow d \mid a$. Thus, $d \mid a \Leftrightarrow d \mid r$.

A.17   Proof of Corollary A.4 on page 344:

This is a consequence of the logical argument $(P \wedge Q) \to (R \leftrightarrow S) \Rightarrow P \to (Q \wedge R \leftrightarrow Q \wedge S)$, where P = "$a > b > 0$" and r = "$a\%b$" > 0, Q = "$d \mid b$", R = "$d \mid a$", and R = "$d \mid r$".

A.18   Proof of Corollary A.5 on page 344:

Let $A = \{d \in \mathbf{N} : d \mid a \text{ and } d \mid b\}$ and let $B = \{d \in \mathbf{N} : d \mid b \text{ and } d \mid r\}$. Then according to Corollary A.4, $A = B$. Therefore, $\max A = \max B$. But, by definition, $\max A = \gcd(a,b)$ and $\max B = \gcd(b,r)$.

A.19   Proof of Theorem A.20 on page 344:

Corollary A.4 guarantees that the loop invariant is always true. The loop stops when $b = 0$, returning a, which is the $\gcd(a,b)$. Therefore, the value returned is also the gcd of the original pair (a,b).

A.20   Proof of Theorem A.21 on page 344:

On the kth iteration, $a_k = q_k b_k + r_k$, where $q_k = a_k/b_k \geq 1$ and $r_k = a_k \% b_k$. Thus $a_k \geq b_k + r_k$. But $b_k = a_{k+1}$ and $r_k = b_{k+1} = a_{k+2}$. Thus $a_k \geq a_{k+1} + a_{k+2}$. Now consider the reverse sequence $\{x_i\}$ where $x_0 = a_m$ and $x_i = a_{m-i}$: $x_0 \geq 1$, $x_1 \geq 1$, and $x_i \geq x_{i-1} + x_{i-2}$ for all i, so $x_2 \geq x_1 + x_0 \geq 1 + 1 = 2$, $x_3 \geq x_2 + x_1 \geq 2 + 1 = 3$, etc. Thus $x_i \geq F_{i+1}$ (the Fibonacci numbers). Thus $a = x_m \geq F_{m+1} \geq \varphi^m$, so $\log_\varphi a \geq m$.

From C++ to Java

This appendix shows how Java concepts correspond to those in C++. It is intended for C++ programmers who are learning Java.

Some important distinctions are:

- In Java, all executable statements must be encapsulated in classes.
- Java uses `Object` elements in lieu of `template` classes.
- Java allows no external functions or variables.
- Java uses references instead of pointers.
- All arguments are passed by value.
- The C++ definition
  ```
  string* s = new string;
  ```
  is equivalent to the Java definition
  ```
  String s = new String();
  ```
- Java uses automatic garbage collection instead of the `delete` operator.

Here is a list of correspondences between Java and C++:

```
bool .....................................boolean

char .....................................N/A

wchar_t ..................................char

short ....................................short

int ......................................int

long .....................................long

unsigned char ............................byte

unsigned short ...........................N/A

unsigned int .............................N/A

unsigned long ............................N/A

float ....................................float

double ...................................double

enum .....................................N/A

string ...................................String
```

```
const.................................. final

goto................................... N/A

pointer ............................... N/A

reference ............................. N/A

pass by value ......................... pass

pass by reference...................... N/A

inline................................. N/A

register .............................. N/A

namespace ............................. package

stream I/O ............................ N/A

printf() .............................. System.out.println()

scanf() ............................... N/A

class.................................. class

struct................................. class

data member ........................... field, instance variable

member function ....................... method

public................................. public

protected ............................. protected

private ............................... private

static................................. static

this................................... this

new.................................... new

delete................................. N/A

template .............................. N/A

operator .............................. N/A

friend................................. N/A

sizeof................................. N/A

typedef ............................... N/A
```

```
typeid ................................... getClass()

virtual .................................. abstract

virtual class ............................ abstract class

virtual function ......................... abstract method

pure virtual class ....................... interface

header file .............................. package

#include ................................. import

vector ................................... Vector

stack .................................... Stack

queue .................................... N/A

deque .................................... N/A

priority_queue ........................... N/A

list ..................................... LinkedList

map ...................................... HashMap

set ...................................... HashSet
```

Appendix C

Java Development Environments

A *development environment* is a set of computer programs that allow you to build a new computer program. The two essential components of any development environment are a text editor and a compiler. Commercial integrated development environments (IDEs) also include a debugger, documentation on the programming language, and other tools.

C.1 THE WINDOWS COMMAND PROMPT

The simplest development environment is free. Use the text editor that comes bundled with your computer's operating system, and download the latest version of Java from the Sun Microsystems website at `http://java.sun.com/`.

If you are using Microsoft Windows, you can use either the NotePad editor or the WordPad editor. Create a file named `Hello.java` containing the text shown in the screen capture below. Save it as a text-only file on the `A:` drive. Then launch the Windows **Command Prompt** from **Start > Programs > Accessories** and execute the commands shown here. This shows how to set your `PATH` variable, if necessary, so that the operating system can find the `javac` compiler command and the `java` execute command. (On this computer, the Java JDK was installed on the **F:** drive.)

For more details, see Chapter 1 in **[Hubbard]**.

C.2 VISUAL CAFE FROM WEBGAIN

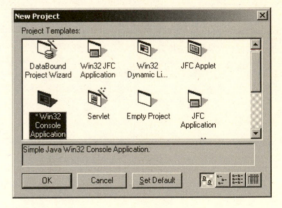

Visual Cafe was originally produced by Symantec Corp. It is now a product of WebGain, Inc. Version 4.0 was released in August 2000.

To create a standard Java application program:

1. Select New Project... from the File menu (or press Ctrl+Shift+N) and then select Win32 Console Application from the New Project dialog box.

2. This creates a new project and defines a class named `SimplCon` like this:

```
/*
    A basic Java class stub for a Win32 Console Application.
*/
public class SimplCon {
    public SimplCon () {
    }
    static public void main(String args[]) {
        System.out.println("Hello World");
    }
}
```

This is a variation of the classic "Hello, World!" program.

356

3. To run the program, select Execute from the Project menu (or press Ctrl+F5). This compiles the code and executes it, producing the output in a classic DOS window.

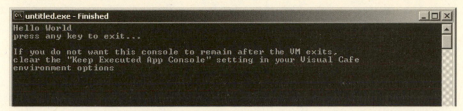

4. Press Enter to close the DOS window.

5. To save your project, click on the project window (the one labeled Project – Untitled) and then select Save As... from the File menu. In this example, we have saved the project as `Project1.vep` on the A: drive. Note that this automatically saves the `SimplCon.java` file in the same directory.

6. To rename your main class, edit both occurrences of the `SimplCon` string in the source code window, and then select Save As... from the File menu. In this example, we have renamed the main class `Main`. Note that this now give you two classes each with its own `main()` method: `SimplCon` and `Main`. Double-click on the file icon named `SimplCon` in the project window to bring it back in its own editing window.

7. A project can have only one `main()` class; that is, only one class whose `main()` method is designated to be the target where execution begins. To see which of the two `main()` methods that you now have in your project is the target, change the `println()` string in the Main class to `"Goodbye, World!"`. Then press Ctrl+F5 to

run your project (or select Execute from the Project menu). The output should be the same `Hello World` message as before, indicating that the target has not changed.

8. To change the target, select Options... from the Project menu to bring up the Project Options window. Then change the listing under Main Class from `SimplCon` to `Main` and click OK. Then run your project again. This time, you should get the `Goodbye, World!` output.

9. Now close the `SimplCon.java` window. Then right-click on its icon in the Project window and select Cut from the pop-up menu (or select Cut from the Edit menu) to remove that class from your project, thereby leaving only your new `Main` class.

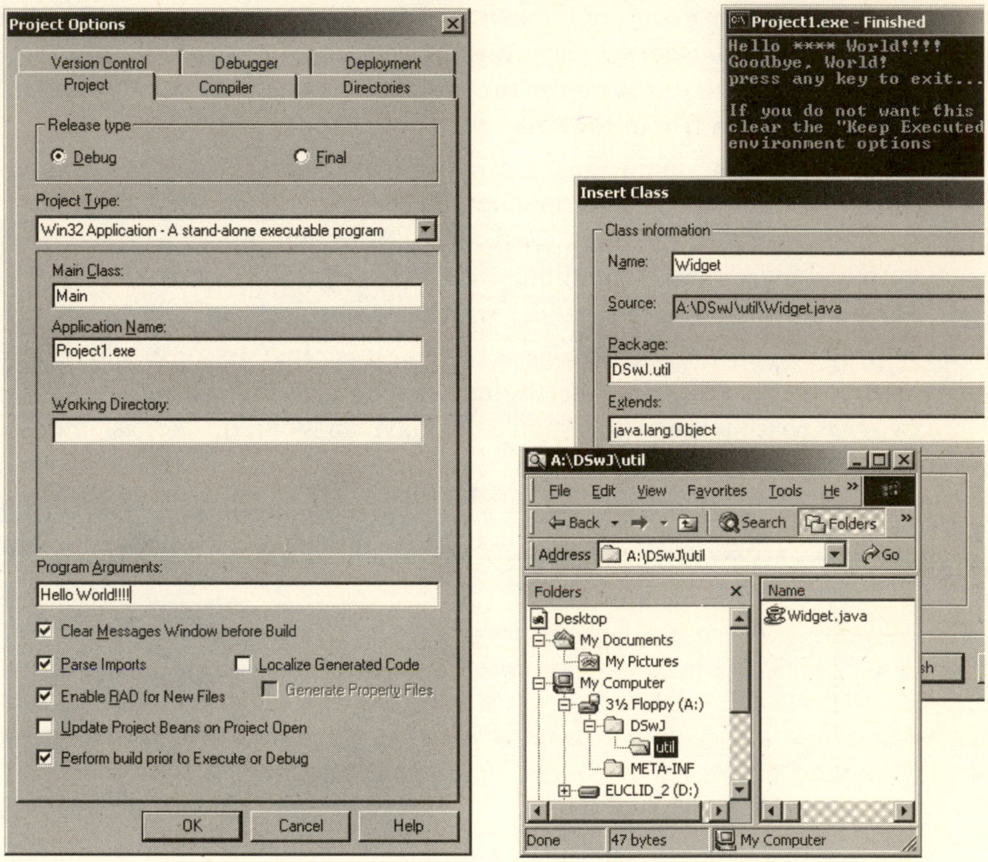

10. Now edit your main class by adding another println statement, so that it `main()` looks like this:

```
static public void main(String args[]) {
    System.out.println(args[0] + " **** " + args[1]);
    System.out.println("Goodbye, World!");
}
```

Then open your Project Options window again (select Options... from the Project menu) and add the text `Hello World!!!!` to the Program Arguments field, as shown here, and click OK. Then run your project again. The output this time should begin with the line

```
Hello **** World!!!!
Goodbye, World!
```

This shows how to use command line arguments. Each string listed in the Program

Arguments field becomes one of the `String` elements of the `args[]` array parameter in the `main()` method.

11. To insert a new class into your project, select Class... from the Insert menu. Name the class `Widget` and enter `DSwJ.util` in the Package field, as shown below at right. Then click on the Finish button, and click Yes as the question about creating a new directory. Then check your project directory to see what was created. A Java package becomes a directory path, with each component being the name of a nested folder. Thus, the package `DSwJ.util` produced the folder named `util` nested within the folder named `DSwJ`, and the new `Widget.java` file is then placed in that inner folder.

12. Double-click on the new `Widget` listing in the Project window to open that source code file. It contains a minimal class outline:

```
package DSwJ.util;

public class Widget
{
}
```

13. Click on the Packages tab at the bottom of the Project window to change it to the Packages view. At the top is the `Main.java` file listed under the `Default Package` package, followed by the `Widget.java` file listed in the `DSwJ.util` package. Below that is a very long list of all the packages in the Java standard library. Scroll down the list to `java.util`, and expand that package entry to list the classes defined within it. Double-click on the `Stack.java` listing. This opens the file, revealing its source code.

14. Select Class Browser from the View menu (or press Ctrl+Shift+C). This opens the Visual Cafe Class Browser window. It has three sections: the Classes listing, the Members pane, and an editing pane below. Right-click in the Classes listing and select Collapse All to "collapse" the folder listings. Then scroll down, just as you did in Step 13, to the `java.util` package, expand that package entry, and double-click on the `Stack` entry. The Members pane then lists all the members of the `java.util.Stack` class. Click on the `push` method to have its source code displayed in the editing pane.

Visual Cafe has all the usual features found in all the other high-tech IDEs:

- color-enhanced editor
- button-controlled debugger
- substantial on-line help

Among its features that distinguish it from other IDEs are:

- meaningful and helpful compiler messages
- a class wizard
- a code helper
- a syntax checker
- a hierarchy editor
- the support for user-defined macros

The on-line help system in Visual Cafe is very good. The Java API Reference... command on the Help menu offers complete listings of all the packages, classes, fields, and methods available. This includes both the standard Java library and the extra libraries provided by WebGain. The Class Hierarchy window presents the enormous inheritance tree, from the `Object` class on down. The Index of all Classes, Fields, and Methods has over 20,000 listings.   The Package Index lists all the 95 packages in the Java, Sun, and Symantec libraries. You can alternate among these indexes by clicking on the tabs at the top of the API Reference window. All the indexes use hypertext for easy browsing. Unfortunately, the API Reference is not up to date. The August 2000 release does not include some of the Java 1.2 classes, such as `java.util.Arrays`.

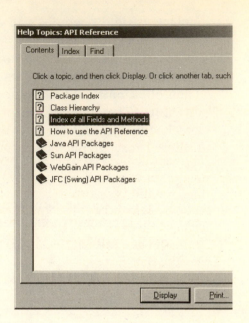

Appendix D

References

Publishers:

Addison-Wesley Publishing Company, Reading, MA, `http://www.awl.com/cs/`
John Wiley & Sons, New York, NY, `http://www.wiley.com/college/eng/comsci/`
Jones and Bartlett Publishers, Sudbury, MA, `http://www.jbpub.com/cs/`
Macmillan, New York, NY, `http://www.macmillan.com`
McGraw-Hill, New York, NY, `http://www.mhhe.com`
O'Reilly & Associates, Inc., Sebastopol, CA, `http://www.oreilly.com`
Oxford University Press, New York, NY, `http://www.oup-usa.com`
Perseus Books, Reading MA, `http://www.perseusbooksgroup.com`
Prentice-Hall, Englewood Cliffs, NJ, `http://www.prenhall.com`
PWS Publishing Company, Boston, MA, `http://www.brookscole.com`
Que Education & Training, Indianapolis, IN, `http://www.mcp.com/resources/`
SYBEX, Alameda, CA, `http://www.sybex.com/`
WCB/McGraw-Hill, New York, NY, `http://www.mcgraw-hill.com`

[Arnold]
The Java Programming Language, by Ken Arnold and James Gosling, Third Edition.
Addison-Wesley, 2000, 0-201-70433-1.

[Bell]
Java for Students, by Douglas Bell and Mike Parr.
Prentice Hall, 1998, 0-13-858440-0.

[Boone]
Java Essentials for C and C++ Programmers, by Barry Boone.
Addison-Wesley, 1998, 0-201-47946-X.

[Budd]
Classic Data Structures, by Timothy Budd.
Addison-Wesley, 2001, 0-201-70002-6.

[Campione]
The Java Tutorial, by Mary Campione and Kathy Walrath.
Addison-Wesley, 1998, 0-201-63454-6.

[Carrano]
Data Sbstraction and Problem Solving with Java, by Frank Carrano and Janet Prichard.
Addison-Wesley, 2001, 0-201-70220-7.

[Chan1]
The Java Class Libraries, Second Edition, Volume 1, by Patrick Chan, Rosanna Lee, and D. Kramer.
Addison-Wesley, 1998, 0-201-31002-3.

[Chan2]
The Java Class Libraries, Second Edition, Volume 2, by Patrick Chan and Rosanna Lee.
Addison-Wesley, 1998, 0-201-31003-1.

[Chan3]

The Java Developers ALMANAC 2000, by Patrick Chan.
Addison-Wesley, 2000, 0-201-43299-4.

[Daconta]

Java for C/C++ Programmers, by Michael C. Daconta.
John Wiley & Sons, 1996, 0-471-15324-9.

[Deitel]

Java How to Program, by H. M. Deitel and P. J. Deitel.
Prentice-Hall, 1997, 0-13-263401-5.

[Goodrich]

Data Structures and Algorithms in Java, Second Edition, by Michael Goodrich and Roberto Tamassia.
John Wiley & Sons, 2001, 0-471-38367-8.

[Gosling]

The Java Language Specification, Second Edition, by James Gosling, et al.
Addison-Wesley, 2000, 0-201-31008-2.

[Grand1]

Java Language Reference, by Mark Grand.
O'Reilly & Associates, 1997, 1-56592-326-X.

[Grand2]

Java Fundamental Classes Reference, by Mark Grand and Jonathan Knudsen.
O'Reilly & Associates, 1997, 1-56592-241-7.

[Harary]

Graph Theory, by Frank Harary.
Perseus Books, 1969, 0-201-41033-8.

[Horstmann2]

Computing Concepts with Java Essentials, by Cay S. Horstmann.
John Wiley & Sons, 1998, 0-471-17223-5.

[Hubbard]

Schaum's Outline of Programming with Java, by John R. Hubbard.
McGraw-Hill, 1999, 0-07-134210-9.

[Kamin]

An Introduction to Computer Science Using Java, by S. N. Kamin, M. D. Mickunas, and E. M. Reingold.
WCB/McGraw-Hill, 1998, 0-07-034224-5.

[Lewis]

Java Software Solutions, Foundations of Program Design, by John Lewis and William Loftus.
Addison-Wesley, 1998, 0-57164-1.

[Liang]

An Introduction to Java Programming, by Y. Daniel Liang.
Que Education & Training, 1998, 1-57576-548-9.

[Preiss]

Data Structures and Algorithms with Object-Oriented Design Patterns in Java, by Bruno R. Preiss.
John Wiley & Sons, 2000, 0-471-34613-6.

[Unicode]

The Unicode Standard, Version 2.0, by The Unicode Consortium.
Addison-Wesley, 1996, 0-201-48345-9.

[Wilson]

Graphs: An Introductory Approach, by Robin J. Wilson and John J. Watkins.
John Wiley & Sons, 1990, 0-471-61554-4.

[Zukowski]

Java AWT Reference, by John Zukowski.
O'Reilly & Associates, 1997, 1-56592-240-9.

Index